PERSPECTIVES ON INTERNATIONAL, STATE AND LOCAL ECONOMICS

PERSPECTIVES ON INTERNATIONAL, STATE AND LOCAL ECONOMICS

GERALD V. LIU
EDITOR

Nova Science Publishers, Inc.
New York

For permission to use material from this book please contact us:
Telephone 631-231-7269; Fax 631-231-8175
Web Site: http://www.novapublishers.com

Library of Congress Cataloging-in-Publication Data

Perspectives on international, state and local economics / Gerald V. Liu (Editor).
p. cm.
Includes index.
ISBN 1-60021-099-6
1. Regional economics. 2. International economic relations. I. Liu, Gerald V.
HT388.P49 2006
330--dc22 2006008466

Published by Nova Science Publishers, Inc. ✦New York

CONTENTS

PREFACE

If all politics are local, then all economics are also international, regional and local. Globalization, for all its mystery and so-called inevitability, has its foundations and bloodlines in urban and regional economics. The economic impacts of poverty, housing, transportation, education, and crime are included. This new book includes within its scope: multiplier and impact analysis, input-output models, growth theory, migration, urban and regional labor markets, urban and regional public policy, regional devolution, small firms policy, and foreign direct investment.

Recent extensive studies of internal control in business have led to the development of a definition capturing both positive and negative aspects of the issue. While the structure of modern organizations often undermines this control, it has become recognized as an essential component of a successful enterprise. Effective governance consists of competent management; implementation of standard policies and processes; maintenance of an appropriate audit program and internal control environment and effective risk monitoring and management information systems. The integrity and reliability of the internal control systems are achieved through clear policies and procedures, process automation, careful selection, training and development of employees and an organization structure that segregates responsibilities. An effective internal control system has inherent limitations no matter how well designed, and therefore, may mitigate but cannot eliminate risks. In addition, there are areas of the Group's business where it is necessary to take risks to achieve a satisfactory return for shareholders, such as investment in the development of new products or acquisition of businesses. Without vulnerability to the risk of opportunism, there is no need to trust. Trust decreases monitoring costs as a result of each party's confidence in the other's performance, even though short-term incentives may favour opportunism. Trust and risk are subjective concepts embedded in a web of social relationships. The organizational culture is an important determinant at the collective level that can shape organizational predispositions. There is strong need for voluntary action. Social capital can facilitate collective action and access to resources; it can stimulate trusting relationships and a culture of confidence between the executive and workforce. Stakeholder relationships minimise shareholder risk, promote innovation, enhance reputation. Trust consists of a cooperative spirit and shared understanding between a company and its stakeholders creates coherence of action, better knowledge sharing, lower transaction costs, lower turnover rates and organisational stability, all leading to increased business value. Chapter 1 discusses the systems of corporate governance and the way they affect control, including a breakdown by relevant factors such as technological advances, sizes and areas of industry and the role of social capital in enhancing trust relations. Trends in definition, practice and application of control are presented with reference to increasing dependence on technology and changes. The interplay of internal control and social capital is explained to highlight internal control's role in risk reduction. A detailed exposition of the effects that relationships between various levels of stakeholders have on control reveals the unique challenges posed to management accountants.

The increasing role of cities in a globalized world, and the interest in linking decision-making at a local level with those decisions made at a global level, dominates the literature on global governance. Chapter 2 looks at the interaction between citizens, an elected mayor or municipal leader, and a firm making decisions to locate in a city on a globalized scale. After discussing the choice for the main three players--citizen, mayor, and firm--, the authors use a dynamic game between these players to better understand the dynamics and uncover key aspects that can be used for policy, while leaving open the question of the *direction of causality*: does governance lead to more globalization or does globalization lead to improved governance at the city level. Empirical examples illustrate the outcome of the dynamic simulation. Using a game-theoretic framework, they show that the dynamics of interaction between citizens, mayors, and firms, within a context of globalization, leads to superior performance of cities. This framework attempts to derive the nature of causality from globalization to good governance and from local accountability to good governance. The analysis shows that both are important, but that the interaction between globalization and good governance should lead to superior performance, over and above that of local accountability by itself, or globalization in the absence of local accountability. They have shown that, when firms try to influence city leaders and go unchecked, it leads to bad outcomes in terms of city performance. The results indicate that history matters, and that a methodology that allows the dynamics over time to be captured, can shed light on some of the difficult issues surrounding urban governance. Such analysis would be relevant to understand the high urbanization rates in Africa which have come with little contribution to increased welfare of urban cities, with limited economic growth for their countries, low levels of foreign direct investment, and with well known challenges in the area of governance. Such a model could shed light on this difficult topic, when used specifically for African cities.

There are several concerns about Estonian regional development because the economic activities have been concentrated into the capital city and the surrounding region, and the municipalities in the borderlands are facing high unemployment rates. Attempts have been made to balance these developments by equalizing the per capita income of local governments across the country. The aim of chapter 3 is to analyse the spatial distribution of central governmental grants to local governments in Estonia and to control whether the gravity model is successful in describing these financial flows. Three hypothesis were tested:

1. There is a positive correlation of the distance from local governments' centre to the capital city Tallinn (and other larger towns) with the per capita unconditional grant flows to local governments;
2. This positive correlation of distance decreases by adding conditional grants;
3. There is a negative correlattion of distance with per capita conditional grant flows to local governments because of higher lobbying costs.

The distribution of income tax as the main revenue source seems to have a geographical pattern. This can be observed graphically and proven by correlation analysis. The central government policy for equalization of local governments' per capita revenues through State Equalization Fund can be seen as successful; the first hypothesis can be accepted. From other side, the distribution of conditional grants is decreasing the equalizing effect of unconditional transfers. The gravity model supports the presence of geographical pattern in grants from central to local governments. However, the negative correlation of conditional grants with distance was not found.

Chapter 4 examines the cost structure of public schools in this paper, using frontier cost models that enable the authors to estimate sources of inefficiency. A two-equation stochastic frontier model is presented that can be used to explain both cost and the sources of inefficiency. Using that model and data for public schools in Nebraska over the period 1989-92, the authors estimate cost frontiers for the districts. Estimated cost frontier information is then used in estimating school district need for purposes of computing state aid, illustrating an important potential application of such information.

Chapter 5 measures the performance of public spending in Italian regions regarding the provision of public services, by constructing a so-called total regional performance indicator for strategic sectors such as general administration, energy, water and sewage, solid waste, and transports for 2001. This composite indicator is then the output measure selected to assess expenditure efficiency for the Italian regions, using the non-parametric DEA approach. The computation of efficiency scores allows to rank the regions and to detect some room for improvement in terms of efficiency gains at the regional level.

Households may undertake housing changes and modifications (HCMs) for two basic reasons – increasing property value and gaining personal utility. In environmentally unfavorable or physically deteriorated neighborhoods, in which no substantial price gain can be expected, HCMs may be motivated mainly by improving personal utility, rather than by maximizing return on HCMs. As a result, in such neighborhoods relatively little accumulation of HCMs may occur. To verify this hypothesis, eight residential neighborhoods in two large cities of Israel – Jerusalem and Haifa, - were analyzed in chapter 6. The incidence of HCMs was found to be related to neighborhood and building characteristics, while the amount of accumulated post-occupancy HCMs helped to explain the variation of selling prices of apartments and houses.

One of the goals of the integration process between EU and MED countries, is the MED countries growth increase. Another goal that the process wants to reach is the increase of intra-area trade by reducing tariffs and non tariffs barriers. The aim of chapter 7 is to verify if a positive relationship between economic growth and international trade in the examined area exist. The empirical evidence (confirmed in this paper) starts from a Johnson model application adapted in the Mediterranean area, by introducing demographic rise. The results of regressions seem to confirm that if the Barcelona integration process goes on, with a constant but continuous increase in trade, Med countries economic growth will also increase. If we exclude from the analysis two countries: Turkey and the Palestinian Authority, we obtain more reliable results.

Under the terms of the Kyoto Protocol on Climate Change, Japan must reduce the emission of greenhouse gases to a target level of six percent below the 1990 base level by the first compliance period covering 2008 to 2012. To achieve this target, the Japanese Government has drafted a national energy plan which calls for the construction of ten additional nuclear power plants. Nuclear power in Japan is regulated by the Nuclear Liability Act (NLA) of Japan. As stated in Article 1, the NLA aims both to promote the sound development of the nuclear energy industry and to protect the victims and the environment from a nuclear accident. In practice, however, the NLA has several weaknesses which prevent it from achieving both policy objectives in a fair, balanced manner. Chapter 8 draws upon the economic analysis of accident law, as well as Japan's first nuclear criticality accident at the JCO plant, to identify these weaknesses and suggest possible remedies, thereby aiding Japan's adherence to the Kyoto Protocol.

In: Perspectives on International, State and Local Economics ISBN 1-60021-099-6
Editor: Gerald V. Liu, pp. 1-59

Chapter 1

THE SYSTEMS OF CORPORATE GOVERNANCE: SOCIAL CAPITAL INFLUENCE ON INTERNAL AND EXTERNAL CONTROL

Giovanni D'orio*[1] *and Rosetta Lombardo
University of Calabria
Arcavacata di Rende, 87036 Italy

ABSTRACT

Recent extensive studies of internal control in business have led to the development of a definition capturing both positive and negative aspects of the issue. While the structure of modern organizations often undermines this control, it has become recognized as an essential component of a successful enterprise. Effective governance consists of competent management; implementation of standard policies and processes; maintenance of an appropriate audit program and internal control environment and effective risk monitoring and management information systems. The integrity and reliability of the internal control systems are achieved through clear policies and procedures, process automation, careful selection, training and development of employees and an organization structure that segregates responsibilities. An effective internal control system has inherent limitations no matter how well designed, and therefore, may mitigate but cannot eliminate risks. In addition, there are areas of the Group's business where it is necessary to take risks to achieve a satisfactory return for shareholders, such as investment in the development of new products or acquisition of businesses. Without vulnerability to the risk of opportunism, there is no need to trust. Trust decreases monitoring costs as a result of each party's confidence in the other's performance, even though short-term incentives may favour opportunism. Trust and risk are subjective concepts embedded in a web of social relationships. The organizational culture is an important determinant at the collective level that can shape organizational predispositions. There is strong need for voluntary action. Social capital can facilitate collective action and access to resources; it can stimulate trusting relationships and a culture of confidence between the executive and workforce. Stakeholder relationships

[1] Email: gio.dorio@unical.it

minimise shareholder risk, promote innovation, enhance reputation. Trust consists of a cooperative spirit and shared understanding between a company and its stakeholders creates coherence of action, better knowledge sharing, lower transaction costs, lower turnover rates and organisational stability, all leading to increased business value.

This work discusses the systems of corporate governance and the way they affect control, including a breakdown by relevant factors such as technological advances, sizes and areas of industry and the role of social capital in enhancing trust relations. Trends in definition, practice and application of control are presented with reference to increasing dependence on technology and changes. The interplay of internal control and social capital is explained to highlight internal control's role in risk reduction. A detailed exposition of the effects that relationships between various levels of stakeholders have on control reveals the unique challenges posed to management accountants.

Keyword: Agency theory; corporate governance; institutions; social capital

1.1. Introduction

Institutions should create order and reduce uncertainty, transaction costs and opportunism which hinder exchange (North, 1990, 1991). "Human wishes and behaviour have been molded or changed through time by institutions and vice-versa" (Pessali and Fernandez, 1999, p. 265). Describing institutions, Thorstein Veblen a hundred years ago declared, " They are the products of his heredity traits and his past experience" (Veblen, 1898, p.390).

According to the theory of property rights, private property rights and corporate ownership structures emerge endogenously as an optimal response balancing benefits and costs (Demsetz, 1967, 1983). Institutional economics however tends to reject this view of optimal outcomes. And the historical record shows that institutional environments are rarely conducive to efficient behaviour.

Recent experiences[2] prove that reasoning in terms of universal "models" to imitate is hazardous. Corporate governance (hereafter CG) and the behaviour of enterprises are central components of each story. Studies of (CG) arrangements conclude that practices change over time, and no single optimal model can be identified (Mayer, 1998; OECD, 1999; Shleifer and Vishny, 1997). The bundle of rights and the quality of their enforcement differ greatly across common law and civil law countries, and among the latter, across French, German and Scandinavian subfamilies. The diverse protection of investors and stakeholders shapes their incentives and leads to differential ownership and financial structures (La Porta et al., 1998, 1999). If management has a good public nature (Stiglitz, 1985; 2000), it requires institutional solutions in order to avoid opportunism, free riding behaviour, and under-supply typical of public goods. The property rights theory and Coase theorem address these issues.

Secure, exclusive, transferable private property rights represent the main element of the incentive system of a market economy. They are the necessary complement of financial discipline and competition, and allow the development of efficient product, factor and financial markets (World Bank, 1996). The Coase theorem moreover shows that the initial allocation of property rights does not matter from an efficiency perspective as long as they are

[2] The Enron and WorldCom affairs that unveiled deep inadequacies of the American corporate governance system, the Parmalat scandal that questioned the virtues of Italian family capitalism, the Asian crisis in 1997 that threw light on the perverse connections between big companies, governments and banks and so on.

clearly defined in the first place, and can be freely and costlessly contracted on and exchanged. On the contrary, poorly defined property rights, the lack of protection against theft and expropriation, the lack of contract enforcement, i.e. weak institutions, are all obstacles to efficiency (Boycko, Sheifer and Vishny, 1995).

Demsetz (1967, p.348) claims that "property rights specify how persons may be benefitted and harmed, and therefore, who must pay whom to modify action taken by persons".

But property rights can not be exhaustive, while transaction and negotiation costs make Coasian contracting often impossible. Complementary formal institutions, including laws, regulations, and accounting rules, prove essential (Nivet, 2004, p.4).

The institutions of CG vary from country to country – in form, substance and most importantly, in how they mutually interact in a given country – they evolve over time. An indicative, hypothetical, list could nevertheless illustrate the main institutions of CG, comprising key "actors" and relevant legislation, regulations, other formal and informal rules, and general accepted business practice. Such a list should distinguish between key institutions of information disclosure and corporate transparency on one hand and those for corporate oversight and control on the other.

In all countries, the institutions of CG serve two objectives: enhance the performance and ensure the conformance of corporations. They facilitate and stimulate the performance of corporations by creating and maintaining a business environment that motivates managers and entrepreneurs to maximise firms' operational efficiency, returns on investments and long-term productivity growth. They ensure corporate conformance with investors' and society's interests and expectations by limiting the abuse of power, the siphoning-off of assets, the moral hazard and the significant wastage of corporate-controlled resources (so-called "agency-problems") that the self-serving behaviour of managers and other corporate insiders can be expected to impose on investors and society in their absence. Simultaneously, they establish the means to monitor managers' behaviour to ensure corporate accountability and provide for the cost-effective protection of investors' and society's interests vis-à-vis corporate insiders. They can be understood, in sum, as serving both to determine what society considers to be acceptable standards of corporate behaviour, and to ensure that corporations comply with those standards.

This work, using a comparative approach, aims at deriving a taxonomy of CG. We will examine in a comparative way the relevant fields for CG and try to understand if there is a process of convergence towards a common set of features or if we will have a divergence of the systems. This issue is particularly relevant for transition and developing economies. In fact, a relevant problem for these countries has been to decide which set of rules about CG to adopt. Ideally, if we consider the legal environment as an important matter, we could split the world into two big areas: one that is governed by a set of "common laws" while the other part is governed by a set of "civil laws". Common law countries developed a market oriented, or "outsider" system of CG while civil law countries developed an "insider" system of CG or, a relationship-based corporate system. As we can easily see the environment is complex.

In fact, just this difference gives us several questions to be answered when we want to implement a system of CG. To asses the efficiency of CG a taxonomy of CG is needed. This is not an easy task since in the literature there is not a clear way to asses which system is the better one. The method used here is to highlight the main features of some systems of CG around the world. This will help to analyse which are the relevant features that a generic system of CG needs to posses in order to be efficient: just considering common law countries and civil law countries we obtain two different systems of CG. If we further complicate the environment (i.e. considering places where there are efficient financial markets or places where there are institutional investors controlling the firms and so on) other problems are still open.

The paper can be ideally divided in three parts: the first one is introductory and regards the question if law matters and, if it does, how it affects the development of a system of CG. The second part, starting from the two main systems of CG, analyse the role of institutions in two hybrid systems as the Italian and the Korean one. Last part of the paper illustrates the main features for each of the examined systems and how the current situation is evolving. More precisely the paper is structured as it follows: in Section 1.2. we analyse the insights that institutional economics offer on the subject and presents some benchmarks on CG and law. In Section 1.3. we discuss how some institutions affect the typical agency relation in CG systems; the role played by institutions to deal with imperfect information and inefficient CG structures are the topic of Section 1.4; section 1.5 contains an overview of social capital as an asset that could reduce agency costs. Sections 1.6 - 1.10 offer a synthesis of the German/European and the UK/US systems, and a brief overview of some hybrid systems in which the role of institutions different from market and law is prominent. In section 1.11 we propose a taxonomy of CG and in Section 1.12 we present an agenda for future research. Section 1.13 concludes.

1.2. Institutional Economics and Corporate Governance: Some Benchmarks

CG is about the control of the resources in firms. It is concerned with the institutions that influence how business corporations allocate resources and returns. A system of CG determines who makes investment decisions in corporations, what types of investments are made, and how returns from investments are distributed (Lazonick and O'Sullivan, 1995). That control should be organized in such a way that investors, managers, employees, and other stakeholders commit resources to the firms on the expectation of a return. The system should discipline management so that objectives of stakeholders are realized.

Systems of CG evolve. In Germany, for example, changes have taken place recently in the bank-based system. Post-war Germany developed into a bank-based system with relational contracting between industrial firms and banks and with long term commitments and trust as the oil in the machine. Banks were important inside shareholders with seats on the board of directors. A second element of Germany system is shared decision making whose logic is the wish to create consensus among the participants. A third element is the insider control system of CG with representatives in banks in the supervisory boards of the industrial firms. During the last decade banks changed strategies from commercial banking based on long-term relations to investment banking. This had implications for the interfirm relations between industry and banks, influencing the insider control system. Investment banking implies deal-based transaction with industrial firms demanding no close ties, flexibility and diversification of the portfolio. Therefore investment banking does not fit well with banks having seats on the boards of industrial firms (see Deeg, 2001). The networks via the board seats become less dense (see Groenewegen, 2004).

Japan can also be characterized as an insider system: banks, industrial corporations, and financial institutions are closely linked, and the development of the system follows a specific path. Fundamental changes in lifetime employment, especially among the younger generation, seem to be occurring.

The changes in the USA also seem path dependent: after the scandals of Enron and others in the USA the reaction mainly has been one of tighter legal regulations as laid down in the Sarbanes-Oxley Act.

Changes such as the ones described above raise the question of the most efficient control of the firm. Who should control the firm? How should the board of directors be composed, and what should be the role of that board in relation to management?

In this section we discuss the insights offered by institutional economics, both the new and the original one.

New Institutional Economics (NIE) departs from the individual who maximizes his or her utility. The instruments are the institutional arrangements of contracts and organizations. In a competitive environment actors are forced to remedy failures, to apply the fitter type of governance structure. Management of firms is disciplined by the competitive pressure of product markets, the market for managerial labour, and the market for corporate control. Government is responsible for the right formal institutional environment of legal rules. According to such a perspective efficient systems of CG are ex-ante created by actors in contractual arrangements (property rights and agency theory) or emerge ex post (transaction cost economics) (Groenewegen, 2004, p.354).

Agency theory builds upon the theory of property rights as developed, among others, by Alchian and Demsetz (1972). The incentive problem arising from a separation between management and ownership should be solved through implicit or explicit contracts, in which individual rights are well specified so costs and rewards are clearly allocated among participants in the firm. How managers behave depends on the contracts they have with the owners. This general idea is elaborated in agency theory resulting in the firm as a multiple of complex relationships (i.e., contracts) between the legal fiction (the firm) and the owners of labour, material and capital input (Jensen and Meckling, 1976). The conflicting interests among stakeholders are brought into equilibrium within a framework of contractual relations. Owners will discipline management through monitoring or bonding contracts, which create incentives for management to serve the interests of the owners, that is, to maximize the values of the firm in the interest of shareholders.

The board is an instrument by which managers control other managers: "if there is competition among top managers themselves…, then perhaps they are the best one to control the board of directors" (Fama, 1980, p. 393). If the contract establishes the incentive correctly, then the managers will monitor each other, which makes the board of directors more like an executive committee. Fama and Jensen (1983) were more explicit about the composition and tasks of the board of directors: a distinction is made between decision management (the initiation and implementation of proposal for resource allocation) and decision control (the ratification and monitoring of proposals). They argued that in noncomplex, small organizations both the decision management and decision control can best be allocated to those who have the specific information in the organization and are also the residual claimants. However, if the organization is large and more complex and the residual claimants are outside shareholders, then management has specific information which is not shared by the owners. In those cases decision management and decision control should be separated: management should be controlled by the board of directors and in case of a large number of shareholders the decision control should be exercised by the board on behalf of the shareholders. In practice, we observe two main systems[3]: one-tier system and two-tier system. Agency theory (AT) does tell us about optimal incentives schemes but does not inform us about the organizational form that will come about (Hart, 1989).

In the AT there is no conceptual distinction between the "inside" and the "outside" of the firm: it is all about contracts that organize input, production and selling. In transaction costs economics (TCE) the firm is conceptualized as a governance structure, which is different from the market and which allows for a clear distinction between "markets and hierarchies". The authority aspect is taken by TCE to be the distinguishing nature of the firm resulting in the hierarchy that economizes on transaction costs in comparison to market contracts (Groenewegen, 2004).

AT and TCE have in common that both work out of the characteristics of bounded rationality and opportunism. Incomplete contracting is central. Meaning that prospective incentive and governance needs will be anticipated and are "folded in" (Williamson, 1985). So, the NIE takes the position that all parties that have a stake in the firm should make contracts to the best of their ability; shareholders should be represented on the board of directors.

Original Institutional Economics (OIE) differ from NIE in scope, method, and significance (Stanfield 1999). In the NIE the individual is the starting point, the approach is methodologically individualistic, and rationality is universal (Mayhew 1989). In contrast, in the OIE the wants of individuals and the resources are endogenous. The change of technology and wants are not random, not subject to a natural law working without human agency, but "change by virtue of influences that are endogenous to the human social system. Since the human social system is fundamentally a system of power and habit, these changes emerge from the exercise of power and habit" (Stanfield, 1999, p.234). Markets are not neutral selection mechanism but are considered to be filters of the interest of specific individuals and groups; individuals and groups attempt to organize markets in such a way that their private interests are best served. Next to this "lower efficiency", institutional arrangements can also serve the "higher efficiency", being the public interest (Groenewegen, 2004, p.357).

What the CG should be and who should control the firm is not an issue of "emergence" but an issue of valuation. Bush (1993) has elaborated the Veblenian distinction between ceremonially and instrumentally warranted values. The former refers to patterns that cohere to the received customs and practices, as well as the prevailing patterns of power and status in the community, the latter to technological innovations that serve the progress of society in general. Instrumental values contribute to the problem-solving process and provide for the "continuity of human life and the non-invidious recreation of community through the instrumental use of knowledge" (Tool, 1979, p.293).

Systems of CG reflect existing values, norms, legal rules, and power structures. Firms are governance structures reflecting ceremonial values, and a pragmatic instrumentalist valuation

[3] The one-tier system is characterized by one board of directors with executives (management) and non-executives as representatives of the owners (residual claimants/shareholders) The two-tier system has a separate supervisory board that monitors management. For further discussion on this topic see section 1.3 and sections 1.6 – 1.9

can show whose interests are served and who do not benefit from existing arrangements. OIE is not value free. On the contrary, all economics is value laden. In general, original institutional economists favour values of democratic decision making serving the interests of all participants. So in the case of the control of firms, the firm is then not a neutral nexus of contracts[4], or the fitter governance structure, but a community stakeholders. Not only capital but also labor, suppliers, the community in the region, and customers have a stake in the firm.

The firm could be looked as a nexus of firm-specific investment rather than a nexus of contracts. These firm-specific investments create room for bargaining and have to be governed after the contracts have been made. For this reson CG can be defined as a set of constraints shaping the ex post bargaining over the joint output of firm-specific investments (Zingales, 1988). The board has to take over the task of governing the firm-specific investments and mediating between possible conflicting interests of financial and knowledge investors in firm-specific assets which cannot be contracted ex-ante (Hosterloh anf Frey, 2005).

Decisions about the control of the firms should be based on a careful, holistic analysis of the firm and of the institutional space available. The firm is not an isolated institutional arrangement without a history and without a context. A firm consists of distinct pattern of behaviour and has institutionally rooted constraints and incentives that create typical strategies, routine approaches to problems, and shared decision rules that produce predictable patterns of behaviour. These patterns are reinforced by similar and complementary patterns in the environment of the firm (Groenewegen, 2004, p. 358).

The basic agency problem formulated in terms of the separation of ownership from control led us to an interesting research field on CG and, particularly, on the efficiency of the various mechanisms for solving this problem and mitigating the costs associated with the resulting conflict of interests. There are five key features that allow us to classify these systems around the world: the legal protection of investors, the level of ownership concentration, the development of capital markets, the market for corporate control, and the effectiveness of boards of directors.

The legal environment is fundamental to explain differences in CG systems and to give an evaluation of CG goodness. What are the features of a legal tradition that define and differentiate it from other traditions? In accord with La-Porta et al. (1998) there are six criteria to consider such as the historical background and development of the legal system, theories and hierarchies of sources of law, the working methodology of jurists, the characteristic of legal concepts employed, the legal institutions and the divisions of law employed. Using these six different categories, we can aggregate the existing systems in two big sets, civil law and common law. Of course these are not the only two existing systems[5] but probably they are the most relevant for a comparative and evolutionary study of investor protection and CG. The common law is formed by judges who have to resolve specific disputes. So precedent from judicial decisions, as opposed to contributions by scholars, shape common law. In the civil law tradition there are mainly three common families of laws and these are the French, the German and the Scandinavian. It seems that the two main systems of CG (the US/UK one and the German/Japanese) follow the two sets of countries divided by

[4]The view of the firm as a nexus of contracts, in which only shareholders carry a residual risk and should therefore have residual ownership and control, is misleading. Firms exist because they can produce what is commonly called synergies (Foss and Iversen, 1997) or quasi-rents (Zingales 1998).

[5]LaPorta (1998) considers even Canon Law, Hindu Law, Muslim Law, Jewish Law and other religious traditions.

the type of law that they use. Let us try to understand more examining which are the similarities between the considered countries, what kind of CG devices a system based on i.e. common law stimulates to develop and if some countries that have a i.e. common law tradition are using some CG devices that are more common in civil law tradition countries. The first issue to examine are shareholder rights and stakeholder (or creditor) rights.

1.2.1. Shareholders or Stakeholders Interest?

Preferences (or tastes), interests, values, and norms are often taken as primitives. Preferences are subjective and personal. They lack cognitive content, and hence are not rationally defensible. One either likes chocolate ice cream or one does not, and there is no point in arguing the matter.

Interests have a pragmatic aspect missing from tastes, and they may be defensible. Interests are related to needs and are constitutive of the good in life. They define what is conducive to human flourishing, and they may diverge from preferences. I have an interest in good health; to accomplish my goal of leading a successful life, I should exercise regularly, but for various reasons I prefer to spend my time some other way. Interest may implicate an ought command, but such a command is only binding in terms of the personal consequences if the command is violated. Interests may also have a social context, such as when we speak of a group interests or the "public interest", in either case indicating what the community in question needs to flourish. An oughtness quality may similarly be implicated, but here this quality is readily associated with shared values (Avio, 2004, p.724).

Values, with references to the property of things that count in choice, are rationally defensible, but the defence of values is typically in terms of a shared way of life. Indeed, the very concept of community implies that some values are held in common. For non trivial values to have an influence on one's life, one must be a member of a community with shared goals and collective aspirations. Values have an associated evaluative quality expressing what is good for a particular culture or an individual. In some instances exit is a viable option.

Norms are rules or principles of action that always have a binary (yes/no) oughtness quality attached. In this they differ from values, which "inform decisions as to what conduct is most desirable" (Habermas, 1995, p.114).

The distinction between the three aspects of human agency, less sharp in practice than in theory, may be made more concrete by considering the death-bed test. What question does each personified agent confront if challenged to sum up his or her life? Homo economicus considers whether he everywhere and in all circumstances chose the best (most efficient) means to satisfy his given preferences. Homo sociologicus additionally asks whether the values she has embraced over her life were defensible within her given form of life. Homo communicans subordinates these questions to moral concerns, that is, whether one acted in accordance with impartial rules freely self-imposed and accettable to all. He is, in effect the ideal man of Adam Smith's Theory of Moral Sentiments. Such a person takes on the generalizable and publicly defensible interests of all (Avio, 2004).

Legal tradition matters for CG and corporate performance because they are systematically related to patterns in the types of legal rights and protection provided to investors. As La-Porta et al. (1998) point out, creditor rights are actually more complex than shareholder rights because in case of financial distress they have to choose to liquidate the firm or they can attempt to reorganise and resuscitate the firm (see also Aoky 1998) and, since there are multiple classes of creditors it is quite probable that different classes of lenders will have different objectives (see Emmons and Schmid 1999).

A possible solution to the dilemma of what to do in case of financial distress is very well examined by Aoki (1998). The author suggests a third way of CG: punctuated CG. In fact, the author builds a model in which, given the presence of a third party as a sort of "umpire" between stakeholders and managers, there will be a different "optimal" type of CG mechanism that can efficiently govern the agency relationship between the parts and management. In the real economic system the "umpire" can be easily interpreted as bank or institutional investors in German/Japanese CG mechanism and in the "market of corporate control" or, in the last instance, the judge for US/UK systems. In some economies this umpire is the Government as well. One of the most powerful results of the work of Aoki is that in his view what he calls "the punctuated contingent governance" (PCG) is superior to the market controlled governance (US/UK). This because PCG triggers the shift of rights to residual outputs and organisational continuation/dissolution from the insiders to a third party agent outside the team. In US/UK system it is an ex ante unidentifiable participant in the market of corporate control that would acquire the residual claimant status. In the event of bankruptcy, liquidation is subject to a court supervised legal procedure. Possible claimants in a bankruptcy are also ex ante not specified. In US/UK systems, potential raiders bid in the market for their own advantage. So they could pursue their own objective despite the interest of shareholders and/or stakeholders. In contrast PCG specifies at the time of initial contracting that the "umpire" must bear costs not only in the bankruptcy region but possibly even greater costs in the bailing out region. Even the German/Japanese system is subject to some critics in the extent of the commitment that the "umpire" can specify ex ante and in the level of independence of the existing "umpire" (bank or institutional investors are usually even stakeholders in the two considered system).

Let us go back to the shareholders rights now. In basically all the existing versions of the Corporate Governance Code done in UK it is specified that the residual claimant is the shareholder and that the manager has to act to represent the shareholder rights (see Maw 1995 and Hampel Code of CG). In La Porta et al. (1998) the civil law countries score better than the common law countries but we have to note that the overall result is again in favour of common law countries and this basically because where the role played by law is high basically there are few rights for shareholder/stakeholder. So, common law countries appear to provide a better CG environment[6]. But we need to consider another implicit actor: the market.

---

[6]Here we would like to stress the word "environment". We are not saying that they provide a better "system" of corporate governance but that the "agent", seen as shareholder more than a stakeholder in these countries, achieves a potentially more "safe" environment. But again, it is important to note that in these countries the principal is the shareholder, that has residual control and residual claim. However, the set of common law countries score a low point in the protection of stakeholder as well. This provide a "good" environment but the "goodness" of corporate governance systems will depend on other factors that we will soon analyze.

1.2.2. Common Law and Civil Law: The Role of Markets in the Two Environments

It is now time to talk of other features distinguishing the two main systems of CG: the role of market of corporate control and the role of financial market. Common law countries have nearly twice the market capitalisation of civil law countries with just few exceptions. Is this event casual or has it got some "evolutionary" connection with the legal environment? La Porta et al (1998) and Emmons and Schmid (1999) have analysed some ratios to understand how much of this phenomenon can explain this difference.

The firms of all 4 groups of countries have a very similar ratio of debt and this is quite surprising since we already saw that common law countries provide better protection to creditors. The way in which the firms finance this debt is different between the sample of countries: in fact, US and Canadian firms issue a significant amounts of bonds but British firms use bank as a source of primary financing, so there is not homogeneity of debt financing between the common law countries. In civil law countries basically banks play a major role in financing firm but even here there are some exceptions. It seems so that the legal environment is not the primary source in differences between different debts by the firm. This result again can be explained with the fact that in US banks cannot own firms' shares in a "relevant" amount and this means that if there are financial troubles the banks cannot recover their debts transforming it in equity (shares).

As previously said, excluding some exception as Japan, South Korea and Taiwan, common law countries have a much more higher market capitalisation than civil law countries. The "exceptions" identified by La Porta et al. (1998) are in a set of Asiatic market with common tradition in the role of financial markets. So, it seems that common law stimulates the evolution of larger market for outside equity and, in some countries, also for corporate bonds. Civil law instead stimulates relatively more bank debts, owner contributed funds and retained earnings. This is an important point and here we need to recall which is the difference of financing with retained earnings, financing with banks and financing through the market. Basically the managers are subject to a different sort of "evaluation" of their investment projects if the financing is with banks that with financial markets. Sometimes the managers use retaining earnings if they do not want, for some reasons, afford the risk of not being financed by external investors. The "different" is referred to the fact that probably the risks that banks are able to play are different from that of venture capitalist or financial market investors. If we use all this small pieces of the puzzles that we are trying to build (and further we go, more complex it becomes), these pieces of evidence on firms' capital structure suggest that bank domination of external financing in civil law countries may reduce firms' flexibility and sometimes (retained earnings) can even stimulate managerial accumulation of power. The fact that civil law does not stimulate the growth of developed capital market becomes quite important when we need to give a sort of evaluation of the potential benefit of bank (or institutional investors or all two together) centred financial system.

1.3. Agency Costs and The Role Played by Markets and Other Institutions

In the classical analysis, the diffused ownership is layered over a basic principal-agent problem: the stockholders' agenda – typically maximizing shareholder value – can be at odds with managers' agendas. In that setting, aligning their interests becomes the typical problem of CG. And the institutions of CG are those repeated mechanisms that tie, or fail to tie, managers to stockholders (Roe, 2004).

This "agency cost", principal-agent, stockholder-manager alignment problem comes in two main varieties. One variety is of diversion, while the other is of competence, "stealing and shirking" in its alliterative form. Managers could divert value from the firm into their own hands: they could have the firm transfer funds to their own bank accounts (or a relative's), or have the firm sell goods at low prices to (or to buy at high price from) entities controlled by them, or more transparently pay themselves (excessively) high salaries.

Well functioning CG institutions put the right manager in the right place and give that manager the right set of incentives and constrains. Compensation, especially stock-based compensation, would seem a quite promising way to align senior managers with shareholders, and thereby reduce the "*vertical*" CG problem[7]. Incentive compensation obviously is an important institution of CG, but it too has its limits. First, with shareholders scattered and not themselves writing the incentive contract, the option may not fully motivate managers but may successfully enrich them. Since the common options contracts seem to fall short of an ideal contract, there are good reasons to think that the options actually used do not resolve the vertical governance problem as well as they could. Second, even if the compensation is nicely attuned to performance, senior managers quickly become rich. But the successful managers not, once they become multi-millionaires, turn the firm over to a new crew of hungry but impoverished managers. They instead continue while wealthy, running the firm. One can question how strongly incentive compensation motivates truly wealth people.

Managers do not act solely for remuneration, but also for the satisfaction of doing a good job. Doing a good job is defined by circumstances, psychology, and culture. Professionals want the firm to do well. They are often acculturated to work for shareholder, and often do so even if the other institutional constraints are not tight. Or, managers who get a new product out, who succeed, who turn a division around feel good about themselves, and in turn shareholders profit. Organization depends on managers' capacity for collaboration, cooperation and trust.

Roe (2004) affirms that the alliterative "stealing and shirking" hides a couple of issues. The first is that each specific CG institution does not uniformly reduce both. Some affect one, some affect the other. "Stealing and shirking" are both costs to shareholders and generally it is correct to lump them together. However, once we evaluate the institutions of CG this is not possible because the institutions affect the two differently. For example corporate lawsuits are geared to handling observed "stealing", but less good at handling "shirking" or managerial error. Corporate disclosure rules, in contrast, are probably better at affecting "shirking" – distant stockholders can see the bottom line results that managers produce, but less good at

[7] Vertical CG regards the relations between minority shareholders and manager. Horizontal CG regards the relations between close control shareholders and minority shareholders.

handling "stealing" (because for very large firms, lots of personal wealth could be obtained from a firm without destroying the corporate bottom line).

Much of the power of an organization comes from routines and embedded information. These give the organization great power and efficiency. Even though bureaucracy often has a pejorative connotation, bureaucracies are effective at routinizing action to create a more powerful output. But when markets or technologies change, the routines and embedded information can weaken the organization. Organizational change is necessary, but insiders often cannot refashion the firm, because they are subject to its old routines and embedded information.

Some CG institutions seek to overcome the free-rider problem, so that large shareholders can focus their ownership and thereby deal better with managerial agency costs. These focusing institutions include a more responsive board of directors, takeovers, blockholders capable of reining in some managerial agency cost, proxy voting and so on.

There are significant differences in the role played by the market for corporate control among various systems. On the one hand, Market-Based Systems are generally characterized by highly active markets for corporate control. Actually, a substantial number of takeovers take place in the US and the UK; and the percent of unfriendly bids is not negligible in these countries.

On the other hand, an active market for corporate control is virtually absent in Bank-Based Systems. For instance, in continental Europe companies usually adopt defensive measures protecting managers and controlling owners, which introduce restrictions into the market for corporate control (Cuervo, 2002). The strength of cross shareholdings and the influence of banks typical of keiretsu represent the main structural barriers to takeovers in Japan. Takeovers are relatively rare in Germany, too.

One of the central topics related to the effectiveness of boards in CG concerns the existence of unitary versus two-tier boards. Firms in Anglo-Saxon countries and in most European countries except Germany have adopted the unitary structure; i.e. there is no distinction between managing and supervisory functions. In contrasts, in systems with a two-tier structure, the existence of both an executive and a supervisory board guarantees that the areas of competence of each of the bodies have been more clearly defined. For example, according to German Law, a public company is obligated to have a two-tier board (see Kaplan, 1997). The independence of the supervisory board is thus assured, since none of its members is allowed to be a member of the managing boarding at the same time. In Japan, although, there is a more complex structure of various committee, the most relevant one acts as a supervisory board, since it is composed of external experts and representatives of the main companies in the Keiretsu[8] (see Kojima, 1994). Another important factor that must be taken into account besides the board structure is the designation of independent or non-executive directors. This practice seems to be increasingly widespread in UK and US firms (see Belcher, 2003).

Markets - the firm's product market, the capital market and the managerial labour market - are often the most important institution of CG. If firm cannot sell its product, it disappears. If firm cannot raise capital, it cannot grow. If firm cannot get and retain good managers (and employees) it will fritter away its resources. This sometimes leads commentators to belittle

[8] For a detailed analysis of the Japan system see section 1.6.2

the importance of other CG institutions, because one of the markets (in some cases all) punishes deviant firms and reward well-performing firms.

But, as Roe (2004) explains, a *markets-are-everything* idea would face three substantial defects. First, as we know, each market is imperfect, sometimes substantially so. CG institutions might pick up the slack where markets cannot reach. Markets can sometimes deal with gross deviations, while other institutions of CG then deal with middle-sized deviations. Markets often draw an outer limit, but not a tight constraint. Second, the other CG institutions can prime or charge-up each one of the markets institutions. Good internal decision making can make the firm react well to market changes, economize on capital, or make sure good managers come, stay and perform. Good CG institutions can feed back and become one of the bases for market place competition in the three markets.

Third, markets may be good for some governance tasks, weak for others. They may be good at limiting some types of "shirking" but be less good at limiting "stealing", especially if the stealing is a small part of the firm's total value[9]. Law and other (non market) institutions are probably more important here than market itself; sometimes they are better and cheaper at governing firms than any market constraint.

The board is the quintessential vertical CG institution[10]. It hires and fires the CEO, makes key business decisions, and reviews the work of the firm's senior managers. Indeed one could see other institutions as primarily interacting with the board, i.e. the devices used by coalesced shareholders once they are means to select a new board. Laws, in the form of rules regulating proxy contests and takeovers, affect the composition of the board of directors. Or information distribution and transparency allow outside stockholders to see what is happening inside the board. Or designing CEO incentive compensation is a tool to align managers with shareholders, but it's a tool that can only be as good as the board makes it (see Roe, 2004).

Distant shareholders (minority shareholders), as Roe (2004) claims, need information about their companies in order to:

a) price their securities and, via that, pricing other CG institutions like incentive compensation or board action, which can be triggered by bad pricing results, come into play;
b) decide whether a corporate control transaction (ousting the board, taking over the company, engaging in a proxy fight) makes sense;
c) decide whether legal action make sense;
d) help capital markets to function properly in CG (by denying or rewarding firms with new capital).

A good information distribution may facilitate allocative efficiency and an accurate information flow helps both allocative efficiency and CG.

The institutions here are the securities law mandates of periodic disclosure (and the penalties for non-compliance). The gatekeepers are those not deeply embedded inside the firm who verify or sometimes warrant the information about the firm. They are lawyers, accountants, securities analysts, underwriters, and outside directors.

---

[9] If a small percentage of a firm's assets is stolen in relation to forgone market opportunities, the market may not deter the manager.

[10] Because a dominant stockholder typically controls the board, the board is less important as an institution of horizontal governance.

Takeovers are not the only means of coalescing shareholders. Proxy fights have one team seeking the votes of other shareholders with a view to gaining control of the board. Leveraged buyouts are another: a management team (or a group of outsiders) borrows heavily to buy out a division of a conglomerate (or an entire firm). Ownership concentrates.

Institutional investors voice is another means of coalescing shareholders. Institutional investors complain to boards, make lists of badly managed firms, and send around proposal on better governance, such as an improved committee structure for boards. Managers and boards then react, presumably, for two reasons: i) many want to do a better job, and if institutional investors have gathered good information, boards can economize by relying on the institutional investors' recommendations of good practice; ii) campaigns by institutional investors could indicate incipient disquiet among the firm's shareholder base. The targeted boards and managers might react because they don't want to activate another CG institution, such as takeover, a proxy fight, or melt-down of the company's stock price (see Roe, 2004).

1.4. Imperfect Information and Inefficient Corporate Governance Structures

Economics of information provides a number of reasons as to why inefficiencies can prevail in both organization and markets. As Akerlof (1970) demonstrated, when information is distributed unequally between sellers and buyers, that sellers of low quality used cars could drive out sellers of good quality used cars. This market failure can be addressed partially by introducing warranties, but the market cannot supply warranties with optimal quality due to "double moral hazard". In other words, it is not in the interest of the sellers to provide optimal warranty given the probability that the buyer's care effort would fall after the warranty (Ugur, 2005).

Information economics has also revealed the implication of information asymmetries for CG quality (Core, 2001). Once the agent does not pursue adequately principal's interest there can be two explanations: a bad state of the world or an agent's opportunistic behaviour. The principal cannot distinguish the case. Agency costs are incurred in order to reduce or eliminate the effect of opportunistic behaviour (moral hazard or adverse selection)[11].

One may argue that information asymmetries and therefore agency costs can be minimised by the emergence of a market for information. However, a developed market for information may lead to lower disclosure quality overall and generate rents that can be shared between managers, the analysts and the institutional investors at the expense of other stakeholders.

Imperfect information provides ample scope for inefficient CG structures to survive even if firms and their stakeholders act rationally. Secondly, CG norms and regulations may fail to resolve even the principal-agent problem between key internal actors of the firm let alone the more general CG problems in the wider world of corporate-stakeholder interactions (Ugur, 2005).

---

[11] Moral hazard exists due to a lack of effort (shirking) on the part of the agent. Adverse selection exists when the agent misrepresents his or her ability or, more generally, does not behave in the manner preferred by the principal.

As Hayek (1945) pointed out, information asymmetries are an inescapable feature of human society. As a result, exchange is hindered either because agents who could benefit from the transaction cannot find each other, or because, having found each other, they do not trust each other enough. Many transactions that would benefit both parties, thereby promoting efficiency, will not take place.

For the institutional economists the transactions between pairs of actors are constrained by an "order", "governance structure" (Williamson, 1985), "institutional environment" or "institutional arrangement (North, 1990) – i.e., a set of explicit (formal) or implicit (informal) rules, which structures transactions between individuals in particular ways. In the widest sense [business] transactions are constrained by or embedded in "ongoing social relations" (Granovetter, 1985, p.53).

Granovetter's concept of embeddedness of actors, that social structure matters, is in effect directed against the zero-transaction-costs world of neoclassical theory. The social structure of markets does not matter in the case of "perfect markets" or its counterpart, "perfect hierarchy". All social relationships are of economic value to actors, make up their "social capital" (Coleman 1988, Sobel 2002). That social relations matter in a much more general sense than economists are used to take in account is known.

Organizational culture in the sense of Kreps (1990) is a focal ("shared") set of rules of appropriate behaviour. Such a self enforcing implicit agreement can be interpreted as a Nash Equilibrium of a repeated game about the endogenous rules of a given super-game. This is an "institutions-as-equilibrium-of-a-game view". It is based on the plausible idea that institutions can only enduringly function when every individual regards it advantageous to adhere to their explicit or implicit rules in the long-run as well (Richter, 2002).

Economic theory and basic common sense suggest that differences in the organization of society should have an effect on economic outcomes: when institutions ensure that a potential investor has property rights over the proceeds from his investments, he is more likely to invest than when he expects the fruits of his efforts to be taken by other parties in the economy or by the government. What is crucial is whether the organization of the society ensures that a broad cross-section of the society have effective property rights, so that those with productive opportunities expect to receive returns from their investments (Acemoglu et al., 2001).

Since economic actors will make investments when they expect to be rewarded for their spending and effort, in a society where property rights are no well enforced, investment and output will be low. Therefore the property rights' degree of enforcement is a central feature of the institutions and the broad organization of a society.

While philosophers find it impossible to formulate universal moral principle, common law theories of CG contracting impose broad duties of competence, loyalty, and care on all stakeholders. These duties require insiders and outsiders alike to explore the economic perspective of other stakeholders and to avoid doing net (i.e., insufficiently compensated) harm to any of them. This principle of no exploitation expresses a "Golden Rule of Corporate Governance". Because it is impossible to build an information and control system capable of truly enforcing due compensation, the rule is only a counsel of perfection. However, it can serve as a touchstone with which to identify weakness in the incentive system under which real world corporation and watchdog institutions operate (Kane, 2004, p.2).

A firm's internal incentive system is "impartial" if it minimizes temptations for its employees (including so-called independent directors) to engage in inefficient, dishonest, or exploitative behaviour. The theory of principal-agent relationships transforms this ethical criterion for fairness into a condition of economic efficiency. The transformation leans on the proposition that in every contract counterparties have incentives to reduce or control conflicts of interest so as to reduce the losses these conflict engender and then share the gains (Jensen, 1994). Costs of principal-agent relationships are minimized when information and corporate-governance systems harmonize the marginal benefits and costs that managerial strategies and tactics confer on different stakeholders.

As the Golden Rule stipulates, incentive compatibility is achieved when information flows and enterprise contracts leave all parties unable to gain an advantage from other stakeholders by acting opportunistically. An enterprise whose incentive system offers specific employees an opportunity to pursue personal short-run advantages at the expense of uninformed others may be characterized as "institutionalizing a temptation to do wrong" .

Watchdogs lower stakeholder coordination costs by designing and enforcing disclosure requirements and by policing managerial behaviour. Internally, a firm's board of directors and auditing team are tasked with developing sound reporting safeguards and detecting deviations from them. Externally, their work is tested by other specialists. These external watchdogs include: outside auditors, stock analysts, credit-rating agencies, standard-setting professional organizations, regulators, government examiners, law-enforcement personnel, and information media (see Kane, 2004).

Watchdogs face incentive conflicts of their own; these conflicts are only partially mitigated by reputation concerns and codes of professional ethics that frown on dishonesty.

1.5. Social Assets and Opportunistic Behaviour

Corporate morality might be seen as an analogy of individual morality. Corporation, like individuals, will benefit from moral behaviour. In general, corporation behaviour will reflect the moral sentiments of its top management. If this is true, stakeholders will be able to assess the moral sentiments of top management with reasonable accuracy.

Corporate morality like individual morality is detectable through reputation and it is reflected in the policies and decisions of the firm and in the nature of its direct dealings with corporate stakeholders.

Economists and moral philosophers since Adam Smith have observed that market economies operate far better where shared values of honesty and integrity prevail than where they do not. As North (1981, p.47) claimed: "strong moral and ethical codes of a society are the cement of social stability which makes an economic system viable".

Circumstances in which agents pursue their own interests at expense of principals is a clear manifestations of opportunism. Situations of opportunism, lack of trust and cooperation are real problems in firm/stakeholder relations .

We can improve efficiency in two ways: increasing the quality of information (less asymmetry and/or more completeness) and fostering trust. To do this, there are basically two solutions: via formal institutions or via interpersonal relationships. Formal institutions, as we saw in section 1.3, are more expensive than interpersonal relationships and quite often they need to be integrated by informal institutions to be effective. So, it can be helpful to analyse the literature on social capital[12] that focuses principally on interpersonal relationships.

One can distinguish two main categories of social capital: structural (roles, rules, precedents, and procedures) and cognitive (norms, values, attitudes, and beliefs). Social capital is an accumulation of various types of social, psychological, cultural, cognitive, institutional, and related assets that increase the amount (or probability) of mutually beneficial cooperative behaviour. This behaviour is productive for others as well as for one's self (Uphoff, 2000).

The component of social capital are therefore many, varied and, in many instances, intangible as they consist of different types of relationship and engagements. Social capital is unlike other assets that economists call capital because investment in its development does not seems amenable to quantified measurement, even in principle. The capital label should be taken somewhat metaphorically as long as the effort involved in building social networks cannot be measured[13].

Much of the interest in social capital stems from effort to understand how social efficient outcomes can occur in environments in which the sorts of condition necessary for the classical First Welfare Theorem are not fulfilled (Durlaf and Fafchamps, 2004).

In other words, the transaction cost paradigm remains the traditional way of thinking about the mechanism by which social capital affects economic performance. When social capital is high, transactions costs are low which makes organizations and governments more efficient which ultimately leads to better economic growth and improved organizational efficiency (La Porta et al., 1997).

One important role for social capital concerns its ability to reduce potential inefficiencies caused by imperfect information.

From different definitions we find in literature, it is possible to distinguish three main underlying ideas: (1) social capital generates positive externalities for members of a group; (2) these externalities are achieved through shared trust, norms and values and their consequent effects on expectations and behaviour; (3) shared trust, norms and values arise from informal forms of organization based on social networks and associations.

An important aspect of social capital is the role played by social norms in determining socially conscious behaviour. The literature on the role of social norms in generating efficient social outcomes is growing (see Ostrom, 2000).

Individuals not only internalize moral norms, such as that of paying their dues, helping others at some costs for themselves; they also practice such norms as those prescribing that they punish people who have hurt them intentionally and even metanorms as shunning people who break agreements, and so forth. Individuals therefore feel shame or guilt in violating the norm and this prevent them from doing so. A general disposition to abide by agreements, to be truthful, to be able to trust one another is an essential lubricant of society.

In cases in which market relationships and nonmarket relationships coexists, a grim norm could be expected prevail, as it involves permanent sanctions – which is a device for

[12] The concept of social capital is used differently by sociologists, political scientists and economists. Views are divided both on definitions, measurement possibilities and significance. In pertaining literature, social capital has been conceptualized in a number of ways.

[13] Many authors take both social and human capital to be embodied in people. However, the critical difference between human and social capital is that education and health can be embodied in one individual regardless of what other people. Social capital requires a form of cooperation among them (Grootaert, 1998).

preventing people from engaging in opportunistic behaviour when short-term opportunities appear from time to time (Dasgupta, 2000)

Social preferences like altruism, fairness, trust, and reciprocity are relevant concepts to explain many forms of strategic interaction involving social dilemma games. These are particularly relevant for public goods and, as we have seen, management has a public good nature.

Several recent studies view social capital as a propensity of people in a society to cooperate to produce socially efficient outcomes and to avoid inefficient non-cooperative traps such as that in the prisoner's dilemma (La Porta et al. 1997).

The presence of social relationships can significantly alter the way effective payoffs are perceived by the players. Non-cooperative behaviour can lead to a reduction of utility in the form of implicit punishment or exclusion from relate "social games": Non cooperation can imply a loss of the benefits accruing to the individual as a result of her being part of a community and which are different from those that give rise to the reputation established in repeated games.

Moral characteristics can foster cooperation if they lead individuals to identify non cooperative behaviour with direct disutility. The mechanism at work in these cases is the presence of moral costs or a loss of self-esteem which prompts individuals to cooperate, especially when there is a reciprocity with a counterparty. Reciprocity does not imply in itself social ties or repeated transactions. In fact, it seems to be generated by the counterparty's trust, therefore a phenomenon which has already happened and not merely anticipated (Basili et al, 2004).

Institutions affect human behaviour. Organizations produce goods and services that are used by society. The rules that determine a society's institutions can be formal or informal. Even when formal rules are similar, informal rules or social capital can explain a significant part of the reason why some societies progress faster than others.

In the following paragraphs we present a selection of cases study.

1.6. Corporate Governance and Social Capital: A Selection of Cases Study

In the literature (see Shleifer and Vishny 1997) we have a broad classification of systems of Corporate Governance in US/UK model and in Continental Europe models (or German/ Japanese). Here, for brevity, we will not illustrate again the two main systems (Corbett 1994; Dimsdale 1994; Hughes 1994; Masuyama 1994; Schneider-Lenne 1994; Dietl 1998 Hoshi 1995 and 1997, Miyajima 1995 and 1998, Teranishi 1995 as references on the German Japanese system and Beecroft 1994; Dietl 1998; Prevezer and Ricketts 1994 among the others for the US/UK system). In section 1.6.1 there will be a short summary of the main characteristics of the German European system of CG. In section 1.6.2 we analyse the Japanese system of corporate governance. These two models are often analysed by the literature (see Shleifer and Vishny 1997 for a review) as "insider" system of CG. Section 1.7 analyses the two "outsider" systems of CG: the US and the UK systems. In Sections 1.8 and

1.9 are analysed the Italian and Korean system since they represent two hybrid systems[14] of the previous "benchmark" models. Finally in section 1.10 there are some situations that needs investigation when we deal with CG in Transition and developing economies.

1.6.1. The German/European and Japanese Models of Corporate Governance

The German and Japanese system of allying decision-making power and availability of information with interested parties has been described as an insider system. In an insider system, the powers of shareholders are diluted and those of banks, suppliers and employees are increased. The role of the banks is more prominent in disciplining company management while that of the stock market is reduced.

In Germany and Japan, financial institutions were allowed to develop in a very different direction from that in the USA (Corbett 1994; Dimsdale 1994; Edwards and Fischer 1994; Hughes 1994; Lomax 1994; Masuyama 1994; Schneider-Lenne 1994; Dietl 1998). In particular, they can hold significant amount of firms' equity and they could be able to provide an effective counterweight to strong managers and ensure that shareholder's interests were pursued (Roe 1994).

Germany has always had a prominent place in the international CG debate. Many German companies are world leaders in their fields and Germany is one of the richest countries in the world. On the other hand, Germany has institutions that often differ substantially from those found in other continental European countries, but even more so from those found in Anglo-Saxon countries. There are several comprehensive accounts of the German CG system. Charkham (1994) and Schmidt *et al.* (1997) provide institutional overviews. Edwards and Fischer (1994) analyse universal banking in Germany, but CG issues play an important role. Franks and Mayer (1996) analyse the role of ownership and control in disciplining management.

The German European model of CG involves three groups of participants at Director level. These include the Executive Board (appointed by the shareholders to run the company), the Supervisory Board (appointed by stakeholders) and the Advisory Board that is formed by independent experts to provide technical and external expertise to assist the company. In this scheme, the Supervisory Board undertakes the job of CG. So the Advisory Board is seen as a separated entity and they must sit or not on the Board of Directors (formed by Executive and Supervisory Boards). They have no specific legal responsibility for the actions undertaken by the firm.

In Germany the large bank-dominated corporate enterprise is only one such structure though it is the one that has dominated attention (Von Thadden 1995). Equally striking from the comparative perspective are the large number of firms with concentrated stockholdings (i.e. by family groups), the importance of cross holdings among firms in industrial groups and the sharp discontinuity in structure between the 30 or so largest firms and the vast middle-tier of German companies. The German CG structure contains a more formalised set of countervailing mechanisms against inside management. While insiders constitute the Managerial Board, this Board was monitored in turn by the Supervisory Board. The latter

[14] Hybrid in the special role played by some institutions such as family, coalition, personal relationships and so on.

included representatives of shareholders and workers, and because of the proxy voting structure, the shareholders' representatives, as a practical matter, were representatives of the main creditor groups, the bank. However, this formal structure seems to perpetuate managerial dominance. Managers' advantages derive from several sources: superior access to information, control over information flow to would-be-monitors, *de-facto* independence in day-to-day decision making and an ability to neutralise conflicting groups by playing them against each other.

The Supervisory Board relies on the Managerial Board for information so it does not seem to control well for these factors. Disclosure requirements have been exiguous but there has been some progress towards new accounting standards. The structure of voting prevents worker representatives from exercising any decisive influence. Also, the separation of Boards permits the Managerial Board to "divide and conquer" that is deal separately with shareholders and labour representatives of the Supervisory Board. While there are advantages to a system that places highly motivated representatives in the Supervisory Board, it appears that the system does not empower these representatives to do much to reduce managers' exercise of discretion. However there is some evidences that the Supervisor Board act as a monitoring device (Poens and Kaplan 1994).

Bank as Monitors

Universal banking is an alternative mechanism to a stock market for risk-sharing, for providing information for guiding investment, and for contesting CG. In Germany, where the stock market has historically been small, banks hold equity stakes in firms and have proxy voting rights over other agents' shares. In addition, banks lend to firms and have representatives on corporate Boards. If a banking relationship is a substitute for the stock market, then interaction with a bank should improve the performance of firms. But, if banks have private information about firms that they lend to and have monopolistic control over access to external capital markets, then bank interests may conflict with those of other equity holders, especially those whose shares are voted by the banks in proxy (see Gorton and Schmid 1996). So, in such a circumstance we can say that in the German system the role played by asymmetric information can be relevant and it is not fully avoided by the structure of CG implemented.

Aside from the structural problems posed by the dual Board, banks are at first cut a puzzling choice for monitoring managers. Though highly sophisticated given the information that they possess, as creditors they pursue substantially different interest from those of shareholders. May be that shareholders would prefer higher risk strategy than those that creditors would pursue. There can be other features connected to the presence of banks as monitoring mechanism, (i.e. some advantages in obtaining funds, preferential channel, or the possibility to stipulate contracts that they incorporate all the information in possession of the banks).

The Board and the System of Interest Representation

A unique feature of the German Board is its fit as a component of the German system of interest representation - codetermination at the firm and possibly with links to the way interest representation works at the government levels. Codetermination can be assessed either as a CG device or as device for facilitating the interest representation with on balance desirable features despite its negative impact on governance. That a third or half of the representative on the Supervisory Board are workers and they have some interests that can be different (if not opposite) from that of manager will move the managers to an attempt to avoid decision making through the Board as much as possible. In this way, the manager will be the only one who will take decisions and all the collective process of decision making will end.

Innovation

A crucial dimension for assessing CG systems is their ability to adapt to changing economic and technological circumstances. Two criticisms of the German corporate model predominate discussion: the difficulties of forming innovative German firms on the model of US venture capital financing for entrepreneurs and the problem of encouraging and monitoring innovation in large firms. The big problem, then is whether banks and large firms can provide proper incentives for innovative entrepreneurial activity.

The role of take-over in the German system has not a very important relevance. A paper from Franks and Mayer (1998) examines the three cases of hostile take-overs in Germany in the post-Second World War period. It describes the important role played by banks in affecting the outcome of the bids: bank representatives were chairmen of the Supervisory Board in all three cases and banks voted a large number of proxies in important decisions affecting the bids. One of the main results of this work is that it reports that shareholders of two of the target firms earned low returns and offers an explanation in terms of bank control and the regulatory regime operating in Germany.

The case of Metallgesellschaft AG (Jayaraman and Shrikhande 1997) is a very useful one to understand how, in practice, the German system of CG works. Metallgesellschaft AG had a serious financial distress that was driving the firm near to bankruptcy: while German CG and bankruptcy laws stimulated the recovery, they could not help in averting financial distress. Specifically, the participation of financial institutions in CG and the legal framework for troubled companies in Germany had a significant role to play in ensuring the survival of Metallgesellschaft AG (Jayaraman and Shrikhande 1997).

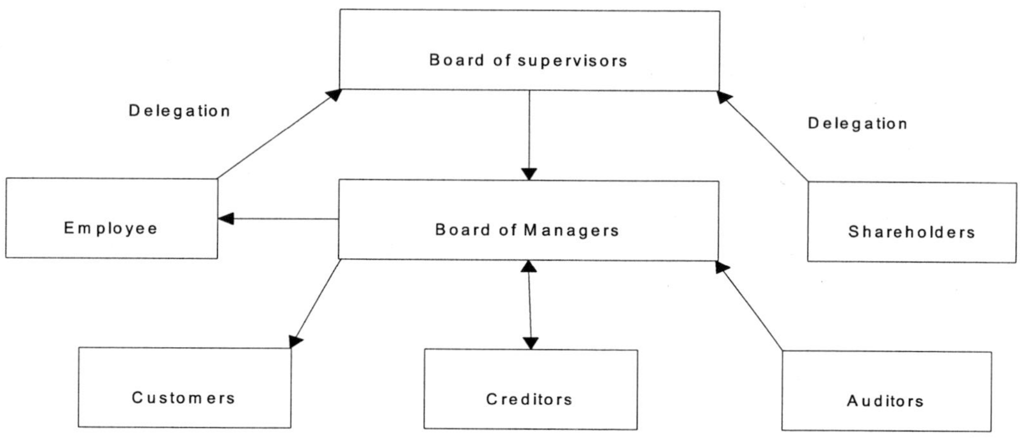

Figure 1 Corporate Governance in Germany

Corporate Governance in Germany: A Summary

In Figure 1 there is a representation of the dual Board structure of the German system of CG with the relationship between the actors of this system. In this system, shareholder concentration is important. We saw that the role played by bank as shareholder is fundamental: on the other hand, the role played by the capital market orientation is not as important as the market for corporate control. In fact, in Germany, the market for corporate control does not really exist (see De Jong 1997). As we saw, mergers are common but friendly and not hostile. During a take-over dialogues between the interested parties are likely to take place (Franks and Mayer 1998). The autonomy of the senior management, given the fact that they are strictly controlled in their actions by the institutional investors, is important. The formal decision making power still resides in the hand of the management but the practical effects of rational discussion, co-determination and consensus formation in the economic domain are working through (see De Jong H. 1997). Probably more important is the role played by the employees since they have a relevant place in the Board of the firm. Employees are a relevant stakeholder in corporate decision making. Their participation in the most important decision that may affect the future of the corporation is the rule, not an exception (see Dietl 1998) The employment involvement in the decision making process is not at discretion of the senior management but it is determined by the law to employ co-determination (see for this point Baums 1993, pg. 152). Two other important features of the German system of CG is the role played by banks (see for a survey on the topic Frank and Mayer 2001)) and the state intervention.

1.6.2. Corporate Governance in Japan

The work of Kojima (1997) is an extensive study of the model of CG in Japan. In this paper there is a presentation of the major characteristics of corporate environment, addressing capital markets and the ownership structure of public corporations. It also discusses internal control mechanisms of corporations and it describes the major features of the external control mechanisms.

Other relevant works in the structure of Japanese CG are Hoshi (1995 and 1997), Miyajima (1995 and 1998), Teranishi (1995). In this section we describe the main features that give to the Japanese model its own peculiarity[15].

> Shareholders have a duty to exercise certain responsibilities as corporate owners. All shareholders have a duty to try to replace dishonourable or incompetent management (source: Japanese Code of Corporate Governance; Corporate Governance Forum of Japan (CGFJ); Corporate Governance Principles - A Japanese View; May 26, 1998)

Shareholders, especially institutions that hold shares in trust for the benefit of others, have a duty to ensure that their investments are sound and that the management of the corporations in which they invest are competent, responsible, and effective leaders capable of producing wealth. This duty requires shareholders to monitor the performance of companies

[15]As a general reference for this paragraph see the Revised Japanese Code of Corporate Governance; Corporate Governance Forum of Japan (CGFJ); Corporate Governance Principles - A Japanese View; March 6 2002.

and to raise questions when company management makes decisions in contrast to the economic interests of its shareholders.

Minority shareholders have a special duty to question management decisions that benefit only one class of shareholders at the expense or detriment of other shareholders. The duty to the people who depend on corporate investment performance for their retirement or other economic well being must outweigh the unpleasantness of pointing out the mistakes of management. The second part of the sentences is more questionable. While it gives to the shareholders a duty more than a right raises the usual and important problem of how do shareholders assess incompetence of management? The problem of excessive cost of getting information and the high "convenience" of free riding is a major threat to the usefulness of the last part of the sentence.

> Japanese Corporate Boards should consider the interests of, and strive for accountability toward, all shareholders (source: CGFJ ibid.).

The Board's focus should be on safeguarding the interests of shareholders and providing them with the highest possible long-term returns on their investment. A Board of Directors should represent all of a company's shareholders. Where a Board is composed mainly of insiders, as is usually the case in Japan, it must take particular care to avoid any conflict of interest and to take into account the interests of minority shareholders. The Board also has the responsibility to ensure that all shareholders are provided with accurate and complete information on the activities of the Board and the corporation.

> Japanese Corporate Boards should use the corporate governance principles developed by the Corporate Governance Forum of Japan as a benchmark of their duties and responsibilities to shareholders (source: CGFJ ibid.).

The Corporate Governance Forum of Japan is a body consisting of representatives from Japanese corporations, institutional investors and academia. It has developed an interim report that promotes a sensible two-step approach to reforming Japanese CG. The first step includes reforms implemented by 2002 while the second step includes more substantive reforms that should be implemented "early in the 21st century".

Figure 2 summarises the Japanese system of CG. We can observe that, as in Germany, the role played by banks is fundamental. In fact, banks can be shareholders as usually they are. In Kim *et al* (1998), the main structure of Japanese economy is an organisation called "keiretsu". "Keiretsu" is a group of corporations and a banks interconnected between them. Usually the bank is at the head of the "keiretsu". This sort of organisation is a direct evolution of what was called in Japan "Zaibatsu", a very similar structure in which the bank was substituted from a family. After the II World War the "Zaibatsu" were extinguished (see Mørck R. and Nakamura 1999 for details) and there was a change in the ownership structure, shifting it from families to banks.

Returning to, we see that shareholders (and so banks) control the Board of Directors that, differently from the German system, here is unique and has not a dual structure. Here the employees are not directly involved in Board decision and they influence more directly the business activity of the firm, as customers and suppliers.

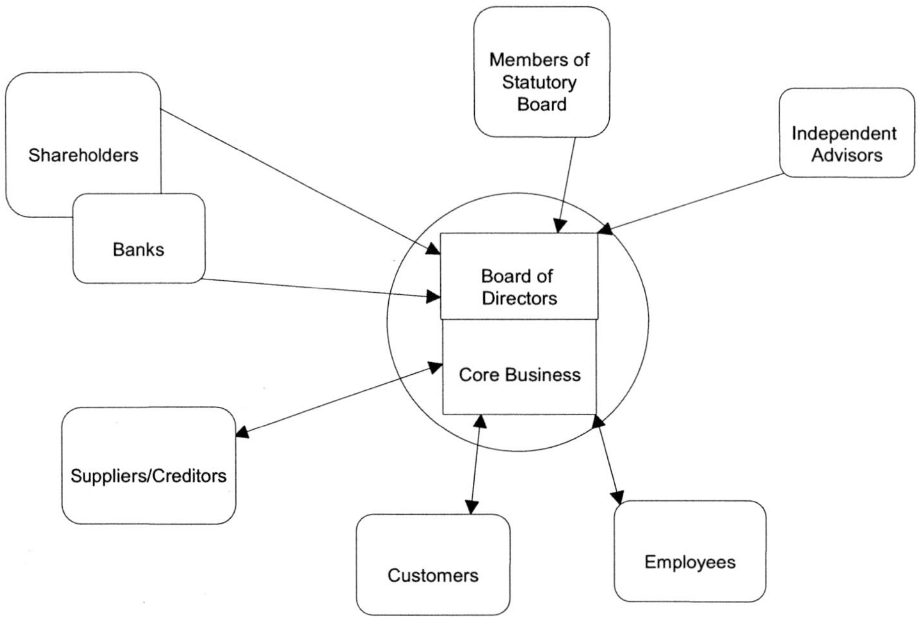

Figure 2 Corporate Governance in Japan

In Japan the relationship between employee and the firm is very strong (see Dietl 1998 among the others as reference) and the loyalty and reliability of employee to "the firm" are based not only on "economic reasons" but, more important, on social and cultural roots. Moral firms, like Japanese firms may solve problems of opportunism in markets and in hierarchies better than do their less moral counterparts. Efficiency within organizations, and efficiency at organizational boundaries may both better achieved through trust and cooperation than through mechanism purporting to efficiently curb opportunism. Moral sentiments may transcend both markets and hierarchies as efficient contracting mechanisms.

According to Yamagishi and Yamagishi (1994) if one party trusts another party owing to assurance that the trusted party has an incentive to cooperate, this is not so much a matter of trust as one of assurance. True trust, they say, exists when the trustor believes that the other party has incentive to cheat but, because of its goodwill, will not cheat. The view that trust can only exist when the trusted party has the opportunity to cheat is quite common. The two authors find, from a series of surveys, that trust is significantly lower in Japan than in the United States. This finding supports their idea that Japanese subjects, who live in a society which is characterized by strong mutual monitoring and sanctioning, have weaker trust and cooperate less in the absence of a sanctioning system than American subjects, who live in a more individualistic society. This suggests that in Japan there are few opportunities to cheat and, thus, few opportunities to develop a sense of trust – a notion contrary to conventional wisdom about Japan.

Japan has a collectivist culture in the sense that people's self-identification tends to be deeply rooted in group membership, for this reasons ostracism (whether from family or from business community) could be a particularly severe for a Japanese. Any gain from dishonesty is quickly overwhelmed by the negative reputation. Collective sanctioning in Japan seems to work as a powerful social instrument for reducing incentives for cheating, as well as for punishing discovered cheaters through social and economic ostracism. Social sanctioning, which is positively combined with institutional sanction, plays a critical role in promoting trust among participants.

A critique of the Japanese system is needed. As we can observe in the Corporate Governance Forum of Japan *(source: CGFJ ibid.),* the standard of accounting in Japanese corporations is not at the international standard. This probably is not a big problem for some shareholders (as banks) that can have a "privileged channel" where to find information but it is a serious problem for small shareholders or minority shareholders for all the reasons that we gave previously. So the Japanese system does not yet provide a good standard of disclosure and correct and substantive information to investors. Moreover, several time the non-executives Directors are not fully independent since some of them have some interests in the company (see Mørck R. and Nakamura 1999). Also, several critiques are done to the role played by Auditors since they do not seem to be independent and they do not have clear criteria to assess the “goodness” of management of the firm. This is partially connected to the previously mentioned standard in accounting.

Last, the Japanese scholars of CG (see as general reference Turnbull S. 2000) are not fully satisfied of the composition and the role played by the Board. This is a problem that is connected in firms where the shareholders are "strong" (see Roe 1994) and it is a partial problem of the system. So, (see Almazan and Suarez 2000) a more independent Board is needed, the separation of the role of CEO and Chairman and last, the effective presence of committees such as nominating and remuneration committees will be major reforms needed for the system to improve its efficiency.

The development of banks and other financial institutions in Germany and Japan is evidence of how differently things could be in the US. In these countries political influences were different and banks and other institutions have been allowed to concentrate equity holdings and play a significant role in disciplining managers. The separation of ownership and control is arguably much less important than in UK/US. So, let us analyse the UK/US systems.

1.7. Corporate Governance in UK/US: A More Decentralised Model

The UK’s CG scheme is slightly different from the German one but with great implication for all the matters connected with legal responsibility in the firm (see Beecroft 1994; Dietl 1998; Prevezer and Ricketts 1994). Under this scheme there is a unitary Board in which there are executive and non-executive members but all Directors have equal legal liability and all of them are fully responsible for the company’s action. In the context of UK CG a strong role is played from an active market for corporate control. In the UK scheme of CG, this has meant accountability to shareholders, subject to legal constraint.

1.7.1. Corporate Governance in United Kingdom

CG in UK is based basically on the Hampel code (February 1998) of corporate governance that is a revision and integration of the two well known "Cadbury report" and Greenbury report" on CG. The key points of the Hampel report that allow us to talk of a "UK way" of CG are concentrated in the area of the general principle of CG, in the Directors' functions and remuneration, in the auditing and accountability and in the role and duties of the shareholders in the Annual General Meeting.

CG lies in the contribution it makes to both business prosperity and accountability. Chairman and CEO roles should be split (source: Hampel Code ibid.). The chairman of a company is responsible for running the Board and the chief executive for managing the business. These are separate roles and should not be combined in listed companies, save in exceptional circumstances, since such a combination represents a very substantial concentration of power in the hands of one member of the Board creating the potential risk that they will exercise undue dominance over decision-making. In the "UK way" of CG non-executive Directors play a key role. A properly constituted Board of independent non-executive Directors alongside the executive Directors is essential.

Even if the importance of independent non-executive Directors cannot be underestimated there could be some real concerns about this point. Firstly, those companies in most need of top quality non-executive Directors will be those that find them most difficult to appoint. It is the responsibility of the business community at large to encourage good executive Directors and other senior officers to contribute to the greater good of UK business by acting as non-executive Directors for other companies. Investing institutions may have a part to play in this where they have concerns on governance issues. Second, independence is essential to the operation and development of good CG. In economies where there are pyramidal structures of property, to find independent Directors it is really difficult.

For the Cadbury Committee's independence means: "*independent of management and free from any business or other relationship which could materially interfere with the exercise of their independent judgement*". A survey about cross appointment of non-executive (see Denis *et al.* 1997) found that many non-executive Directors were far from independent. Clearly it is not sufficient to pay lip service to the Committee's recommendation that the majority of non-executive Directors should be independent. If progress is to be made without regulation, non-executive Directors should not only be independent, but should be seen to be independent.

In Figure 3 there is a summary of the structure of CG in United Kingdom. As already pointed out several times, here we have that the presence of "suppliers of debt capital" does not influence in a direct way (as in Japan or Germany) the Board of Directors. Here, the only direct and strong influence to the member of the Board derives from the presence of active shareholders or, better from an efficient market for corporate control. Today the most updated Code of Corporate Governance in UK is the Turnbull Report. Basically it combines the Hampel report and the Cadbury Report. The guidance requires companies to identify, evaluate and manage their significant risks and to assess the effectiveness of the related internal control system. Boards of Directors are called on to review regularly reports on the effectiveness of the system of internal control in managing key risks, and to undertake an annual assessment for the purpose of making their statements on internal control in the annual report.

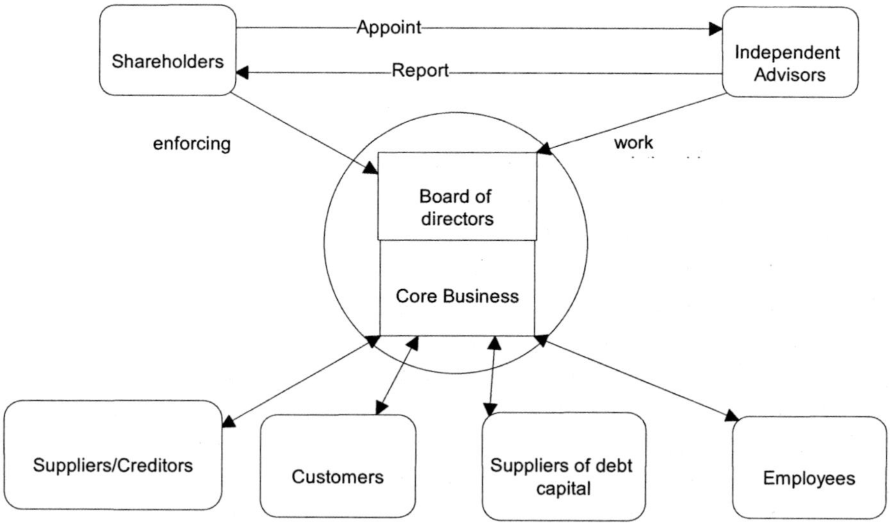

Figure 3 Corporate Governance in UK

The UK has an effective external system of CG, the oldest of Europe. It is not easily exportable to Continental Europe since the UK has the most effective stock exchange market and its system of CG strongly relies on the stock exchange market.

1.7.2. Corporate Governance in US

There is strong evidence that the separation between ownership and control is not the result of a natural economic evolution but rather a deliberate political choice of the US to have weak financial intermediaries, which were prevented from playing an active role in CG (Roe 1994). There has been a long political tradition in the US of eliminating concentrations of financial power. Throughout the 19th century, the banking system was highly fragmented and unlike every other industrialising country the US failed to develop large banks with extensive branch networks. This was due to the political influence of the numerous small banks that feared they would be put out of business if forced to compete with large banks. In the 20th century the political influence of small banks again prevented the development of a nation-wide system that could play a strong CG role (Glass-Steagall Act).

The other institutions that could potentially have developed a large equity stake in firms and offset the power of managers were insurance companies, mutual funds and pension funds. Insurance companies were prevented because in this way will be avoided that they gain too much power and influence. The desirability of diversifying holdings led to regulations that made restrictions of the quota that a mutual fund could hold. Also the desirability of prohibiting insider dealings led to regulations, which made it undesirable for mutual funds to become more involved in CG. Pension funds could potentially play an important role but the fact that their manager controls firms' pension funds means that they are reluctant to do this. Any firm's fund that interfered in another firm's affairs could expect that its own affairs might be subject to the same type of interference.

1.8. THE ITALIAN WAY: A NON-EXPLICITLY-EXISTENT SYSTEM

In Italy, the possible way to separate ownership and control has not been based on a unique model but on a set of different models for the different kind of enterprises involved. This can be seen as the way in which the system was self-organising given the fact that in Italy there has never been a law in CG issue before the Draghi OPA law.

1.8.1. A Brief Description of the Actors of the Italian System

For all the *individuals firms* the individual exerts control with a majority of voting rights. A *hierarchical group control* is the most frequent CG model. *Family control* is the second most relevant model. *Coalition control*: is a model quite similar to the previous one but more complex. The trust-link between entrepreneurs and investors can be interpreted as a Japanese Keiratzu and might further be forged with formal agreements. The *financial supervision* model was basically absent among Italian manufacturing firms in 1992 since the Banking law was not allowing the banks to own a relevant quota of shares in a firm.

Important components of Italian economy are "Groups". A group is a set of companies with separate legal status, which are all subject to the direct or indirect control[16] Another source of separation between ownership and control are shareholders agreements. The separation between ownership and control may be obtained also by circular holdings, a device which is in place when a company A holds shares in company B, which holds shares in company C, which in turn holds shares in A. Circular holdings are neither prohibited nor limited by the Italian law. Hierarchical groups have been a very common device for the separation between ownership and control of listed companies in Italy. The State itself in the past used pyramiding for its own industrial activities. The "Chinese boxes" system has been widely accepted by the Stock Exchange Market. *Interlocking directorates* are not subject to any limitation under Italian law. They are not relevant for antitrust purposes. It is also to note that no indirect disincentive against such separation tool comes from the legal regime of directors' conflict of interests: the case law has in fact greatly relaxed such regime.

1.8.2. Corporate Governance and the Legislative Decree 19/01/03nr. 6: The Alternatives

The Italian system of CG does not fit in either of the categories of the well-known distinction between bank-based and stock exchange based systems. Instead, it can be ranked among the first group of the more recent distinction between insider-dominated and out-sider dominated systems. All the distinctive variables of this group indicated by La Porta et al. (1998) can be found in the Italian system:

- Italian firms depend heavily on bank finance;

---

[16]The ways to obtain the direct or indirect control in a group are several and theyare not defined directly by the Italian law: The most common ways (see Bianchi et al. 1998) are: through one or more lines of control - of one leadership - an individual, a coalition of individuals or a government body.

- banks have never played an important role in the CG of firms;
- financial markets have historically been shallow and small;
- ownership and control are concentrated;
- the role of the state is important;
- groups of firms are very widespread and used as a mechanism to separate ownership and control;
- there are conflicts of interest between minority and majority shareholders;
- boards of directors play a limited role;
- the market for corporate control is not active,
- hostile take-overs are difficult and unlikely.

The possible way to separate ownership and control has not been based on a unique model but on a set of different models: the system was self-organising given the fact that in Italy there has never been a law on CG issue. The model is actually based on the following devices:

- Hierarchical group. The most frequent CG model; it accounts for 52 per cent of manufacturing activity and is more frequent among larger firms.
- Family control. The second most relevant model. This is the case where family links exist among controlling shareholder.
- Coalition control: is a model quite similar to the previous one but more complex. The trust-link between entrepreneurs and investors is based on their sharing common values (belonging to the same industrial district, to the same political party etc.).
- Financial supervision. Financial guarantees to non-controlling shareholders are represented by the presence of financial companies with privileged information exerting monitoring (banks, merchant banks, institutional investors etc). This model was basically absent among Italian manufacturing firms in 1992 since the Banking law did not allow the banks to own a relevant quota of shares in a firm.

Under Italian Law two main types of company may be incorporated: S.p.A. (Società per Azioni) and S.r.l. (Società a responsabilità limitata).

S.p.A. is the normal form for larger companies (joint stock companies). An S.p.A. may be listed on the Stock Exchange although the absolute majority are not. It is however necessary for a company to be an S.p.A. in order to be listed thereon.

S.r.l. in practice corresponds to a closely held limited company. It is the kind of structure which is more suited to small-to-medium sized enterprises where limited liability is required. This is by far the most common type of company used by Italian entrepreneurs and that most frequently chosen by foreign parent companies when setting up their subsidiaries in Italy.

The governance structure of corporations is two-tired: the managing board (consiglio di amministrazione) has the function of ratifying decisions that have been previously taken by the controlling group, and is supplemented by a board of auditors (collegio sindacale) who are responsible for internal monitoring. Directors can either be executive or non-executive and there is only a limited number of external directors. They tend to meet only a few times a year and the meetings are frequently of poor quality. In addition, information is generally scarce and incomplete. Even though board members and managers are supposed to use the "agent's diligence" in the management of the company, responsibility is effectively taken only in cases of insolvency or incidents of criminal significance.

The board of auditors is composed of either three or five members (sindaci) who are to be chosen among certified public accountants (revisori contabili). The latter are elected by the assembly of shareholders and cannot be revoked without cause before the end of the term. Listed firms are also subjected to an external monitoring and sometimes the two forms of control overlap giving rise to several problems of competence.

Until the Reform of Company Law which was introduced by Legislative Decree 19 January 2003 No. 6 (hereafter the Reform), many of the rules governing an S.p.A. were also applicable to an S.r.l.

By the Reform the legislator has clearly manifested its intention to regulate smaller enterprises in a totally different manner by stressing the importance of the personal contribution provided to the company by shareholders. To a certain extent, this type of company has been equalled to a limited liability partnership but it is still characterised by its capital being divided into intangible shares, which are not represented by certificates.

1.8.3. Corporate Governance in S.P.As

The traditional structure of Italian companies is based upon a clear-cut distinction between different functions assigned to three separate bodies.

The General Meeting of Shareholders, which is responsible for approval of the balance-sheet, the appointment of directors and the determination of remuneration for directors and statutory auditors.

The Directors; this organ may be represented by a sole director or by a Board of Directors and is in charge of management

The Board of Statutory Auditors which invigilates on compliance by the company management with the law and the articles of association, on respect by the management of rules of correct business administration.

According to the Reform, Statutory Auditors will no longer control the company accounts, a function which is now exclusively entrusted to external auditors.

The assignment of the company's functions to three bodies has traditionally been compared with the division of powers in a modern state. Along with this traditional structure the Reform has however introduced two alternative management and control systems, respectively deriving from the German/French and English experience and recommended by the EU Council Regulations on the "European Company By-laws" dated 8 October 2001.

1.8.4. The "Dualistic" System (S. 2409 Ff., Civil Code)

This alternative provides for

a) a Management Board, with the same type of responsibilities as those which are attributed to the BOD and

b) a Supervisory Board whose tasks are wider than those of Statutory Auditors, in that it sees to the appointment and revocation of Management Board members and to the approval of the company's accounts. The Supervisory Board is also exclusively enabled to promote actions in liability against members of the Management Board and to waive such actions by way of settlement out of court. Consequently in a company managed in accordance with this two-tier system the functions of the Shareholders' Meeting are confined to appointing and revoking members of the Supervisory Board.

1.8.5. The "Monistic" System (S. 2409 Ff. Civil Code)

According to this system, management is entrusted to a regular Board of Directors at least one third of which must be represented by independent members. Supervision is attributed by the Board to a Management Control Committee whose members are chosen from among independent directors. In companies which make recourse to the capital market, the Committee must be formed by no less than three members and at least one member must be a registered auditor.

In both types of governance, save for small unlisted companies, supervision of accounts is invariably entrusted to an external auditor or auditing firm.

1.8.6. Corporate Governance in S.r.ls

In the view of the legislator an S.r.l. should be the swiftest and most flexible tool in the hands of shareholders. A much greater degree of discretion has thus been recognised to shareholders by the Reform, particularly in laying down the rules for the administration of their company.

Articles of associations will be set forth by shareholders in accordance with their needs. Therefore, they will be less formal and quite probably be drawn up in the form of contracts.

In line with this very flexible structure, the managing body of an S.r.l. may be freely shaped by shareholders by way of recourse to some alternative solutions

- a Sole Director
- a traditional Board of Directors collectively acting as a committee, presided by a Chairman and by a Managing Director
- a Board of Directors not acting as a committee, formed by a plurality of members having the same powers. Depending on the shareholders' choices, such directors may operate

a) severally: this alternative, however, carries with it the power of each director to veto resolutions proposed by the other directors;

b) severally on certain issues (for instance in matters concerning the day-to-day business);

c) jointly;

d) jointly on certain matters (for instance as regards the so called "extraordinary administration").]

Supervision of accounts will be entrusted to a Board of Statutory Auditors or to a sole auditor only where the company share capital is in excess of € 120,000 or when the turnover or the size of an S.r.l. are beyond a certain threshold determined by law.

1.8.7. Corporate Governance, Accounting and Auditing After the Parmalat Scandal

Was it a forged Bank of America document, allegedly patched together by a Parmalat executive using a scanner and a fax machine, that reveals a troubling aspect about Italian capitalism - the lack of effective financial control over its family-owned companies ?

In Italy, dissatisfaction with the state of CG has seriously increased in recent years and the previously analysed Reform has not changed at all the general feeling about the "quality" of CG. After the privatisation process started in 1988, the Italian system of CG has begun to move towards the U.S. system without reforming three important features that are different between the two systems:

1. the role of institution and institutional investors[17] in controlling management;
2. the different ability to fill in gaps in contingent contracts due to the a less efficient Italian legal system and the absence of protection for investors' rights in Italy;
3. the control model of medium and large firm[18];

The main critics that the Italian system collect is that the duty of loyalty is not an operational concept and that courts have no expertise or inclination to provide protection for non-controlling investors[19]. The Reform did not affect this two points and the words experts have used to describe it are "feeble" and "toothless". That is particularly vulnerable in an economy dominated by family-run businesses and lubricated by social ties. Although Parmalat was a public company, the Tanzi family controlled it, which is the pattern with many of Italy's large concerns, including Fiat, Prada and Benetton. The Italian government last year decriminalized "false accounting". As a result, Parmalat prosecutors are having to turn to other statutes.

Parmalat rarely explained its finances to stock analysts, and because it was family-run it was exempt from certain disclosure requirements. Consob, Italy's securities and market regulator, is viewed as understaffed and ineffective and now the Italian Parliament is discussing a new reform to create a Super Consob and "to protect save".

---

[17] See Dietl (1998) for a good survey on the role played by institution and institutional investors in an efficient CG system.

[18] The success of the Italian economy is due mostly to the large number of small firms that perform very well. A small firm is one with less than 20 workers and in Italy this kind of firm represents 98% of the total number of firms. The solution to corporate governance issue in small firms environment is the simplest possible: they lack the separation of ownership and control that generates agency problems and that basically defines the corporate governance puzzles in more complex systems. Is there a link between these two facts? For sure we cannot exclude it.

[19] *See on this point Barca 1995, see also Macey 1998*

In the latest annual corruption perception index by the nonprofit Transparency International, Italy ranked second to last among EU states, edging only Greece. Chile, Botswana and Bahrain were among the 34 nations seen as less corrupt than Italy. Rules require enforcement, and Italy's reputation does not inspire confidence: Parmalat as the final drop that caused the collapse of trust in Italian saving and investment plan.

1.8.8. What More than Only Criticisms?

In Italy, dissatisfaction with the state of CG has increased in recent years. This is probably due to the process of privatisation conducted in Italy with the creation of millions of new (and very fractionated) shareholders that, probably do not have the feelings of being protected of the actual structure of CG. In fact, the Italian system of CG is very similar to the U.S. system but there are several differences with the role of institution and institutional investors in the two ways of Governance (see Boot et al. 1998) and with the structure of economy. The success of the Italian economy is due in large part to the large number of small firms that perform very well. The solution that these small firms find to the problem of CG is the simplest possible: they lack the separation of ownership and control that generates agency problems and that basically defines the CG puzzles in more complex system.

The big differences and the main critics that the Italian system collect are connected to the low ability to fill in gaps in contingent contracts due to the poor legal system and absence of protections for investors' right[20]. The fact that the duty of loyalty is not an operational concept in Italy makes that Italian CG does not perform very well in terms of its ability to resolve agency problems (see Barca 1994, see also Macey 1998).

The exit device has also been unavailable. The failure of financial and non-financial institutions to act as advisers or intermediaries and the high concentration of ownership, have prevented this development. Company law, securities law and investment regulations do not provide a framework for institutional investors to play much of a role in CG. The information available to the shareholders is also inadequate. Corporate bodies have exercised no independent monitoring. The board of directors in Italian companies is generally fully identified with controlling shareholders. One of the main characteristics of the Italian model, the system of State-Owned enterprises has come under particular attack and in 1992 a process of privatisation was initiated. Major problems have been encountered in replacing the old system with alternative devices (see Barca 1998).

In Italy we also observe a lack of financial institutions exercising, interim and ex-post monitoring via share or debt capital or via financial services. No other financial institutions have taken over the role of banks in the ownership structure of Italian companies, partly due to the absence of pension funds as a consequence of the country's broad coverage pay-as-you-go public pension system.

In the absence of financial institution, fiduciary duties and the market for corporate control, the CG in Italy has relied on three main actors (see Barca 1998): the state, pyramidal groups and the family and/or coalition control.

[20] In Italy there is not a specific law or a set of recommendations for Corporate Governance. The main document that is used to infer some principles of corporate governance is the law for the OPA (offerta publica d'acquisto) done from the Draghi Committee. This is a very recent law ,1998, but it is subject to numerous critics and there is already a need to revise it. See Bianchi et al. 1998

The state has directly controlled a major stake. De facto it has held about 80% of the commercial banking system's deposits and an even larger stake of long-term lending banks (see Barca 1994). The politicisation of capital investment decision inevitably results in sub-optimal decision about capital allocation in CG system. So the State activism in the sector is seen much more in a political way that in an economic way.

In private firms the role of active actors is fundamental in system as the Italian one. But institutional investors in general and even banks are characterised for the lack of activism Italy's particular bankruptcy law plays an important role in explaining this behaviour (see Barca 1994). Banks do not appear particularly active in soliciting the adjustment of companies' ownership structures. The thin and underdeveloped stock market also does not provide the appropriate arena for involvement of the other financial intermediaries in CG (see Ferri and Pesaresi 1996).

Another device of control in Italy is pyramidal control. This way of achieving separation puts the interests of minority shareholders in all subsidiaries of the groups at particular risk. The head of pyramid look to the group as a whole but the shareholder of a particular firm of the group wants good performance for his own firm. The company at the top of pyramid if private have been governed by family control[21] and coalition control[22] (see Bianco et others 1997).

But is the Italian system of CG subject only to criticisms? The Italian experience may offer some insights of general use especially in analysing transitional economies. When a crisis occurs, all three models - family, coalition and state - tend to reduce the risk that signals of bad performance might too easily unsettle an allocation of control, even when there is no misallocation. This is possibly one of the main advantages of Italian Governance environment. On the other hand, due to lack of continuous monitoring, these models may increase the risk of the opposite error: that a misallocation of control, though signalled by bad performance, does not lead quickly enough to transfer control.

The relative independence of management from ministerial bureaucracies (see Perrow 1995) can be another extraordinarily effective tool in separating ownership and control and this can play an important role in States where the all or the majority of corporations are in public hands. To avoid the collusion between managers and bureaucracies are needed sanctions: the political market replaces the market for corporate control. For the Italian model of CG to work, state owned enterprises must not be "limited" with special social objectives. Finally, if there is no functioning political market to guarantee democratic change of parties[23] in power and if the "mission" culture of public manager is eroded the system is bound to degenerate: top managers and political overseers will inevitably capture one other. The last possible advantage of the Italian system is that it provides strong incentives for the managers to make the firm-specific human capital investment necessary to develop specialised skills. Managers in these small firms can make these investments secure in the knowledge that they will not be exploited.

---

[21] An ownership structure in which the non-controlling owners belong to the same family as the entrepreneur 22% of total capital (see Barca 1994).

[22] Where the entrepreneur and the non controlling owners share a common value and/or are linked through contracts (13%) (see Bianco et al. 1997).

[23] This is not the case of Italy of course but in some transition economies there are still some problem of existence of a sort of "political market".

1.9. THE KOREAN SYSTEM OF CORPORATE GOVERNANCE

The Korean case, for some methodological aspects, is quite similar to the Italian one. It also shows some similarities with what has been done in the process of reunification in Germany since that now in Korea a similar project is under process. For these two reasons, and for the peculiarities that CG has in Korea, it is worth briefly describing the Korean system of CG.

One peculiarity of this system is a particular type of industrial organisation called "Chaebol". A "Chaebol" can be defined as a set of firms each one of them with an independent and different legal status, but all of them connected in a way that they form a group, the Chaebol, which has no legal status. A "family" usually controls the Chaebol in its wholeness. The firms that are in the same Chaebol are usually connected one with each other by a relevant and interconnected cross-shareholding. In this way, a "family" is able to control with a minority share, usually around 10th % of the capital (see table 1 in the work of Lee 1999) of the group, all the "Chaebol". For a detailed description of the way in which "Chaebol" works see the paper of Lee (1999) and, among the many others, the work of Cho (1992).

The economic system in Korea is not only Chaebol. Even if it represents the more "fashionable" way to organise property there are other ways to "own" a firm. In fact, we have also the presence of firms directly managed by the owner and firms that, given the very fragmented ownership structure between thousands of shareholders, are managed by professional managers.

The last two types of industrial organisations are similar to the others all over the world so, it is better to concentrate now on the unique features of the "Chaebol". The "Chaebol" has two main contrasting characteristics: from one side it allows to keep at a very low level the agency costs deriving from the employment of professional managers that are not directly involved with the ownership of the firm, from the other side it generates very high costs deriving from the fact that the group is controlled by minority shareholders. Korea is not the only place in the world where this is true. As we have seen in Italy this is also sometimes allowed in three different ways: with pyramidal groups, with the presence of shares that have particular voting rights and with cross shareholding.

The Korean "Chaebol", concentrates all these three methodologies in a unique organisational form (see Bebchuk e al. 1999).

A general opinion (see Lee 1999) is that, even if the Chaebol seems to work in an effective way when the economic cycle is in a positive period as growth, it is not able to give exhaustive answers to firm's problems during recession.

We saw which could be the analogies with the Italian system. Now we can find some with the American and with the Japanese system. The Chaebol structure is similar in its shape with the big American enterprises characterised by an M-form of organization. In fact, the single firms of the chaebol have little autonomy from the headquarter. Just like the single division of American firms with an M structure. In the Japanese keiretsu the autonomy of the single components of the group is bigger either with respect to the general headquarter or with respect to the other components on the same horizontal line in the productive process.

When we draw the analogy with the American M-form firms we could observe an important evolutionary aspect of the economic process of organisation. The M-form of the

American firms is nothing more than an evolution of the U-form (see Williamson 1975); even the Korean Chaebol is an evolution of U-form firms but it has evolved towards an organisational form similar to the one that Williamson (see Williamson 1975) called "X-form" (see Cho 1992). As it is noted in the work of Cho, a X-form develops when a U-form evolves for a process of expansion towards new business sector or business sectors that are different from the one present in the enterprise. As we said, new business activities in the Chaebol often mean creation of new firms, and this because it is easier in this way to raise new investment capitals. As a further incentive this means that the amount of capital supplied from the headquarter of the Chaebol is certainly smaller than the capital that the single firm has to invest to create a new branch in a M-form organisation.

In this case, and this will be useful later on when we will discuss the evolutionary approach, we have that the same organisational U-form has generated two evolutionary paths, the M-form typical of American enterprises and the X-form typical of Korean enterprises and, in a wide sense, even of the Japanese one.

The reason why the evolutionary path of the Korean system has evolved toward this direction is mainly due to the role played from the capital market in Korea. In particular is fundamental to highlight the role of the banks and of the institutional investors. To understand the different role played from these financial institutions is a key step to understand how a system can evolve toward a direction instead of another.

Conclusions and a Critique of the Korean System

The main systems of CG are characterised either from an efficient capital market or from a set of institutional investors that use the option "voice" to control the firm's management. The Korean system has not a well-developed and efficient capital market and, at the same time, has passive institutional investors. Even if we draw some analogies in the ownership structure with the Italian economic system, we cannot observe in Italy a so anomalous situation even if, for a certain period of time the Korean system was working with very high rate of growth.

The role played by the Government in this growth process was very relevant. Even without any direct investment, it helped the firms to raise the necessary capital to start several investment projects, some profitable some not. In the moment in which the Government decided to switch from this kind of distorsive policies to some more market oriented the system collapsed. Here the aim of this study is not to find reasons for the Asian crisis for Korea but the previous analysis is useful to highlight the low flexibility of the Chaebol organisation during crisis years. In fact, some changes in the external environment caused a very deep crisis for the difficulty of the system to react to these changes. Furthermore the initial crisis of some firms, given the cross shareholding present in the economic system, caused a chain reaction that reduced consistently the economic power of one of the most active Asian tiger.

Actually Korea is developing a process of transition from a system of CG organised with Chaebol to a system in which the separation between ownership and control is real and not artificial. Two kinds of measures are used to sustain the development of these new organisations. The first one is just the real separation between ownership and control obtained with the creation of Foundations that hold the majority of shares but that they do not interfere with the day-by-day management. The second process actually in act is the dissolution of collective organisations such as Chaebols (see Hyun 1999). What it seems necessary during this process is the reinforcement of the minority shareholders' rights, an increase in the monitoring function from institutional investors and the entrance in the Board of external non-executive directors independents from the ownership and management of the firm.

This is necessary to avoid some of the pathologies that characterised other transition economies when they decide to implement ex-novo some CG systems just copying one of the two existing macro-models or when they tried to accelerate the evolutionary process of the CG system during the transition from a planned (or State) economy to a market economy. The last point gives us the chance to consider some issues about CG and transition economies.

1.10. Corporate Governance in a Transition Context: A Short Note

For several transition economies, the privatisation programs have been nothing if not controversial. For some countries they have been described as purely cosmetic (e.g. see Intriligator (1994), Arrow et al. (1996)). Critics pointed on several aspects but the one that has come in for the most criticism concerns the massive advantages given to enterprise managers and other employees in acquiring shares in their firms (e.g. see Frydman and Rapaczynski (1994) or Earle and Estrin (1995)). One of the main objectives of the privatisation program in transition economy was the need for extensive restructuring of most of the industrial enterprises. One way to promote a programme like this involves a strong presence of outsider entrepreneurs (foreign entrepreneurs or a mix between local and foreign entrepreneurs).

The role of CG in this case is clear. It is important in these transition economies to state who is the residual claimants of the firm and what kind of discretion has the manager in this case. Again here it is a problem of "exit" and "voice" (see Lowenstein 1999) where the option exit seems quite easy achievable but it involves sometime big losses (let us do not forget how many households sold the share that they received for a month ration of bred) and the option of "voice" it is absolutely impossible to be used for lack in the information system, excessive cost of judicial action and excessive power of the manager of the firm. The important point here is that several firms have been put in to the market without a public sale but with a voucher sale without a "strong and direct" willingness to buy from the shareholder. The system of price was not yet present and were it was, was not properly working.

In several transition economies, developing a CG system for state-owned enterprises has not been a main point of reforms (see Roland 1995; see also Berglof 1995). In the last year something is slowly changing. Several Presidential decrees in Russia have formed a State Property Committee, sector governing agency, have stated the duties of director of state-owned enterprises, regulate contracts with state-owned enterprises managers and established several ways to represent state interest in the Board of directors (see Litwack 1995). However, clear mechanisms of manager's responsibility to the state as an owner are not yet adequately enforced.

Transition economies ownership structure calls for consideration of the extent of concentration of ownership (as emphasised by analysts of CG in the West; see, e.g., the summary in Shleifer and Vishny (1995)), and also demands attention to the identity of various types of owners[24]. In transition economy we can distinguish five important categories of owners: the state, managers, non-managerial employees, individual outsiders, and institutional investors[25].

A set of different measures seems necessary to provide for market transformation of the transition economies. Between them, the corrections in the property rights aimed at establishing efficient CG can play a fundamental role (see Akamatsu 1995). The target of these corrections have to move the management of joint–stock companies under the control of the owners of capital and making them maximise two objectives: profits (in the short run) and the net worth of the firm (in the long run). To do this we need a solution to two problems. The first one is the introduction of legal mechanisms providing for shareholders to fulfil their functions as business owners. As previously said, these mechanisms are being instituted and the task is to complete it successfully and quickly. Under current conditions, the second problem is probably the main one: the introduction of a system that would guarantee a market-compatible style of asset management by a specific owner, the State. We cannot forget that, even after massive programs of privatisation, in several transition economies the government is still the main owner.

This behaviour, therefore, turns out to be a natural way to operate in an irrational economic system. But it is also true that continuing such actions can only freeze the existing impasse.

1.11. A Taxonomy of Corporate Governance

Most of the economic literature on CG focuses on the main characteristics of different systems of CG but in few works there are attempts to define what is a "good system of CG". Actually there are definitions about different systems but there is not a clear attempt to provide a precise and policy-oriented definition of what constitutes "good corporate governance". The existing literature is trying to understand the consequences on growth, development and efficiency of the "continental system" of CG and of the UK/US system of CG but this debate misses insights that could be gained from transition countries undergoing fundamental structural, social and economic reforms.

One of the most widely accepted explanations for the different patterns of CG across countries is based on the role played by laws in protecting investors (La Porta et al., 1998, 2000). In short, these authors conclude that common law countries protect investors better than those with civil law. Following this general idea, scholars have tried to identify the main legal feature using several indices in order to measure the effectiveness of laws across countries.

In paragraph 0 we saw which are the main differences in CG system deriving from a different legal system. As we noted, usually a Common Law system conducts to an "outsider system" (see UK and US experience in this work but even Canada) while a Civil Law system conducts to an "Insider system" (see Japan, Germany in this work but basically all the EU countries with the hybrid Italian Experience). Markets basically rule outsider systems. Insider

[24]We have to take in consideration that the objectives pursued from each category of owner are different; furthermore the constraints faced by different types are different.

[25] Within the last group, banks, investment funds, domestic firms, and foreign investors are also considered.

systems by “actors” that can be, in the different cases, banks, financial institutions, Government, Institutional Investors, Groups or pyramidal groups and so on. But which are the factors that we have to consider to be able to derive a taxonomy of CG? As a first differentiation we can start talking of Internal factors and External factors (see also Collected Paper 1999). In Picture 1 we can see these factors in details. Some systems of CG rely on internal devices, others instead rely on external devices. Among American corporation law scholars, contemporary appreciation of the distinctive features of the worldwide CG models has proceeded in two stages. The first stage, exploited by Roe (1994) study of the political origin of corporate finance accomplished an intellectual paradigm shift. The work of Roe (1994) shows just that several systems can exist and be the best possible solution for each different country. Recalling some categories of evolutionary economics, conceptions of multiple equilibrium reached by divergent evolutionary pathways, which had been hinted at in some theoretical, were shown to have stunning real-word embodiments in the divergent corporate systems. So, to talk of a taxonomy of Corporate Governance does not mean that we have a unique system of CG but that we can have more systems that can be equally efficient if they respect some features that we will shortly illustrate.

The broad picture of several radically different corporate systems presented more a set of ideal types than a complete description of the corporate world. Each system spawned deviant case and evolutionary "mutations", which thrived in their peculiar economic niches. Further, each system involved complex trade-offs between the competing virtues of a governance system: flexibility vs. stability, innovativeness vs. predictable success. Finally, the systems have been subject to contemporary economic pressures such as globalisation, the dissemination of the new production methods and the collapse of welfare-state regimes that made the stable post-war equilibrium appear to be mere temporary stopping points on the way to some yet unspecified but brave new world.

In Table 1 we made an attempt to classify the systems of CG previously analysed. Here it has been considered the two main systems of CG and a third way represented by countries that are half way through (i.e. Italy and Korea). We need now some considerations for the taxonomy: a system that has not a liquid and large financial market or a market for corporate control very developed needs a high concentration of shareholding and this is true for all the questions regarding the capacity to enforce “voice” since exit is not possible or it is very expensive. So, our taxonomy could say that: if a system has similar characteristics to the Japanese German one, we can classify its efficiency looking to these two variables simultaneously.

An economic system that has a very fragmented ownership and a small financial market is less efficient than a system that has a concentrated ownership and a small financial market. The prices to pay in this case are mainly three: the minority shareholders, if in conflict with the controlling shareholders, are usually less protected in civil law countries and they cannot use at small costs the option “exit”. Furthermore the role played by takeover is very low but in this case this is not much important since shareholders are able to control management easily and they do not need an external device as market for corporate control to do it.

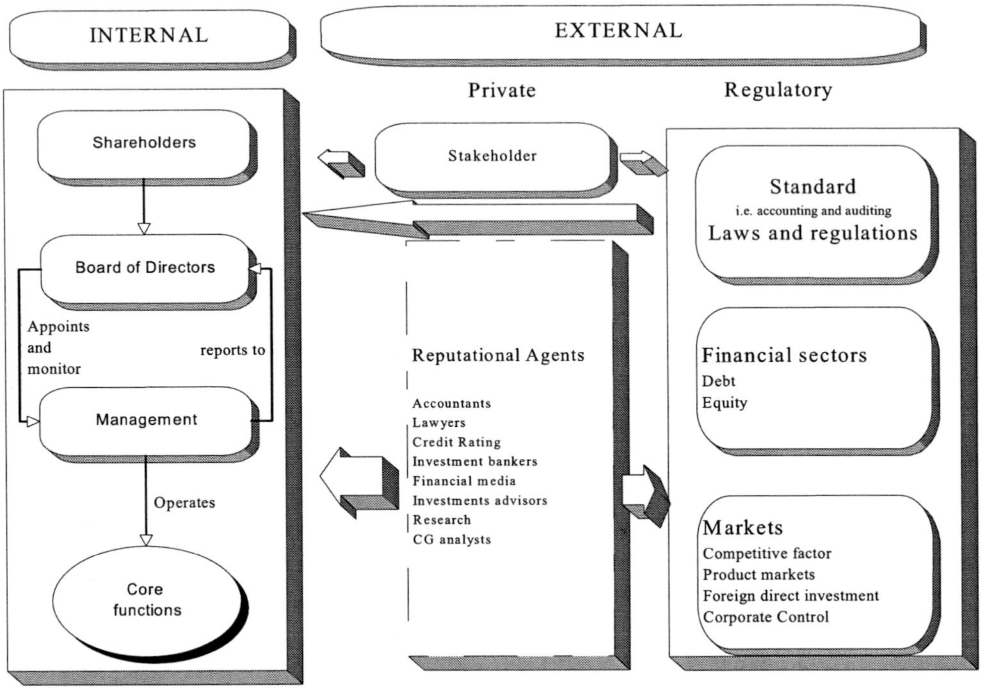

Source: own adaptation on AAVV (1999)

Figure 4 Internal and external factor involved in CG system

At the same time the role played by the Board is not crucial in Insider controlled systems. If the main shareholders are Banks, we see a strong concentration in debt and equity. This can be good for the firm that has more facilities to obtain capital but it can create several problems connected with the role played by the institutional investors. With outsider control, the role played by institutional investor is low. In fact mainly the market of corporate control controls management. The device "Exit" is not expensive. The role of take-over is fundamental. So we find another criterion of our Taxonomy: in countries in which we have developed markets and highly fragmented ownership the role played by take-overs is fundamental. So we can classify countries in this set by the role played by anti takeover law and we can state that the efficiency of system of outsider CG is influenced by the "goodness" of take-over law. Even these systems may have some costs: the sometimes excessive regulation in the field of mechanisms for separating control and capital base (so we will say that outsider systems with a inelastic regulation are worst of outsider systems with an elastic[26] regulation). Again, we can furthermore classify our outsiders systems by the role played from the market of corporate control and state that: if the ownership is very fragmented, to avoid very high costs of agency between manager and shareholders, we need big and liquid market for corporate control. As a critical note, for transition economies that have followed the UK/US system of CG, we had really bad consequences in countries such as ex Soviet

[26] It seems that the words "elastic" and "inelastic" are connected respectively with common law and civil law where, as seen in the US experience, the role played by Judges has been foundamental to develop a deep regulation of takeover and presence of Banks in the Risk capital of firms.

countries and partially all the transition countries that used vouchers to privatise. In that place, were the market for corporate control was small or, in several cases non existent, manger have done everything they could do to pursue their own interests with several small shareholders left with just piece of papers without value in their hands.

Table 1 – Types of corporate governance and financial system.

	Insider-dominated	**Half Way**	**Outsider-dominated**
	Germany - Japan	*Italy - Korea*	*US – UK*
Share of control-oriented finance	High	Medium	Low
Financial markets	Small, less liquid	Medium, liquid	Large, highly liquid
Share of all firms listed on exchanges	Small	Medium	Large
Ownership of debt and equity	Concentrated	Concentrated	Dispersed
Investor orientation	Control-oriented	Control-oriented but with changes deriving from mass-privatisation	Portfolio-oriented
Use of mechanisms for separating control and capital base	Frequent	Frequent but limited in the past from regulation	Limited (often by regulation)
Dominant agency conflict	Controlling vs. minority shareholders	Controlling vs. minority shareholders	Shareholders vs. management
Role of board of directors	Limited	Important	Important
Role of hostile take-overs	Very limited	Limited but in some cases important (see Telecom Italia)	Potentially important
Specialised financial institutions	Universal banking	Universal banking	High presence
Banks, merchant banks, institutional investors	Important and active role	Not very developed but developing now	Not a fundamental role
Fiduciary duties, courts and law firms	Not very developed	Not very developed	Highly determinants
State ownership	Medium	High but in strong reduction	Low
Contracts and implicit rules (based on trust)	Based on civil law	Based on civil law	High developed and based on common law[27]

In a paper by Fox and Heller (1999) it is noted that Russian industry has performed very poorly since privatisation. The authors of the paper agree in general with the existent literature in Russian privatisation that explain this poor performance in terms of "continued bureaucratic meddling, poor macroeconomic and tax policy and low human capital" but at the same time they try to understand which kind of effects a poor system of CG had on Russian economic performance. Russian economic system, in the view of Fox and Heller (1999) gives poor incentives to the "loosely constrained" managers, this is its mean problem. If managers receive low incentives this raises several problems connected with the non-maximisation of profit and with the non-pro rata distributions. For what it concerns the non-maximisation of profit, the Russian situation is very varied.

[27] The role played by court is enormous in economy as US. As example, the work of Barca 1995 examines the role played by Chancery Court of Delaware and by the other courts in the US starting from the breakthrough required in the formalistic English Common Law system in order to introduce the more flexible principles of "Roman aequitas" (see Barca 1994).

We saw that all the previous mentioned misconduct of the management conduct the firm to a sub-optimal level of profit. The important feature to point out is that this level of sub-optimality is going to affect to kind of people: shareholders in primis and the entire community after them. This level of sub-optimality is sometimes given to strong incentive for managers to pursue a sort of private benefit maximisation (when they have as reference point a set of "biased" stockholders or when they are not easily controllable and their action cannot be enforced in court) or the risk aversion of manager can just cancel the weak incentive that they have to identify and implement positive net present value projects.

As earlier pointed out, the sub-optimality of profit is not the only lack caused by a "bad" system of CG. There are problems connected with the distribution of the productivity ratio. In fact sometimes firms fail to prevent diversion of claims and this happens particularly when some residual owners of a firm manipulate corporate, bankruptcy and other laws to shift ownership away from other residual claimants. The most common way to achieve this is by diluting shares held by outside minority shareholders. Again, the failure of CG in transition economies can teach as how important is in a "good" system of CG to protect minority shareholders. This process of misappropriation become even more dangerous when some residual owners privately appropriate assets and opportunities[28] belonging to the firm but leave the firm's formal ownership structure basically intact.

The main explanations of these sets of non-maximisation of profit and non-pro rata distribution can be connected with lack in CG system. This lack includes the low level of corporate transparency, the lack of effective adjudication of corporate law violations, weak enforcement of judgements and the absence of a network of trust among transition businessman. To understand why all this happen it is important to understand which was the role of initial conditions at the time of privatisation, the initial boundaries of privatised firms and the initial allocation of firm's shares primarily to insiders and finally the bargaining dynamics that have followed. Our final question will be if path dependence had a strong influence in the "failure" of the economic transition[29]. Something has to be noticed however. The domestic Russian (and basically of several transition economies, excluding Poland, see Coffee 1999) privatisators and their foreign advisers believed it "politically" necessary to move in the quickest possible way. The reformers hoped, and now it seems to be just a very naive hope, that resources would naturally flow their highest value users after markets were established. For sure they underestimated the roadblocks that the initial starting conditions would continue to impose for resource reallocation (see Bebchuk and Roe 1999). Coffee pointed out that a "more prudential and cautious program of privatisation gives better results because the risks of market failure and political corruption that may result when control seekers are tempted to bribe and seduce the judicial and regulatory systems to achieve the private benefit of control is too high" (Coffee 1999).

We can use the information about concentration in D'Orio (2000, 285) to build the information in Table 1. Here the only anomaly is the low value of concentration in Japanese

---

28 That is strictly connected to the previous mentioned problem of firm unable to implement positive net present value project just because the manager has the opportunity to implement that project with another firm in which he has some indirect interests.

29 Failure in terms of economic results, efficiency gain and growth of the involved economies, we not not expressing a political view and a social welfare, were other variables as freedom of speech and so on are very important

firm. The value contained could be misleading and induce us to classify Japan as a country with low value of concentration (lower than UK).

Table 2 - Ownership and Voting power: structure and consequences

	Where	Advantages	Disadvantages	Agency conflicts	Possible way to limit disadvantages
Dispersed Ownership and Dispersed Voting Power	US and UK	Portfolio diversification and liquidity; take over possibility	Insufficient monitoring: free riding problem	Management vs. shareholders	Laws or incentives to limit free riding; different role of institutional investors
Dispersed Ownership and Concentrated Voting Power	Countries where a stake holder can collect proxy votes and shareholder coalitions are allowed	Monitoring of management; portfolio diversification and liquidity	Violation of one share one vote; reduced take over possibilities; different objectives between shareholders	Controlling block holders vs. small shareholders	More power to markets; increase exit devices; laws to limit pyramidal groups
Concentrated Ownership and Dispersed Voting Power	Any company with voting right restrictions i.e. Italian co-operatives	Protection of minority rights	Violation of one share one vote; low monitoring incentives; low diversification; low liquidity; higher cost of capital; reduced take-over possibilities	Management vs. shareholders	More power to the markets; different and more important role of institutional investors as inv. Funds
Concentrated Ownership and Concentrated Voting Power	Continental Europe, Japan, in any company after take over so some Italian companies after privatisation	High monitoring incentives	Low portfolio diversification; low liquidity; reduced take-over possibility	Controlling block holders vs. small shareholders	Development in financial markets

Source: own adaptation of Crama et al. (1999) Table 2

The Japanese system is based on "keiretsu" that we can now define as an organisation of cross-shareholding and interconnected shareholding. So, to analyse the Japanese case, more than to check the concentration in the single firm, it could be more useful to check for the level of concentration in a "keiretsu". So, taking this point into account we can easily classify Japan as a country with concentrated ownership even if the type of concentration is different from the German one. This could be another parameter to classify insiders systems of CG as we did when we made a critical note on the dynamic efficiency of Japanese and Korean CG. In D'Orio (2000) we can find the whole set of values that we used in this work to classify the countries in for what it concerns the presence of fragmented or dispersed ownership and with a note on the role played by the state. The reason why we did not considered Italy in the first column of Table 1 is due to the massive programme of privatisation that Italy conducted from 1995 till today. Several programmes of privatisation in Italy produced a high fragmented ownership (see Telecom Italia with the deriving 1999 takeover, see ENI, see Autostrade and so on (for a detailed information in this area see Bertero and Rondi 1997). Finally we can summarise some possible conclusion about Ownership concentration and Voting Power. As we saw previously, ownership can be concentrated and dispersed, voting power can be, as well, concentrated and dispersed.

In Table 2, there is a classification of countries and the advantages and disadvantages of the 4 resulting possible systems. Two themes can be the guide to develop CG taxonomy. One theme is that CG system serves diverse and potentially conflicting functions of which three are important in the present context. First, the CG regime has to monitors senior managers to assure that they are making decisions that are in some sense value maximising for the enterprise. Second the CG regime has to facilitate contracting between the corporation and its stakeholders.

Third the CG regime has to serves a set of political functions (these are sometimes merely symbolic, as perhaps is the case with board representation for workers). Other times, these governance regimes achieve concrete outcomes that are chosen for political rather that economic reasons, or aim at achieving results for the economic system considered from a macro or developmental perspective.

The second theme is the interaction between "ecology" and background conditions, including the background legal regime and the CG features of particular firms. The background regime may select for some particular features even in the same country and it permits a wide range of alternative structures to emerge.

A possible graphical explanation of the three features that have to be analysed to understand CG, taking in to account the existing systems of CG is shown in Figure 5.

A point like A is a vertex of maximum and is for sure a global maximum in the representation but probably no system will be in that point. This is quite easy to explain since even if we are in the point were the solution to agency problems are solved at the maximum level, we do not have a problem of CG anymore even if the system is not able to fill gaps in contracts at all. The opposite situation is absolutely the same. A system that is able to fill perfectly every gap in contracts has not a problem of CG anymore because every situation can be regulated by a contract. So, even if A is a point of maximum, there are for sure other maximum and the historical experience is showing that the two "big" system of CG are specialising themselves to achieve one of the two other maximum while a system as the Italian one is trying to move towards a point in which the incentives given to the human factor are long-run oriented.

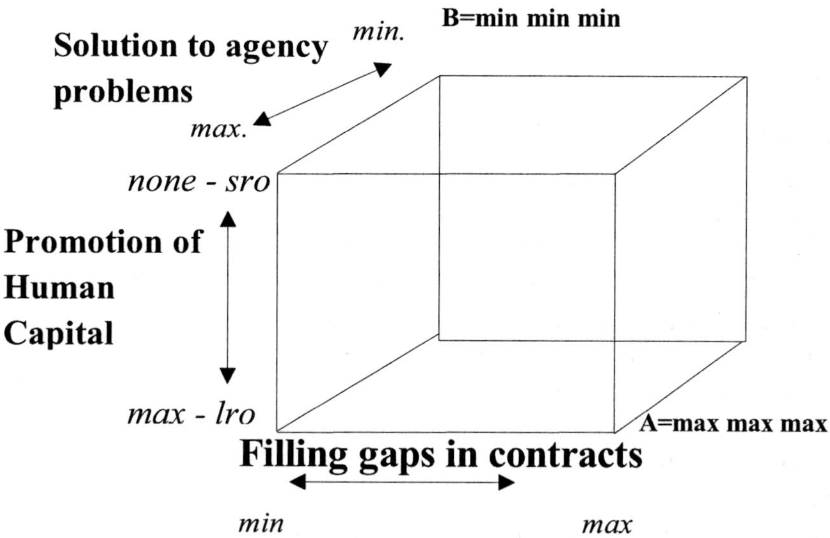

Figure 5 Some important features of Corporate Governance

But to do this (for the Italian system) could not be enough to have an efficient CG system. Any governance environment can be interpreted as providing a solution to the conflict of interest between investors and entrepreneurs by resorting to different mixes of the following seven devices:

In Table 1 are also analysed the presence and the type of specialised financial institutions in the three systems of CG studied, the role played by fiduciary duties, courts and law firms, contracts and implicit rules and finally the presence of Government as shareholder.

So, to the tools analysed in Figure 5 one should add state ownership. In the continuum of devices available to cope with the separation between ownership and control, state ownership can be interpreted as a model in which the state raises capital directly through taxation and finances entrepreneurs by entrusting political authorities with the power to safeguard the interest of investors. Each of these devices provides a second best compromise between the controlling interest of entrepreneurs and the monitoring interest of investors.

Hostile take-overs can be facilitated by specific public offer rules or discouraged by anti-take-overs statutes; the extent of activism by institutional investors depends on their own CG and on the means they are provided within shareholders' meeting and so on. One of the starkest differences between the US and Germany/Japan is the frequency of such hostile take-overs. Since World War two, for instance, only four successful hostile take-overs have occurred in Germany. They are almost as rare in Japan.

The effects of any given mix of CG devices can be evaluated on two different grounds: static efficiency and dynamic efficiency. Static efficiency i.e. the ability to bring about an allocation of control as close as possible, given the technology and the skill of all agents to efficiency, i.e maximising innovation and human capital investment. Dynamic efficiency the ability to guarantee a degree of control mobility that creates enough of an incentive for people to improve their skill, given their endowment of talents.

In recent decades, German and Japanese firms did exceptionally well while US corporations stagnated. This has not always been the case and the reverse has often been true in the past. The UK presents an interesting contrast to the US. It has a similar separation of ownership and control in corporations but very different financial institutions. The banking system is concentrated and although the Bank of England has wide powers of intervention there are no explicit restrictions on the activities that banks may undertake. Insurance companies have also not been barred from playing an important governance role but have not. Some of these issues are addressed briefly but for the thesis that the political factors are of primary importance to be completely convincing more is needed. After all, the political nature of the UK situation is very different yet the separation of ownership and control seems to be similar to the US. If it is historic traditions and custom in the UK that led to the separation of ownership and control why could it not be the same factors in the US?

1.12. An Agenda of Research: Complexity and Corporate Governance

Competition between animals in the same specie and between different species caused that just the best animal and the best species survived in the years. This kind of Darwinian approach can be used to explain, even in economic environment, why some firms survive while some others disappear. Firms that survive in competitive environment are presumed to have optimal governance structures[30] since that they are able to adapt to different and dynamic environment.

Questions that are still open in the literature (see Kole and Lehn 1997) refer to the dynamic of governance structure. How fast these structures change during the time, how suddenly they adapt to change in the environment and how much it cost to adapt this structures to the firms in particular and to the society in general and, much more important, is the long-run survival of a firm related to its choice about which system of governance to adopt? All these questions are still open and partially explainable with a combined use of the Darwinian approach and the transaction costs model.

The most industrialised countries of the world exhibit big differences in the primary mechanism of CG. These differences in finance and governance are not simply accidents of history but a result of major differences in the legal and regulatory environments of the countries' financial systems.

1.12.1. An Evolutionary Approach to the Corporate Governance Question

There are of course many characteristics that could be considered when we differentiate between the existing systems of CG. The number of characteristics is N. Here we suggest four:

a) Ownership structure (fragmented 0 / concentrated 1);
b) Ability and capability to fulfil and enforce contract (unable 0 /able 1);
c) Management (family 0 / professional 1);

[30] For a "Darwinian" approach to theory of firms' organization see Alchian (1950) and Kole and Lehn (1997).

d) Control of management (big institutional investor 0 / market 1)

The "control" variables are of binary type, which can be coded as 0 or 1. In this way, for instance, the incentives that the considered economic system gives are or long run or short run. Even considering just four characteristics and restricting each to only two possible values, the total set of all possible combinations contains 16 combinations of Governance characteristics and a four-bit string can label each one of them. The dynamic of each single variable in the cube will follow the following scheme:

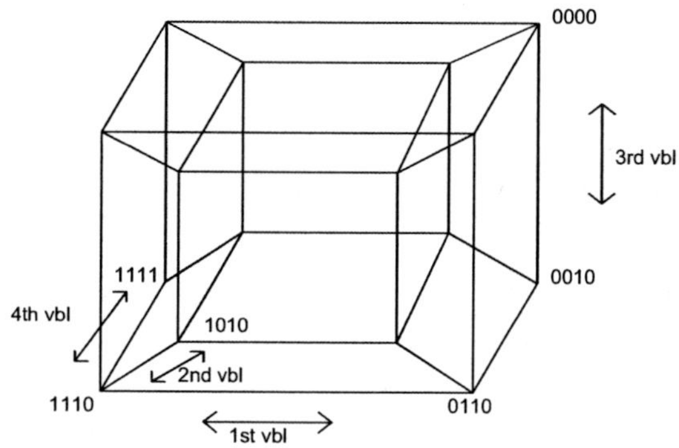

Figure 6 A graphic of the evolutionary approach to Corporate Governance

Each type of governance can be changed to another just changing one of the four bits.

Each vertex, labelled with the corresponding bit string represent one of the combinations of characteristic and each is linked to the four other types that differ from it by a single bit being switched from 0 to 1 or viceversa.

Suppose the capacity of each organisational type to accomplish a particular task under determined condition is a well-defined property. We could then define for each type the capacity to maintain throughput as the type's "fitness". Being fit relatively to a particular task need not necessarily imply overall fitness of the CG system. For example, a system that is "fit" regarding the capacity to give long run incentives but that is not able to solve agency problems probably cannot be defined fit in overall. Such fitness would be distributed across the various members of the ensemble; CG system types could be ranked according to that capacity from the best one (1) to the worst one (A^N).

If the economic system searches for fitter types by alteration of single bits at each of the margin, the hill-climbing process can be thought as an adaptive walk between adjacent vertices on the fitness landscape. The algorithm described is just one of the many possible algorithms. If we had an extra condition that each step must improve the ranking in which we are, a walk started from any of the vertex will reach a local optimum that, by definition, will be the highest ranking of the neighbourhood. One of the problems of this algorithm is that once arrived to a local optimum, to keep on using this procedure will stake the system in the local optimum precluding the achieving of the first best. So a possible different path could be the one to accept to achieve a "reasonable" loss in the short term to be able to arrive to a global optimum. In this case, the use of this algorithm is worth if the present value of the global optimum minus the lost that we sustain to achieve it is bigger than the value that we achieve in the local optimum.

Another algorithm that could be used is to modify more than one bit each step, for instance to change at the same time ownership structure and type of incentives given. This kind of algorithm is not very recommended for a theoretical reason. A walk that is constrained to pass via one-mutant neighbours is a "plausible limiting case of a population's adaptive flow under mutation, selection and recombination" (Westhoff et al. 1996, 5). It has been shown (Gillespie, 1983; 1984) that such constrained walk correspond to a population in which the rate of finding "better" point is quite low compared with the fitness differentials between the less and more fit alleles (Gillespie, 1984). If the product of population size and mutation rate is low compared with the rate of finding fitter variants, the population jumps with different probabilities to one or another of the fitter neighbours. So the algorithm based on a multiple change in the 4-string digit can result less helpful in explaining the process of CG as result of an adaptive process under selection, mutation and recombination.

Path dependence of this sort of reform is very important. In the case of transition economies, the rich array of deviant behaviours flesh out a framework of pathologies that help us to understand which are the potential risk of a CG failure for the real economy. This analytic tool helps us to give more precision to the often vague notion of CG failures. Sometimes it is quite easy to analyse the costs of poor CG but to tell the mechanisms by which the poorly incentived managers are causing social welfare losses it is very hard given the possibility of "moral hazard" and "adverse selection". The understanding of the role of too powerful stakeholders or managers or a non efficient market of capital and corporate managers can suggest a powerful set of reform, or better, can avoid future failure when we are in presence of a CG reform, for CG systems. In accord with Bebchuck and Roe (1999)[31], we see concretely that initial conditions matters for subsequent CG development (see also Schmidt R.H and Spindler G. 1999). To try to implement a set of rules as the US rules of CG with the presence of hostile takeover threat, share price-based management compensation schemes, board elections, shareholders approval of certain extraordinary transactions, ex post court review, the managerial labour market and other reputation incentives and so on cannot be enough if the initial conditions of the considered economy (or better country) are different. This is due to the path dependency of several rules and, more specifically corporate rules, some grounded of course in efficiency but the other grounded on interest groups politics. In transition economies we see this two salient initial conditions: uneconomic firm boundaries and competing groups of insider owners. Again, to use the concept that managers have to take in to account stakeholders wealth[32] when there are competing groups of insider owners, can be very dangerous for the efficiency of the firm.

It is possible to learn some lessons from the failure of the CG system in transition economy. A decent legal and enforcement infrastructure capacity must precede or at least accompany privatisation of large firm. It is quite relevant as well if this kind of legal environment has to be based on Common Law or on Civil Law. This sort of setting depends on the past tradition of the country that we are considering. Hayek (1960) argued for the superiority of the English tradition of Common Law with respect to the French Code Napoleon Civil Law legal tradition. This basically because common law provides superior property rights protections across the board, leading to faster economic growth not merely through its impact on financial markets but on all commercial activities There is after all a

[31] They use an example of two countries facing different conditions at time T0 but the same conditions at T1.

[32] That is basically the benchmark of all the German/Japanese types of CG systems.

substantial difference in the ideas motivating the common law and the civil law traditions. The judges who played a leading role in shaping English Common Law System were deeply concerned with protecting property and contract rights. If in our hypothetical transition economy the judges have different targets we could be in trouble with our system of CG relying in a common law system with dreadful consequences for growth, foreign investment and so on.

1.13. Conclusion

The institution in general responds to two distinct problems, one of vertical governance (between distant shareholder and managers) and another of horizontal governance (between close, controlling shareholder and distant shareholders). CG institutions, principally those that align managerial and shareholder interests, and secondarily those that prevent massive diversions of value from dispersed shareholders to the insiders are needed to stabilize the corporation. CG institutions have another role. Players outside the corporation can affect the corporation: if corporate arrangements appear unfair, then the outsiders can intervene through political institutions: they can ban some arrangements, raise the costs of others, and subsidize others. They can everywhere in the world. When they do so, they can deeply affect the institutions of CG (Roe, 2004).

The principal institutions are: the market, the board, gate-keeping, coalescing (via takeover, proxy fight and shareholder voice), incentive compensation, professionalism, lawsuits, capital structure, and bankruptcy. We have considered just some of them synthetically; however we can say that the institutions of CG are not just organizational and technical. They are, or they are affected by political institutions and by social factors such as social capital and social norms as well. Legislators can pass any number of rules. These will be of no avail until we realise that the market realities themselves have changed vastly during the last few years. There is strong need for voluntary action. This comes from personal commitment to ethics, social values equity, fairness, transparency, rule of law, legitimacy.

Social capital is an important influencing factor of manager incomes; it can be trusting relationships and a culture of confidence between the executive and workforce. The recruitment of manager is often based on strong ties. A recruitment procedure where individuals recruit one another produces trust. Established norms can be re-enforced by owners or CEOs when they select what they consider to be loyal and talented people. Hence a mobilization-oriented network can be instrumental for high salaries.

In the case of asymmetric information trust becomes a substitute for other selection rules in the recruitment of top executive. Trust is in this context interpreted in Williamson's terminology as "calculative" trust – trust justified by expectations of positive reciprocal consequences however loosely coupled to a specific significant other. In this context, a manager who violates a rule of an implicit or explicit agreement may suffer from a bad reputation among significant other managers. This may in turn reduce the willingness of these managers to use their referral capacity for the violating manager (Lombardo, 2005).

As a group, a board of directors combines a mix of competencies and capabilities that collectively represent a pool of social capital for their organization. The social capital contributed by the directors is a measure of the value added by the board in executing its governance function.

The central premise of social capital is that social network (of which board of directors and corporate organizations are examples) has value. Social capital arises from the idea of civil society, civic engagement and democratic governance, referring to the collective value of social networks and the inclinations that arise from these networks for the people in them to do things for each other (norms of reciprocity). The term social capital encompasses a wide variety of specific benefits that flow from the trust, reciprocity, information and cooperation associated with social networks. Social capital creates value for the people linked by the social ties created by these networks and can have flow-on effects beyond the immediate connection as well. Applying this thinking in the corporate context, a board can be viewed as exemplifying such a social network.

Under the social responsibility concept, the governance role of the board is expanded beyond the narrower idea of maximisation of shareholder welfare alone, to include the ethical treatment of the organization's stakeholders.

The differences across countries in how firms are financed and how their managers are held accountable to shareholders have long been the subject of intense academic scrutiny (see for a review Mayer 1998). Only recently however have these issues become a top policy topic. In the United States there is ongoing debate about the best methods of financing and governing firms. In deciding how to fashion their financial market, policy makers have to determine which is the optimal way to organise their corporate sectors. They clearly would benefit from understanding the factors behind the different corporate finance and governance systems in the industrialised countries. Even a normal observer can see significant differences in how firms are financed and governed. US firms rely heavily on corporate securities markets to finance investments whereas for Japanese and German firms, intermediaries (banks) have traditionally been the most important source of external finance (see on the topic the collection volume of Black and Moersch 1998).

In Japan and Germany, corporate finance markets have been substantially deregulated in recent years. Other countries, such as France and Italy, are considering vast privatisation programmes and changes in their financial systems. And the formerly communist countries are putting in place entirely new systems of property rights, business law and financial markets.

As we saw in 0, one important mechanism is high ownership concentration. If a firm's ownership is concentrated in the hands of a few investors, each will have sufficient incentive to invest in acquiring information and monitoring management. Large shareholding also confer the ability to exert control over management, through either voting power or board representation, or both. In contrast, firms in Japan (see Kim et al. 1998) and (especially) Germany exhibit much higher degrees of ownership concentration than the US. Ownership is very heavily concentrated in German firms. These large shareholders in Japanese and German firms are primarily banks, other financial institutions such as life insurance companies, and non-financial corporations. In US, even if there is a large growth of mutual fund holdings in recent years, direct individual holdings remain relatively more important.

Privatisation leads to efficiency for the new possibility to take-over and make some improvement in the firm if we are in presence of active shareholders and efficient capital market and for the possibility of bankrupt of inefficient firm.

In this paper we conducted a short analysis of comparative CG. We tried to understand why there can be diversity of CG mechanism, although, in the long run, less effective governance mechanism may be weeded out through competition among firm in product markets (Aoki, 2001).

The idea of the paper was not that to give very deep details on the structure of each individual country but to supply some useful devices to understand which are the characteristics of CG that are common between different countries and those characteristics that are similar. Moreover we did a description of some systems that are not fully conductible to the US/UK system or to the Japanese/European system but that they present some interesting features such as Italy and South Korea. The reason why we analysed Italy is because it is the only nation in the group of the G7 that has not a specific set of rules regarding the regulation of CG. We noted that the Italian system solved this problem with a sort of self-organisation in a way so that the agency problems have been reduced with the creation of small enterprises owned and, at the same time, managed from the same or form a group of investors connected by families' links. The Korean system shows its own peculiarities when we observe the way a "Chinese boxes" system reacts to an economic crisis or to a strong foreign competition. Furthermore we did a short analysis on what is happening in transition and developing economies to try to understand in how many "imitative" process and "evolutionary" process are on their way in these countries.

After that we tried to contribute a bit in the process of defining a taxonomy of CG. At the actual state of the world, we can observe rather more than a taxonomy of a single "perfect" system, we can observe two different systems: an insider one and an outsider. Each one of these systems can be efficient if they respect the features that we analysed in the devoted paragraph. The question now is if we will keep on having two main systems or if they will evolve in a third common one or if one of them will incorporate the other.

This can be the starting point of a new interesting question on CG: whether or not there is a convergence between the different systems around the world and which are the evolutionary path of each system.

Using Kauffman nK model could be helpful to contribute to the question that is now puzzling many researchers in the field: is there a process of convergence between the main systems of CG or is there a process of polarisation around the two main systems of CG? To find all the possible paths of evolution and the possible convergence and divergence of the systems of CG will be the next challenging adventure.

REFERENCES

Acemoglu, D., johnson s. and robinson j.a. (2001), *Institutions and Economic Development*, mimeo

Alchian, A. (1950). *Uncertainty, Evolution and Economic Theory* Journal of Political Economy, June 1950 58(3) pg. 211-21

Akamatsu, N. (1995). *Enterprise Governance and Investment Funds in Russian Privatization*; in Aoki,-Masahiko; Kim,-Hyung-Ki, eds. Corporate governance in transitional economies: Insider control and the role of banks. Economic Development Institute Development Series. Washington, D.C.: World Bank, 1995, pages 121-83.

Akerlof, G. (1970), The Market for Lemons: Quality Uncertainty and the Market Mechanism, *The Quarterly Journal of Economics*, vol.84, pages 488-500

Aoki M., (1998). *"An Information Theoretic Approach to Comparative Corporate Governance"*; Paper provided by Stanford University, Department of Economics in its series Working Papers nr. 99004

Aoki, M. (2001). *Toward a Comparative Institutional Analysis*, Massachusetts Institute of Technology

Arrow, K.J. ET AL. (1996). *"Joint statement of Russian and American Economists"* Nezarisimaya Gazeta, 1st July, summarised in M. D. Intriligator, "A new economic policy for Russia", Economics of transition vol. 5, nr. 1, 1997.

Avio K. L. (2004). A Modest Proposal for Institutional Economics, *Journal of Economic Issues*, vol.XXXVIII, pages 715-745

Barca F. (1994). *Allocazione e riallocazione della proprietà e del controllo delle imprese: ostacoli, intermediari, regole;Il mercato della Proprietà e del controllo delle imprese: aspetti teorici ed istituzionali*; BANCA D'ITALIA Numero speciali dei contributi all'analisi economica;1994

Barca , F. (1998). *Some views on U.S. Corporate Governance*" Columbia Law Review, Vol. 1998, No. 1

Barca, F. and Trento, S. (1997). *State Ownership and the Evolution of Italian Corporate Governance*; Industrial-and-Corporate-Change; 6(3), September 1997, pages 533-59.

Basili, M., Duranti C. and Franzini, M. (2004), Networks, Trust and Institutional Complementarities, forthcoming in *Rivista di Politica Economica*

Baums T., (1993). *" Takeovers versus institutions in corporate governance in Germany"*; edited in Prentice D.D. Holland P.R.J. (1993); Contemporary issues in CG; Clarendon Press

Bebchuk, L., Kraakman, R. and Triantis, G. (1999). *Stock pyramids, Cross ownership and dual class equity: the creation and agency costs of separating control from cash flow rights*; Discussion Paper nr. 249; Harvard Law School, Olin Center for Law, Economics and Business 1999

Bebchuk, L.A. and Roe, M.J (1999). A theory of path dependence in corporate governance and ownership; Columbia law school; The centre for Law and Economic studies; Working paper no. 131; November 1999

Beecroft, A. (1994). *The Role of the Venture Capital Industry in the UK*; in Dimsdale,-Nicholas; Prevezer,-Martha. Capital markets and corporate governance.. Oxford and New York: Oxford University Press, Clarendon Press, 1994, pages 195-208.

Belcher, A. (2003). The Unitary Board: Fact or Fiction? *Corporate Ownership and Control*, vo.1, pages 139-148.

Berglof, E. (1995). *Corporate Governance in Transition Economies: The Theory and Its Policy Implications*; in Aoki,-Masahiko; Kim,-Hyung-Ki, eds. Corporate governance in transitional economies: Insider control and the role of banks. Economic Development Institute Development Series. Washington, D.C.: World Bank, 1995, pages 59-95.

Bertero E, Rondi, L., (1998). *"Managerial discretion and investment decision of state-owned firms: evidence from a panel of Italian companies"*; Working paper nr. 7/1998; CERIS-CNR

Bianchi, M., Bianco, M. and Enriques, L. (1998). *Ownership, pyramidal groups and separation between ownership and control in Italy*; Preliminary research output by

European Corporate Governance Network; forthcoming in Barca and Becht (eds.) Ownership and Control: A european perspective Oxford University Press

Black, S. W. and Moersch, M. eds (1998). Competition and convergence in financial markets: The German and Anglo-American models; *Advances in Finance, Investment and Banking*, vol. 5. Amsterdam; New York and Tokyo: Elsevier Science, North-Holland, 1998, pages xix, 406

Boot, A. W. A, Macey J. R., (1998) Objectivity, Control, and Adaptability in Corporate Governance; Working paper Social Science Research Network.

Boycko, M., Shleifer A. and Vishny, R. (1995). *Privatizing Russia*, Cambridge, Mass, MIT Press

Bush, P. D., (1993). The Methodology of Institutional Economics: A Pragmatic Instrumentalist Perspective, in Marc R. Tool (Ed.), *Institutional Economics: Theory, Method, Policy*, Boston: Kluwer Academic Publishers, pages 59-107.

Charkham, J., (1994). *"Keeping Good Company: A study of Corporate Governance in Five Countries"*, Oxford University Press, 1994, Oxford

Cho, D.S. (1992). *A study of the korean chaebols*; Seoul: Maeil Business News Press

Coase r. (1937). On the Nature of the Firm, Economica, pages 386-405

Coffee, J.C. Jr. (1999). Privatisation and Corporate Governance: the lessons from security market failure; Columbia law school; Working Paper nr. 158; October 1999

Coleman J. S. (1988), "Social Capital in the Creation of Human Capital", *American Journal of Sociology*, 94 (Suppl.): S95-S120.

Collected papers (1999). Corporate Governance: a Framework for implementation; World Bank

Corbett, J. (1994). *An Overview of the Japanese Financial System*; in Dimsdale,-Nicholas; Prevezer,-Martha. Capital markets and corporate governance.. Oxford and New York: Oxford University Press, Clarendon Press, 1994, pages 306-24.

Core, J. E. (2001). A Review of the Empirical Disclousure literature: discussion, *Journal of Accounting and Economics*, vol.31, pages 441-456

Crama, Y., Leruth, L., Renneboog, L. and Urbain, J. P. (1999). *Corporate Governance structures, control and performance in European market: a tale of two systems.* Tilburg University Working Paper December 1999

Cuervo, A. (2002). Corporatew Governance Mechanisms: A Plea for Less Code of Good Governance and More Market Control, *Corporate Control: An International Review*, 10

Dasgupta P. (2000). Economic Progress and the Idea of Social Capital, in Dasgupta P. and Serageldin I. (Eds) *Social Capital: a Multifaceted Perspective*, Washington D.C., The World Bank, pages 325-424

Deeg R. (2001). *Institutional Change and the Uses and Limits of Path Dependency: The Case of German Finance*, MaxPlanck Institute for Social Science, discussion paper 01/6

De Jong H., (1997). The governance structure and performance of large European corporations; *Journal of Management and Governance*; Vol. 1 1997 Fall

Demsetz H. (1967). Toward a Theory of Property Rights, in *American Economic Review*, 57, pages 347-359

Demsetz H. (1983). The Structure of Ownership and The Theory of The Firm, *Journal of Law and Economics*, 26, pages 375-390

Denis, D.J., Denis, D.K., Sarin A., (1997). *"Ownership structure and top executive turnover"*; Journal of Financial Economics 45, 1997, pages 193-211

Dietl H. M. (1998). *Capital Markets and Corporate Governance in Giappone, Germania and the United States*; London and New York, Routledge 1998

Dimsdale N.H. (1994). *A Postscript on the Draft Report of the Cadbury Committee*; Dimsdale,-Nicholas; Prevezer,-Martha. Capital markets and corporate governance.. Oxford and New York: Oxford University Press, Clarendon Press, 1994, pages 42-49.

D'orio, G. (2000). Privatisation and Corporate Governance. Efficiency and managerial behaviour: the UK experience; University of Naples PhD Thesis; Department of Public Economics

Durlaf S. N., fafchamps m. (2004). *Social Capital*, NBER Working Paper 10485

Earle, J. S. and Estrin, S. (1996). *Privatization versus Competition: Changing the Behaviour of Russian Enterprises*, CEP Working Paper no. 316.

Edwards, J. and Fischer K. (1994). *Banks, Finance, and Investment in Germany*, Cambridge: Cambridge University Press

Emmons, W. R. and Schmid, F. A. (1999). *Corporate governance and corporate performance*; Working paper; Federal Reserve Bank of ST. Luis; W.P 99-018 September 1999

Fama, E. F. (1980). Agency Problems and the Theory of the Firm, Journal of Political Economy, 88, pages 288-307

Fama, E. F. and jensen m.C. (1983). Separation of Ownership and Control, *Journal of Law and Economics*, 26, pages 301-325.

Ferri G and Pesaresi n. (1996). *The Missing Link: Banking and Non Banking Financial Institutions in Italian Corporate Governance*, Fondazione Eni Enrico Mattei Note di Lavoro: 04/96, February 1996, pages

Foss, N. J. and Iversen, M., (1997). *Promoting Synergies in Multiproduct Firms: Toward a Resource-based View*, Department of Economic Strategy, Copenhagen Business School

Fox, M. and Heller, M. (1999). *Corporate Governance: lessons from transition economy reforms*; proceedings of the conference Corporate Governance: lessons from transition economy reforms held at The William Davidson Institute; University of Michigan Business School; December 1999

Franks, J. and Mayer C. (1996). Hostile Takeovers and the Correction of Managerial Failure, *Journal of Financial Economics*, 40, pages 163-181

Franks, J. and Mayer C. (1998). Corporate Ownership and Control in The U.K., Germany and France, *Journal of Applied Corporate Finance*

Franks, J. and Mayer C. (2001). Ownership and Control of German corporation, *CEPR discussion paper nr. 2898*

Frydman, R. and Rapaczynski, A. (1994). *Privatization in Eastern Europe: Is the State Withering Away*?, CEU Press

Frydman R., Gray C. W. and Rapaczynski A. eds.(1996). *Corporate governance in Central Europe and Russia Volume 2. Insiders and the state*. Budapest: Central European University Press; Oxford, University Press, New York, (2) 1996

Gillispie, J. H. (1983). *A simple stochastic gene substitution model*; Theoretical Population Biology 23, 202 1983

Gillespie J. H. (1984). *Molecular evolution over the mutational landscape*; Evolution 38; 1116

Granovetter M. (1985). Economic Action and Social Structure: the Problem of Embeddedness, *American Journal of Sociology*, vol.91, n.3, pages 481-510

Groenewegen J. (2004). Who Should Control the Firm? Insights from New and Original Institutional Economics, *Journal of Economic Issues*, vol.XXXVIII, pages 353-361

Grootaert C. (1998). Social Capital: the Missing Link? *The World Bank Social Capital Initiative Working Paper* No.3

Habermas J. (1995). Reconciliation Through the Public Use of Reason: Remarks on John Rawls Political Liberalism, *Journal of Philosophy*, vol.92, pages 109-131

The Hampel Report, The Final Report (1998) *The Committee on Corporate Governance and Gee Publishing Ltd.*, January.

Hart O. (1989). An Economic Perspective On The Theory Of The Firm, *Columbia Law Review*, vol.89, no.7, pages 1757-1774.

Hayek, F.A. (1945). The Use of Knowledge in Society, *American Economic Review*, vol.35, n.4, pages 519-530

Hayek, F. A. (1960), The Constitution of Liberty, Routledge and Kegan Paul, London, trad. it., La società libera, Vallecchi, Firenze 1969.

Hoshi, T. (1995). *Cleaning up the Balance Sheets: Japanese Experience in the Postwar Reconstruction Period*; in Aoki,-Masahiko; Kim,-Hyung-Ki, eds. Corporate Governance in Transitional Economies: Insider Control and the Role of Banks. Economic Development Institute Development Series. Washington, D.C.: World Bank, 1995, pages 303-59.

Hoshi, T. (1997). *Benefits and Costs of Giapponeese System of Corporate Governance*; Global-Economic-Review; 26(3), Autumn 1997, pages 77-95

Hosterloh, M. and Frey, B.S. (2005). *Shareholder Should Welcome Employees as Directors*, Working Papers Series ISSN 14-24-0459, WP No.228, Institute for Empirical Research in Economics, University of Zurich

Hughes, A. (1994). *The 'Problems' of Finance for Smaller Businesses*; in Dimsdale,-Nicholas; Prevezer,-Martha. Capital Markets and Corporate Governance, Oxford and New York: Oxford University Press, Clarendon Press, 1994, pages 209-34.

Hyun, O. S. (1999). *Korean's Corporate Governance System: Applying new remedies* Articolo inserito negli atti della conferenza " Corporate Governance in Asia: a comparative perspective." Hjosted by OECD, KDI e World Bank 1999

Intriligator, M. D. (1994). "Privatization in Russia Has Led to Criminalisation", Australian Economic Review, No. 106, pp. 4-14, April-June, 1994.

Jayaraman,-Narayanan; Shrikhande,-Milind, (1997). *"Financial Distress and Recovery at Metallgesellschaft"* AG: The Role of Corporate Governance and Bankruptcy Laws; Financial-Practice-and-Education; 7(2), Fall-Winter 1997, pages 7-18

Jensen, M. C. (1994). Self-Interest, Altruism, Incentives, and Agency Theory, *Journal of Applied Corporate Finance*, (Summer)

Jensen, M. C. and meckling w. (1976). Theory of the Firm: Managerial Behavior, Agency Costs, and Capital Structure, *Journal of Financial Economics*, no.3, pages 305-360.

Kane, E. J. (1994). *Role of Watchdog Institutions in Corporate Governance*, Mimeo, March (2004), Boston College

Kaplan, S. (1997). Corporate Governance and Corporate Performance: A Comparison of Germany, Japan and the U.S., *Journal of Applied Corporate Finance*, vo.9, pages 86-93

Kim, K. A.; L., Piman, (1998). *"A Test of the Two-Tier Corporate Governance Structure: The Case of Japanese Keiretsu"*; Journal-of-Financial-Research; 21(1), Spring 1998, pages 37-51

Kojima, K. (1994). Corporate Governance in Germany, Japan and United States: A Comparative Study, *Kobe Economic and Business Review*, 38, pages 171-243

Kojima, K. (1997). *"Japanese corporate governance: An international perspective"*; Kobe Economic and Business Research Series, no. 14. Kobe: Kobe University, Research Institute for Economic and Business Administration, 1997, pages xii, 173

Kole, S. and Lehn, K. (1997). Deregulation, the evolution of corporate governance structure, and survival, *American Economic Review*, papers and proceedings, May 1997 vol. 87 no. 2 pages 421-425

Kreps, D. M. (1990), Corporate Culture and the Economic Theory. In J.E. Alt and Shepsle, K.A. (Eds), *Perspectives on Positive Political Economy*, Cambridge, Cambridge University Press

La Porta, R., De-Silanes, F. , Shleifer, A. and Vishny, R. W. (1997). Trust in Large Organizations, *American Economic Review*, vo.87, n.2, pages 333-338

La Porta, R., Shleifer, A., Vishny, R. W. and Lopez-De-Silanes, F. (1998). *Law and Finance*; Journal of Political Economy, Vol. 106, No. 6, December Harvard University, Harvard University, University of Chicago and Harvard University

La Porta R., Lopez-De-Silanes F., Shleifer A., and Vishny R.W. (1999). Corporate Ownership Around the World, *Journal of Finance,* 54, pages 471-517

Lazonick, W. and O'sullivan M. (1995). Organization, Finance, and International Competition, *Industrial and Corporate Change*, 4, n.1, pages 1-49

Lee, K. (1999). Corporate governance and growth in the Korean Chaebols: A microeconomic Foundation for the 1997 crisis; Seul National University; working paper May 1999

Litwack, J. M. (1995). *Corporate Governance, Banks, and Fiscal Reform in Russia*; in Aoki,-Masahiko; Kim,-Hyung-Ki, eds. Corporate governance in transitional economies: Insider control and the role of banks. Economic Development Institute Development Series. Washington, D.C.: World Bank, 1995, pages 99-120.

Lomax, D. (1994). *The Role of the Banks*; in Dimsdale,-Nicholas; Prevezer,-Martha. Capital markets and corporate governance.. Oxford and New York: Oxford University Press, Clarendon Press, 1994, pages 161-78.

Lombardo, R. (2005). *Management Compensation and Corporate Governance*, in Madhav Mehra, Ed., Making Corporate Governance Work Better, London, World Council for Corporate Governance, MM Publishing, pages 170-179

Lowenstein, L. (1999). Corporate governance and the Voice of the paparazzi; The Center for Law and Economics Studies; Columbia University school of law; Working paper no. 132; February 1999

Macey J. R. (1998) Measuring the Effectiveness of Different Corporate Governance Systems: Toward a More Scientific Approach *Bank of America Journal of Applied Corporate Finance*, Vol. 63, No. 2, 1998.

Masuyama, S. (1994). *Role of Giapponeese Capital Markets: The Effect of Cross-Shareholdings on Corporate Accountability*; in Dimsdale,-Nicholas; Prevezer,-Martha. Capital markets and corporate governance, Oxford and New York: Oxford University Press, Clarendon Press, 1994, pages 325-41.

Mayer, C. (1998). *Financial Systems and Corporate Governance: A Review of the International Evidence*; Journal-of-Institutional-and-Theoretical-Economics; 154(1), March 1998, pages 144-65.

Mayhew A. (1989). Contrasting Origins of the Two Institutionalism, *Review of Political Economy*, pages 319-333

Miyajima H. (1995). *The Privatization of Ex-Zaibatsu Holding Stocks and the Emergence of Bank-Centered Corporate Groups in Giappone*; in Aoki,-Masahiko; Kim,-Hyung-Ki, eds. Corporate governance in transitional economies: Insider control and the role of banks. Economic Development Institute Development Series. Washington, D.C.: World Bank, 1995, pages 361-403.

Miyajima H. (1998). *The Evolution and Change of Contingent Governance Structure in the J-Firm System--An Approach to Presidential Turnover and Firm Performance*; Economic-Review-(Keizai-Kenkyu); 49(2), April 1998, pages 97-112.

Mørck R. and Masao Nakamura, (1999). *"Japanese Corporate Governance and Macroeconomic problems"*; Harvard Institute of Economic Research; discussion Paper Number 1893 February 1999

Nam, I. C., Kang Y., and Kim J. K. (1999). "*Comparative corporate governance trend in Asia*" atti della conferenza su Corporarate Governance in Asia: A comparative perspective; hosted by OECD, KDI and the World Bank

Nivet J. F. (2004). Corporate and Public Governance in Transition: the Limits of Property Rights and the Significance of legal Institutions, in *The European Journal of Comparative Economics*, vol.1, n.2, pages 3-21

North D. C. (1981). *Structure and Change in Economic History*, New York, Norton

North D. C. (1991). Institutions, Journal of Economic Perscpectives, 5, pages 97-112.

North D.C (1994). Economic Performance Through time, *American Economic Review*, 84, pages 359-368

Oecd (1999). *OECD Principles Of Corporate Governance*, Mimeo, April, Parris

Osterloh M., Frey B. S. (2005). *Shareholders Should Welcome Employees as Directors*, Working Paper Series, ISSN 1424-0459, Institute for Empirical Research in Economics, University of Zurich

Ostrom E. (2000). Collective Action and the Evolution of Social Norms, *Journal of Economic Perspectives*, vol.14, pages 137-158

Pessali H., and Fernandez R.G. (1999). Institutional Economics at the Micro Level, *Journal of Economic Issues*, 33, n.2

Poens, K. S. N., (1994). *"Top executives, turnover and firm performance in Germany"*, 10 J.L Econ and Org 142, 1994, pages 148-55

Prevezer, M., and Ricketts M. (1994). *Corporate Governance: The UK Compared with Germania and Giappone*; in Dimsdale,-Nicholas; Prevezer,-Martha. Capital markets and corporate governance. Oxford and New York: Oxford University Press, Clarendon Press, 1994, pages 237-56.

Richter, R. (2002). *On the Social Structure of Markets*, Paper to be presented at the 6th Annual Meeting of The International Society for New Institutional Economics (ISNIE9, Cambridge, Massachusetts, September 27-29, 2002

Roe, Mark J. (1994). *Strong managers, weak owners: the political roots of American Corporate finance*; PRINCETON, N.J.; Princeton University Press 1994

Roe, Mark J. (2004). *The Institutions of Corporate Governance*, discussion paper N.488, Harvard Law School, Cambridge, MA

Roland,-Gerard (1995). *Political Economy Issues of Ownership Transformation in Eastern Europe*; in Aoki,-Masahiko; Kim,-Hyung-Ki, eds. Corporate governance in transitional economies: Insider control and the role of banks. Economic Development Institute Development Series. Washington, D.C.: World Bank, 1995, pages 31-57.

Schmidt, R.H. and G. Spindles, (1999). "*Path dependence, corporate governance and complementarity – A comment on Bebchuk and Roe*" Working paper nr. 27 JW1999 Goethe University

Sobel, J. (2002). Can We Trust Social Capital, *Journal of Economic Literature*, vol.40, pages 139-150.

Smith, B. R. D.,(1996). "*Establishing Effective Oversight over Public Enterprises: The Role of Boards: The Case of Canadian Railways*"; in Pannier,-Dominique, ed. Corporate governance of public enterprises in transitional economies. Technical Paper, no. 323. Washington, D.C.: World Bank, 1996, pages 120-26

Schneider-Lenne,-Ellen-R. (1994). *The Role of the German Capital Markets and the Universal Banks, Supervisory Boards, and Interlocking Directorships;* in Dimsdale,-Nicholas; Prevezer,-Martha. Capital markets and corporate governance.. Oxford and New York: Oxford University Press, Clarendon Press, 1994, pages 284-305.

Shleifer, A. (1997). Government in Transition, *European Economic Review*, 41, pages 385-410

Shleifer A. and Vishny R. W. (1997); *A Survey of corporate governance*, paper presented at the Nobel Symposium on Law and Finance, Stockholm, Sweden, August; published in 1997 in The Journal of Finance, Vol. LII No. 2 June 1997 Pg. 737-783

Stanfield, R. R. (1999). The Scope, Methods and Significance of Original Institutional Economics, in *Journal of Economic Issues* 33, n0.2, pages 231-255

Stiglitz J. E. (1985). Credit Market and the Control of Capital, *Journal of Money, Credit, and Banking*, 17, page 133-152

Stiglitz J. E. (2000). Wither Reform? Ten Years Of The Transition, in Pleskovic B. and Stiglitz B. (eds.) , *Annual World Bank Conference on Development Economics* 1999, Washington D.C., World Bank

Teranishi J. (1995). *Savings Mobilization and Investment Financing during Giappone's Postwar Economic Recovery*; in Aoki,-Masahiko; Kim,-Hyung-Ki, eds. Corporate governance in transitional economies: Insider control and the role of banks. Economic Development Institute Development Series. Washington, D.C.: World Bank, 1995, pages 405-33.

Tool M. R. (1979). The *Discretionary Economy: A Normative Theory of Political Economy*, Santa Monica, Calif.: Goodyar Publisher Co

Turnbull S., (2000). "*Corporate Governance: theories, challenges and paradigms*"; SSRN Working paper nr. 22 09 54.

Ugur M. (2005). *Improving Corporate Governance Quality Challenges and opportunities*, in Madhav Mehra, Ed., Making Corporate Governance Work Better, London, World Council for Corporate Governance, MM Publishing, pages 278-290

Uphoff N. (2000). Understanding Social capital: Learning from the Analysis and Experience of participation, in Dasgupta P. and Serageldin I. (Eds) *Social Capital: a Multifaceted Perspective*, Washington D.C., The World Bank, pages 215-252

Veblen T. (1898). Why is Economics Not an Evolutionary Science?, *The Quarterly Journal of Economics*

Von Thadden, Ernst Ludwig, (1995). "*Centralized Decentralization: Corporate Governance in the German Economic Transition*"; in Aoki,-Masahiko; Kim,-Hyung-Ki, eds.

Corporate governance in transitional economies: Insider control and the role of banks. Economic Development Institute Development Series. Washington, D.C.: World Bank, pages 253-92

Westhoff F. H. Yarbrough B. V. and Yarbrough R. M. (1996). *Complexity, Organization and Stuart Kauffman's The origin of Order*; Journal of Economic Behaviour and Organization; Vol. 29 (1996) 1-25

Williamson O. E. (1975). *Markets and Hierarchies: Analysis and Antitrust Implications*, New York: Free Press

Williamson O. E. (1983). Organisational form, residual claimants and corproate control; Journal of Law and Economics 26 351-380

Williamson O. E. (1985). *The Economic Institutions Of Capitalism*, New York:The Free Press

World bank (1996). *World Development Reports 1996: From Plan To Market*, Oxford, Oxford University Press

Yamagishi T and Yamagishi M. (1994). Trust and commitment in the United States an Japan, *Motivation and Emotion*, vol.18, pages129-166

Zingales L. (1998). Corporate Governance, in P. Newman (Ed.), *The New Palgrave Dictionary of Economics and Law*, vol.1, pages 497-503, London: Macmillan

In: Perspectives on International, State and Local Economics ISBN 1-60021-099-6
Editor: Gerald V. Liu, pp. 61-84

Chapter 2

CITIZENS, MERCHANTS AND MAYORS: THE MAIN PLAYERS OF AN EVOLVING SYSTEM OF GOVERNANCE AT THE CITY LEVEL

Frannie Léautier and Séverine Dinghem
The World Bank
North America - United States

ABSTRACT

The increasing role of cities in a globalized world, and the interest in linking decision-making at a local level with those decisions made at a global level, dominates the literature on global governance. The paper looks at the interaction between citizens, an elected mayor or municipal leader, and a firm making decisions to locate in a city on a globalized scale.

After discussing the choice for the main three players--citizen, mayor, and firm--, we use a dynamic game between these players to better understand the dynamics and uncover key aspects that can be used for policy, while leaving open the question of the *direction of causality*: does governance lead to more globalization or does globalization lead to improved governance at the city level. Empirical examples illustrate the outcome of the dynamic simulation.

Using a game-theoretic framework, we show that the dynamics of interaction between citizens, mayors, and firms, within a context of globalization, leads to superior performance of cities. This framework attempts to derive the nature of causality from globalization to good governance and from local accountability to good governance. Our analysis shows that both are important, but that the interaction between globalization and good governance should lead to superior performance, over and above that of local accountability by itself, or globalization in the absence of local accountability. We have shown that, when firms try to influence city leaders and go unchecked, it leads to bad outcomes in terms of city performance.

Our results indicate that history matters, and that a methodology that allows the dynamics over time to be captured, can shed light on some of the difficult issues surrounding urban governance. Such analysis would be relevant to understand the high urbanization rates in Africa which have come with little contribution to increased welfare of urban cities, with limited economic growth for their countries, low levels of foreign direct investment, and with well known challenges in the area of governance. Such a model could shed light on this difficult topic, when used specifically for African cities.

1. Introduction

The increasing role of cities in a globalized world, and the interest in linking decision-making at a local level with those decisions made at a global level, dominates the literature on global governance. We look at the interaction between citizens, an elected mayor or municipal leader, and a firm making decisions to locate in a city on a globalized scale. We derive the key aspects of such an interaction in a manner to draw policy conclusions.

In a sister paper (see Kaufmann, Léautier, and Mastruzzi, 2004), we show through empirically-based exploration, the key determinants of the performance of cities. In particular, we explore and show empirical evidence of the dynamic pressures from globalization and accountability that result in better performance at the city level. In that paper, we left open the question of the *direction of causality*, between governance leading to more globalization or globalization leading to improved governance at the city level.

There is also a specific link between the performances of utilities, whether they are water, electricity, garbage collection, or sewerage services and the quality of local governance. The concept of universal public service is fairly recent; beforehand, utilities such as water distribution, sewerage collection, gas, public light, and electricity were provided to groups of populations with a high density, which economically justified the minimum investments – whether public or private - needed for service provision, hence the importance of the *municipal scale* when dealing with utilities. For discussion on the link between utilities and local governance see Estache and Kouassi, 2002. In this paper, we use a dynamic game between three players--citizen, mayor, and firm--to better understand the dynamics and uncover key aspects that can be used for policy.

2. Historical Background and Strategic Trends in City Governance

We look at the historical origin and trends of interactions between citizens, mayors, and firms in order to derive the starting point of the dynamic game as well as verify and illustrate the conclusions with empirical examples.

The Constitution of Cities

The city is a relatively recent form of social organization, having existed for the last 10,000 years. The origin of cities passes through at least three distinct phases.

The **first phase** of urbanization began between five to six thousand years ago. Records of the first largest cities date between 3,500-4,000 B.C. in Mesopotamia and most cities, such as Jericho in 7000 B.C. are known to have grown from villages[1]. These settlements depended

[1] Taken from http://www.faculty.fairfield.edu/faculty/hodgson/Courses/city/origins/

largely on agriculture and domesticated animals. However, as the civilizations grew in size and trade routes grew in number, these settlements became centers for merchants, craftspeople, traders and government officials. The division between "town" and "country", "urban" and "rural" had begun. The need for governance and organized government had also begun. As for utilities and service provision, the construction of aqueducts, storage tanks and water distribution systems for consumption have been documented as early as 2000 B.C. in Qumrân. The technologies involved during this period had already been used in Jericho by the Hashmodean kings, and were the first documented evidence of *providing services to a community*. Earlier use of utility services, such as the network designed by the engineers of Herod the Great, were aimed at providing water to a single residence: the king's winter palace[2].

The **second phase** in the development of cities was during the industrial revolution in Europe around the middle of the 18th century. Large numbers of people moved from rural areas into cities to supply labor for factories. During this period, the number and the population of cities multiplied tremendously. At the same time, this period is characterized by the empowerment of city representatives, whereby cities gained regional and feudal independence to establish a more direct relationship to existing central governments. In France, municipalities become the basis of the administrative organization and are particularly numerous, even by today's standards[3]..

The **third phase** began after the Second World War. The largest and fastest growth in the world's urban population has taken place in the decades since 1950 and globalization, as measured by the interconnectedness of economies, contributed even further to the fast Space of urbanization. The need for managing local and global interests became more apparent.

Governance at the Local Scale

As cities grew, they needed more and better organization and management. Particularly around managing trade between large agglomerations, organizing and managing religious activity, organized defense, transport and communications, and organized government[4].

A number of authors have looked at the performance of cities particularly during the second and third phases of urbanization. De Long and Shleifer (1992) for instance look at European cities from 1000 to 1800, comparing their economic performance as a function of the regime of rulers. They find that cities that were ruled by princes - assumed to be representing badly governed and usually centralized regimes with extortionist tax structures - did more poorly than cities ruled by merchants or parliaments, such as Venice, Florence or Amsterdam. The main argument is that princes seek to maximize influence and revenue and prevent other regimes from coming up, while merchants would seek to maintain and expand the flow of commerce. Parliaments and other citizen voice-based regimes would seek to limit tax burdens and maximize economic growth. Our paper demonstrates that in the dynamic

---

[2] Source: Les Manuscrits de la Mer Morte, André Paul (Bayard Editions / Centurion, 2000)

[3] Today there are 36,565 for metropolitan France, among which around 32,000 comprise less than 2000 inhabitants (see graph 1 in annex 2). In comparison, there are 14,727 municipalities in Germany, 8,070 in Italy, 8,027 in Spain and 522 in the UK.

[4] Taken from http://www.un.org/cyberschoolbus/habitat/units/un02pg01.asp

interactions between a citizen, a mayor (ruler in the case of De Long and Shleifer), and a firm (merchant in the case of De Long and Shleifer), we can expect different equilibria depending on the type of mayor. This is an insight we will revisit in the next sections.

A study by Rauch (1994) looks at the performance of cities in the U.S. during the Progressive Era, which covers roughly the first two decades of the 20th century. During this period, there was a wave of municipal reforms, which transformed the governments of many cities. These reforms were mainly aimed at getting better performance since the political model of city management was not leading to the expected results. Rauch finds that when cities are managed by more Weberian institutional structures, as opposed to predatory ones where the mayor rules totally, they make decisions to allocate resources for longer gestation periods, such as investments in infrastructure. The evolution of a Weberian structure at the city level to ensure improved performance of cities from the point of view of services to citizens is of keen interest to us.

Henderson and Venables (2004) develop a model that evolves the dynamics of city formation in countries whose urban population is growing steadily. They consider the forward looking behavior of city managers in the specification of investments in housing and urban infrastructure assets. This paper allows the comparison of governance related measures to financial constraints in the performance of cities, where performance is measured by efficient size. Their results on the role of governance are of particular interest to us.

The Mayor

The office of the Mayor has existed as early as the fifth century in some cities and has changed dramatically over the years[5]. The title of mayor was given to the head of the Corporation (Council) much later in the 19th century. The role of the mayor however has not changed much since the Middle Ages. The mayor was acknowledged then as the "first citizen" of the town and had a council to assist him. He also was the custodian for peace and would preside over civil and criminal courts.

Mayoral powers at the time included: (a) power to regulate the private sector such as ensuring the size of loaves of bread and seizing bread of unlawful size as well as holding the bakers responsible[6]; (b) power to arrest those disturbing the peace[7]; and (c) power to compel persons to go into service, and to deal with labor issues such as matters relating to servants and apprentices[8]. Through the past centuries, the role of the mayor has evolved to include a legally recognized role within a national setting with well developed political and civic responsibilities. The degree of regulation of mayoral activity varies across cities and countries, as does the relationship between mayors, citizens, and firms. The power of the mayor in common law countries has been tremendously reduced throughout the centuries and today's mayor in such countries does not have as much power as a mayor in 15th century Europe. In Roman Law countries, especially the ones that introduced prerogatives to decentralize central government functions, mayors have gained financial and political

---

5 See references to the mayor in the web-page of Royal Borough of Kingston upon Thames at http://www.kingston.gov.uk/council_and_democracy/.../history_of_the_office_of_mayor.ht

6 Lamarde, William. Stack of Statutes. 5 Henry V c.6

7 Lamarde, William. Stack of Statutes. 2ED.II c.3

8 Lamarde, William. Stack of Statues. 5 Eliz. I c. 4.

independence. Moreover, in the Middle Ages, the mayor was mostly a representative of the feudal power and not often chosen by his peers. So there has indeed been a revolution in the degree to which citizens actually participate in choosing mayors over the centuries in both Common Law and Roman Law countries. A history of interactions between citizens, merchants, and mayors has lead to this evolution, all pushing towards improved governance and better delivery of services.

A study by INSEE (see Besson, 2002) also shows the importance of the mayor's role and powers in local governance. French history saw the mayor's role shift from being a *representative of the State* – which was the case almost since the French Revolution as he was not elected but nominated by the central government until 1848 – to *a local representative*, with a large degree of autonomy and a local budget since the beginning of the decentralization process of 1982. Following the trend, investments conducted at the local level increased significantly since the three decentralization laws of 1982, 1983 and 1986: the volume of investments carried out by municipalities increased by 14.9% in 1988. Between 1978 and 1993, the local investments in education and schools went up by 7.5%. By contrast, the share of direct municipal investment in infrastructure has decreased by 11.2% as the municipalities delegate public infrastructure services to the private sector. This helped reduce the debt burden of local administrations which decreased from 9% to 7.5% of the Gross National Income. The INSEE study also shows that the volume of investments made by a municipality is strongly influenced by the electoral cycle.

3. Model Specification

This section is devoted to the modeling of the possible interactions between three main players that are critical to the city's development. We define the city as a geographically bounded space where interactions take place between *citizens*, a *mayor* (or municipal authority), and *private firms*, as the main actors of the local economy. The outcomes of these interactions can be observed as the performance of a city from the point of view of: (a) quality of life, which is of interest to the citizens; (b) a good business address in terms of getting access to markets or quality services, from the perspective of the firm; and (c) a well-governed place where the resources needed to improve quality of life and offer good services are available, and the political support to continue is there, from the mayor's point of view. We observe the achieved performance of a city, which is the outcome of interactions between the three players. We develop the general case and expand from it with special cases.

The General Case

To model this process, we start the game off with a citizen in a city that has an existing endowment of quality of life and quality of governance. We denote a city-type by h^t, which represents a history of performances of the city over a time period t. When looking at a collection of cities from the outside, a city-type would be an observation from a feasible set of city-types $H = \{h^0, h^1.....,h^T\}$.

All players (citizen, mayor, and firm) observe $h^t = a^0, a^1, \ldots, a^{t-1}$ for all $t \geq 1$, as h^t comes from realized choices of actions at all time periods before t. In such a specification, we assume that the actions a^t of the players create the city performance profile h^t.

For the purposes of this paper, we use the Hirschmann (1970) framework to derive the actions of the citizens and their message bearing content to the mayor. Hirschmann's framework assumes that citizens seek to maximize their utility, through three options: ***exit*** if not happy with the quality of life package offered by the city by physically leaving the city or seeking alternative sources of service provision including self-provision; be ***loyal*** to the city and stay, consuming services offered by the municipality; and use ***voice*** to vote the mayor out of office or lodge complaints to the municipality and get services fixed.

The mayor observes the citizen's choice and responds following a governance framework, where he/she can ***ignore*** the demands and preferences of the citizens; or can ***satisfy*** them by responding to the demands of the citizens. A municipality that functions on a Weberian basis would have a mayor that relies on the council which is broadly representative of the views of citizens. Other types of structures would be more political and respond to shorter term gains by the mayor, such as re-election or other benefits, such as in Rauch (1994). Our model follows the Weberian/Rauch principle.

A firm observes the outcome of the choices of citizens and mayors, and chooses its response. We look at a firm that is seeking to invest in a city outside of its headquarters on a global scale. Such a firm has three options based on the observed information about the city: ***exit***, do not locate in city or, if there, decide to leave; ***locate*** and conduct transparent business in the city; and locate and seek to ***influence*** the local politics through bribes, state capture, and other forms of influence.

Citizens, mayors, and firms discount future utilities using a discount factor $\partial > 1$. The discount factor $\partial = e^{-r\nabla}$, where r is the rate of time preference and ∇ is the period length (a normal period to consider being the electoral cycle for a mayor which is about 5 years).

The utility for a citizen i is:

$$U_i = E_\sigma(1-\partial)\sum_{t=0}^{\infty}\partial^t g_i * \sigma^t(h^t)) \qquad (1)$$

where E_σ is the expectation with respect to the distribution over infinite histories of city performance that is generated by a strategy profile σ. We denote the null history by h^0, to represent a new city where residents have just moved in, or where a new mayor has just been elected. Which means the message of the citizen to the mayor represented by the series of choices of the citizen influence the utility of the citizen, and the citizen is impacted by the real quality of life of the city, the response of the mayor to their messages, and the choices made by firms. We use the convention (U_i, S_i, σ_i) for the utility, strategy, and choices of the citizens, respectively for the whole game and (g_i, a_i, α_i) for the stage game building block for a repeated game.

The utility expressions for the mayor and for the firm have a similar form, with notation j for the mayor and k for the firm. The theorem is detailed in Annex 1.

With such a structure, we define the payoff structure for the citizen as:

$\underline{v}_i$ = exit ; $\underline{v}_i + \theta$ = voice; and v_i = loyal

The payoff structure for the firm is:

$\underline{v}_k$ = exit; $\underline{v}_k + \varepsilon$ = influence; and v_k = locate

And the payoff structure for the mayor[9]:

v_j = ignore citizen; $v_j + \varphi$ = ignore firm; and v_j = satisfy citizen and firm

These strategies are a Nash Equilibrium for any $T > R.I$ and for $T > R.I(\max_a g_i(a) - \underline{v}_i)/\varepsilon$ the average payoffs are within 2ε of v where R denotes a repeated cycle (Benoit and Krishna (1985)).

The mayor will play "satisfy" in T-1 at the minimum, to ensure citizens play "loyal" at T when facing a re-election. A firm will either "exit" or "locate" if play by the mayor is "satisfy", within a well-governed system. But the firm can also play "influence" at T-2 if the mayor has no chance of getting "loyal" from citizens (in a situation where it is the mayor's last term in service for instance). If a firm plays "influence" and the mayor can provide some services to the firm, then it is a worthwhile strategy for the mayor and the firm at period T-2.

Global And Local Cities within a Responsive Governance Framework

In this section, the definitions of a Global City and a Local City refer to a framework developed in Kaufmann, Léautier, Mastruzzi (2004). A global city is one which is connected to activities in other countries through trade, finance, and intense communication (telephone, internet, tourist travel), while a local city is one with minimal interactions with other cities, but does serve as a regional or urban-rural center.

The pattern of choices that comes from a game such as developed in the previous section can be classified into the following main types of results.

The Case of a Global City

A Global City, which is well performing and well governed would have an end state that comes from a mapping of:

(loyal/voice, ***satisfy firm***, locate) ➔ (loyal/voice, ***satisfy citizen***, locate)[10]

---

[9] We assume that refusing influence by firms in the short run is better than ignoring citizens, since they may applaud the mayor for not being influenced by firms. [this can be discussed, especially if accepting influence by the firm is not known by the citizens…]

[10] The end state is described under the form of (citizens' choice, mayor's position, firm's strategy).

A Global City, which is well governed but poorly performing would have an end state that comes from a mapping of:

(voice, ***ignore firm***, locate) ➔ (voice, ***satisfy citizen***, locate/exit)

A Global City, with state capture or other forms of influence would have an end state that comes from a mapping of:

(loyal, ***ignore citizen***, influence) ➔ (loyal, ***satisfy firm***, locate)

A Global City can become a Local City that is well governed and well performing, with an end state that comes from a mapping of:

(loyal/voice, ***ignore firm***, influence) ➔ (loyal/voice, ***satisfy citizen***, exit)

This means that the city was able to attract some firms at earlier time periods (perhaps through perfectly legitimate reasons) and does well to meet the needs of its local residents, but cannot attract companies to locate there permanently. However, such a city is not responsive to negative influence such as bribes or state capture, and hence is a well governed local city, with little interest to outside firms.

The Case of a Local City

A Local City which is well governed but poorly performing, such that no companies locate there and the citizens have to self-provide services or do with poor performance would have an end state that comes from a mapping like:

(voice, ***ignore firm***, influence) ➔ (voice, ***satisfy citizen***, exit)

A poorly governed and poorly performing Local City, where the residents are not getting the services they need and are also not able to get a response from their mayor to their concerns would have an end state that comes from a mapping of:

(voice, ***ignore firm***, exit) ➔ (loyal/voice, ***ignore citizen***, exit)

Generalizing from these mappings, we can say an observed outcome of a set of actions taken by a citizen, mayor, and firm would represent a distinct strategy path which defines the city-type h^{t+1} which we would evolve into the set $H = \{h^0, h^1, ..., h^T\}$ where $H = T(a_i, a_j, a_k)$. The observer of a data set which is an outcome of such strategic choices would see a city-type h^t with probability $p(h^t)$, where $p(h^t) > 0$ for every T and $p(h^t) + p(h^1) + ... + p(h^T) = 1$.

The general form of the payoff function for the mayor is $U_j(a_i, a_j, a_k)$ since the mayor has to respond to the messages from citizens and the strategic choices of firms, but is also influenced by the history of his responses. Such responses could include having been re-elected because he made citizens happy, having had to respond to unsatisfied citizens who complained, or having had to deal with firms who left the city for other locations or decided not to locate in the city. A special case of the mayor who ignores messages from the citizens - representing a bad governance framework - would have a response that is based on the following utility function, since they will ignore the message sent by the citizen:

$$Max \sum p(h^t) U_j(h^t, a_j, a_k) \tag{2}$$

The payoff for the firm is $U_k(h^t, a_j)$ which like the citizen depends on the real quality of life profile of the city - rather than the message from citizens to their mayor - and the response of the mayor. We will look at a special case where the mayor sends information to the firm so as to signal good governance and a good business address.

Using the payoff structure developed in the last section we see that the mapping (loyal, satisfy firm, locate) is superior to the mapping (voice, ignore firm, influence) which in turn is superior to (exit, ignore firm, exit). We can express this as:

$$(v_i + v_j + v_k) > \{(v_{\underline{i}} + \theta) + (v_{\underline{j}} + \varphi) + (v_{\underline{k}} + \varepsilon)\} > (v_{\underline{i}} + v_{\underline{j}} + v_{\underline{k}}) \tag{3}$$

Firms and Citizens Responding When Mayor's Action is Not Observed

We look at a special case where the citizen takes the lead action, and the firm is an observer. This case would be relevant for multi-national firms making decisions to locate in a given city. In such a case, the mayor's action is not observed. The firm looks to see whether the citizen is "loyal" and deduces that the mayor could have played "satisfy citizen", which is the expected response in a well-governed framework. If the firm observes that the citizen has used "voice" it can deduce that this is an indication that the mayor can be "influenced". Such a special case would be relevant to an outside firm that is looking at imperfect information. Such a firm would have access to public information such as "Mayor X has been re-elected to a second term" or "Citizens of City Y have demonstrated against the mayor for poor garbage collection". The actions of citizens can convey information to firms.

We develop an extensive form of this game (Gibbons, 1990) which is shown in Figure 1. For purposes of simplicity, we do not include the pay-off structure in the figure.

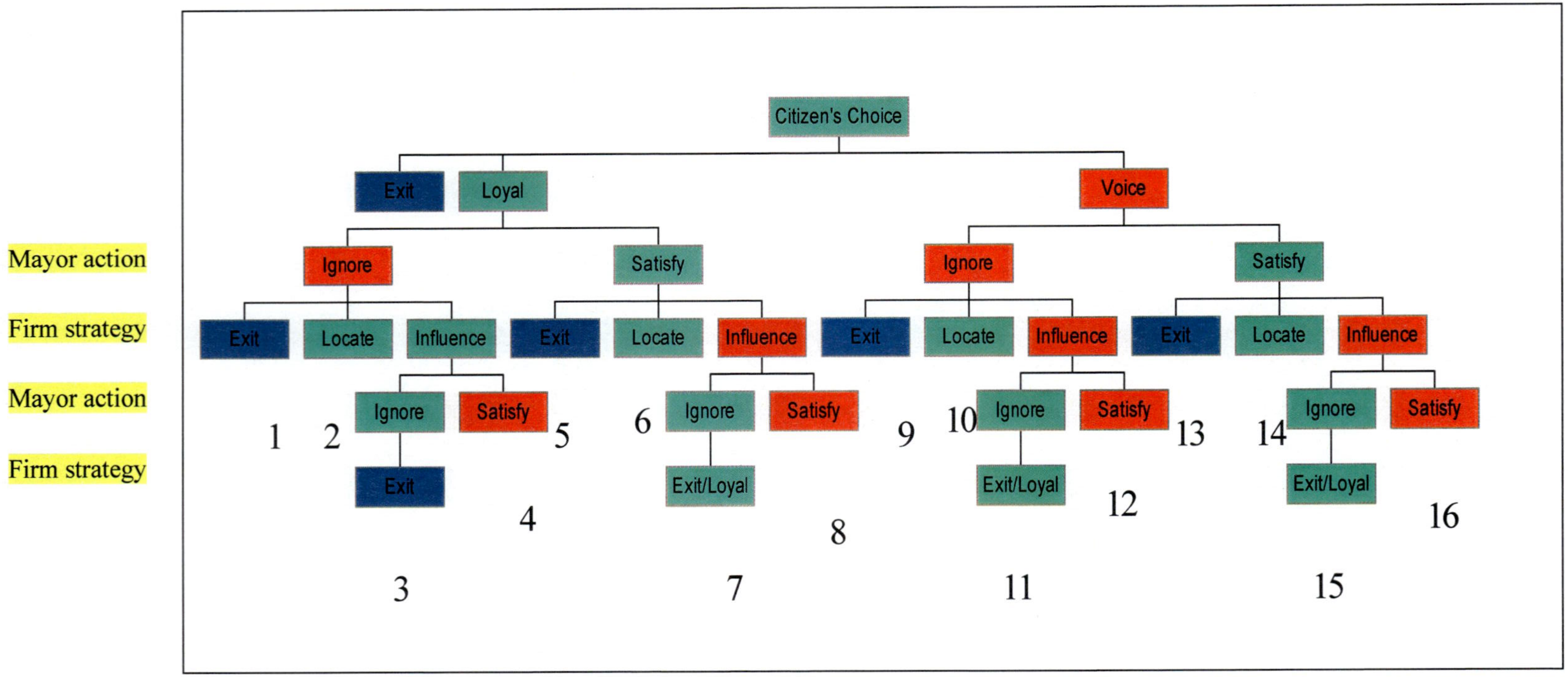
Mayor action
Firm strategy
Mayor action
Firm strategy
Citizen's Choice
Exit
Loyal
Voice
Ignore
Satisfy
Ignore
Satisfy
Exit
Locate
Influence
Exit
Locate
Influence
Exit
Locate
Influence
Exit
Locate
Influence
Ignore
Satisfy
Ignore
Satisfy
Ignore
Satisfy
Ignore
Satisfy
Exit
Exit/Loyal
Exit/Loyal
Exit/Loyal
1
2
3
4
5
6
7
8
9
10
11
12
13
14
15
16

Figure 1

From Figure 1, we see that there are 17 distinct outcomes that result from this game, labeled from 0 to 16. Some outcomes (shown in red) lead to an end state of corrupt cities, that may perform poorly for their citizens but well for the firms (4 and 12), or well for their citizens and firms, but firms have influence over the mayors (8 and16) and have captured them. While other outcomes (shown in green) lead to an end state of well-performing and well-governed cities (6, 7, 14, and 15). Other outcomes which are shown in blue, lead firms to exit after receiving more information (3 and 11) and or to firms deciding not to come on the basis of existing information (1, 5, 9, and 13). One outcome (0) leads to no city at all as the citizens exit. Henderson and Venables (2004) also find the conditions under which such a result can be obtained, using a different specification of a dynamic model with forward-looking behavior.

In such a game, the outcome at the city level of strategies 1, 3, 5, 9, 11, and 13 would be to have no foreign companies investing in the city. We called such cities "local city" in the definition employed in Kaufmann, Léautier, and Mastruzzi (2004) and also in the discussion in the last section. A well-governed and well performing local city would be represented by outcome 3 and 11, which despite having the mayor responding to citizens needs, companies decided not to locate there, for reasons other than governance. A poorly governed global city, would be represented by the outcomes from strategies 4, 8, 12, and 16.

Let us look now look at the payoff functions of some of the sub-games. At the first stage of the game, or in a sub-game where we observe the citizen, we would have an extended form as shown in Figure 2 below.

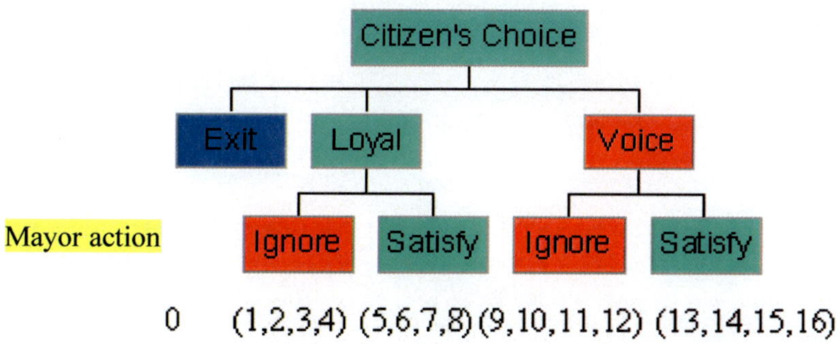

Figure 2

The history of the sub-game in Figure 2 would be visible in the performance of the city at the end of the game, which would be unique to a particular mapping, and a function of the payoff structure. We represent such performance as a simple sum of the payoffs of the three players at the end of that stage. The city performance for the respective paths would be:

Map 0: Citizen "exit" at the first stage: v_i

Map (1,2,3,4): Citizen "loyal" followed by "ignore" by mayor: $(v_i + \underline{v}_j)$

Map (5,6,7,8): Citizen "loyal" followed by "satisfy" by mayor: $(v_i + v_j)$

Map (9,10,11,12): Citizen "voice" followed by "ignore" by mayor: $\{(\underline{v}_i+\theta)+\underline{v}_j\}$

Map (13,14,15,16): Citizen "voice" followed by "satisfy" by mayor: $\{(\underline{v}_i+\theta)+v_j\}$

From this sub-game, we can see that the mappings have the following ranking in terms of city performance, if θ is small:

$$(v_i+v_j) > \{(\underline{v}_i+v_j)+\theta\} > (v_i+\underline{v}_j) > \{(\underline{v}_i+\underline{v}_j)+\theta\} > v_i \tag{4}$$

The superiority of good governance, that is when a mayor is responsive to their citizens is shown in that Map (13,14,15,16) is superior to Map (1,2,3,4). But it is possible for the mayor to hedge and ignore the citizen in this first stage, since Map (9,10,11,12) is superior to Map (5,6,7,8), and the mayor can also be proactive and respond to citizens' needs before they voice concerns, since Map (13,14,15,16) has the best possible city performance.

With such a sub-game, we can now look more carefully at the stage where we introduce the firm's choices. Since the firm is an observer and would have seen the city performance history, we would have one simple choice. If citizens are exiting, then a rational firm would exit as well. We do not develop Map 0 any further. We explore the other Maps in more detail in order to see why a poor governance framework would be more superior to a good governance framework in the first stage. This is shown in Figure 3 and 4.

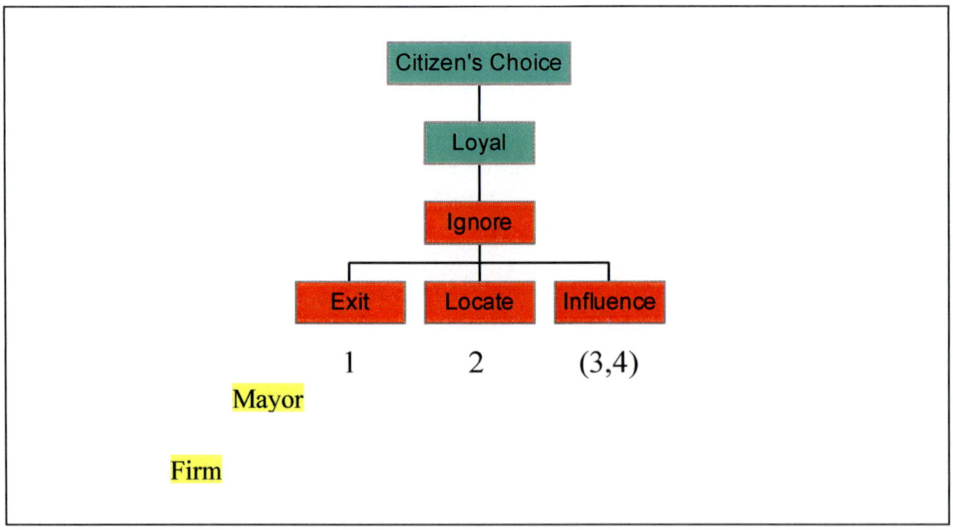

Figure 3

Map 1 at Stage 2 is the outcome of (loyal, ignore, exit): $(v_i+\underline{v}_j+\underline{v}_k)$

Map 2 at Stage 2 is the outcome of (loyal, ignore, locate): $(v_i+\underline{v}_j)+v_k$

Map(3,4) at Stage 2 is the outcome of (loyal, ignore, influence): $\{(v_i + \underline{v}_j) + \underline{v}_k + \varepsilon\}$

With ε being small, we see that Map 2 is superior to Maps 1 and (3,4), and even in stage 2 of the game, there is still a preference for a bad governance framework, where the mayor ignores the citizens whose loyalty she has, and firms choose to locate there, without at first influencing the mayor. This is possibly due to imperfect information at this stage. We do not know if the citizen is loyal to the mayor because the mayor delivers good services or because the citizens are apathetic.

We also look at the special case of "voice" which we develop in the sub-game in Figure 4. City performance at stage 2 following a "voice" play by a citizen is shown below:

Map 9 at Stage 2 is the outcome of (voice, ignore, exit): $\{(\underline{v}_i + \theta) + \underline{v}_j + \underline{v}_k\}$

Map 10 at Stage 2 is the outcome of (voice, ignore, locate): $\{(\underline{v}_i + \theta) + \underline{v}_j + v_k\}$

Map (11,12) at Stage 2 is the outcome of (voice, ignore, influence):
$\{(\underline{v}_i + \theta) + \underline{v}_j) + (\underline{v}_k + \varepsilon)\}$

Comparing Map (3,4) to Map (11,12), we see that the city performance, as represented by the total pay-off structure at the end of stage 3 of the game, is poorer when "influence" by the firm follows a map of (loyal, ignore) than when "influence" by the firm follows a map of (voice, ignore). This result, shows that citizen voice counts as a deterrent to bad governance even if firms try to influence the mayor and we are not yet certain of the choice of the mayor in the following stage of the game. The beginnings of good governance creeping into the influence of city performance can be seen at the end of stage 3 of the game.

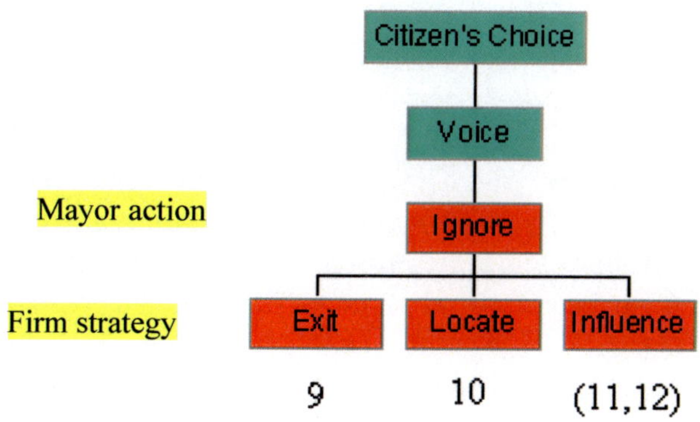

Figure 4

Using the terminal states only, we can derive the following conditions for influence and their governance implications. A poorly performing but well governed city would be one with the following mapping structure: (voice, satisfy citizen, influence, satisfy firm, voice, satisfy citizen). A well performing, but poorly governed city (such as with state capture) would be one with a mapping of: (voice, satisfy citizen, influence, satisfy firm, loyal, satisfy citizen).

As long as the mayor gives the citizens what they need, even if she receives bribes from firms, the city will be well performing, as firms and citizens will stay.

The analysis in this section provides us with sufficient impetus to see if there is empirical proof of the dominance of good governance in the context of globalization. From the analysis, we should expect good governance to interact positively with globalization - having firms locating in a city -, but also to have less impact when citizens and firms have options for exit, i.e. when they can self-provide a service like telephones or electricity. We also should expect a U-Shaped curve when comparing city size and city performance. This is because well-performing cities that are small, could be small because they have a framework of governance that does not allow influence by firms. If a medium city is badly governed, it would eventually lose citizens and company activity, and hence would shrink in size. For a medium size city to grow, it would have to be well-governed. In such a simple framework, medium sized cities should have the worst performance. An empirical test of this result indeed shows that this is the case, as can be seen in the following section.

4. Empirical Evidence

Empirical Evidence Based on Cities Characteristics

To test the theoretical framework in Figures 1 through 4 using empirical evidence, we employ a data set that has been constructed from various sources. These data were used extensively in a sister paper by Kaufmann, Léautier, and Mastruzzi (2004) and we refer to specific results in this paper for which the theoretical framework offers additional proof. We look at four types of data from an observation of city histories: (a) the quality of life as experienced by a citizen; (b) the observed quality of governance of the city; (c) the observed pattern of firms' decisions to locate in a city; and (d) the type of information firms would have access to prior to making a decision to locate in a city.

For measures of what a citizen would be looking for, we use a ***quality of life index*** developed by Mercer 2002, which is a database using survey data from 215 cities with assessments and evaluations of 39 key quality of life determinants, grouped in the following categories: political and social environment, economic environment, socio-cultural environment, medical and health considerations, schools and education, public services and transportation, recreation, consumer goods, housing, and natural environment. In this database, New York City has an index of 100. Zurich has the highest quality of life, and Brazzaville has the lowest.

For the ***quality of governance*** by the mayor, we use three indicators derived from various sources including: control of corruption, bribery in utility, and state capture. These indicators are developed in detail in Kaufmann, Kraay, and Mastruzzi (2004).

For the ***decision by the firm to locate*** or not in the city, we use data from Taylor and Walker (2004) which is a data base that measures the number of offices of major advertising, accounting, and financial firms in each city for 161 cities in 114 countries. We also use data from other sources such as A.T. Kearney (Foreign Policy, 2002) who use a composite index of globalization, which we use as a proxy for ***stable dynamics when firms have chosen to locate*** and stay in a city. The Kearney globalization index builds on indicators of trade, finance, personal contact, and information exchange.

For the ***type of information a firm may have about a city prior*** to its decision to locate there, we use city level indicators constructed through internet searches of city population, whether a city has a website or not, availability of data on budget and business regulations in such websites, and dummies for whether the city is the country's capital (for political influence) or a port (for ease of export).

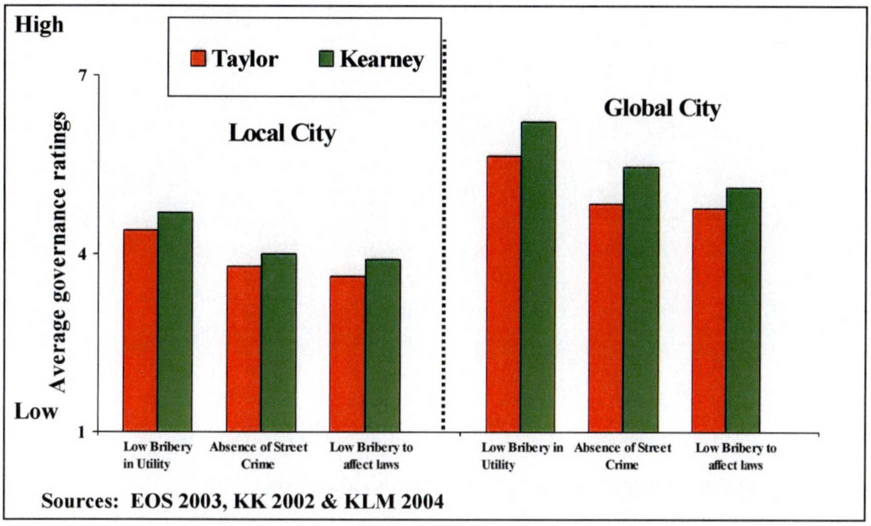

Figure 5. global Firms, Citizens and Mayors

We find evidence that strategies 3, 7, 11, and 15 in Figure 1 are superior to strategies 4,8,12 and 16, as shown in Figure 5. In other words, the positive dynamics of interaction between the citizens push for local accountability and firms push to get influence, but within a well-functioning municipal governance in a globalized world, are evident when you look at the fact that global cities achieve higher governance ratings than local cities, as shown in Figure 5. Global cities are better governed than local cities, because the added pressure by firms, for good governance, in addition to the pressure by citizens, makes a difference. We also see that country level globalization (using the Kearney composite) is more superior to city level globalization (using the Taylor index), but this difference is more profound for global cities than for local cities[1]. This result is evidence that the interaction across many cities and many firms leads to better governance outcomes than within a single city. Furthermore, evidence that when firms try to influence city mayors, it does not lead to long-run capability to stay in the city and perform (that is it eventually leads to exit and hence lower levels of globalization) is shown in Figure 6. We see that high globalization is strongly associated with high governance at the city level when looking at variables such as illegal party financing, diversion of public funds, or the quality of the postal system.

[1] The Kearney Composite is for country-level globalization measures, whereas the Taylor Index is for specific cities. See Kaufmann, Léautier, and Mastruzzi (2004) for more detail on the indices.

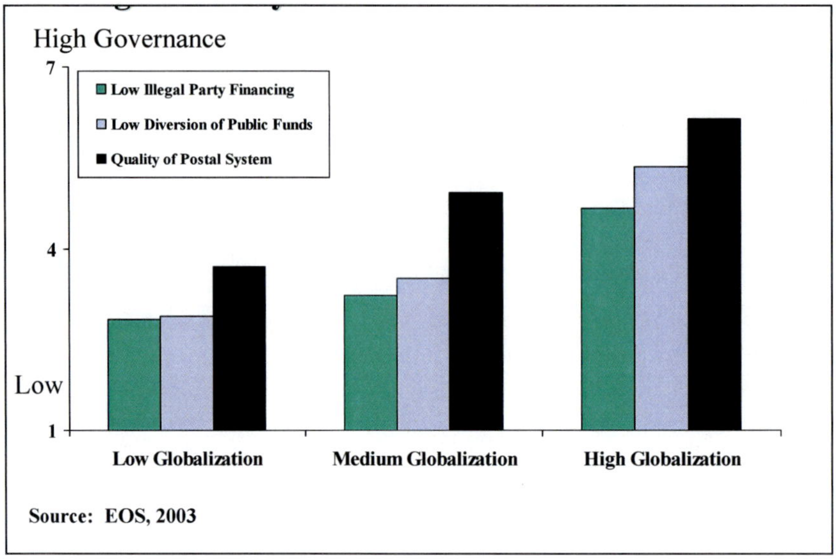

Figure 6. City Covernance and Globalization

There is strong evidence that when mayor's satisfy the needs of their citizens and are not corrupt and influenced by firms, the quality of life is good (see Figure 7).

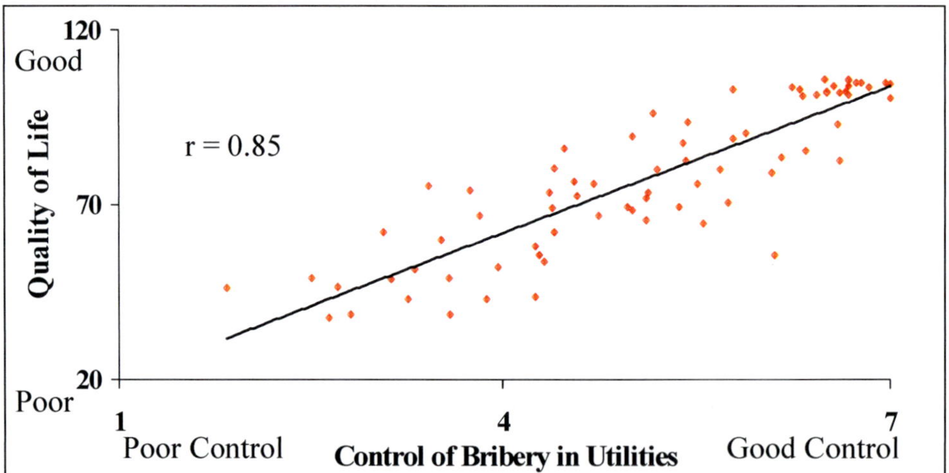

Sources: Bribery in Utilities: EOS 2003, 271 cities (from KLM database); Quality of Life: Mercer 2002, 215 cities. Mercer's survey provides an evaluation of quality of life in 215 cities. The study is based on detailed assessments and evaluations of 39 key quality of life determinants, grouped in the following categories: Political and social environment; Economic environment; Socio-cultural environment; Medical and health considerations; Schools and education; Public services and transportation; Recreation; Consumer goods; Housing, and Natural environment. Quality of Life Index: New York City = 100 (Highest: Zurich, Lowest: Brazzaville); Sample city overlap: 116.

Figure 7. Quality of Life vs. Corruption at City Level

But quality of life is also better when cities are more globalized, which means the added pressure from firms to improve performance does have an influence on the outcome of city performance (see Figure 8).

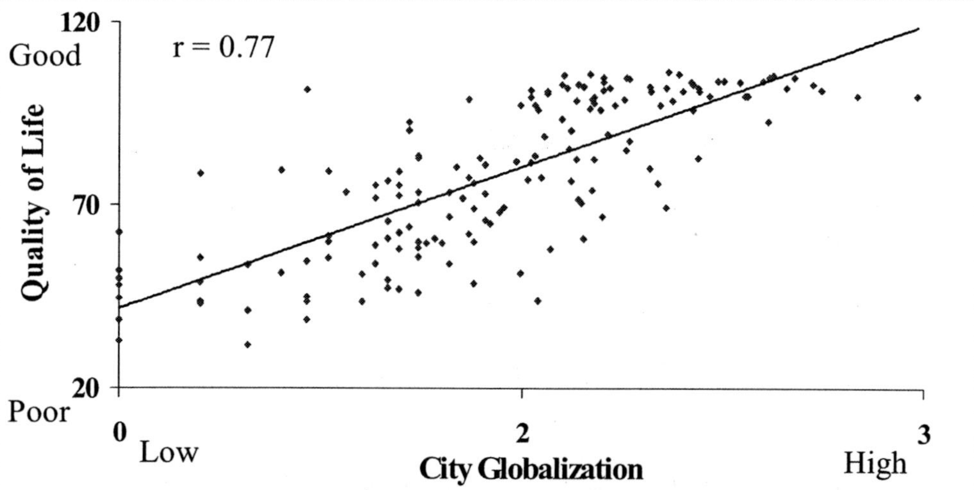

Sources: City Globalization: Taylor 2001, 261 cities (from KLM database); Quality of Life: Mercer 2002, 215 cities. Mercer's survey provides an evaluation of quality of life in 215 cities. The study is based on detailed assessments and evaluations of 39 key quality of life determinants, grouped in the following categories: Political and social environment; Economic environment; Socio-cultural environment; Medical and health considerations; Schools and education; Public services and transportation; Recreation; Consumer goods; Housing, and Natural environment. Quality of Life Index: New York City = 100 (Highest: Zurich, Lowest: Brazzaville); Sample city overlap: 162.

Figure 8. Quality of Life vs. City Globalization

A more detailed econometric analysis also shows that the theoretical framework developed in section II does indeed have merit when looking at the dynamics of choices made by citizens and firms at the city level.

We see that, whether a city has a website or not makes a difference in the quality of its governance which is of interest both to its citizens and to firms locating there. But whether the city's website has the information a firm needs to set up a business is much more important as a variable both in terms of size as well as significance in explaining the differential performance of cities across a number of key indicators of governance. Whether a city is global or not also matters. It is to be noted that a global city was derived from the definition of Taylor which is the number of firms who have located in the city.

The importance of prior information to firms also shows up when you look at the quality of services provided at the city level as shown in Table 1. Cities with a website have better quality of services than those that do not. Furthermore, if a citizen can get access to information on the budget (a measure of transparency and accountability) or there is information on how to start a business (a measure of good response to firms in a transparent manner) than the services are also higher. These data show that good governance (represented by the ***satisfy*** response by the mayor to ***voice***) leads to better outcomes at the city level.

The French Experience to Improve Local Governance

In addition to the empirical underpinnings of city level governance provided in the first section, the following examples in France illustrate a dynamic interaction between citizens, mayors, and firms that can lead to different types of equilibria. These cases concern certain large water municipal contracts in France. They are of particular relevance as France is the country that has the largest number of municipalities given it's the size of the territory and the number of citizens, as detailed in Annex 2.

Table 1: City Performance by Prior Information to Citizens and Firms NON-OECD SAMPLE (274 Cities) Average Ratings

CITY PERFORMANCE	CITY WEB PORTAL					
	City has a Website		Web has information on budget		Web information on how to start a business	
	No	Yes	No	Yes	No	Yes
Access to Sewerage (%, UN)	44%	54%	46%	70%	45%	72%
Access to Water (%, UN)	62%	68%	63%	92%	62%	90%
Access to Electricity (%, UN)	75%	76%	75%	91%	74%	93%
Access to Telephone lines 1 (%, UN)	84%	93%	86%	99%	86%	95%
Overall Number of Cities	210	58	262	6	256	12

Source: Constructed from data taken from the UNCHS Urban Observatory data in City Performance and from a web-search on whether a city has a web-site and what is posted in it. For more detail on the data see Kaufmann, Léautier, and Mastruzzi (2004).

Context

Decentralization has given greater power and has provided important public resources to local government, transferring key welfare state responsibilities to management at the level of cantons and regions. In the absence of an equivalent development in a posteriori controls, decentralization has given local politicians powers that they are not always able to successfully manage and has also extended the opportunity for corruption. France has been involved in a transition to a managerial model of public administration, with the opening of previously public functions to private contractors. In the late 1970s, 75% of the municipalities in France were managing their water services through "*régies municipales*". Twenty years later, 80% of the water distribution was managed by the private sector - the number of contracts signed with the municipalities peaked between 1982 and 1992. Over 500 contracts were terminated in 1997, 2% of them chose a different operator.

There has also been a sharp increase in public-private capital companies which have been the origin of a number of infamous affairs.

Examples of Bad Governance at the Local Level

Since the implementation of decentralization law in the 1980's, local politicians have become involved in illicit exchanges related to various practices. Several cases have been disclosed, raising public dissatisfaction and triggering new laws and regulations to mitigate bad governance risks as illustrated in Box 1. These cases were built on very different examples of bad governance practices, whether they were based on bribery charges or illicit party financing methods, not only at the municipal level but also sometimes at the government level.

Box 1: Examples of French water affairs

Questionable competition practices

In 1980, the two main French water companies, Lyonnaise des Eaux and Générale des Eaux, were condemned to pay each a compensation of FRF 2 million for collusion in the bids for the concession of Versailles, Martinique and French Guyana.

Fraudulent practices are not the only issue when dealing with public service delegation; unfair measures to competition or to the consumers also provide examples of bad governance. In 1990, CGE paid an entry right of FRF 550 million to the municipality of Toulouse for its water concession. At the same time, CGE inherits a burden of FRF 770 million of debts and liabilities from the previous municipal régie.

The Noir-Botton affair: bad governance and mayor's personal profit

The Noir-Botton Affair (1992-1998) concerned the financing of political campaigns and personal advantages given to the former mayor of Lyon, now dismissed, by his daughter-in-law, who was involved in show business. Benefits included the distribution of gifts to obtain broadcasts and the bankruptcy of a firm providing him with financial resources.

Other scandals involving the financing of political parties at the national and local scales also implicated French private companies and political representatives : in 1984, there were 69 verdicts condemning political and elected representatives for corruption-related charges; this figures almost doubled in 1987 (which had 133 condemnations) to reach 286 condemnations in 1997[2].

The Carignon and the Boucheron affairs: bad governance and political party financing

The Carignon Affair (1996) is also illustrative. It involved the former mayor of Grenoble, who was charged with manipulating competition for public contracts, thereby obtaining personal benefits and financing his political career.

In July 1989, Alain Carignon, mayor of Grenoble and a Minister, decides to privatize the municipal water services without a bidding process. From then on, the water price is increased from FRF 4.85 to FRF 13.59 [3] (at the end of 1995), although the network did not need any major investments or renewals. In 1994, French magistrates found that the water service was privatized in exchange for contributions by Lyonnaise des Eaux to the electoral campaign of Alain Carignon and other gifts totaling over FRF 19 million. They prosecuted Carignon, his main advisor at the city hall and two executives of Lyonnaise. In 1995 and 1996, they were convicted of paying and/or receiving bribes and condemned to prison remaining on probation. The courts also ruled that the consumers could claim compensation of a total of FRF 300 000 as COGESE (spell out acronym) used various methods including factitious accounting to inflate the price of water charged to consumers.

As a consequence, Grenoble water services were partially turned back to the public sector in 1996 and the water tariff dropped by 11%. The COGESE water company returned fully to the public in 2000.

In July 1997, a junior French minister Jean-Michel Boucheron was jailed for two years, with a further two suspended, and fined FRF one million for taking bribes from companies bidding in public tender. Boucheron reportedly had received fees of FRF 327 000 for a fictitious job by Générale des Eaux in exchange for giving the utility a water concession in Angoulême. He was also found guilty of taking bribes of FRF 500 000 in 1986-89 from various companies.[4]

---

[2] www.ifrap.org

[3] USD 0.75 to 2.2 per cubic meter

[4] www.foe.co.uk "Dirty Water"

Reactions to Bad Governance

These infamous cases triggered numerous reactions at the citizens' level, which caused raising public concern about public service delegation to the private sector. Not only were the cases judged in a court of law, but they also initiated a number of laws that were passed with a view to fight and limit bad governance practices and outcomes.

Box 2: Examples of people's reaction to prevent bad governance

- Law N 92-3 (January 3, 1992) – aka "Water Law" – shifts accounting responsibilities to the municipal level and introduce accounting measures aimed at controlling the fair cost-recovery of water services at the municipal level;
- Law N 92-1282 changes the procedures, in particular the bidding process, to award water concession and water contracts;
- Law N 93-122 (January 29, 1993) – aka "Sapin Law" is passed to prevent corruption and bring more transparency in the public bidding process. The law makes it compulsory to adopt competitive bidding for public service delegation contracts and imposes a strict regulatory framework for the content of these contracts: the concessionaire has to prepare an annual report including the accounts of the of such contracts to 20 years;
- November, 18, 1994: National Water Day when the National Water Price Observatory is created by the Minister of Environment, Michel Barnier;
- Law N 95-101 (February 2, 1995) – aka "Barnier Law" makes annual report including a price analysis compulsory in the water sector (for both municipal and private operators), forbids entry rights (cf. Toulouse), sets stricter limits on the duration of the contracts, and introduces the possibility to sue companies and municipalities which are not compliant with these requirements;
- December 19, 1996: publication of the DGCCRF[5] report in the evolution of the price of water in France from 1991 to 1996;
- January 27, 1997: publication of the Cour des Comptes (National Audit Department) on "The management of water and wastewater services by municipalities" criticizing local governance;
- August 7, 1998: The administrative court of Grenoble cancels the city concession renegotiation with Lyonnaise des Eaux because of its non compliancy with the competition regulations applicable to public services;
- December 22, 1999: the High Council of Public Sector recommends the creation of a water and urban services regulation authority to control the transparency of the water market;
- July, 17, 2002: The Conseil de la Concurrence (Competition Board) publishes a report on the water market in France, focusing on the level of competition prevailing in the sector;
- 2002 – 2004: several major water concessions terminate and are re- bided. The water tariff have significantly decreased in several large municipalities in France.

[5] Direction Générale de la Concurrence, de la Consommation et de la Répression des Fraudes (General Council for Competition, Consumption and Fight against Fraud)

OTHER ILLUSTRATIONS OF BAD GOVERNANCE AT THE LOCAL LEVEL

Other examples include the case of transportation services in suburban Montreal during the 1800's, as described by Boone (1996). As a result of a contest between competing street car firms to serve the city of Montreal, and the existing poor governance of the city, with serious divisions within the municipal council, citizen pressure did have an impact on one particular mayor. The mayor of Mile End Village tore up half a mile of the Montreal Street Railway Company's track in protest of the behavior of the companies. The majority of citizens, despite having clamored for street car service, applauded his heroics.

These historical illustrations provide impetus for the study of the dynamics of choices between citizens, mayors, and firms. We use them to see what type of equilibrium can emerge. In particular, can a "bad governance (corrupt mayor) good company (delivering services)" equilibrium exist and if yes is it unstable? Can we see a shift to good governance and well performing companies as a result of a small perturbation (such as more political awareness from voters)? What are the chances that a citizen response using "voice" will emerge? Are solutions like the Bangalore Agenda Task Force[6], where civil society interacts with the state to improve governance emergent? Can we explain the empirical finding for U.S. municipalities by Warner and Hefetz (2003) indicating that municipalities relying more on private companies to deliver services also rank lower on voice and equity measures?

In this paper, we have developed a game-theoretic model to uncover the dynamics between citizens, mayors, and firms in a globalized context. Our main reason for focusing on a globalized context is the rather seamy side to globalization, which co-exists with the benefits of globalization. The intensification of the exchanges and increased exposure and demands of citizens for good governance also comes along with more sophisticated and "hidden" ways for bad governance. Typically: examples of financial crime and money laundering on the international scale make it more and more complex to dismantle money embezzlement and corruption in countries that are already exposed to bad governance and lack of transparency. In other words, globalization could be an "amplificatory" factor to good or bad governance, i.e. cities / regions with good governance tend to become even more efficient, and on the other hand cities that are suffering from bad governance where it is difficult for the citizens to "exit" (most African cities or old industrial centers in Europe and Central Asia) are getting into even worse situations.

5. CONCLUSIONS AND FURTHER RESEARCH

In this paper, we have attempted to show using a game-theoretic framework, that the dynamics of interaction between citizens, mayors, and firms, within a context of globalization, leads to superior performance of cities. This framework attempts to derive the nature of causality from globalization to good governance and from local accountability to

[6] The Bangalore Agenda Task Force is a Bangalore-based citizens monitoring initiative that generates report cards on public services using systematic city-wide feedback from citizens. See Paul, S., Holding the State to Account, Books for Change, Bangalore, 2002.

good governance. In fact, our analysis shows that both count, but that the interaction between globalization and good governance should lead to superior performance than local accountability by itself,or globalization in the absence of local accountability. We have shown that, when firms try to influence city leaders and go unchecked, it leads to bad outcomes in terms of city performance.

What firms and citizens know, in terms of what is publicly available, also matters in terms of improving the possibility of good governance and hence of a better quality of life. There are other barriers to good governance, which are removed when one has better access to information about the city. Better information leads to increased means to control public accountability. We have not in this paper looked at other forms of information access such as the media's role as a watchdog which are well studied by others. What comes out of our work is that Cities can do a lot using technology to improve the access to information.

Our results also indicate that history matters, and that a methodology that allows the dynamics over time to be captured, can shed light on some of the difficult issues surrounding urban governance. Such analysis would be relevant to understand the high urbanization rates in Africa which have come with little contribution to increased welfare of urban cities, with limited economic growth for their countries, low levels of foreign direct investment, and with well known challenges in the area of governance. Such a model could shed light on this difficult topic, when used specifically for African cities. We hope to do such research at a later stage.

REFERENCES

Benoit, J.P., and V. Krishna, "Finitely Repeated Games", *Econometrica* 53: 890-904.

Besson, Danielle « *L'investissement des administrations publiques locales – Influence de la décentralisation et du cycle des élections municipales* » INSEE Première, October 2002

Chandernagor, André « *Les maires en France – XIXème-Xxème siècles* », Fayard 1993

Cour des Comptes « *La gestion des services publics locaux d'eau et d'assainissement* », January 1997

De Long, B.J., and A. Shleifer, "*Princes and Merchants: European City Growth before the Industrial Revolution*", NBER and Harvard University, March 1992; revised December 1992.

Durkheim, Emile « Les communes françaises du Moyen-Age » *L'Année sociologique nr.* 6, 1903

Duval, Guillaume, « Etat des lieux », *Alternatives Economiques*, April 1996

Estache and Kouassi, "Sector organization, governance, and the inefficiency of African water utilities", *Policy Research Working Paper*, The World Bank, 2002

Francillon, Claude "Grenoble conclut un nouveau contrat d'eau avec la Lyonnaise", *Le Monde*, March 24, 1996

Fudenberg, D., and J. Tirole, *Game Theory*, MIT Press, 1991.

Georges, Jocelyne, « *Histoire des maires 1789-1939* », Editions Christian de Bartillat, 1990

Gibbons, R., *Game Theory for Applied Economists*, Princeton University Press, 1992.

Henderson, V.J., and Venables, A.J., "The Dynamics of City Formation: Finance and Governance", Centre for Economic Policy Research, *Discussion Paper No.* 4638, www.cepr.org. 2004. ISSN 0265-8003.

Hirschmann, A. O., *Exit, Voice, and Loyalty: Responses to the Decline in Firms, Organizations, and States*, January, 1970.

Inciyan Erich, "La Générale des eaux reconnaît des financements politiques illégaux", *Le Monde*, October 26, 1996

Kaufmann, D., Léautier, F., and Mastruzzi, M., "*Governance and the City: An Empirical Exploration into Global Determinants of Urban Performance*", 2004

Léautier, F. and Lemer, A. "Perspectives on Globalization of Infrastructure", *WBI Working Papers*, 2003

Le Wino, Frédéric, "Le scandale du prix de l'eau*", Le Point*, April, 30, 1994

Paul, André « *Les Manuscrits de la Mer Morte* », p.114-116, Bayard Editions / Centurion, 2000

Paul, S., *Holding the State to Account, Books for Change*, Bangalore, 2002.

Pujas, Véronique "Working paper : Corruption via party financing in France" (*workshop on corruption and political party funding* in La Pietra – Italy), October 2000

Taylor, P.J., and D.R.F., Walker. "World City Network: Data Matrix Construction and Analysis." From the GaWC Research Group and Network, Data Set 6. Online at *http://www.lboro.ac.uk/gawc/*. Based on primary data collected by J.V. Beaverstock, R.G., Smith and P.J. Taylor (*ESRC project "The Geographical Scope of London as a World City"*).

Warner, M. and A. Hefetz, "Contracting: Theoretical Propositions, Empirical Realities", *Presented to the Economic Policy Institute*, Washington DC, April 4, 2003.

ANNEX 1

Theorem: Fudenberg and Tirole (1991). The terminal state of such a game, where citizens, mayors, and firms choose from the set of actions shown above is Nash Equilibrium.

Proof: Fix a Nash Equilibrium at α^*, which is a building block of a repeated game where the citizen, mayor, and firm are playing over a fixed time period T (mayoral electoral cycle over 5 years). All three players must play (loyal, satisfy, locate) at this stage since doing so increases their period-T payoff and since there are no future periods in which they will be punished, by earning less than their reservation utility. This is true for any period history h^T that has positive probability under α^*.

The static equilibrium for each player is $\alpha^*(i)$ with the terminal reward phase being $g_i(\alpha^*(i)) > v_{-i}$. At this stage, each player receives strictly more than their reservation utility (min-max value) v_{-i}.

For a repeated cycle R (with R large enough) each player prefers payoff v_i followed by the R-cycle terminal phase of (loyal, satisfy, locate), to getting the largest possible payoff

$\max_a g_i(a)$ in one period and then being min-maxed for R.I periods (Fudenberg and Tirole, 1991).

Select a small ε such that $v+\varepsilon;\varepsilon>0$ and $\{a(t)\}$ is a deterministic cycle of length $T-R.I$ whose average payoffs are within ε of payoff v. Each player plays according to the deterministic cycle (loyal, satisfy, locate). If any player deviates from this path when there are more than R.I periods left, then min-max that player for the remainder of the game. If player agrees with $\{a(t)\}$ until there are R.I periods left, then follow the R-cycle terminal phase for the remainder of the game.

ANNEX 2

There are 36,565 municipalities in France, among which 31,927 villages of less than 2,000 inhabitants. These villages represent about 25% of the population (around 15 million inhabitants).

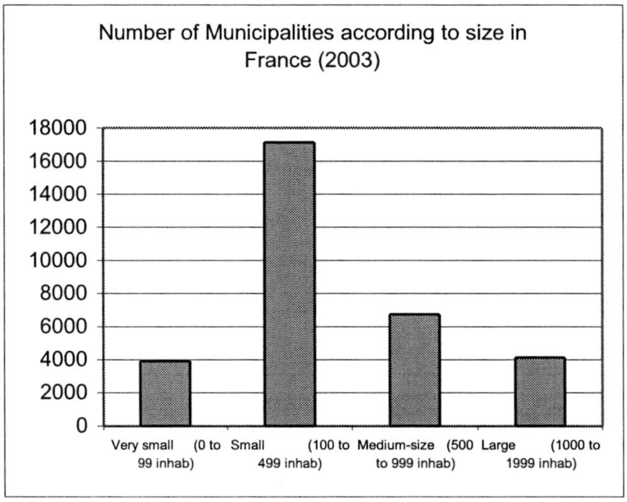

In: Perspectives on International, State and Local Economics ISBN 1-60021-099-6
Editor: Gerald V. Liu, pp. 85-114

Chapter 3

SPATIAL DISPARITIES IN CENTRAL GOVERNMENTAL GRANTS TO LOCAL GOVERNMENTS*

Janno Reiljan, Kairi Andresson,and Kadri Ukrainski
FEBA, University of Tartu
Tartu, Estonia

ABSTRACT

There are several concerns about Estonian regional development because the economic activities have been concentrated into the capital city and the surrounding region, and the municipalities in the borderlands are facing high unemployment rates. Attempts have been made to balance these developments by equalizing the per capita income of local governments across the country. The aim of this article is to analyse the spatial distribution of central governmental grants to local governments in Estonia and to control whether the gravity model is successful in describing these financial flows. Three hypothesis were tested:

1) There is a positive correlation of the distance from local governments' centre to the capital city Tallinn (and other larger towns) with the per capita unconditional grant flows to local governments;
2) This positive correlation of distance decreases by adding conditional grants;
3) There is a negative correlattion of distance with per capita conditional grant flows to local governments because of higher lobbying costs.

The distribution of income tax as the main revenue source seems to have a geographical pattern. This can be observed graphically and proven by correlation analysis. The central government policy for equalization of local governments' per capita revenues through State Equalization Fund can be seen as successful; the first hypothesis can be accepted. From other side, the distribution of conditional grants is decreasing the equalizing effect of unconditional transfers. The gravity model supports the presence of geographical pattern in grants from central to local governments. However, the negative correlation of conditional grants with distance was not found.

INTRODUCTION

Several articles have been analyzing the financing system of Estonian local governments[1] (see e.g. Ulst, 2000; Lauritsen, 2000; Reiljan et al., 2003; and others). In those articles, it is generally found that in Estonia the financial situation of the local governments has been destabilised over the last few years and has in many cases even deteriorated. On one hand, the number of functions assigned to local governments has grown, on the other, local governments lack a stable legally determined income base, which would enable them to make long-term plans for local development and effectively manage diverse local issues (Reiljan et al., 2003).

As argued by Lauritsen (2000), the functions legally assigned to local governments are fully (renovating local roads, requirements on school canteens, implementing the Law on unemployment insurance) or partly (teachers' salaries, allowances, social benefits) without the financial coverage. According to Ulst (2000), Estonian fiscal system is more centralized than those of other countries, including the Baltics. In the situation, where the total grants to local governments in average accounted for one third of their total income in 2002 and earlier, many problems arise. Firstly, one can consider insufficient economic and political autonomy, and high dependency of local governments from the central government. Secondly, the flows and targets of the support grants can be unpredictable. Thirdly, the high share of grants and the eligibility conditions for grants can lead to the lack of motivation of local governments to search for alternative income sources. Fourthly, the local government officials can become indifferent towards managing or not managing the local matters.

The issue of financing Estonian local governments remains very topical because the administrative system reform in this field is not completed and there are several unsolved problems concerning the design of the reform. One very difficult task comprises the possibility at the same time to balance finances of local governments and maintain the proper incentives for local governments to raise their own revenues.

Raus and Trasberg (2003) have shown that there is a certain relationship between the income tax revenues (part of which is the largest own revenue source for local governments) and the location of the local government in Estonia. The highest per capita revenues from income tax have been concentrated in Tallinn (the capital city) and its surroundings. The lowest revenues are spread to the borderland, mainly to northeastern and southern parts of Estonia.

The aim of this article is to analyse the spatial distribution of central governmental grants to local governments and to control whether the gravity model is successful in describing these financial flows in Estonia. To achieve this aim the following steps are undertaken. At first, general description of the system of financial relations of central and local governmental levels is given containing the discussion concerning the distribution of the functions between central and local governments and the centralization of Estonian municipalities' fiscal capacity. After that, analysis of the conditional and unconditional grants used by central government is performed. Thereafter, the chapter is assessing the geographical pattern in income of Estonian municipalities and addressing the question, whether the current grant system has influenced the geographical disparities in income of municipalities.

---

[1] Throughout the article, municipalities and local governments are used as synonyms for Estonian local governments.

There are three hypotheses tested. First, whether there is a positive correlation of the distance from local governments' centre to capital city Tallinn (and other larger towns) with the per capita unconditional grant flows to local governments; second, whether this positive correlation of distance is decreasied by adding conditional grants; and third, whether there is a negative correlattion of distance with per capita conditional grant flows to local governments because of higher lobbying costs. The hypotheses are formally tested by using the gravity model approach of respective financial flows.

In this article, the data set comprising the budgets of Estonian local governments in detail from the period of 1996-2002 is used (Database of..., 1996-2002). The data set contains 247 cross section units including 43 towns and 204 rural municipalities. In this article, only the data for 2002 are included into the correlation and gravity analysis. The comparative statistical analysis is done in Euros. In addition, the Regional Database of Statistical Office of Estonia is used to include more general indicators for analysis.

Public Revenues, Expenditures and Economic Geography

The main reason for supporting decentralization in the administration of revenues is the comprehension that local governments compared to central governments are managing more effectively local matters. This is an explanation offered by theory of fiscal federalism (Oates, 1999). Decentralization of tasks must be accompanied by an increase in the local governments' autonomy in such areas as local tax revenues and other receipts, budget execution and debt management (de Mello, 2000). The main advantages for decentralising the revenues are listed in table 1.

Local governments in comparison with central government:

1) have higher interest in influencing the structure of local economic activities (e.g. land tax, local taxes);
2) can be more effective in raising some types of revenues (e.g. own revenues of local public institutions as fees and revenues from additional services);
3) have better knowledge about local fiscal needs and fiscal capacities and therefore are more effective in managing debt and income from assets.

The first two points can in addition be associated with higher efficiency in enforcing revenue regulations by officials in close proximity and greater willingness of taxpayers and users of public sector services to pay to local governments. The idea is based on the assumption that a lower-level government unit is likely to possess better information about citizens' preferences than the higher-level, larger government with many other concerns (Hamilton, Slutsky, 1997). Especially in larger countries (like US) local governments have greater legitimacy when deciding over investments and other expenditures for providing services. As a result, taxpayers can see the direct link between taxes and services (Silverman, 1992).

Table 1. Reasons of decentralization of some public receipts (authors' table)

Reasons Receipts	Primary Reasons	Secondary Reasons	Disadvantages
Land tax and local taxes	Influencing the structure of local economic activities	1) Higher efficiency in enforcing revenue regulations 2) Greater willingness of firms and households to pay to local governments	1) Competition to attract firms and human capital 2) Temptation to increase tax rates and fees
Own revenues of local public institutions	Effective in rising revenues		
Loans and income from assets	Better knowledge about local fiscal needs and fiscal capacities	Shorter recognition, decision and institutional lags	1) High debt burden 2) Dependence on financial cycles

The tax bases that would be easy and inexpensive for local governments to administer are few and they are usually very narrow (de Mello, 2000:366). Therefore, most of the taxation remains by central government and some of the collected revenues are transferred to local governments. Intergovernmental grants are policy instruments, which can be used for different purposes. According to Oates (1999:1126), mainly following functions are discussed in the literature: the internalization of spillover benefits to other jurisdictions, fiscal equalization across jurisdictions, and improved overall tax system. The intergovernmental grants can be conditional or unconditional. Conditional grants are mainly fulfilling the first function: they act like Pigouvian subsidies for ensuring that the spillover benefits to other municipalities are taken into account by decisions of local policy-makers (Oates, 1999:1127). The unconditional grants are mainly used for equalizing the revenues of the local governments in order to ensure that all municipalities would have the same level of public services with the same tax effort (Borck, Owings 2003:140). This is done usually by transfers based on a formula, which takes into account the „fiscal need" and „fiscal capacity" of the municipalities. These formulae should ensure disproportionate transfers to municipalities with high fiscal needs and low fiscal capacity (Oates, 1999: 1127). It is not clear, however, whether these equalizing grants are indeed welfare improving. Some authors argue that this enables poorer regions to compete with richer ones (who could in absence of such transfers enjoy economic growth at the expense of poorer ones). Other authors argue that these grants are holding back the development of poorer regions by impeding the interregional flow of resources (both, migration and immigration) in response to cost differentials. (Oates, 1999:1127–1128) The question addressed is, whether there are some possibilities to influence the location of firms by public spending and to avoid the regionalization of an economy.

In the literature, some interesting approaches can be found, where the old theories of location are elaborated to solve this question. In Krugman's original core-periphery model, the stable equilibrium is achieved in conditions of complete specialization, that is the manufacturing will concentrate and the core and periphery regions will emerge (Krugman, 1991). Trionfetti (1997) modifies the core-periphery model of Krugman by adding public expenditure to the model[2]. He finds that the location of the industry depends on the nature and level of public expenditure. Public expenditure in this model creates a new and independent source of geographical dimension, through a backward linkage that is overriding the

[2] Even Trionfetti uses Krugman's model to explain the international location of industries there is no reason, why the model cannot be used to describe the location of national industries. The analysis of Trionfetti is brought in the style, which is more suitable for intra-country analysis.

agglomeration forces. The analysis of the model shows, that the existence of public expenditure even in small amounts, results in stable equilibrium in conditions of incomplete specialization regardless of existence of transportation costs (Trionfetti 1997:115). To influence the allocation of production, public expenditure is an effective instrument in this model: It is sufficient to act on the allocation of public expenditure rather than on the level[3]. Trionfetti also analyses the role of specific intergovernmental grants in his model. Governments have three possibilities for grants: unconditional grants (pure transfers), conditional grants (tied aid) and joint expenditures[4]. In each case there can arise many possibilities of shifting the production in favour of one or another region[5]. Trionfetti (1997:115) concludes that transfer policies do not influence the location *per se*. The results show that in order to have an impact on location, the transfer policies should imply a change in the overall allocation of public expenditure.

There are no unique empirical results to justify the theoretical discussions above. Many of them find that politics has significant effect on the distribution of grants. Generally, it is found that although central governments are transferring funds to local governments, it appears the reasons are other as mentioned in the theoretical discussion earlier (see the review of the empirical literature in Borck and Owings, 2003:140–141). As noted by Oates (1999), many programs seem to be linked with spillovers, but the size of these programs seems not to be justified on efficiency grounds. The other rationales found in literature for grant distribution are for example, the design of the decision procedures and the political influence of representatives of recipient municipalities. Borck and Owings (2003) are discussing the lobbying procedure by adding the dimension of geographical distance from state government. To receive these grants, local government officials have to contact and lobby the state officials/politicians. Since transport and time costs increase (and similarly lobbying costs) with distance, the grants obtained should fall with distance. Their empirical results confirm this hypothesis.

From the discussion above, we can conclude, that although intergovernmental grants are designed for improving economic welfare, empirical results are showing that the practical implementation of these transfers has other reasons and outcomes. The spatial aspect of intergovernmental transfers is expressed by the desirability of intergovernmental grants in order to balance the regional development in peripheral regions, but considering the politics

---

[3] For example, let's take a situation, where regions are interested in increase of production of good A and are indifferent about the production of good B. If both governments will act exactly in the same way in allocating their expenditures, nothing would happen. Now, the government of the region 1 changes its behavior and increases the share of its expenditure on domestic good A. As the result region 1 will get a larger share of good's A production.

[4] It must be mentioned that there is no significant difference, whether centrally directed grants or grants between local governments are considered. The grants from central government can be interpreted as redistribution of local governments' revenues and as the bondage to give grants to less developed regions.

[5] Here some examples of Trionfetti's model (1997) are discussed. If the governments of two regions tend to prefer to consume locally produced good A then unconditional grants from region 2 to region 1 (or from central government to region 1) lead to an increase in number of firms producing A in region 1. If the governments prefer to consume imported good A then there will be a decrease in number of firms producing good A in region 1. In the case of conditional grants from region 2 to region 1 it is possible that local government can still act in the way that will lead to increase in number of firms producing a good A in region 1. For instance is this true in the situation where government 2 spends a large portion of its tax revenues on locally produced good A, and government 1 uses the received grants to purchase good B from region 2.

the distribution of grants could result in lower level for periphery regions because of higher lobbying costs.

FUNCTIONS OF CENTRAL AND LOCAL GOVERNMENTS IN ESTONIA

There are three main functions of fiscal policy, which are mostly discussed in the literature, (e.g. see Bird, 1999; Cangiano and Mottu, 1998) – allocation, distribution and stabilization. According to the theory of fiscal federalism the distribution and stabilization functions are seen as the functions of central government (Oates, 1999:1121). The decentralization or centralization of allocation function depends on the government's priorities: differences in the preferences of the inhabitants (or firms) or presence of large economies of scope in provision of public services.

However, one must not forget that these three functions mentioned above are seen as the main fiscal functions of the central and local governments in a stable and closed economy. In reality these functions are often inferior to other aims of central government. In the case of Estonia the central government main goals during most of the transition period were democratization, introducing the market economy and achieving the external stability (see as well Figure 1).

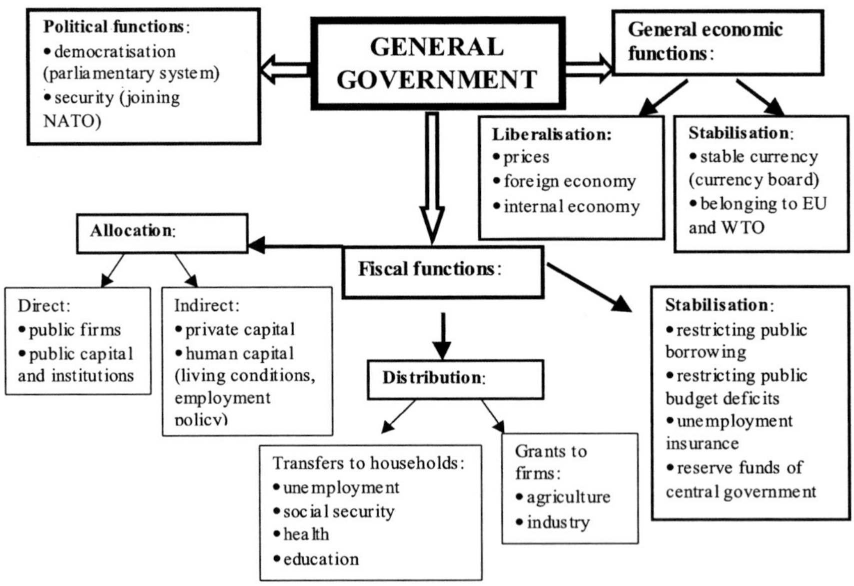

Figure 1. Functions of Estonian general government (authors' figure)

The fiscal functions of central and local governments were underlying to main political stream of *laissez faire* policy. However, from the fiscal functions, brought on Figure 1, we can say that the most important fiscal functions in Estonia are the allocation function (spending/investments into infrastructure, education) and distribution function (especially transfers to households). The importance of these functions has increased in last years. When one decomposes the structure of general government expenditures, one can see that in 2002, approximately 40% of total expenditures can be associated with the subsidies and other current grants (see Estonian Statistical Office, 2002). One good example of government's orientation on passive redistribution is the labour market policy. Especially in last years the unemployment benefits accounted for more than 60% of total expenditures on labour market policies (see Paas et al., 2002). As will be discussed later in this chapter, different grants and transfers play an important role in the income of the Estonian local governments as well.

In Estonia, local governments' areas of responsibility are determined by the Local Governments Organization Act (1999). According to Reiljan et al., (2003) the division of responsibilities in the public sector in 2001 compared to the 1993 has shifted slightly towards increased responsibilities of local governments. In 2001, some additional responsibilities were shifted to local governments: salaries of teachers in primary and secondary schools, school transport, salary of a municipal doctor, responsibility for emergency services[6]. However, the functions of local governments are legally not very explicitly determined. According to a survey conducted by the Ministry of Internal Affairs, local governments' responsibilities were already in the mid 90ies regulated by almost 450 different laws and legal acts that had assigned to them over 400 different tasks (Moll, 1997).

The functions described on the figure 2 are not performed in all local governments. The responsibilities are depending on the presence of appropriate educational, social or cultural institutions within the local government. From one aspect, such a division of functions doesn't encourage local governments to broaden the scope of their public services, but provides a way to live at the expense of neighbouring local governments. Local governments could settle the accounts among themselves, but as widely discussed in Estonian media, they are reluctant to pay for tuition for the children studying in other local governments (the problem is more important for larger towns like Tallinn and Tartu). One reason for this reluctance is certainly the gap between the fiscal need and the fiscal capacity. This problem will be elaborated later on. Described problems lead to the issue of appropriate assignment of tasks and finances in multilevel governments, especially with the respect to the design and effects of horizontal and vertical grants.

Structure of Income and Expenditures of Local Governments in Estonia

In the structure of revenues of Estonian local governments, in 2002 the state allocations played an important role. The transfers in general amounted for a third of the revenues; another third was received from the personal income tax.

In 2002 the Equalization Fund (unconditional grants) accounted for 37% of all transfers to local governments budgets (e.g. in 2001 this was 27%). However, those local governments who are not entitled to get state support should cover these expenditures from their own revenues. The largest part of income transfers (around 40%) consists of targeted (conditional) grants on education, as teachers' salaries are being paid out of the local budget since 2001 (Ministry of Internal Affairs, 2002).

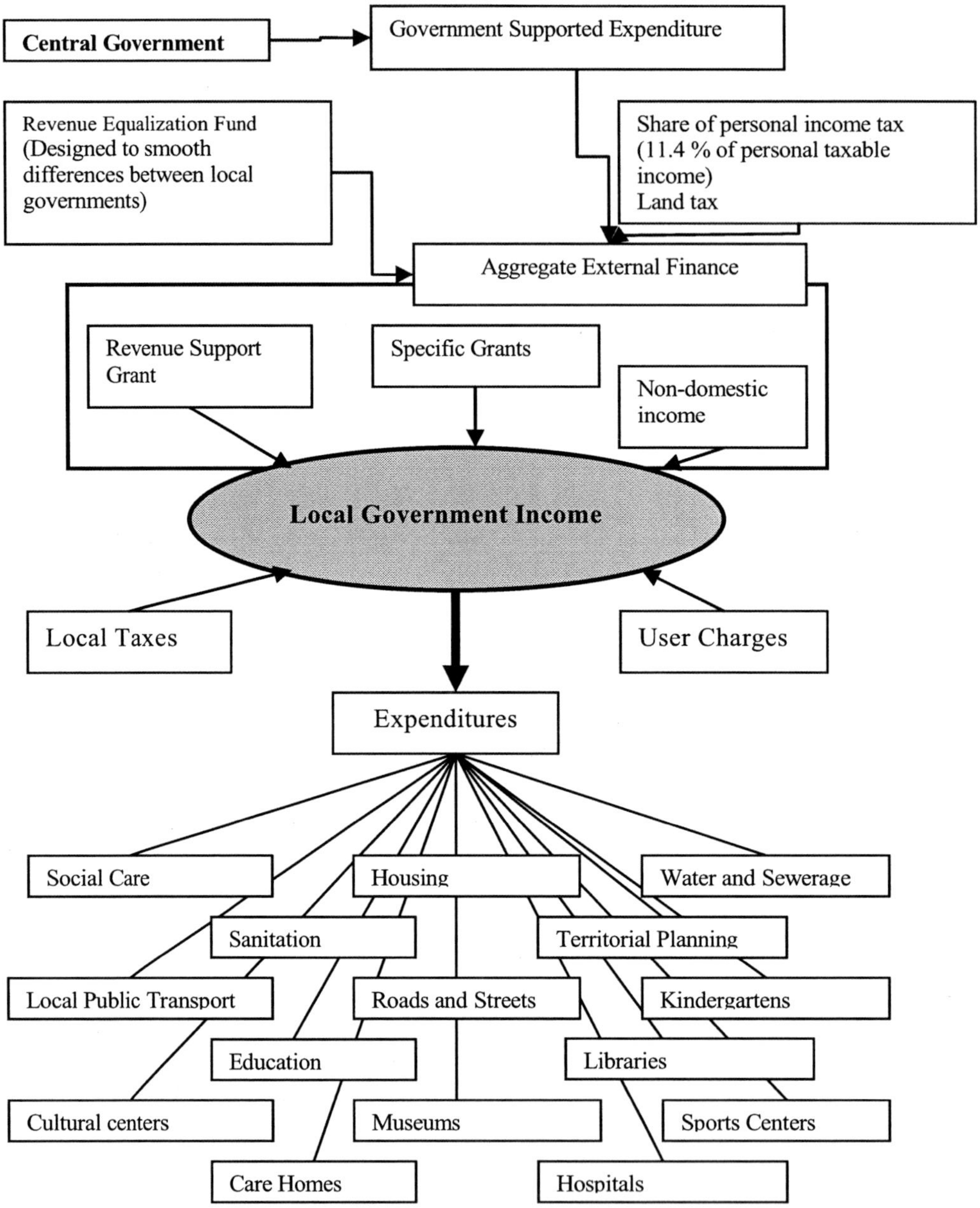

Figure 2. The system of financing local government functions (authors' elaboration of Pacione 2001)

The income bases of towns and rural municipalities have been built up by the central government in the way that in more than 90% of the municipalities, unconditional support from the State Equalization Fund plays considerable role. This could be seen as a financial instrument for safeguarding the administrative authority of the centre.

[6] The main functions of Estonian local governments for today consist of the activities in the fields of social care, housing, water and sewerage, sanitation, territorial planning, local public transport, roads and streets, kindergartens, education, libraries, cultural centers, museums, sport centers, care homes, hospitals.

In Estonia the tax income accounted for 38.4% and state budget allocations for 32.8% of the revenues in 2002 (Database of... 1996-2002). At the same time, here has to be noted, that the size of allocations depends on the level of a particular local government's own revenues – the higher the own per capita revenues of local governments, the fewer per capita allocations it will receive. This impedes the initiative of local governments to increase their revenues from other sources and improve the tax base. The number of local governments with high own revenues that do not depend on the central government's Equalization Fund is less than 10% of all local governments.

The sources of tax revenues can be generally divided into two parts:

1) state taxes (imposed by law, paid either in full amount or partly into the local budgets).
2) local taxes (imposed by the local councils).

From state taxes, 56% of the revenues from personal income tax[7] and 100% of land tax receipts are paid into local budgets. The municipal council has the right to set the land tax within the prescribed margin, which in 2002 was 0.8-2.0% of the assessed value of land. There are additionally fees that have to be paid on the use of natural resources and on special use of water to the budget of local governments. The share of such receipts is generally small, but very important for some local governments (who's per capita revenues are raised significantly by these payments – those local governments are mainly in the region of northeastern Estonia and receive fee for oil shale exploitation). The Local Taxes Act (1994) allows local councils to impose several local taxes: head tax, sales tax, boat tax, advertising tax, motor vehicle tax, animal tax, entertainment tax, and road and street closure tax. During the period of 1996–2002, only head tax was not used by any of the local governments of the country; in 2002 only two municipalities had income from boat tax, other two from the motor vehicle tax and seven from sales tax. The most popular taxes were advertising tax and street closure tax (Database of..., 1996-2002).

The main source of revenue for Estonian local governments is personal income tax, which in 2002 provided 34.5 % of the total revenues of local governments (see Figure 3). Land tax accounted for 3.3 % and other local taxes only for 0.6 % of the revenues. There are several factors explaining the low level of local taxes. The administration of local taxes is problematic and expensive, while tax evasions are difficult to control. Additionally, relatively low income base, tax competition, and some other reasons discourage the local governments using widely other taxes to increase their income. The initiative of local governments to collect local taxes is considerably obstructed by current financing scheme (increased own revenues will immediately reduce the amount of unconditional allocations paid from the Equalization Fund). This issue remains the biggest problem of reforming the financing system of Estonian local governments – how to smooth the revenues at the same time increasing the incentives of local governments to improve their performance. Here, one must not ignore the fact that the income levels of the population are extremely different across municipalities of Estonia and therefore the implementation of additional taxes can be politically risky.

---

[7] Since 2004 there is a change in the scheme – local governments are receiving 11.4% from the taxable personal income and central government 24.6%. Currently proposed personal income tax abatement (from 26% to 20%) in 2007 would occur on account of central government revenue part.

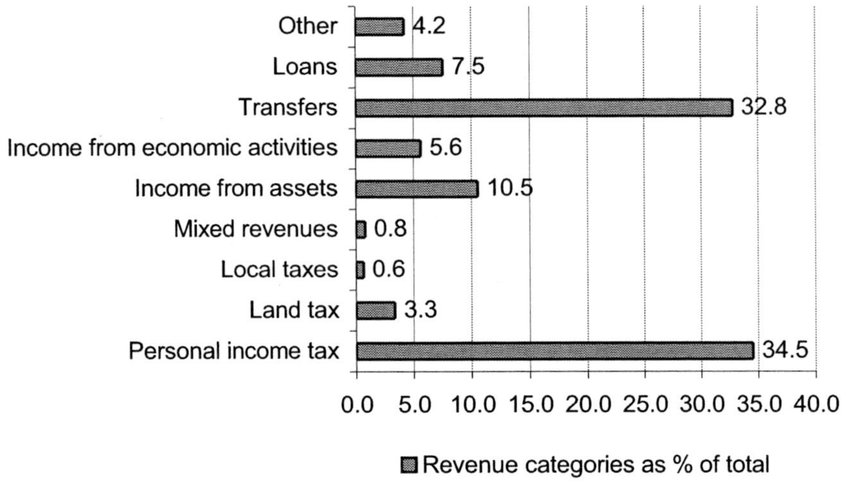

Figure 3. The Structure of Revenues of Local Governments in 2002 (Database of… 1996-2002; calculations by authors).

In addition to the aforementioned, also investment support to local governments (6.7% of revenue transfers in 2002) through the national investment programme and allocations by the ministries (altogether around 13% of transfers in 2002) belong to revenue transfers. Besides that there are allocations from local governments unions and sponsors, receipts from other municipalities for services provided to them, receipts from international organizations and from other funds and foundations, which all comprise relatively small amount of revenue transfers (Database of…, 1996-2002). Evidently, the investments and also current revenues of local governments are determined by central governments (the financing system in this aspect is centralized in Estonia and the grants received depend from the lobby work of local government officials).

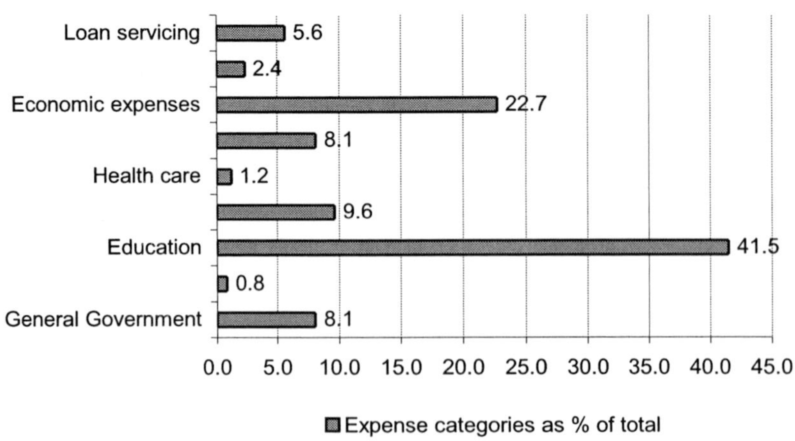

Figure 4. The structure of local governments expenditure in 2002 (Database of… 1996-2002; calculations by authors).

The structure of the expenditures of local governments in Estonia is shown in Figure 4. In 2002, no doubt the largest item of expenditure for Estonian local governments was education. The next important category of expenditure was economic expenses (infrastructure, sanitation, planning and constructing activities, and so forth). The expenses of general administration, culture and sport and social welfare were equally around 10%, the share of health care was only slightly above 1% of the overall expenditures. Among other costs the largest were loan-servicing costs (5.6% of total expenditure), from which most was used for repayment of loans and smaller amounts for interests payments (Database of... 1996-2002).

The level of local governments' income as the weighted average revenue per inhabitant in different groups of local governments is shown in table 2 (as the weight the number of inhabitants was used). In order to ensure better comparability, the 2001 and 2002 revenues are given without central government allocations for teachers' salaries, which from 2001 onwards are paid from the local budgets.

Table 2. Weighted average per capita revenues of local governments in 1996-2002 (EUR), adjusted to CPI

Type of municipality by number of inhabitants	Average per capita revenue						
	1996	1997	1998	1999	2000	2001	2002
Tallinn	265	237	268	289	268	418	466
Towns, >10,000	207	250	243	257	291	272	298
Towns, <10,000	234	273	287	300	323	348	388
Rural municipalities, >3000	190	224	249	270	253	270	313
Rural municipalities, 1500-3000	199	255	285	301	279	292	318
Rural municipalities, <1500	239	308	330	340	321	325	347
Estonian average	225	248	265	282	282	326	362
Real growth of per capita revenues (1996=100), %	100	110	117	125	125	145	161
Real growth of GDP, %	100	110	115	108	116	124	131

Source: Database of..., 1996-2002; own calculations

When grouping local government units, the types of the local government (town or rural local government) as well as the number of inhabitants were taken into account. As the revenues are given in constant prices of 1996, we can consider these figures as real income. We can see that the real income of the local governments in Estonia has been growing. The growth rate was highest in 2001 (15.2%) and lowest in 2000 (0.0%). Looking at the dynamics by different groups, we can see quite substantial differences. In Tallinn, the real income growth was very significant in 2001, the growth was driven by increase in income from assets (growth in share from total revenues from 10% to 31%, primarily because the increase in selling shares). This has also pushed up the average level of income from assets in Estonia. Even the revenues from assets in Tallinn decreased in 2002, the total income level increased due to sudden increase of revenues from economic activities (growth from 0.1% of total revenues to 8.1% of total revenues)

In general, the variance of real income between the groups is relatively high, which characterises the instability of the income base. In 2000, the real income in Tallinn and rural municipalities (even in the smallest ones) decreased, whereas the real income in towns (excl. Tallinn) grew considerably. In 2001, the situation was the opposite: in parallel with the decrease of real income in towns (excl. Tallinn), the real revenues in rural municipalities and in Tallinn increased. In 2002, the revenues of local municipalities grew in all groups. On average the real growth rates of local government *per capita* revenues in Estonia slowed down constantly until 2000 (from 10.4% in 1997 to 0.0% in 2000). However, in 2001 and 2002 the growth rates were again more than 10% (Database of... 1996-2002; own calculations).

Estonian local governments' revenue structure by main revenue sources during 1996 – 2002 is shown in table 3. The main income source, as also discussed earlier in this chapter, is personal income tax. The second largest income source has shifted form transfers from the State Equalization Fund to revenues from assets. We can observe that mostly the trend for revenues was upward, but the growth rates are unstable. The highest differences in growth rates can be seen in the case of loans and revenues from assets.

Table 3. Weighted average revenue per capita of local governments by revenue sources in 1996-2002 (EUR), adjusted to the CPI

Revenue sources	Average weighted revenue per capita						
	1996	1997	1998	1999	2000	2001	2002
Personal income tax	108	120	132	137	132	135	145
Revenues from assets	8	15	15	16	28	55	44
Transfers from the State Equalization Fund	33	30	28	29	31	32	38
Loans	36	20	21	24	22	25	32
Income from economic activities	6	9	10	10	11	11	23
Land tax	9	11	11	12	13	14	14

Source: Database of..., 1996-2002; own calculations

It appears that the larger the local government is, the higher its level of average income from personal income tax and *vice versa* – the smaller the local government, the higher the amount of transfers per inhabitant from the State Equalization Fund. This tendency can be identified by looking at the correlation matrix (see table 4). We can see that there is positive correlation between number of inhabitants in local government and *per capita* receipts of income tax, and negative correlation of number of inhabitants and support flows (as both, for total support and for Equalization Fund flows). In addition, we can see the high negative correlation between income tax revenues and receipts from State Equalization Fund

In Tallinn the average revenues from personal income tax considerably exceeded those in other municipalities. Compared to the smallest rural municipalities, the average revenues from personal income tax *per capita* in Tallinn were almost two and a half times higher. At the same time, in 2001 the revenues from the income tax *per capita* in smaller towns and larger rural municipalities were higher than those of larger towns. Generally, in real terms, the receipts from personal income tax have been increasing constantly. The growth was negative only in Tallinn in 1999 and in all other groups except small towns in 2000. During the years 1997-1999 and in 2001-2002 the receipts from personal income tax grew in rural municipalities even faster than in towns.

Table 4. Correlation matrix for per capita revenues of local governments in year 2002

	All support (per capita)	Income tax (per capita)	Equalization Fund (per capita)	Number of inhabitants
All support (per capita)	1.000			
Income tax (per capita)	-0.195***	1.000		
Equalization Fund (per capita)	0.322***	-0.771	1.000	
Number of inhabitants	-0.117*	0.193***	-0.193***	1.000

***p<0.01, **p<0.05, *p<0.1

Source: Database of... 1996-2002; own calculations

For the smallest municipalities, the allotments from the State Equalization Fund are as big as their revenues from personal income tax. In other types of local governments, they are not so important revenue sources. Tallinn received no support from the State Equalization Fund until 2002[8]. In 1997-1998 the growth of the allotments from the State Equalization Fund was negative in real terms, while towns experienced a particularly substantial decrease. In 2000 a notable increase in transfers took place in real terms, which was again significant in towns (excl. Tallinn). In rural municipalities the growth was more modest. Due to these changes, in 2000 the real revenues from the Equalization Fund were almost at the same level as in 1996. However, as Reiljan et al. (2003) point out, during these years several new functions were assigned to local governments. In 2001 the allotments from the Equalization Fund to rural municipalities decreased to a certain degree, while the transfers to towns, on the contrary, increased. The growth was most remarkable in larger towns. In 2002, the state support increased in all groups and again the larger towns gained at most.

The income from assets increased during 2000 and 2001, and decreased in 2002. In 2000, the growth was particularly high in larger towns (178.5%), but it was also considerable in smaller towns (60%). Only in larger rural municipalities the growth rate was negative (-5.7%). In 2001, the growth was highest in Tallinn, as it was mentioned earlier, but rural municipalities too experienced quite a considerable growth of income from assets. The growth rates were negative only in larger towns (-55.1%), that experienced a significant growth in 2000. In 2002 the growth was on average negative in all groups, except the smallest rural municipalities (Database of... 1996-2002; own calculations).

The level of Estonian local governments' expenditures by main expenditure categories during the years 1996–2002 is given in Table 5. In order to ensure better comparability the 2001 and 2002 expenses are given again without central government allocations for teachers' salaries. As shown earlier in this chapter, the main expenditure category of local governments has been expenditure on education (over the whole period). It is followed by expenses on economic affairs and general administration expenditures. As in the case of revenues the changes in expenditures are quite stochastic. Only expenditures on defense and public order have been constantly decreasing, except in 2001 and 2002 when emergency services became to an area of responsibility of local governments. In this paper we will shortly analyse only the dynamics of four biggest types of cost: expenditures on education, economic affairs, social security, general administration, and culture and art.

---

[8] However, all the resources received in 2002 from State Equalization Fund were meant for paying subsistence allowances

Table 5. Local governments' per capita expenditures in 1996-2002 (EUR), adjusted to the CPI

Expenditure areas	Weighted average expenditures per inhabitant						
	1996	1997	1998	1999	2000	2001	2002
Education and science	85	88	97	103	97	102	115
Economic affairs	56	52	54	64	60	74	91
Social security and welfare	9	23	23	24	24	31	33
General administration	26	26	27	28	28	30	32
Culture and art	14	16	20	21	20	22	26
Recreation and sport	4	4	5	7	9	12	13
Health	4	3	4	4	4	5	5
Defense and public order	1	1	1	1	1	3	3

Source: Database of... 1996-2002; own calculations

In average, expenditures on education have been growing (except year 2000). However, the trends in different size-groups of municipalities are different. In all groups years with growth trend alternate with the declining trend. There are some variations in *per capita* expenditures on education between different groups (in 2002, 101 EUR in larger towns and 143 EUR in smaller towns). Nonetheless, it can be observed that these expenditures tend to be on average higher in smaller municipalities (in smaller towns and smaller rural municipalities). As smaller local governments also have smaller schools in general, this shows the existence of certain fixed costs, which do not depend on the number of pupils in a particular school. As a result, the present state system of financing schools on the basis of the expenses per pupil puts smaller municipalities (especially those who have several schools) into worse conditions (Reiljan et al., 2003).

Expenditures on economic affairs have likewise varied, both in Estonian average figures as well as within different groups of municipalities. It can be observed that in general these expenditures have been higher in towns than in rural municipalities, although recently the differences have been somewhat decreasing. This is not surprising, considering that a large part of these expenditures is spent on public maintenance services such as keeping streets clean, electricity and car transportation and so forth (in Estonia on average about 50%). Tallinn is exceptional leader in this area (in 2002 the total expenditure accounted more than half of all-Estonian expenditures or in *per capita* real terms this spending was 176.3 EUR) (Database of..., 1996–2002; authors' calculations).

The expenditures on general administration have grown in real terms during all the years concerned, but the growth has been slower than the growth of total expenditures. However, in some years in some of the groups of municipalities the level of expenditures also decreased. Per capita expenditures on general administration are certainly higher in smaller municipalities and the differences are quite significant. In 2002 the expenditures in this area were lowest in larger towns (on average 23 EUR per inhabitant in real terms) and highest in the smallest rural municipalities (on the average 57 EUR per inhabitant). The difference is thus two and a half times. This refers to the possibility that the amalgamation of the smaller municipalities might save at least general administration costs (Reiljan et al., 2003).

It is somewhat surprising that since 1998, the general administration expenditures in Tallinn have been higher than in other larger towns; in 2002 the difference was quite substantial – respectively 32 EUR compared to 23 EUR per inhabitant in real terms. If we would look at the administration costs' share in Tallinn's total revenue, it is stable at 7% level (except 2000, when it was 9%). However, if we look at these costs' share in Tallinn's revenues from personal income tax, then there is clear tendency of increase (from 10% in 1997 to 16.5% in 2002).

Social welfare expenditures grew considerably in 1997, when local governments first started to pay subsistence allowances. However, as the funds for these allowances are allocated from the state budget, there was no actual increase in local governments' expenditures. Later on the social welfare expenditures have been relatively stable, and have risen again in 2001 and 2002). Throughout the period, social expenditures were highest in smaller rural municipalities. In 2002, the average per capita social welfare expenditures were 32.7 EUR. Until 2001 the lowest per capita social welfare expenditures were those of Tallinn (in 2000 only 16.7 EUR in real terms, which rose to 35 in 2002) (Database of..., 1996-2002; own calculations).

In 1997-1999 spending on culture and art grew (except in Tallinn and medium size rural municipalities in 1999). In 1998 the growth was particularly high, but in 2000 the expenditure decreased only to be followed by a new increase in 2001 and 2002. The level of expenditures on culture is highest in smaller rural municipalities (Database of... 1996-2000; own calculations).

It is interesting to observe (see Table 6), that there is positive correlation of *per capita* administration costs with *per capita* economic affairs, education and health care costs.

Table 6. Correlation matrix for per capita expenditures in 2002

	Inhabitants	Education and science	Economic affairs	Social security and welfare	Administration	Recreation and sport	Health
Inhabitants	1.000						
Education and science	-0.011	1.000					
Economic affairs	0.163***	0.093	1.000				
Social security and welfare	0.004	0.071	0.008	1.000			
Administration	-0.085	0.243***	0.535***	0.062	1.000		
Recreation and sport	0.095	0.044	0.07	-0.097	-0.106*	1.000	
Health	0.118*	0.028	0.217***	-0.079	0.159**	-0.053	1.000

***p<0.01, **p<0.05, *p<0.1

Source: Database of... 1996-2002; own calculations using

This could be a sign of general inefficiency of some municipalities. For example, from 15 municipalities with highest per capita administration expenditures and per capita expenditures on economic affairs are seven the same municipalities. However, many of them are islands or belonging to the problem-regions of Estonia. In first case the high expenditures on economic affairs could be a sign of pecularity of the islands (higher transportatioin costs, fixed administration costs of small municipalities, for example). In the second case this could be a sign of unfinished communal reform and high costs on communal services. Therefore, the inefficiency should be studied with more caution and case-by-case in the future.

SPATIAL DISTRIBUTION OF ECONOMIC ACTIVITY IN ESTONIA

As already shown in preceding parts of this chapter, the main income of local governments in Estonia is received from personal income tax. Raus and Trasberg (2003) already pointed out that there seems to be some geographical pattern in local governments' receipts from personal income tax in Estonia in 2001. If we look on the Figure 5, we can see that in 2002, these receipts are still somewhat higher in surroundings of bigger cities, especially around Estonian capital, Tallinn. In addition, there seems to be higher wealth in regions located next to bigger roads and in tourism regions. The lowest income is associated with Estonian regions in south and north-east. On the Figure 5 we can see that the per capita personal income tax receipts of local governments seem to have geographical pattern with core economic region around Tallinn and with periphery on the southern and eastern borderlands.

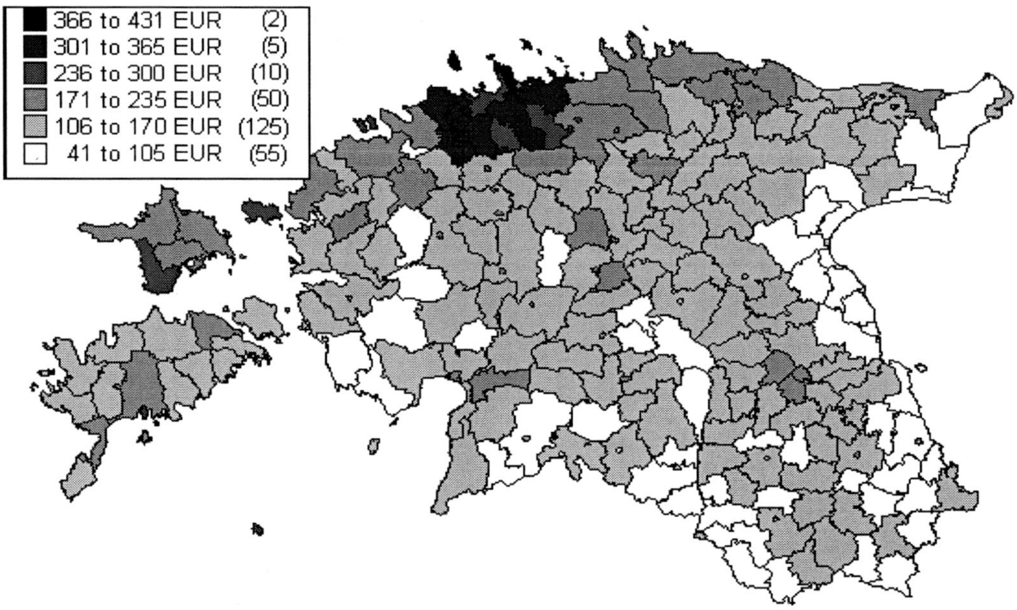

Figure 5. The geography of local government's personal income tax receipts in 2002

The reason for differences in local governments' per capita income tax receipts is the unequal distribution of economic activities in Estonia. The regional location of economic activities and core-periphery rationale is discussed widely in the theoretical literature[9]. However, in the case of Estonia, the older theories of firm locations are not always

[9] The location theory is mostly dealing with the location of firms and this through the relation between transportation costs and scale economies. Most known authors in the theory of location are von Thünen, Lösch, Christaller, Krugman and Venables. Von Thünen related the location of agricultural production to the market (Lindermann 1999). Lösch (1940) introduces trade-off between increasing returns to scale and transport costs (as transports costs diminish, the effects of economies of scale become more pronounced). Upon a large decrease in transport costs, the economic landscape is characterized by a small number of large-scale productive units (Gerard-Varet, Thisse, 1997, p. 25). Krugman and Venables (1995, p. 876) develop another model where regional differentiation is driven by the interaction between scale economies and transport costs. However, compared to earlier authors they discuss international location of firms.

appropriate. The economic policy during the period of belonging to Soviet Union and the collapse of CMEA (The Council for Mutual Economic Assistance) afterwards left Estonia with certain industries, large agricultural sector and the labour force not corresponding to the comparative advantage.

As we can see from Table 7 there seems to be high concentration of all kinds of economic activities in Tallinn and its surroundings (Harju County) and in some larger towns (Tartu, Pärnu). There can be observed some smaller economic centres with higher concentration of economic activities and positive growth of population[10], but these tendencies in Tallinn seem to be superior.

Table 7. Distribution of economic activities in between counties in 2002[11] (%)

Economic activity In counties	Population	Entrepreneurs*	Enterprises	Employed	Employees Inhab in working age (15-74)	Total assets	Foreign Trade	Accommo-dated tourists
Estonia	100.0	100.0	100.0	100.0	100.0	100.0	100.0	100.0
Harju **	38.2	49.5	51.2	43.8	54.3	70.0	74.4	63.8
Incl. Tallinn	29.1	42.9	43.1	33.9	47.0	61.8	59.8	62.4
Tartu	10.9	9.7	9.7	10.6	7.7	5.0	5.0	5.9
Incl. Tartu city	7.4	6.6	n.a.	n.a.	n.a.	n.a.	3.9	5.5
Pärnu	6.8	6.5	6.2	6.3	5.0	3.8	4.6	11.1
Incl. Pärnu city	3.4	3.3	n.a.	n.a.	n.a.	n.a.	3.3	8.9
Ida-Viru	12.9	6.1	7.4	11.9	12.2	8.9	4.3	0.9
Lääne-Viru	4.9	4.9	5.2	4.8	4.4	2.9	2.0	2.7
Other	26.3	23.2	20.3	22.6	16.4	9.5	9.7	15.5

* registered in the commercial register (non-official statistics) ** Tallinn is included here as part of Harju county, so are, respectively Tartu and Pärnu included in county figures.

Source: Statistical database, calculations by authors

Most of the rural side (central and southern regions) and formerly industrial north-east of Estonia can be seen as periphery, where the economic activity, employment and population have drastically decreased compared to Soviet period.

THE ROLE AND DESIGN OF STATE REVENUE EQUALIZATION FUND FOR LOCAL GOVERNMENTS

As discussed earlier in this chapter, until today we can observe mostly vertical conditional and unconditional grants in Estonia; conditional and unconditional grants are still not used on horizontal level. In the case of conditional grants the local governments are mostly too dependent on central government policies. Central government is deciding the location of education, health, public order, and culture and sport institutions. In Estonia

10 For the population and employees mobility and growth, see Tammaru, 2001.

11 Here the counties are used instead of local governments, because respective statistics is not available for local governments.

approximately 50% of all internal and external grants can be associated with central government before-mentioned policies.[12]

Under the scheme of joint expenditures[13], the governments of the regions pool their revenues and delegate the spending decision to an *ad hoc* authority (like local governments' union). In Estonia the grants for joint expenditures do not play any important role. From inter-municipalities transfers in 2002, only 0.43% was meant to finance the joint events and 0.57% was directed through the local governments' unions. 99% of the inter-municipalities grants (or 4% of all central, local and international grants and aid) were the payments for the services (mostly education) bought from other municipalities.

Unconditional equalising grants are very important for the budgets of municipalities in Estonia. Municipalities are entitled to get support from the State Budget trough the State Equalization Fund and as allocations earmarked for specific purposes. In distributing the payments from the Equalization Fund, the formula for calculating the subsidy to local government in 2002 was following (Budget Law, 2002):

$$T_n = ((m * a_k - a_n) * 0{,}9 * c_n) + \frac{T_s}{\sum T_s} * 338400000;$$

where:

m – subsidy level coefficient derived from the size of subsidy fund;

a_k – the per capita sum of average receipts of income tax to local government in 2000 and 2001, estimated land tax for 2002 and estimated resource tax in all municipalities;

a_n - the per capita sum of average receipts of income tax to local government in 2000 and 2001, estimated land tax for 2002 and estimated resource tax in respective local government;

0.9 - revenues are supplemented at amount of 90%;

c_n - population of local government unit

T_s – finances allotted to the respective local government for subsistence allowances in 2002 (T_s = 0,7**tt*2001+0,3*tt*2000); where *tt* represents the respective number for 2001 and 2000).

By analysing the structure of revenues of Estonian local governments in 2002, we found that the main income came from personal income tax[14], followed by total transfers and grants (see Figure 3). The other income sources are already much smaller than these two income categories. The initiative of local governments to levy local taxes is considerably obstructed by the fact that increased own revenues will immediately reduce the amount of allocations paid from the State Budget.

The main purpose of the allocations from State Equalization Fund is to equalise the per capita income of local municipalities in order to guarantee the municipalities with lower income base the sufficient resources for fulfilling their tasks. However, as one can see from

---

[12] Almost 80% of these grants are funds to finance education.

[13] This scheme was separately included in Trionfetti's model (1997).

[14] 56% of total personal income tax receipts are going to local budgets and 44% to central government budget, which means that 11.4% of personal taxable income is directly given to the local governments' budget as already noted on the figure 2.

the basis formula of the grant distribution, the principle takes into account only the revenues' side of local governments. The per capita costs are overseen. This can lead to the situation where some municipalities get "unfairly" high increase in income, even this is not corresponding to their actual costs. On another side there will be the municipalities, who still will have to search for alternative means of finance. To overcome this problem the ministry of finance has in 2004 established slightly different fund allocation principle by formula, which accounts also for some costs as well[15]. This new system of grants will redistribute the current grants somewhat in favour of municipalities, who have more pupils, social aid beneficiaries, or both.

To get some imagination about the disparities in local governments' revenues and costs, we tried to find out in which areas the gaps of finance after conditional grants are the largest. As revenues, we counted all own incomes of appropriate institutions[16]; targeted grants from ministries, other local governments and other institutions/funds, which could be directly linked to appropriate activity (to be short, we call these revenues „conditional revenues"). In the case of costs we included conditional grants as well. However, because of insufficient aggregation of the data we could not identify all targeted grants. These unidentified grants are included in the "Other grants". After rearranging the data in this way we can see in which fields the „conditional revenues" form bigger and in which fields smaller part of the fiscal need (see Table 8).

Table 8. Disbalances of revenues and costs of Estonian local governments (2002, in th. Euros)

No	Revenue/cost article	Revenues (conditional)	Costs	Revenues–Costs	Revenues to Costs (%)
I	Economic activities	16482.3	172171.3	-155689.0	9.57%
II	Education	138406.3	330820.8	-192414.5	41.84%
III	Culture and sports	11262.1	74398.4	-63136.3	15.14%
IV	Health	201.8	9348.5	-9146.6	2.16%
V	Social security	37361.1	63334.9	-25973.8	58.99%
VI	Defense and public order	4769.5	6545.3	-1775.8	72.87%
VII	Environment	7948.3	3468.3	4479.9	229.17%
VIII	Administration	859.4	62333.7	-61474.3	1.38%
Sub-Total (rows I to VIII)		217290.7	722421.2	-505130.4	30.08%
IX	Loans	60689.1	43511.6	17177.5	139.48%
X	Foreign transfers	655.9			
XI	State Equalization Fund (excl. subsistence allowances)*	73602.2			
XII	Other grants	6013.9	1783.0	4230.8	337.28%
XIII	Other revenues,** and costs	438681.1	5970.3	432710.9	7347.77%
Total (rows I to XIII)		796932.9	773686.0	23246.9	103.0%

* subsistence allowances are added to social security costs, ** incl. taxes, fees, mixed revenues, revenues from assets, financial revenues and so forth.

Source: Database of..., 1996-2002; calculations by authors

[15] The formula for payments from State Equalization Fund in 2004, see [https://www.riigiteataja.ee/ert/act.jsp?id=691962] (in Estonian)

[16] These own revenues cover only the minor part of the appropriate costs. For example, the own incomes of education and science institutions cover approximately 4% of their costs.

As we can see from the table 8, in absolute terms the highest disparities of fiscal need and "conditional revenues" can be observed for education, economic activities and culture and sports. In relative terms the "conditional revenues" are covering the smallest part of the costs in the fields of administration, health and economic activities. We can see that approximately 505 Mill. Euros of costs has to be covered by local governments. Most of these costs have to be covered through "Other revenues", 15% through Equalization Fund and the smallerst part through "Loans".

The situation, where a local government is depending on conditional grants from central government (in the case of Estonia in education and social security, both in absolute and relative terms), has a significant impact on its autonomy in making decisions about the use of the revenues. The possibility to rely on their own income would give local governments the freedom to decide how to use their resources. In contrast, allocations from the State Budget are often targeted, which reduces local governments' autonomy in designing their expenditure structure (de Mello 2000). Especially the dominance of the conditional grants can lead to the non-optimal allocation of the resources for the local government. Unconditional grants, serve for filling the gaps between the fiscal need and the expenditure need due to functions assigned to the local governments.

Now we take similar approach as it was used in Table 8, that is we calculate the differences between "conditional revenues" and actual expenditures of some activities. However, this time the per capita terms are considered. On figure 6 we have geographically mapped the gaps in finance of education. As we can see, predominantly the most under-financed regions are bordering to each other. Especially in the district, where the density of population is higher (surroundings of Tallinn) the financial gap is higher. This could have many explanations:

1) Central government is forcing the richer municipalities to finance some fields (in this case education) by themselves;
2) The economies on scale in financing education do not work,
3) It is an additional sign of chronic deficit in finance in transition economy.

This analysis is quite rough and in the future must be adjusted to specific costs (for example using number of pupils in local government). However this gives us some insight about regional gaps in finance. By analyzing respective gaps in other branches (e.g. culture and sports, economic activities and so forth) there seems to be as well similar pattern as shown by Figure 6, that the municipalities with lower (or higher) gaps are bordering to each other. This example shows that the fiscal need after conditional grants is not uniformly spread and does not seem to have any similar geographical core-periphery pattern as the regional development.

The main failures stemming from high proportion of grant-income discussed earlier can be divided into two groups:

1) Failures of all grants:
   a) Reluctance of local governments to increase own revenues using local taxes.[17]

[17] From one side, this can be desirable for central government of Estonia, when the main aim is to follow *laissez faire* policy. From another side, this lowers the local governments' initiative and investment activity for

b) When grants are not depending on the level of local government fiscal needs (in Estonia the case of State Equalization Fund until 2004), then some municipalities will be "over or under financed" compared to their actual costs.

c) Local government can instead of solving problems by concentrating on lobby.

d) Political and economic dependence on central government.

2) Failures of conditional grants.

a) Decreased autonomy in determining the public activities in current local government.

b) From the point of view of local government non-optimality in expenditure, investment composition, or both.

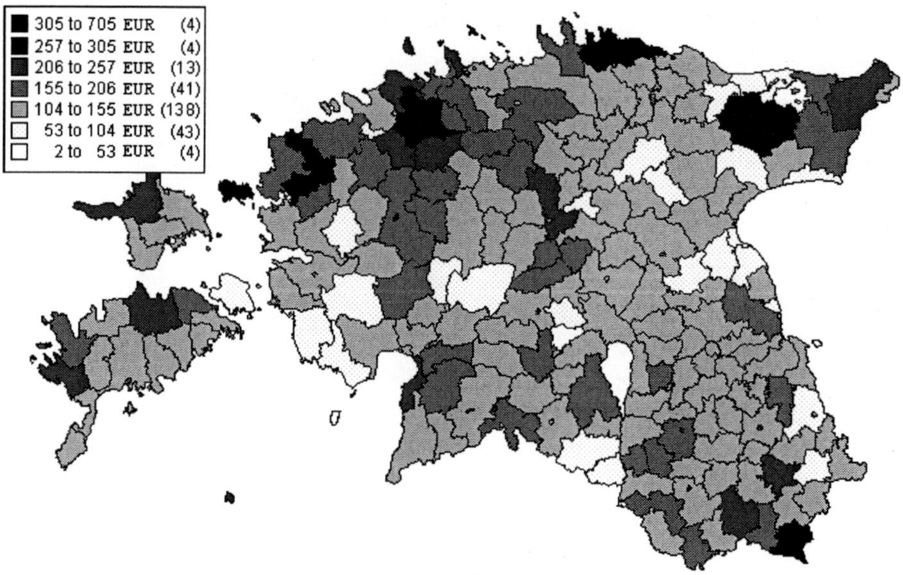

Figure 6. Regional per capita gaps in finance of education in 2002

When the main aim of central government in Estonia was to increase equality in fiscal base of local governments, then how successfully this aim was accomplished? One possibility to analyse the inequality of the municipalities is to use the coefficient of inequality expressed by following equation.

$$Ratio \quad of \quad inequality = \frac{revenues \quad of \quad 40\% \quad of \ poor}{revenues \quad of \quad 20\% \quad of \ rich}$$

To calculate the coefficient we arrange data based on the per capita incomes. The numerator is calculated as follows, based on number of inhabitants we take 40% of Estonian population in poor municipalities, find the total income of these municipalities (by multiplying per capita income with number of inhabitants in each local government and then

promotion of economic development (or accelerating the land reform). The reason, an increase in tax revenues would lead to the decrease in support allotments.

summarising these total revenues of poor municipalities)[18]. The denominator is calculated in similar way. The higher coefficient means higher equality.

Table 9. Total revenues of rich and poor regions (in thousands of Euros) and inequality ratios in 2002

Per capita revenue article	Without Tallinn[19]			With Tallinn		
	40 poor	20 rich	Ratio	40 poor	20 rich	Ratio
Income tax	47214	48718	0.969	69686	79508	0.876
Income tax + Equalization Fund	87613	57156	1.533	127029	80537	1.577
Income tax + all grants	105312	81057	1.299	155489	109314	1.422

Source: Database of... 1996-2002; calculations by authors

Table 10. Per capita weighted average revenues of rich and poor regions (in Euros) and inequality ratios in 2002

Per capita revenue article	Without Tallinn			With Tallinn		
	40 poor	20 rich	Ratio	40 poor	20 rich	Ratio
Income tax (per capita)	121.31	250.34	0.485	127.03	289.86	0.438
Income tax + Equalization Fund (per capita)	225.10	293.70	0.766	231.55	293.61	0.789
Income tax + all grants (per capita)	270.57	416.51	0.650	283.43	398.53	0.711

Source: Database of... 1996-2002; calculations by authors

As we can see from Table 9 the allocations from State Equalization Fund tend to increase the equality of local municipalities' revenues. However, the other grants will reduce this equalization effect. If we look at the differences in average per capita incomes of poor and rich, we can see that the per capita income tax receipts of poor regions form only 44 of appropriate revenues of rich ones (see Table 10)[20].

If we look at how the central government has actually succeeded in equalizing the local governments' income on regional level (initial own revenue distribution was presented on the Figure 5), we can see that at least in the case of total income from personal income tax and State Equalization Fund grants there are less governments in the lower (compare with Figure 7) and more in the average income level groups. However, as we can see, there are still some cluster-regions with low income and regions surrounding Tallinn have still higher income than most of other regions in Estonia.

However, if we look at all per capita grants (figure 8), that is grants from central government and from other local governments, we can see that the number of poorer municipalities is increased. The picture seems to be similar to Figure 5, where we mapped the distribution of the per capita income tax revenues. There are still poorer regions in northeast, south and center of Estonia. The difference from earlier distribution of income is that small islands and some of poor regions have gained and the surroundings of Tallinn have lost.

---

[18] To get exactly 40% or 20 % of population some municipalities are included only partly.

[19] Because Tallinn accounts almost for one third of the Estonian population the inequality ratio is calculated both as excluding as including the incomes of Tallinn.

[20] To calculate the coefficients we take the appropriate weighted average *per capita* income of poor regions and divide by weighted average *per capita* income of rich regions.

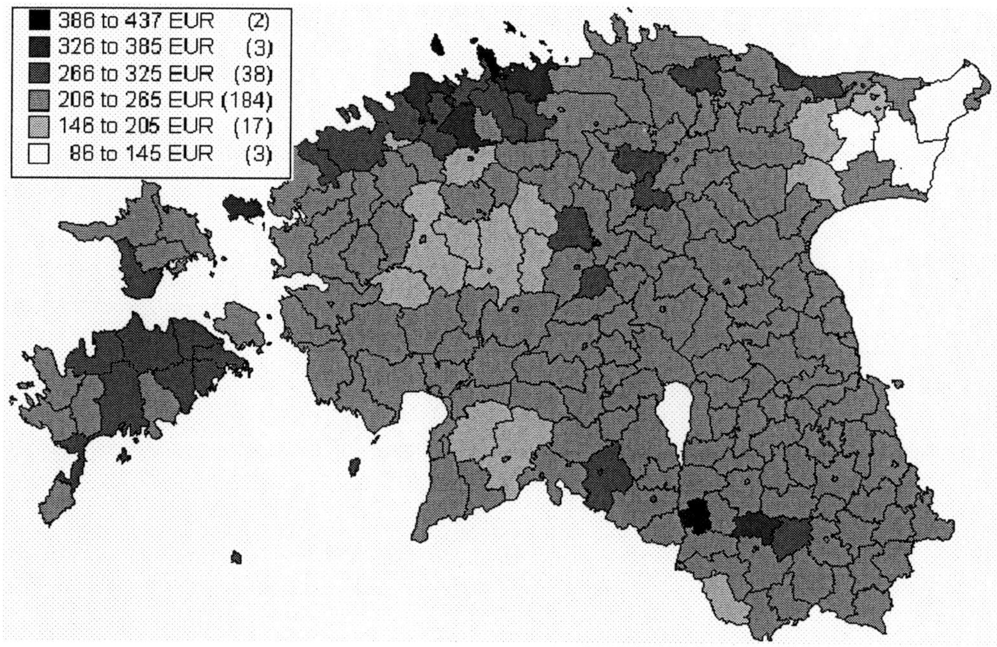

Figure 7. Per capita revenues from income tax and State Equalization Fund (unconditional grant) of local municipalities in 2002

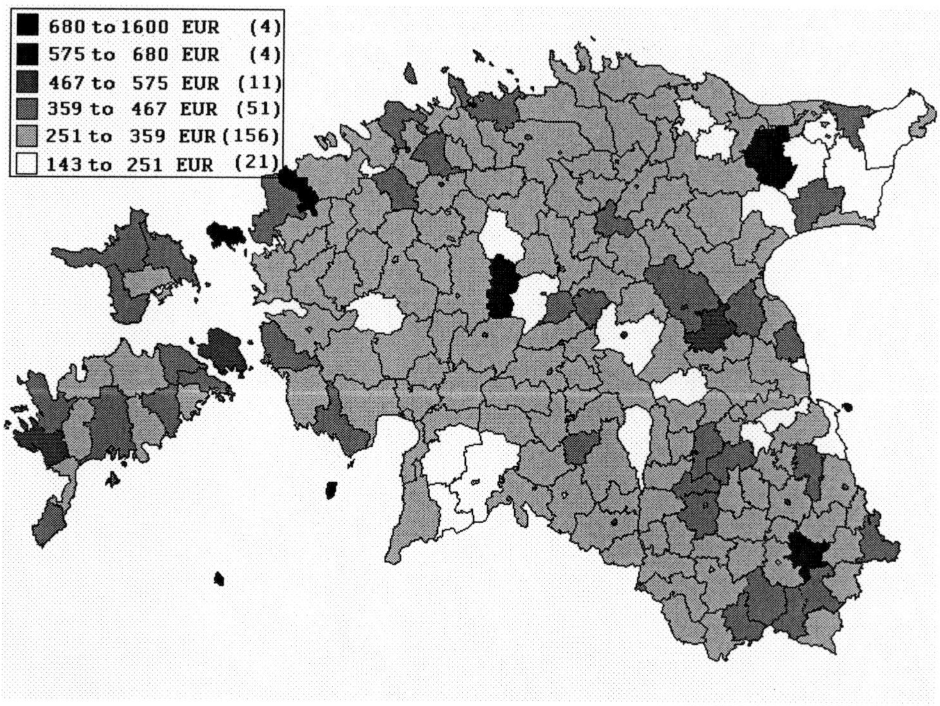

Figure 8. Per capita revenues from income tax and total grants of local municipalities in 2000

After taking into account all (conditional and unconditional) grants, the picture is different, there are emerging poorer regions in northeast and southwestern part of Estonia, which could indicate lower lobbying power and less conditional grants to those peripheral municipalities.

Table 11. Abbreviations used in correlation and regression analysis

ADMtoINCTAX	administration costs divided by income tax revenues
TOTALGRANTpc	the total per capita grant
C	Constant
CITY	dummy (=1) for urban local government
COUNTDIST	distance (in km) between municipalities' center and county's center
DEPEND	dependency rate in appropriate local government
DIST	distance (in km) between municipalities' center and Tallinn
DU130PAOTH	dummy (=1) for local government located in range from 1 to 30 km away from its county's center (excluding surroundings of Tallinn and Tartu)
DU130TLL, DU130TA, DU130PA	dummy (=1) for local government located in range from 1 to 30 km away accordingly from Tallinn, Tartu or Pärnu
DUCIT10000	dummy for cities with more than 10 000 inhabitants
DUCIT200010000	dummy for cities with number of inhabitants between 2000 and 10 000
DUMM	different dummies, which describe location or size of the local government
DUMUN20004000	dummy for non-urban municipalities with number of inhabitants between 2000 and 4000
DUMUN4000	dummy for non-urban municipalities with more than 4000 inhabitants
DUMUNLES2000	dummy for non-urban municipalities with less than 2000 inhabitants
ISLAND	dummy (=1) for municipalities located on island
LnDIST	logarithm of the distance (in km.) between municipalities' center and Tallinn
LnTOTALGRANTpc	logarithm of the total per capita grant
LOANtoINCTAX	loans divided by income tax revenues (%)
LnOWNREVpc	logarithm of the per capita revenues excluding grants
LnUNCGRANTpc	logarithm of the per capita grants from State Equalization Fund
LnCONDGRANTpc	logarithm of the per capita grants excluding Equalization Fund
LnXpc	logarithm of the per capita state Equalization Fund grants or total grants
NONEST	percentage of the non-Estonians in population
SmallISLAND	the dummy (=1) for municipalities located on small islands (Ruhnu, Kihnu, Vormsi, Piirissaar)
UNCGRANTpc	the per capita grants from State Equalization Fund
CONDGRANTpc	the per capita grants excluding Equalization Fund
UNEMPtoINHAB	official number of unemployed divided by number of in inhabitants

Table 12. Correlation matrix (pair wise) [21]

	DIST	COUNT-DIST	UNC Grantpc	TOTAL Grantpc	COND Grantpc	DEPEND	Admto-inctax	Unemp-toinhab
Dist	1.0000							
Countdist	0.0706	1.0000						
Uncgrantpc	0.5973***	0.3057***	1.0000					
Totalgrantpc	0.3348***	0.2834***	0.3216***	1.0000				
Condgrantpc	0.1496**	0.1949***	-0.0019	0.9463***	1.0000			
Depend	0.5019***	0.4329***	0.4930***	0.3156***	0.1650***	1.0000		
Admtoinctax	0.2783***	0.3601***	0.2661***	0.3938***	0.3250***	0.5041***	1.0000	
Unemptoinhab	0.1232*	-0.0310	0.2234***	0.0727	0.0019	-0.0251	0.1309**	1.0000

***p<0.01, **p<0.05, *p<0.1

Source: Database of... 1996-2002; calculations by authors

[21] For the abbreviations see Table 11.

GRAVITY ANALYSIS OF INTERGOVERNMENTAL GRANTS

As analyzed in earlier sections in this chapter, economic development and hence the own income base are reflecting a certain core–periphery pattern in Estonia. By the theoretical discussion and the observed dynamics in data, we would prove the validity of three following hypotheses:

1) There is a positive correlation of the distance from local governments' center to Tallinn (and other larger towns) with the per capita unconditional grant flows to local governments;
2) This positive correlation of distance is becoming weaker by adding conditional grants;
3) There is a negative correlattion of distance with per capita unconditional grant flows to local governments because of higher lobbying costs in distance. The rationale for the third hypothesis follows the idea of Borck and Orwings (2003).

If we do the simple correlation analysis, we can see that distance from economic and political center does matter. There is negative correlation of distance of local government's center to Tallinn (and to county's center) with the per capita income from personal income tax (see Table 12). If the policy of the central government is to reduce the differences in geographical income distribution, then there would be a positive correlation of distance with the per capita flows of support to local governments, what can be indeed seen from Table 12.

One of possibilities to include distance into regression analysis is to use gravity model. The main idea is derived from physics – there is a gravitational force between the bodies, which is positively depending on the masses of the bodies and negatively depending on the distance between them. Gravity type models are very popular in order to analyze the flows of goods, services, or both (see Frankel, Stein and Wei, 1995; Helliwell, 1996) and migration (see Greenwood and Hunt 2003). In last years there has been done some research about foreign investment flows (see Buch, Kokta, Piazolo, 2003; Ng, Tuan, 2003) using gravity models.

In this part we concentrate us on the central government's state equalization fund grants and total grants flows to local governments. Therefore the differences between donor and recipient are not analyzed, as it suggested in the case of modeling international trade (see Egger, 2002). Grants should flow to the districts with lower own revenues. This should be true when government is interested in equalizing the per capita income of local governments[22]. General logarithmic econometric specification of the gravity model describing the per capita grant receipts of municipalities is brought in following equation[23].

$$LogXpc_j = \beta_1 + \beta_2 * LogOWNREVpc_j + \beta_3 * LogDIST_j + \beta_4 * DUMMIES_j + u_j$$

---

[22] The modification of gravity model is now the assumption that the weaker the local government is the more support it must attract. Firstly, this means that the lower is own income the higher are support flows. Secondly, because the more distant regions have lower *per capita* income from personal income tax, they should have higher income from grants.

[23] For the abbreviations see Table 11. Some measures (like ADMtoINCTAX or UNEMPtoINHAB) were used in following gravity model, but did not give significant nor robust results. Dependency rate seems to have geographical pattern itself.

Using cross section analysis in econometric analysis has its disadvantage. Namely, from cross-section parameters we get valid predictions of the comparative statics if the economy is in the equilibrium (Schmalensee, 1989). This assumption does not hold in the case of Estonia. Namely, in Estonia the reform of local municipalities' size, revenues and responsibilities is still unfinished. Therefore, we must interpret the results with some caution.

In the case of State Equalization Fund the main aim was to equalize the per capita income of municipalities. As we can see from the Table 13 the gravity model describes more than 70% of the variations in per capita State Equalization Fund flows to the municipalities. We can see that municipalities' distance from Tallinn has positive and significant impact on support flows. In addition, the bigger cities and surroundings of some bigger cities have lower per capita State Equalization Fund income than in average other municipalities do. The absolute value of the coefficients of dummies, which describe belonging to the surroundings of Tallinn, Tartu and Pärnu, is highest for Tallinn, lower for Tartu and smallest for Pärnu. This means that even the surroundings of Tallinn, Tartu and Pärnu are all, in average, getting less grants than other regions of Estonia the tendency is to equalization of the municipalities, where economic activity is lower.

In the case of total per capita grant flows we can see that gravity model has already smaller power of description (see Table 14). However, the tendencies are similar to the ones of State Equalization Fund distribution, that is more distant municipalities have higher, and the bigger cities and surroundings of some bigger cities have lower income from grants. What we can see additionally is the higher grant-income of islands` municipalities.

The correlation of distance with total state grant flows and the conditional grant flows are both lower than that of Equalization Fund (see Table 12), but their are all positive. In addition, the coefficients of distance variable in the model describing total per capita grant flows compared to the model of describing state support flows remained in all model designs lower, but positive. The last argument must be treated with some caution. We cannot directly compare the magnitude of the coefficients, because the scales of depending variables are different (the total support flows are in average higher than unconditional grant (Equalization Fund) flows).

Table 13. Results of estimated gravity models for State Equalization Fund

	LnUNCGRANTpc	t-statistic-*	LnUNCGRANTpc	t-statistic*
C	14.260	10.240	14.583	10.290
LnDIST	0.355	5.020	0.320	4.270
DUCIT10000			-0.282	-2.320
DUCIT200010000			-0.245	-2.250
DUMUN 4000			-0.296	-2.520
LnOWNREVpc	-1.058	-7.220	-1.073	-7.260
DU130TLL	-1.240	-3.480	-1.139	-3.180
DU130TA	-0.306	-2.960	-0.271	-2.750
DU130PA	-0.218	-3.110	-0.217	-2.920
CITY	-0.196	-2.620		
R^2	0.724		0.733	
F-statistic	47.69		43.07	
Obs.	247		247	

*the t-statistics are White heteroscedasticity-consistent

Even in the case of modeling conditional grant flows separately gives us a positive relationship between the distance and grant flows (see Table 14). This seems to contradict our third hypothesis of existence of lobbying costs because of the physical distance. However, the issue remains unclear, because there is a positive correlation of conditional grants with own revenues of municipalities. Additionally, there seems to be an evidence for lobbying costs because of the cultural distance – the regions with the higher proportion of non-Estonians are getting fewer grants. This could be explained by the lower Estonian language skills of non-Estonians. The last arguments should be controlled using less aggregated data and including the variables to describe the appropriate institutions.

Table 14. Results of estimated gravity models for all support funds

	LnTOTAL GRANTpc	t-statistic *	LnTOTAL GRANTpc	t-statistic *	LnTOTAL GRANTpc	t-statistic *	LnCOND GRANTpc	t-statistic *
C	8.926	8.68	8.865	8.6	9.108	8.62	3.328	2.50
LnDIST	0.230	4.38	0.239	4.89	0.217	4.13	0.199	2.55
DUCIT10000	-0.410	-4.17	-0.416	-4.12	-0.414	-4.21	-0.480	-2.80
ISLAND			0.122	1.4	0.115	1.25		
SmallISLAND	1.561	7.18	1.546	6.93	1.590	7.09	1.933	8.65
DUMUNLES2000	-0.188	-2.58	-0.177	-2.31	-0.195	-2.59	-0.726	-6.30
DUMUN20004000	-0.294	-3.9	-0.284	-3.6	-0.300	-3.9	-0.796	-6.08
DUMUN4000	-0.463	-4.74	-0.453	-4.53	-0.464	-4.71	-0.851	-5.58
LnOWNREVpc	-0.244	-2.27	-0.242	-2.24	-0.260	-2.36	0.412	2.95
LOANtoINCTAX	0.005	2.91	0.005	2.94	0.005	3.04		
DU130TLL	-0.556	-2.89	-0.549	-2.88	-0.559	-2.92	-0.696	-2.81
DU130TA	-0.345	-2.68	-0.358	-2.74	-0.329	-2.53	-0.779	-2.87
DU130PA	-0.149	-2.28			-0.141	-2.17	-0.229	-1.73
DU130PAOTH			-0.092	-1.78				
NOTEST							-0.011	-3.38
R^2	0.543		0.545		0.546		0.351	
F-statistic	21.9		22.5		20.6		20.78	
Obs.	247		247		247		247	

*the t-statistics are White heteroskedasticity-consistent

The gravity model has explicitly shown the existence of regional pattern in financial support flows in Estonia, however it does not give a clear answer, how much different grants are influencing the income equality of municipalities.

Conclusion

In Estonia traditional fiscal functions (allocation, distribution and stabilization) are at a great extent underlying other main general government goals (democratization, liberalization and security). In addition, the number of functions assigned to local governments has grown, but local governments lack a stable legally determined income base, which would enable them to make long-term plans of local development and effectively manage diverse local issues. The responsibilities of local governments are dependent on the presence of appropriate educational, social or cultural institutions within the local government. This doesn't encourage local governments to broaden the scope of their public services, but provides a way to live at the expense of neighboring local governments.

In Estonia the main reasons for the need of redistribution of the local governments' income are differences in income base between municipalities, increase of number of functions assigned to local governments, which was often not followed by the increase of funds, and differences in the presence of appropriate educational, social or cultural institutions within the municipalities.

Estonian local governments are depending on different conditional and unconditional transfers. The aim of unconditional grants is to equalize the financial capacity of all local governments. However, the main unconditional grant source (State Equalization Fund) is not distributed on the basis of actual costs of local governments, but takes into account only the revenue side. Since 2004, some education and social security expenditure needs are taken into account and thereby the distribution of funds is expected to be more fair. From the other side such a method of finance makes the local governments even more dependent on presence of appropriate institutions and reduces local initiative. Conditional grants are similarly distributed in accordance with central government's policy, local governments can influence their receipts by lobbying work.

Regarding of financing different fields, the highest gaps in finance after conditional revenues (grants) can in absolute terms be observed in education, economic activities and culture and sports. In relative terms the costs are prevailing highest revenues highest for administration, health and economic activities. The gaps seem to have a regional pattern – the municipalities with lower (or higher) gaps are often bordering each other.

The differences of income tax distribution seem to have a geographical pattern. This can be observed graphically and proved by correlation analysis. The central government policy of equalization of local governments' per capita revenues through the State Equalization Fund can be seen as successful. From the other side, the distribution of conditional grants is decreasing the equalizing effect of unconditional transfers. However, the negative correlation of conditional grants with distance was not found. The gravity model supports the presence of geographical pattern in grants from central to local governments.

REFERENCES

Bird, R.M. (1999) Fiscal Federalism. In Cordes, J.J., Ebel, R.D., Gravelle, J.G. *The Encyclopedia of Taxation and Tax Policy*. Washington: Urban Institute Press, pp. 151-154.

Borck, R., Owings, S. (2003). The political economy of intergovernmental grants. *Regional Science and Urban Economics*, Vol. 33, pp. 139–156.

Buch, C. M.; Kokta, R. M.; Piazolo, D. (2003) Foreign direct investment in Europe: Is there redirection from the South to the East? Journal of Comparative Economics, Vol. 31, Issue 1, pp. 94-109.

Cangiano, M., Mottu, E. (1998). Will fiscal policy be effective Under EMU?, *IMF Working Paper* WP/98/176, 32 p.

Database of Budget Execution in Local Governments (1996–2002). (Kohalike omavalitsuste eelarvete täitmise aruanded (1996–2002)), Tallinn: Ministry of Economic Affairs

De Mello, Jr, L. R. (2000) Fiscal decentralization and intergovernmental fiscal relations: a cross-country analysis. *World Development*. Vol. 28, No. 2, pp. 365-380.

Egger, P. (2002). An Econometric View on the Estimation of Gravity Models and the Calculation of Trade Potentials. *World Economy*, Vol. 25 Issue 2, pp. 297-312.

Frankel, J., Stein, E. and Wei, S. (1995) Trading Blocs and the Americas: The Natural, the Unnatural and the Super-natural. *Journal of Development Economics*, Vol. 47 Issue 1, pp. 61-95.

Gerard-Varet, L.-A., Thisse, J.F. (1997). Local Public Finance and Economic Geography. *Annales D'Economie et de Statistique*, No. 45, pp. 19-35.

Greenwood, M. J.; Hunt, G. L. (2003) The Early History of Migration Research. *International Regional Science Review*, Vol. 26, Issue 1, pp. 3-37.

Hamilton, J.H., Slutsky, S.M. (1997). Decentralizing Taxation and Public Expenditure within a Federation. *Annales D'Economie et de Statistique*, No. 45, pp. 199-218.

Helliwell, J.F. (1996) Do National Borders Matter for Quebec's Trade?. *Canadian Journal of Economics*, Vol. 29, Issue 3, pp. 507-522.

Jha, S., Swaroop, V. (2000) Fiscal Effects of Foreign Aid in a Federal System of Governance: The Case of India. – *Journal of Public Economics*, Vol. 77, Iss. 3, pp. 307-330.

Krugman, P. (1991) Increasing Return and Economic Geography. *Journal of Political Economy*, Vol. 99, Issue 3, pp. 483-499.

Krugman, P., Venables, A.J. (1995). Globalisation and the Inequality of Nations. - *Quarterly Journal of Economics*, Vol. 110, Issue 4, pp. 857-880.

Lauritsen, F. (2000). *Kohaliku omavalitsuse kohustuslike ülesannete maksumuse hindamine. Eesti Vabariigi Siseministeeriumi ja Taani Kuningriigi Siseministeeriumi kohaliku omavalitsuse arendamise programm Eestis. Lõpparuanne.* (Tallinn: Eesti Regionaalarengu Sihtasutus, Taani Kommuunide Liit)

Lindermann, S. (1999). *Theorie und Empirie kommunalen Wirtschaftsförderwettbewerbs: Eine Konkurrenzanalyse in den neuen Ländern*. Baden-Baden: Nomos Verl.-Ges.

Local Governments Regulation Act. (1999). (Kohaliku Omavalitsuse Korralduse seadus.) *Riigi Teataja I*, 82, 755.

Local Taxes Act. (Kohalike maksude seadus).(1994). *Riigi Teataja I,* 68, 1169.

Lösch, A. (1940). *Die Räumliche Ordnung der Wirtschaft*. Jena: Gustav Fischer Verlag.

Ministry of Internal Affairs of Republic of Estonia. (2002) Functions of the Local Governments. [www.sisemin.gov.ee], in Estonian.

Moll, M. (1997). Report in PHARE Public Development Programme ES 9502.

Ng, L.F.Y.; Tuan, C. (2003). Location decisions of manufacturing FDI in China: implications of China's WTO accession. *Journal of Asian Economics*, Vol. 14, Issue 1, pp. 51-72.

Oates, W.E., (1999). An essay of fiscal federalism. *Journal of Economic Literature*, Vol. 37, pp. 1120–1149.

Paas, T., Eamets, R., Rõõm, M., Selliov, R., Jürgenson, A., Masso, J. (2002). Labour flexibility and migration in the EU eastward enlargement context: the case of Baltic States. *Ezoneplus Working Paper.* No 11, 79 p. (http://www.ezoneplus.org/archiv/ezone plus_wp_eleven.pdf 20.01.2004)

Pacione, M. (2001). Georgaphy and public finance: planning for fiscal equity in metropolitan region. *Progress in Planning*, No 56, pp. 1-59

Raus, T.; Trasberg, V. (2003) Regionaalsed Tuluerisused. pp. 283-303. In Kaldaru, H (Ed.) *Eesti regionaalarengu sotsiaalmajanduslik käsitlus.* Tartu: Tartu University Press.

Reiljan, J.; Timpmann, K.; Olenko, K. (2003) Key issues in developing the public administration system of Estonia before joining the European Union. *Tartu Ülikooli majandusteaduskonna toimetiste seeria*, No. 17, 2003, 68 p.

Budget Law. (2002). (2002. aasta riigieelarve seadus). *Riigi Teataja* I 2002, 15.01; 4,8.

Schmalensee, R. (1989) Inter-industry studies of structure and performance. In: Schmalensee, R., Willig, R.D. (Eds.), *Handbook of Industrial Organization*, Vol. 2, Amsterdam: North-Holland.

Silverman, J., M. (1992) Public Sector Decentralization. Economic Policy and Sector Investment Programs. *World Bank Technical Paper, Africal Department Series*, No. 188, 111 p.

Tammaru, T. (2001) Eesti linnade mõjualad ja pendelränne. Lõpparuanne. TÜ: Rahvastikuministri büroo, 203 lk.

Trionfetti, F. (1997) Public Expenditure and Economic Geography. *Annales d'Economie et de Statistique*, No. 47, pp. 101-120.

Ulst, E. (2000) Eesti kohalike omavalitsuste tuludebaasi analüüs. Leping LMJRI 10699, EMFA komponent PA-3 lõpparuanne.

In: Perspectives on International, State and Local Economics
Editor: Gerald V. Liu, pp. 115-140
ISBN 1-60021-099-6

Chapter 4

PUBLIC EDUCATION COST FRONTIER MODELS: THEORY AND AN APPLICATION

John E. Anderson
Department of Economics, University of Nebraska, Lincoln, NE
Mahbubul Kabir
Division of Business and Economics, Lyon College, Batesville, AR

ABSTRACT

We examine the cost structure of public schools in this paper, using frontier cost models that enable us to estimate sources of inefficiency. A two-equation stochastic frontier model is presented that can be used to explain both cost and the sources of inefficiency. Using that model and data for public schools in Nebraska over the period 1989-92, we estimate cost frontiers for the districts. Estimated cost frontier information is then used in estimating school district need for purposes of computing state aid, illustrating an important potential application of such information.

Key Words: education cost functions, frontier estimation, education finance, education aid, fiscal disparity
JEL Classification: H41, H77, I21, I22, D24

INTRODUCTION AND BACKGROUND

Over the past two decades across countries and regions serious questions have been raised about performance in the public education sector. In the United States, growing reluctance on the part of taxpayers at the local level to pay increasing taxes has become pervasive. School district expenditure, its mode of funding, and social equity effects on educational outcomes have all been the subject of numerous studies. In particular, a number of recent studies have examined the economic efficiency of public schools. One of the common analytic tools used in these studies is the estimation of the cost structure of the educational production process. Knowledge of cost structure and estimates of efficiency should shed light not only on the expenditure side, but also on efforts to derive useful policy implications for the funding and equity in public education.

School districts in Nebraska, like many other states, have been dependent on property tax and state/federal aid for their funding. Believing that school district funding was too dependent on the property tax, and desiring to achieve additional equity across districts, a commission was instituted in 1988 in Nebraska to formulate policies for financing, expenditure, and equity. Part of the motivation for the commission was a desire to avoid court-ordered reform due to perceived inequality in funding across districts, as had been experienced in a number of states in the previous decade. It was perceived to be time to overhaul the state aid mechanism for funding public schools, taking into account appropriate measures of school district need and resources.

The Nebraska school aid formula was revised in 1990-91 to rationalize state aid, basing aid on the difference between school district need and resources. The definition of district need prescribed was quite primitive, simply defining need as the average expenditure of districts of roughly similar size. Districts were classified by size, with the two largest districts in the state, Omaha and Lincoln in their own classes. Hence, district need was simply defined as district expenditure for these specific districts. Districts in classes composed of more than one district, have need defined as the average expenditure of the districts in the respective class size. This approach to state aid funding is not unique to Nebraska, but does illustrate the critical role to be played by proper estimates of school district need.

Within this context, our paper is an attempt to study the cost structure and efficiency of each of the Nebraska school districts included over the period of 1989-92. The new element in this research approach is to focus on frontier cost, rather than on average function cost, to derive insights about the cost structure and efficiency performance of Nebraska school districts. In this paper, we first present a summary of the underlying theory of public education cost function estimation and vis-à-vis its implications in understanding efficiency and fiscal disparity in public education. Then, we suggest an alternative method of cost function modeling and estimate the proposed cost frontier model in the case of Nebraska school districts. We explain the usefulness of the cost frontier approach in exploring cost structure and in measuring efficiency of public education. Finally, we suggest ways to improve public education finance mechanisms, intended to address fiscal disparities across districts, by examining the potential use of frontier cost estimates of district need in the state aid formula.

Theory of Public Education Cost Function Estimation

The Average Response Function and the Concept of a Frontier Function

The approach adopted in this paper to examine cost and fiscal issues of Nebraska school districts is different from that used in prior studies based on ordinary least squares (OLS) estimation of educational cost structure. Various econometric methods have also been suggested in the literature to improve the unbiasedness, efficiency, and consistency of estimators. See Downes and Pogue (1994), for example. For non-statistical frontier methods, see Klitgaard and Hall (1975), Levin (1976), Sengupta and Sfeir (1986), McCarty and Yaiswarng (1993). For parametric statistical frontiers, see Barrow (1991), Wyckoff and Lavinge (1991), and Chakraborty *et al.* (1996).

OLS estimation of a cost function for school districts involves fitting an average response function through the scatter of school district points. The implicit educational production technology estimated by this method is thus an average technology for school districts in the sample. Estimated coefficients for the variables of such a cost model reflect an average technology, not a technology reflecting the best that can be done with given resources. Farrell (1957) first recognized that the traditional econometric techniques (represented by the so-called average response function of OLS) used in many production and cost studies did not base their estimations on the microeconomic definitions of cost and production functions. His idea was to fit a curve that would pouch all the observed points above the curve, in the case of a cost function, or envelope all the observed points below the curve in case of production function. Hence, Farrell's suggested frontiers represent the best available technology and his concept of a frontier function was used to develop methods to measure the efficiency of enterprises. However, the average response function has been the focus of the mainstream econometric literature in production and cost economics. If we assume all firms are efficient then no doubt, such an average function would be adequate for describing the efficient technology involved. If inefficient production units exist, then Farrell's frontier concepts are not only relevant, but also necessary for conducting appropriate analysis. It is our contention that such methods are appropriate in estimating public education cost functions.

Advantages of Stochastic Frontier Modeling

A statistical deterministic cost frontier can be adopted from Afriat (1972) written as log [C] = log [C(y, p)] + u, where log [C] is the natural logarithm of cost per pupil and u is a nonnegative random variable ($u \geq 0$, i.e., strictly one-sided distribution) representing cost inefficiency effects. Output is denoted y and input prices are denoted p. Here, the cost frontier is the non-stochastic part, log [C(y, p)] = C^f, and as such it is called the deterministic frontier. In this case, residuals are entirely attributed to inefficiency. The most damaging criticism cast on this model is that it ignores the regular noise term. For this reason and others cited in Coelli (1995), econometricians have abandoned the deterministic frontier for efficiency measurement.

In a stochastic cost frontier model there are two error terms: one symmetric and another asymmetric. Schmidt (1985-86) explains that the first term is a regular symmetric noise term representing "events not under the control of the firm, such as luck, weather, etc." The error term is assumed to be independently and identically distributed normal with zero mean and constant variance: $v \sim iid$ N $(0, \sigma_v^2)$. Second, cost inefficiency effects are captured in an asymmetric error term u, independent of v, and are assumed to be arising from an *iid* truncated-normal or exponential distribution ($u \geq 0$; half-normal or exponential, as in Schmidt and Lovell (1979)). The stochastic frontier model is represented as:

$$\log [C] = \log [C(y, p)] + (v + u). \quad (1)$$

The combined error term $(v+u)$ has a range of -ά to + ά, but the distribution is skewed and has a non-zero mean, given by the mean of the composite error term $(v+u)$. Addition of a noise term provides superiority for the stochastic model, in comparison with a deterministic frontier model. A stochastic model allows us to conceptualize both favorable and unfavorable random conditions (v) separately from inefficiency effects (u). This feature provides a way to measure efficiency less arbitrarily than a deterministic model.

The composite nature of the error term in the stochastic model also has very helpful implications in the analysis of school district cost structure. For example, Bradbury *et al.* (1984) and Downes and Pogue (1994) included environmental cost factors in cost models, and thus tried to identify the cost differential between local jurisdictions (municipalities, school districts, cities and towns) because of uneven environmental cost factors. In the case of education, it might be that in one school district there is an extra cost of $R per pupil due to a particular environmental cost factor such as the presence of special-need students. There may be agreement among state and local officials that this $R per pupil should be covered by the state aid formula. However, it is reasonable to ask under what random favorable or unfavorable conditions a particular school district is operating. It could be that the school district is operating under a favorable condition that helps the school district save cost in the amount of $Q per pupil. In this situation, the school aid formula should be adjusted for the required expenditure of $R per pupil to $(R-Q) per pupil. In a similar way, it can be argued that the adjusted extra cost per pupil would be $(R+Q) in an unfavorable situation. The opportunity to account for random favorable and unfavorable conditions in the environment of school districts is possible because of the composite error structure $(u+v)$ in stochastic cost frontier and it can then be instrumental in adjusting the school aid formula. Thus, besides providing an efficiency measure for school districts, the stochastic cost frontier approach has significant potential for rationalizing school aid.

A geometric exposition of cost frontier concepts, following Battese (1992), is illustrated in Figure 1. C^f represents the deterministic part of a cost frontier in the figure. Three school districts denoted with scale subscripts i, j, and k, illustrate three possible situations in terms of their relative size of inefficiency and random favorable/unfavorable condition with which they are operating. School district k's stochastic cost frontier lies above the corresponding deterministic part, indicating a random unfavorable operational condition $(v_k > 0)$. Inefficiency u_k contributes to placing district k further above the deterministic cost frontier C^f. In the case of school district i, the stochastic cost frontier is below the deterministic frontier line implying a random favorable condition $(v_i < 0)$. However, inefficiency of the school district i offsets the favorable condition $(u_i > v_i)$ and causes the observed cost to be higher than the deterministic cost frontier. School district j's situation is similar $(v_j < 0)$ to school district i, except that j's efficiency level is relatively better $[(u_j/v_j) < 1$, and $|(u_i/v_i)| > 1]$ than school district i, resulting in an observed cost lower than the deterministic cost. This description of the relative size of u and v terms helps illustrate the potential of the stochastic frontier function in addressing the issue of fiscal disparities among school districts.

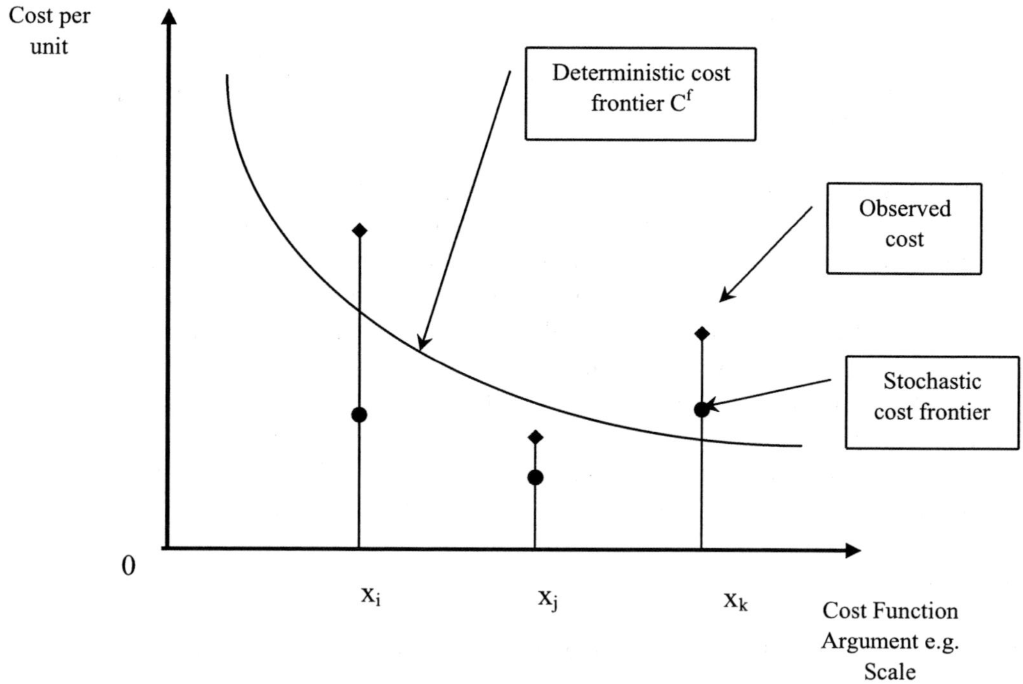

Figure 1: Cost Frontier Illustration

Nature of Inefficiency and Frontier Model Specification

Favorable and unfavorable conditions are random, by definition, so they should not affect the specification of the model. As long as inefficiency effects are random they too should not cause any serious concern for misspecification of the model. However, if we assume that observed inefficiency is systematically dependent on controllable factors, and if we do not incorporate those factors in the cost model, then it is quite likely that the omission of these factors will cause specification errors. Factors systematically causing inefficiency eventually affect cost. In this situation if we could at least account for the fixed portion of inefficiency, it would then certainly improve the quality of estimations. However, attempts to incorporate those variables directly within the cost function might bring in other econometric problems (e.g., multicollinearity). With completely deterministic inefficiency (different from the concept of deterministic frontier), however, OLS estimation would suffice if we could include the variables that systematically affect inefficiency. Unfortunately, one limitation of this approach is that the inefficiency effects cannot be singled out. A one-equation stochastic frontier model is obviously irrelevant when inefficiency effects are modeled with a systematic component only. But if the inefficiency effects consist of systematic and random components, then we need to be more careful about specification. In this circumstance, a one-equation stochastic frontier model would seem to be more vulnerable to misspecification.

Reifschneider and Stevenson (1991) addressed the question of "whether inefficiency occurs randomly across firms, or whether some firms have predictably higher levels of inefficiency than others." They argued "if efficiency ... is not totally random, then it would be possible to identify factors that contribute to the existence of inefficiency." They developed a single-step maximum likelihood estimation (MLE) technique similar to, but independent of, the Kumbhakar *et al.* (1991) technique. Their empirical results for the cost frontier of an electric utility suggest that including both systematic and random components in the inefficiency error term is superior. A two-equation model, including equation for inefficiency effects, as proposed by Kumbhakar *et al.* (1991) and Reifschneider and Stevenson (1991) (extended further to panel data by Battese and Coelli (1993)), appears to be better conceptualized to handle the anticipated specification problem. The first equation of a two-equation model can be written as equation (1) where $v \sim iid\ N(0, \sigma_v^2)$, and u comes from the distribution $N(\delta Z, \sigma_u^2)$ which is truncated at zero. Z is a column vector of firm-specific factors that explain the systematic part of firm inefficiency and δ is a row vector of corresponding parameters. In the second equation the error term u is specified as

$$u = f(\delta Z) + w, \quad (2)$$

where w represents the random component of inefficiency, distributed as a normal random variate $N(0,\sigma_u^2)$, truncated at $-f(\delta Z)$. This two-equation model has another important aspect. It can address heteroskedasticity that may be present in the inefficiency distribution. In the public school cost function context, it is likely that the variance in cost per pupil is not constant, but depends on school district size.

Battese and Coelli (1993) adopted and extended the Kumbhakar *et al.* (1991) model of $u_i \sim N(\delta Z, \sigma_u^2)$ in light of Huang and Liu (1994). Then Coelli (1994) developed a computer program called *Frontier 4.1* for the numerical solution of the model. Battese and Coelli (1993) and Coelli and Battese (1996) extended this approach for panel data. Under the assumption that inefficiency effects are stochastic, the panel data model allows a distinction between intertemporal variation in technical efficiencies and technical change over time. Within the two-equation stochastic frontier framework, Huang and Liu (1994) emphasized the notion of non-neutral shifting of the average response function by allowing the interaction between firm-specific variables and the right hand side variables of the frontier function. Their paper suggests that a discovery of non-neutral shifting of the average function in an empirical investigation would further weaken the usefulness of the average response function as an analytical tool. In this case, OLS cannot even indicate the shape of the frontier function.

Therefore, it is an empirical matter to determine whether an OLS model with only deterministic inefficiency, a one-equation stochastic model, or a two-equation stochastic model, is best supported by the data. Theory suggests that the two-equation model may be more promising in analyzing school district cost structure and in deriving aid formula implications.

Basic Questions and Methodological Issues Raised in the Studies on Education Production Process

Hanushek (1979, 1986) has noted that since Coleman *et al.* (1966) outlined "a bewildering array of technical and esoteric issues" and revealed "apparently contradictory results" on the production process of primary and secondary schools in the United States, there have been many economic studies researching the production, efficiency and cost structure of public education. The basic questions addressed in those studies are: What factors do influence students' performance? What are the determinants of educational cost structure? Are the schools operated efficiently? However, the results of these studies are surrounded by considerable controversy, as observed by Hanushek (1987). Researchers often find that the most excruciating part of analysis lies in the methodological issues involved.

Hanushek (1979, 1986), Woodhall (1987a,1987b), Verry (1987), and the Walberg, Cohn and Bray entries in Husen and Postlethwaite (1990) provide a detailed and encyclopedic discussion of the conceptual and empirical issues commonly faced in estimating econometric models of public schools. In terms of model specification and policy focus, an earlier group of cost studies including Riew (1966), Cohn (1968, 1975), and Hough (1981) relied on a quadratic cost function in student numbers and linear in other variables (factors that might influence cost of education), with a specific focus on scale economies. This group of studies recognized the importance of other factors, but only implicitly. Except for instructional cost, other cost factors are not pursued to the extent of implicating policy issues. Jimnez (1986), alluding to the Fox (1981) review, characterized most of the previous cost studies (studies of 1960s and 1970s) as being engaged in *ad hoc* formulation of functional form and specification. He claimed to have specified a flexible (translog), multi-product (primary and secondary school services), quality-adjusted short run cost function based on sound economic criteria--assuming that schools are efficient and minimize cost in the short run. Jimnez used average student performance in standardized test to control for what he called students' socioeconomic backgrounds and innate abilities. However, environmental cost factors (socioeconomic characteristics of communities (SEC)) were not considered explicitly. Gyimah-Brempong and Gyapong (1991) used a canonical regression technique and a Cobb-Douglas production function to investigate the effects of socioeconomic characteristics (SEC) of communities as inputs in the production of high school education in Michigan. They found positive and significant impacts of SEC.

In an earlier study on the fiscal condition of Nebraska school districts, Ratcliffe *et al.* (1990) adopted the methodology of Bradbury *et al.* (1984) and examined the relationship between cost of educational services and environmental cost factors (including socioeconomic characteristics of the communities), controlling for the level of school output (fiscal resources and demand variables). They found five factors (special education students, transportation costs, proportion of elementary and secondary students, economies of scale, and interclass cost differences) which are not controllable by school officials, but do appear to have influence on the cost of public education in Nebraska. The study did not use average teacher salary or test scores as explanatory variables for educational cost. They argued that a test score "inevitably leaves out many of the services provided by a school district." Ratcliffe *et al.* (1990), like Bradbury *et al.* (1984), presumably believed that variation in teacher salary would be reflected in the variation of environmental cost factors. In order to be comprehensive, the study claimed to have controlled for educational output (including school quality) by including variables that influence voters' decisions about school output.

An Alternative Method For Public Education Cost Function Modeling

Frontier Approach to Estimation of Production and Cost Function of Education

In order to examine scale economies in California public school districts, Sengupta and Sfeir (1986) estimated a nonparametric production frontier by linear programming and a parametric "average" production function by standard regression (OLS). Overall economies of scale estimated by a production frontier indicates a higher level of economies of scale for schools close to the frontier than the schools further off from the frontier. An average production function, as it is estimated by standard regression, is not susceptible to the differential scale economies across school size. Thus, Sengupta and Sfeir argued for a frontier function to use in capturing the differential scale effects of small and large schools. In their study, the estimated production frontier appears to have been placed neutrally downward from the average production function except for the input denoting average class size. This raises an important concern. Had the frontier not been a neutral shifting of the average function, the effect of explanatory variables estimated from the average function might not be reliable. This suggests that the importance of estimating the frontier function lies not only in efficiency analysis, but also in the need to understand the effects of individual explanatory variables when the operation of a school district is close to the frontier.

Barrow (1991) estimated statistical one-equation stochastic cost frontier models for local educational authorities in England. While developing the model he referred to Darlington and Cullen (1984) and Levitt and Joice (1987), where the importance of socioeconomic variables had been emphasized. Barrow maintained that "the socioeconomic background variables appear to be more important statistically than variables relating to input quantities such as the pupil-teacher ratio." He used the average cost per pupil in schools as dependent variable, and the number of students as scale factor, performance in "O" level exams as output, and proportions of pupils receiving free meals, from low socioeconomic background, with additional educational needs as socioeconomic variables. He argued that socioeconomic variables could be thought of as "correcting the exam performance variables to give a measure of value added rather than gross output." It is interesting to recall that Jimnez (1986), on the contrary, used test scores to purge out the differential effects of socioeconomic background of students. Barrow's socioeconomic variables appear to have been conceived as environmental factors. To the best of our knowledge, Barrow's piece was the first published article of this type where a stochastic cost frontier was used to assess efficiency of schools. However, he did not elaborate on how the estimated cost frontier of schools could be used to guide policy analysis of fiscal issues so important for the operation of local educational authorities.

Model Specification

In case of school districts, unlike regular manufacturing plants (in technological sense, which usually operate in isolation from the community), there are compelling reasons to search for other factors that influence the cost of public education. In cost functions, disparities in local conditions have implications for spending and are characterized as uneven environmental cost factors in Bradbury *et al.* (1984), as community attributes in Downes and Pogue (1994), or as quasi-inputs in Hughes (1988). This is a unique aspect of the technology involved in producing local educational services and it needs careful recognition in econometric model specifications.

The distinction between a direct cost function and an indirect expenditure function, as described in Downes and Pogue (1994), is a helpful notion to discuss the variables that determine local expenditure. We would argue that when variables are put into a cost function under the umbrella of environmental factors, it implies that the measures of outputs and/or input prices are not complete. Thus, in practice, we get a quasi-cost or quasi-expenditure function. However, there is one good aspect of having an incomplete measure of outputs and/or input prices. It allows us to focus on uneven environmental cost factors and helps to formulate policies to address each cost factor. Therefore, depending on the purpose of the study, availability of data, and empirical testing of the specifications, one should decide whether a quasi-cost or quasi-expenditure function would be appropriate. Given the purpose of the present paper, models of quasi-cost functions for Nebraska school districts have been formulated and estimated.

Conceptual Structure for Cost Models of Nebraska School Districts

Given the situation in Nebraska school districts, it is reasonable to assume that school districts minimize their expenditure per pupil in order to meet ever-increasing budget pressures. Assuming cost minimizing behavior by school districts and modeling inefficiency with random and systematic components, we apply the Battese and Coelli (1993) two-equation model and write the cost frontier as:

$$\log [DPP_i] = \log [C(S_i, p_i, ENF_i)] + v_i + u_i \tag{3a}$$

$$u_i = \delta Z_i + w_i. \tag{3b}$$

Where log $[DPP_i]$ is the natural logarithm of disbursement per pupil, S_i is a vector of educational services, p_i is a vector of input prices, and ENF_i is a vector of environmental cost factors. C(.) is the cost function and the v_i's represent a noise term assumed to be *iid* $\sim N(0, \sigma_v^2)$. Here, the nonnegative inefficiency effects, the u_i's, are assumed to be independently distributed as truncated (at zero) normal distributions with constant variance σ_u^2 and means δZ_i. Means are a linear function of school district specific characteristics (and time, if panel data). Z_i is a column vector of explanatory variables for inefficiency effects (including interaction between variables in the cost function and any other plausible variables; Huang and Liu, (1994)), δ is a row vector of unknown parameters, and w_i follows a truncated normal distribution (truncated at $(-\delta Z_i)$): $w_i \sim N(0, \sigma_u^2)$. The cost efficiency is defined as: Efficiency =

(Actual cost/ Frontier cost). This is computed as the exponential function of ($\delta Z_i + w_i$). The point estimator for cost inefficiency (u_i) is the expected value of $e^{(\delta Z_i + W_i)}$, given ($u_i + v_i$).

Ratcliffe *et al.* (1990), in the case of Nebraska school districts, and Barrow (1991) in case of cost frontier for local educational institutions, are both helpful in identifying particular variables for specification of the cost frontier for Nebraska school districts. Unlike the districts in the California system, school districts in Nebraska have control over cost per pupil. Therefore, disbursement per pupil DPP, measured as current expenditure per pupil, is an appropriate measure of educational costs in Nebraska.

Enrollment and other variables have been considered as outputs (including test scores, and quality adjusting variables), as suggested by Lewis and Chakraborty (1996) and discussed in the *International Encyclopedia* (1990). In the cost specification for Nebraska school districts, average daily membership (ADM) is considered an output and captures the important issue of economies of sale. Graduation rates (GR) in Nebraska school districts appear to be a measure of wastage (of resources) or repetition (of students in class). It indicates a measure of the flow of students in the school districts. Since there are no standardized test scores available for Nebraska school districts, and available graduation rates are just an indication of what proportion of students fulfill the basic requirements to graduate, interpretation of graduation rates as a proxy for measure of "wastage and repetition," as suggested by Loxley (1987), seems to be helpful. In some studies, such as Jimnez (1986), standardized test scores have been used to control for students' socioeconomic backgrounds and abilities. Lewis and Chakraborty (1996) used the graduation rate as a measure of output. Ratcliffe *et al.* (1990) notes several studies that used test scores to adjust for the quality of students. Barrow (1991) and Downes and Pogue (1994) used test scores as measures of output.

As an input price, average salary for full time equivalent teachers (AVGS) is a standard argument in a cost function. However, some empirical studies, such as Ratcliffe *et al.* (1991) and Bradbury *et al.* (1984), have not used any measure of input price. They argued that not putting an input price (such as teacher salary) in the cost function would allow environmental factors to reflect both the direct effect of cost factors on expenditure and an indirect effect via input prices. It may be argued that putting input prices in the cost function would help to isolate the direct effect of the environmental factor on the expenditure. Moreover, it is important to remember that teacher's salary constitutes a significant portion of educational cost. There are studies, however, that include teacher salary and other composite input prices in the educational cost function: Jimnez (1986), Downes and Pogue (1994), and Lewis and Chakraborty (1996).

The proportion of special-need category students (PSP), like students with limited English proficiency (LEP), is an environmental cost factor (ENF). This type of variable has been widely investigated in the literature. For example, Downes and Pogue (1994) examined the effects of LEP on cost per pupil in Arizona elementary and secondary public schools. Ratcliffe *et al.* (1990) found that in case of Nebraska school districts the proportion of special education students was an important cost variable. Understanding the effects of this variable on educational expenditure has potential to provide tools for adjusting school aid formulae. ADM can be also considered as one of the environmental factors, in the sense that economies of scale contribute to the cost side of fiscal disparities, as in Ratcliffe *et al.* (1990).

The Z vector can include any variable that explains the observed cost of inefficiency. An interesting aspect of this set of variables is that it can accommodate interaction between the regular right hand side variables of the cost function and other exogenous variables. Thus, it can help to unravel any non-neutral shifting of the average response function, as described in Huang and Liu (1994). Interaction between educational experience of teachers (EDX) and the size of the school district (ADM) has been hypothesized to be a promising variable for explaining cost inefficiency for Nebraska school districts.

FRONTIER MODEL ESTIMATION FOR NEBRASKA SCHOOL DISTRICTS

Two-Equation Stochastic Cost Frontier Models

The software package, *Frontier 4.1,* described in Coelli (1994), was used in this study to estimate the parameters of the two-equation cost frontier model and the inefficiencies of Nebraska school districts. The crucial empirical question that needs to be settled prior to embarking on the frontier cost analysis is: do we need to go beyond OLS, or is any form of stochastic cost frontier at all required? In the traditional average response function (OLS), school districts are assumed to be fully efficient, i.e., the u_i term is not present in the model. Inefficiency effects incorporated in a two-equation stochastic cost frontier model enables investigation of the causes of inefficiencies. Moreover, the capacity of such a model to accommodate interactive terms facilitates empirical testing of the OLS specification and its ability to reveal the shape of the cost frontier in the presence of inefficiency. When inefficiencies systematically affect costs, improved specification of the cost structure can be obtained using the two-equation model. The two-equation panel data model also facilitates ordering the school districts by their estimated inefficiency in each time period. This is not permitted in the one-equation frontier panel data model, as noted by Battese and Coelli (1992, 1993). The panel model helps us examine the dynamics of relative efficiency changes over time. Thus, the two-equation cost frontier model should provide more reliable estimates of cost structure parameters and inefficiency of the school districts.

Cross Section Models

The model for the 1989-90 and 1991-92 cross sectional data is specified as:

$$LDPP_i = \beta_0 + \beta_1 LADM_i + \beta_2 LADM_i^2 + \beta_3 LGR_i + \beta_4 LAVGS_i + \beta_5 LPSP_i + u_i + v_i \quad (4a)$$

$$u_i = \delta_o + \delta_1 (EDX*LADM)_i + w_i \quad (4b)$$

The names of the variables are as described above, with the initial letter L here indicating natural logarithm. In the case of the 1990-91cross-section model specification, however, an alternative model is used for reasons that will be explained later. Tables 1 through 6 present the results of cross section estimation.

Table 1: Maximum-Likelihood Estimates of Parameters of Stochastic Cost Frontier and Inefficiency Models for Nebraska School Districts in 1989-90 (Cross Section Models)

Variable	Parameter	General Model	Preferred Model	OLS
Stochastic Cost Frontier				
Constant	β_0	1.069	2.077	3.746
		(1.137)	(2.52)	(3.83)
Log (ADM)	β_1	-0.9103	-0.9401	-1.039
		(-16.768)	(-17.75)	(-16.68)
[Log (ADM)]^2	β_2	0.0538	0.0558	0.0625
		(14.143)	(15.04)	(13.88)
Log (GR)	β_3	0.0389	0.0299	0.0697
		(0.998)	(0.7300)	(1.54)
Log (AVGS)	β_4	1.047	0.9588	0.8162
		(11.22)	(11.41)	(8.12)
Log (PSP)	β_5	0.0373	0.0443	0.0541
		(1.742)	(2.09)	(2.45)
Inefficiency Model				
Constant	δ_0	0.8230	0	---
		(2.877)		
EDX * Log (ADM)	δ_1	-0.0206	-0.0245	---
		(-2.243)	(-2.10)	
Variance Parameters	$\sigma^2=\sigma^2_u+\sigma^2_v$	0.0812	0.2002	0.0159
		(3.28)	(2.67)	
	$\gamma=\dfrac{\sigma_u^2}{\sigma_u^2+\sigma_v^2}$	0.9065	0.9680	0
		(30.97)	(83.33)	
Log-Likelihood Function		203.16	202.04	181.07
* LR test of the one-sided error (H_0: γ=0)		44.18	41.94	---
With number of restrictions		3	2	---

Estimated asymptotic t ratios are given in parentheses below the parameter estimates.
Level of significance = 5%,
* Likelihood ratio test (LR).

Table 2: Generalized-Likelihood Ratio Tests of Hypotheses for Nebraska School Districts in 1989-90 (Cross Section Models)

	Hypothesis Testing with Reference to the General Model			
Null Hypotheses	Log-Likelihood	χ^2 Statistic	Critical Value	Decision
$H_0 : \gamma = \delta_0 = \delta_1 = 0$	181.07	44.18	7.82	Reject H_0
$H_0 : \gamma = \delta_0 = 0$	181.46	43.40	5.99	Reject H_0
$H_0 : \delta_0 = 0$	202.04	2.24	3.84	Accept H_0
$H_0 : \delta_1 = 0$	196.12	14.08	3.84	Reject H_0
$H_0 : \delta_0 = \delta_1 = 0$	192.35	21.62	5.99	Reject H_0
(Given Restriction: $\delta_0 = 0$)	**Hypothesis Testing with Reference to the Preferred Model**			
$H_0 : \gamma = \delta_1 = 0$	181.07	41.94	5.99	Reject H_0
$H_0 : \delta_1 = 0$	192.35	19.38	3.84	Reject H_0
$H_0 : \gamma = 0$	181.46	41.16	3.84	Reject H_0

Level of significance = 5%.

Table 3: Maximum-Likelihood Estimates of Parameters of Stochastic Cost Frontier and Inefficiency Models for Nebraska School Districts in 1990-91 (Cross Section Models)

Variable	Parameter	Alternative Model	Preferred Model	OLS
Stochastic Cost Frontier				
Constant	β_0	3.38	3.09	5.87
		(3.18)	(2.90)	(6.01)
Log (ADM)	β_1	-0.8372	-0.9252	-1.017
		(-3.42)	(-16.43)	(-18.20)
[Log (ADM)]^2	β_2	0.0496	0.0549	0.0611
		(3.31)	(14.00)	(14.99)
Log (GR)	β_3	-0.2643	-0.2493	-0.3441
		(-2.45)	(-2.40)	(-3.42)
Log (AVGS)	β_4	0.9225	0.9791	0.7846
		(7.68)	(10.61)	(8.47)
Log (PSP)	β_5	0.0555	0.0560	0.0577
		(2.72)	(2.93)	(3.07)
Inefficiency Model				
Constant	δ_0	1.46	0.6669	---
		(2.00)	(2.47)	
EDX * Log (ADM)	δ_1	---	-0.0162	---
			(-1.65)	
EDX	δ_2	-0.0296	---	---
		(-0.4536)		
Log (ADM)	δ_3	-0.2187	---	---
		(-1.98)		
Variance Parameters	$\sigma^2 = \sigma_u^2 + \sigma_v^2$	0.0357	0.0582	0.0138
		(0.7430)	(1.88)	
	$\gamma = \frac{\sigma_u^2}{\sigma_u^2 + \sigma_v^2}$	0.8049	0.8649	0
		(3.40)	(9.76)	
Log-Likelihood Function		212.37	212.74	200.18
* LR test of the one-sided error (H_0:γ=0)		24.38	25.11	---
With number of restrictions		4	3	---

Estimated asymptotic t ratios are given in parenthesis below the parameter estimates.

Level of significance = 5%.

* Likelihood ratio test (LR).

Table 4: Generalized-Likelihood Ratio Tests of Hypotheses for Nebraska School Districts in 1990-91 (Cross Section Models)

Null Hypotheses	Hypothesis Testing with Reference to the Preferred Model			
	Log-Likelihood	χ^2 Statistic	Critical Value	Decision
$H_0 : \gamma = \delta_0 = \delta_1 = 0$	200.18	25.11	7.82	Reject H_0
$H_0 : \gamma = \delta_0 = 0$	200.92	23.64	5.99	Reject H_0
$H_0 : \delta_0 = \delta_1 = 0$	205.54	14.40	5.99	Reject H_0
$H_0 : \delta_1 = 0$	206.78	11.92	3.84	Reject H_0
$H_0 : \delta_0 = 0$	211.28	2.92	3.84	Accept H_0
	Hypotheses Testing with Reference to the Alternative Model			
$H_0 : \delta_3 = 0$	211.66	1.42	3.84	Accept H_0

Level of significance = 5%.

Table 5: Maximum-Likelihood Estimates of Parameters of Stochastic Cost Frontier and Inefficiency Models for Nebraska School Districts in 1991-92 (Cross Section Models)

Variable	Parameter	General Model	Preferred Model	OLS
Stochastic Cost Frontier				
Constant	β_0	3.856	4.621	6.53
		(3.73)	(4.74)	(6.39)
Log (ADM)	β_1	-0.951	-0.975	-1.049
		(-16.20)	(-18.05)	(-18.94)
$[\text{Log (ADM)}]^2$	β_2	0.0573	0.0590	0.0641
		(14.02)	(15.53)	(16.00)
Log (GR)	β_3	-0.1930	-0.1930	-0.2074
		(-1.759)	(-1.785)	(-1.81)
Logs (AVGS)	β_4	0.8923	0.8248	0.6717
		(9.61)	(9.30)	(7.33)
Log (PSP)	β_5	0.0270	0.0289	0.0404
		(1.29)	(1.394)	(1.949)
Inefficiency Model				
Constant	δ_0	0.5979	0	—
		(2.92)		
EDX * Log (ADM)	δ_1	-0.0156	-0.0177	—
		(-1.75)	(-2.379)	
Variance Parameters	$\sigma^2 = \sigma_u^2 + \sigma_v^2$	0.0560	0.1164	0.01360
		(2.22)	(3.12)	
	$\gamma = \dfrac{\sigma_u^2}{\sigma_u^2 + \sigma_v^2}$	0.8542	0.9344	0
		(13.94)	(37.18)	
Log-Likelihood Function		214.40	212.93	202.99
* LR test of the one-sided error (H_0: γ=0)		22.82	19.88	—
With number of restrictions		3	2	—

Estimated asymptotic t ratios are given in parenthesis below the parameter estimates.

Level of significance = 5%.

*Likelihood ratio test (LR).

Table 6: Generalized-Likelihood Ratio Tests of Hypotheses for Nebraska School Districts in 1991-92 (Cross Section Models)

	Hypothesis Testing with Reference to the General Model			
Null Hypotheses	Log-Likelihood	χ^2 Statistic	Critical Value	Decision
$H_0 : \gamma = \delta_0 = \delta_1 = 0$	202.99	22.82	7.82	Reject H_0
$H_0 : \gamma = \delta_0 = 0$	203.02	22.76	5.99	Reject H_0
$H_0 : \delta_0 = 0$	212.93	2.94	3.84	Accept H_0
(Given Restriction: $\delta_0 = 0$)	**Hypotheses Testing With Reference to the Preferred Model**			
$H_0 : \delta_1 = 0$	205.84	14.18	3.84	Reject H_0

Level of significance = 5%.

A likelihood ratio (LR) test of the one-sided error in conjunction with the high value of γ indicates that OLS estimation is not an adequate representation of the cost structure for the Nebraska school districts observed over the three years. An LR test of the hypothesis that there is no systematic component in the inefficiency distribution, H_0: $\delta_0 = \delta_1 = 0$, is rejected. An LR test for the presence of a stochastic element of inefficiency was also conducted. In order to do so, δ_o was set equal to zero ($\delta_o = 0$) and the interactive variable (EDX*LADM) was relocated from the inefficiency model to the cost function. Then the OLS regression of the cost function was run. The test statistic rejects the null hypothesis H_o: $\gamma = \delta_0 = 0$, and supports the existence of a stochastic element of inefficiency. The t ratio for β_6 (EDX*LADM) in the cost function (not reported in the table) is very low (with the asymptotic t = -0.4649 insignificant) indicating that inefficiency is stochastic. Thus, inefficiency consisting of systematic and stochastic components does exist (H_0: $\gamma = \delta_0 = \delta_1 = 0$, H_o: $\delta_o = \delta_1 = 0$, H_o: $\gamma = \delta_o = 0$, and H_o: $\gamma = \delta_1 = 0$ are all rejected) in Nebraska school districts.

Except for coefficient β_3, the estimated β coefficients have expected signs and are reasonably significant judging by the asymptotic t ratio. Our estimated negative β_1 and positive β_2 coefficients reveal a concave cost function with respect to scale (ADM). Unlike the other two years, hypothesis testing for the intercept term (δ_0) in the inefficiency model, H_o: $\delta_o = 0$, is rejected in 1990-91. In the inefficiency model it appears that the interactive variable (EDX*LADM) is significant by the asymptotic t ratio, and has the expected negative sign. The negative sign implies that the scale efficiency is dominant over the efficiency changes associated with the relative change in educational experience of teachers. The hypothesis that the interaction between educational experience of teachers and scale of operation does not explain inefficiency (H_0: $\delta_1 = 0$), is also rejected by the likelihood ratio test. Thus, the inclusion of EXS (EDX*LADM) term in the inefficiency model is supported by our data. Therefore, as expected, average educational experience of teachers and scale of operation in an interactive form, (EDX*LADM) helps explain the observed inefficiencies of the schools districts.

The evidence indicated by the LR test (and also by the asymptotic t ratio) that an interactive variable (EXS) can explain inefficiency, suggests a non-neutral shifting of the cost frontier with respect to educational experience of teachers and scale of operation, as described in Huang and Liu (1994). Thus, we have confirmation that the cost function estimated by OLS cannot even indicate the shape of the cost frontier for Nebraska school districts. The stochastic cost frontier with an explicit model of inefficiency effects emerges as a superior model.

Panel Data Model

Panel data allows incorporation of a time dimension in the cost frontier model. In terms of model structure, a two-equation panel data model is an extension of the two-equation cross section model, as described in Battese and Coelli (1993), with the inclusion of the time variable (YR) in the cost function as well as in the inefficiency model. The panel model estimated is:

$$LDPP_{it} = \beta_0 + \beta_1 LADM_{it} + \beta_2 LADM_{it}^2 + \beta_3 LGR_{it} + \beta_4 LAVGS_{it} + \beta_5 LPSP_{it} + \beta_6 YR_{it} + u_{it} + v_{it} \quad (5a)$$

$$u_{it} = \delta_o + \delta_1 LEDX_{it} + \delta_2 LADM_{it} + \delta_3 YR_{it} + w_{it},\ t = 1,2,\&3 \text{ years.} \quad (5b)$$

Results are presented in Tables 7 and 8. With panel data, the hypothesis, H_o: $\gamma = 0$ is overwhelmingly rejected. Thus, as in the cross section models, the panel data model does not suggest OLS estimation of the cost function to be appropriate for the data. Testing for stochastic inefficiency effects indicates that the effects are random (H_o: $\gamma = \delta_0 = \delta_2 = \delta_3 = 0$, is rejected). As inefficiency exists, and is stochastic in nature, the inclusion of a time variable both in the cost frontier function and the inefficiency effects model is permissible.

Estimation results of the model indicate that with the exception of LGR and YR variables in the cost frontier function, all the β coefficients are significant judging by the asymptotic t ratios. Signs for β_1 through β_5, with the exception of that of β_3, are consistent with those of the cross section models. The absolute value of the estimated coefficient for the variable graduation rate is similar to that of the 1989-90 cross section model. The value of the coefficient for the average teacher salary variable is estimated to be very close to that of the 1991-92 cross section model. The intercept β_o in the panel data model is estimated to be in the vicinity of the 1990-91 and 1991-92 estimates, but higher than that of the 1989-90 cross section model. Estimated values of the other β coefficients are similar to those of the cross section models.

The positive coefficient for the year variable (β_6) in the cost frontier function implies that the cost frontiers moved up over time. Since all the input prices are not held constant in the model, a positive β_6 might also reflect increasing input prices. Thus, it is consistent with the general concern that there is an increasing trend of the cost of education in Nebraska school districts. It is possible that the time variable (YR) might also pick up other effects, such as reforms in the funding and distribution of state aid to school districts in Nebraska.

In the efficiency model (preferred model), the LEDX variable appears to be highly significant, but the YR and LADM variables are not. As expected, signs of the explanatory variables in the inefficiency model are negative. A negative coefficient for the time (YR) variable in the inefficiency model indicates that individual school districts are catching up with their corresponding frontier costs. This is certainly a desirable outcome. However, a regressive technological change indicated by the positive coefficient of the time variable (YR) in the cost frontier, should be a serious concern for policy makers. Teachers' educational experience and larger scale school operation appear to have positive effects on the cost efficiency of school districts. Scale efficiency was also observed in the case of 1990-91 cross section data. Hypothesis tests for β_6 (YR) = 0 and δ_3 (YR) = 0 are both rejected, and δ_1 (LEDX) = 0, is rejected too, while the hypothesis H_o: δ_o = 0 is accepted. Results of hypotheses testing are presented in Table 8.

Table 7: Maximum-Likelihood Estimates of Parameters of Stochastic Cost Frontier and Inefficiency Models for Nebraska School Districts in 1989-90 Through 1991-92 (Panel Data Models)

Variable	Parameter	General Model	Preferred Model	OLS
Stochastic Cost Frontier				
Constant	β_0	3.64	3.77	5.13
		(6.51)	(6.47	(4.18)
Log (ADM)	β_1	-1.004	-0.9853	-1.0164
		(-26.08)	(-26.16)	(-13.29)
[Log (ADM)]^2	β_2	0.0603	0.0593	0.0621
		(22.06)	(22.03)	(11.20)
Log (GR)	β_3	-0.0159	-0.0246	0.0215
		(-0.3674)	(-0.5814)	(0.255)
Logs (AVGS)	β_4	0.8403	0.8237	0.6853
		(14.54)	(13.47)	(5.47)
Log (PSP)	β_5	0.0452	0.0448	0.0397
		(3.02)	(2.98)	(1.46)
YR	β_6	0.0128	0.0105	-0.0081
		(1.84)	(1.68)	(-0.6785)
Inefficiency Model				
Constant	δ_0	-3.28	0	—
		(-2.45)		
Log (EDX)	δ_1	-0.2287	-1.454	—
		(-0.5645)	(-8.48)	
Log (ADM)	δ_2	0.01233	-0.0414	—
		(0.4430)	(-0.7595)	
YR	δ_3	-0.3909	-0.2528	—
		(-8.64)	(-1.85)	
Variance Parameters	$\sigma^2_u=\sigma^2_u+\sigma^2_v$	0.3873	0.4311	0.0761
		(16.23)	(19.41)	
	$\gamma = \frac{\sigma_u^2}{\sigma_u^2+\sigma_v^2}$	0.9769	0.9807	0
		(567.06)	(482.95)	
Log-Likelihood Function		593.38	593.13	-104.37
* LR test of the one-sided		1395.51	1395.03	—
error (H_0: γ=0)		Rest=5	Rest=4	—
Number of iterations		51	100	

Estimated asymptotic t ratios are given in parenthesis below the parameter estimates.
Level of significance = 5%.
* Likelihood ratio test (LR).

Table 8: Generalized-Likelihood Ratio Tests of Hypotheses for Nebraska School Districts in 1989-90 to 1991-92 (Panel Data Models)

Null Hypotheses	Hypothesis Testing with Reference to the General Model			
	Log-Likelihood Value	χ^2 Statistic	Critical Value	Decision
$H_o : \gamma = \delta_0 = \delta_1 = \delta_2 = \delta_3 =$ o	-104.37	1395.51	11.07	Reject Ho
$H_o : \delta_0 = 0$	593.13	0.50	3.84	Accept H_o
$H_o : \gamma = \delta_0 = \delta_2 = \delta_3 = 0$	-102.63	1392.02	9.49	Reject H_o
(Given Restriction: $\delta_0 = 0$)	**Hypotheses Testing with Reference to the Preferred Model**			
$H_o : \delta_3 = 0$	591.01	4.24	3.84	Reject Ho
$H_o : \beta_6 = 0$	590.54	5.18	3.84	Reject H_o
$H_o : \delta_1 = 0$	566.64	52.98	3.84	Reject H_o
$H_o : \delta_2 = 0$	591.91	2.44	3.84	Accept H_o

Level of significance = 5%.

It is interesting to note that contrary to the cross section models, the panel data model does not support the idea that the multiplicative interaction between LADM and EDX (or LEDX) would explain the inefficiency effects. In the model for explaining inefficiency we have LEDX, LADM, and YR variables. No interaction between scale of operation and other variables has been accommodated in an explicit way. Hypothesis testing for the interaction term, ((EDX*LADM) or (LEDX*LADM)), does not support their inclusion in the model. Interactive terms like, EDX*LADM or LEDX*LADM, do not appear to be good explanatory variables for the inefficiency model. However, in the panel model we can see that the interaction between educational experience of teachers (EDX) and scale of operation (ADM) has been taken into account in an implicit way. The form of interaction (log(EDX *ADM) = log EDX + log ADM = LEDX + LADM) is different than that in the cross section models. Thus, the panel data model also indicates that the inefficiency effects cause a non-neutral shifting of the cost frontier.

Since the panel data are for three years only, it is not surprising that the educational experience of teachers would explain the larger part of the inefficiency in school operation than the time variable (YR) does. However, inclusion of the time variable in the inefficiency model does provide insights into the dynamics of the relative change in the efficiencies of the school districts over time.

USE OF COST FRONTIER ANALYSIS

Rankings of School Districts by Efficiency Estimates

Based on the preferred cross section model for each of the three years, cost efficiency of each of the 274 Nebraska school districts was estimated. School districts were arranged in a descending order of their estimated inefficiency (higher rank indicates a higher level of efficiency). We observe that school districts rated most inefficient at one point of time do not always remain so during the three years of this study. For example, Santee Public Schools was the most inefficient school district in 1989-90, but in 1990-91 it improved its position to the fifth rank and maintained that ranking through 1991-92. Some school districts have exhibited tremendous improvement in terms of cost efficiency. Loup County Public Schools was in fifth position in 1989-90, and then improved to eighteenth position in 1990-91, and then improved further to the sixtieth position in 1991-92. We find that from 65 to 82 percent of Nebraska school districts fall in the range of 10 percent or less inefficiency (65.69 percent in 1989-90, 78.46 percent in 1990-91, 81.28 percent in 1991-92). The number of schools with inefficiency of more than 10 percent declined over the years of our study (34.31 percent, 21.54 percent, and 18.72 percent). In addition, the percentage of districts with more than 15 percent inefficiency declined by about 50 percent over the three year period (17.53 percent, 10.60 percent and 8.51 percent).

Improvement over time in the cost efficiency of the school districts is clearly evident. The number of districts with more than 10 percent inefficiency diminished over the years. For the years 1989-90 and 1991-92, the mode of the distribution was not in the most efficient range (1.05). This observation provides *ex post* evidence supporting our assumption of a general truncated distribution for inefficiencies. Here, it is important to note that the built-in distributional assumption of the two-equation model conforms to the observed empirical results. However, this is not evident in the case of the 1990-91 efficiency distribution.

Efficiencies of the 274 school districts were also estimated using the two-equation panel data model and arranged in a descending order. Estimates of inefficiency by the panel data model appeared to be higher than those estimated by the cross section models. In the inefficiency range of beyond 10 percent, there were 33.59 percent, 27.65 percent, and 24.83 percent school districts in 1989-90,1990-91 and 1991-92 respectively. Evidently, there has been a trend of improvement in terms of cost efficiency of school districts. In fact, this is consistent with the negative coefficient of the time (YR) variable appeared in the inefficiency effect model of the cost frontier. This trend was also noticed with the pooled cost efficiencies estimated by the three cross section models. Thus, the cost frontier estimation reveals the dynamics of change in school efficiencies. Spearman rank correlation coefficients presented in Table 9 indicates a close association between the cross section and panel data correlations for a given year. However, a less clear association between the rankings by either model is observed when there is more time difference.

Table 9: Spearman Rank Correlation Matrix for Rankings of Nebraska School Districts by Cost Efficiency*

	Cross-section Ranking 1989	Cross-section Ranking 1990	Cross-section Ranking 1991	Pooled Ranking 1989	Pooled Ranking 1990	Pooled Ranking 1991
Cross-section Ranking 1989	1.0000					
Cross-section Ranking 1990	0.81394	1.0000				
Cross-section Ranking 1991	0.76670	0.81581	1.0000			
Pooled Ranking 1989	0.96345	0.72143	0.74529	1.0000		
Pooled Ranking 1990	0.81875	0.82410	0.81834	0.86010	1.0000	
Pooled Ranking 1991	0.72194	0.70241	0.95272	0.75905	0.84389	1.0000

* The null hypothesis that there is no association between rankings is rejected.

Aid Formula Implications for Nebraska School Districts

Bradbury *et al.* (1984) calculated the cost index for each of the local jurisdictions in their Massachusetts study. In order to calculate the cost index, their method was to predict "what each community would have spent if it had average resources, average demand and average population change, but retained its own values for the cost variables." Then the predicted expenditures were divided by the mean per capita expenditure for all 351 cities and towns in Massachusetts. An index value above one indicated extra cost incurred for adverse environmental cost factors specific to that community. It is obvious in this case, however, that the cost index calculated by Bradbury *et al.* (1984) is based on an average community.

The cost frontier approach can help reduce fiscal disparities in two ways. One way is to adjust the cost index calculated for a local jurisdiction by its efficiency estimates. For example, as indicated by Bradbury *et al.* (1984), in Boston there was 40 percent more expenditure per person compared to a community with average characteristics. Now, if it is known that the cost efficiency index for Boston municipal services is, say, 1.3, then it is fair to suggest that the intergovernmental aid associated with Boston's cost index of 1.4 must be scaled down by its cost inefficiency of 30 percent.

Ratcliffe *et al.* (1990) combined the five cost factors, "that are largely outside the control of school officials and that influence the cost of public education in Nebraska" into a single cost index for each school district in the state. As explained above, the cost indices for Nebraska school districts can now be adjusted using the estimated cost efficiencies and may then be used in the school aid formula used for offsetting the fiscal disparities among Nebraska school districts. This adjustment would help impose financial and operational discipline on the school districts.

The other way in which the efficiency estimates can be used to reduce fiscal disparities is to incorporate the efficiency factor directly into the intergovernmental aid formula. This approach is obviously not dependent on an average school district concept. It assumes that we can calculate the most efficient cost level for the operation of a particular school district on the basis of that district's inefficiency quotient. The most efficient cost level calculated on the basis of a stochastic cost frontier is unique for a particular school district. Thus, there is no need to compare with an average school district. An additional advantage is that it allows considering all of the factors in their unique value for that school district. Thus, the judgmental issue as to which factors to include as the environmental cost factors and which to retain at their average value, as in Bradbury *et al.* (1984) footnote 10, can be avoided.

The results of the computation presented below in Table 10 illustrate the above idea. The intergovernmental aid formula can make an attempt to offset the fiscal disparity by focusing on the frontier cost rather than on actual cost. Calculation of frontier cost has taken into account the systematic adverse factors. Moreover, it has accounted for any random unfavorable or favorable conditions. It is often argued that in order to avoid encouraging inefficiency intergovernmental aid should not compensate for controllable factors. By the same token, intergovernmental aid should not compensate for inefficient operation of school districts. As we know, for example, the Hayes Center public school district spends an extra $1320.35/pupil due to inefficient operation. This knowledge could help to save a quarter of a million dollars per year ($236,871/year) in intergovernmental aid. Similar calculations show inefficiency costs of $5.56 million/year for the Omaha public schools and $4.31 million/year for the Lincoln public schools. For Kearney and Chadron public schools the cost of inefficiency amounts to $0.43 million and $0.15 million per year respectively.

Table 10: Effect of Incorporating Efficiency Factor Directly into the School Aid Formula

Hayes Center Public Schools in 1989-90	
Cost Efficiency	1.244 (based on cross section model)
Actual Cost	\$6731.62/pupil = $f(y_i, p_i, ENF_i, \beta)\exp(v_i + u_i)$
Frontier Cost	\$5411.27/pupil = $f(y_i, p_i, ENF_i, \beta)\exp(v_i)$
Cost of Inefficiency	\$1320.35/pupil

All costs are in current $ of 1989-90.

Splitting the composite error term into its constituent pieces reveals information about the random favorable and unfavorable condition in which school districts operate. This information has obvious bearing on the designing of state aid formulae for school districts. The following will explain the procedure of estimating the dollar value of the random favorable or unfavorable condition. The term $f(y_i, p_i, ENF_i, \beta)$ can be obtained by inserting the actual value of the arguments (y_i, p_i, ENF_i) in the estimated regression function. Thus, exp (v_i) can be calculated, from which the cost or benefit for the unfavorable or favorable condition respectively can be estimated. As examples, the results of this calculation for selected Nebraska school districts are presented in Table 11. Such information for each school district can be utilized for adjusting the school aid formula, which would help minimize the state aid cost. Moreover, this would help modify the approach presently taken to mitigate the fiscal disparities among Nebraska school districts.

Table 11: Sample Calculation Illustrating the Usefulness of Splitting the Composite Error Term (Cross Section Data 1989-90)

	Omaha	**Lincoln**	**Kearney**	**Ainsworth**	**Kimball**	**Falls City**
Actual Cost	4631.79	4478.13	3335.21	4008.55	5239.50	4045.08
Efficiency Factor	1.030	1.037	1.031	1.060	1.139	1.061
Stochastic Frontier Cost	4492.95	4317.10	3233.17	3781.29	4596.45	3811.79
$f(y_i, p_I, ENF_i, \beta)$	4778.88	4417.82	3446.13	3627.93	4197.25	3756.94
Cost of Inefficiency	138.84	161.03	102.04	227.26	643.05	233.29
Benefit of Favorable Conditions	285.93	100.72	212.96	—	—	—
Cost of Unfavorable Conditions	—	—	—	153.36	339.20	54.85

All costs and benefits per pupil are in current $ of 1989-90.

SUMMARY AND CONCLUSIONS

In this paper, we have proposed the use of a two-equation stochastic frontier model for the estimation of school district cost and have estimated such models using both cross section and panel data for Nebraska school districts. Our results indicate that stochastic frontier models can contribute a great deal of insight regarding school district cost and sources of inefficiency. First, the usual OLS method of estimation is clearly rejected with a stochastic frontier model being clearly superior. Based on both our cross section and panel data estimations, there are scale economies apparent in school district cost. The cost frontier drops with the increase of school district membership and is concave in shape. Furthermore, teachers' educational experience appears to exert a positive effect on cost efficiency of school districts. A large part of the estimated inefficiency across school districts is explained by differences in teacher experience. In the cross section models, the interaction between district membership and teacher experience helps explain the observed inefficiencies of the school districts and suggests a non-neutral shift of the cost frontier. The panel data models also indicate that the inefficiency effects cause a non-neutral shifting of school district cost frontiers. However, the form of interaction is different in the panel data models than that in the cross section models. Teacher educational experience and larger scale both have positive effects on the cost effectiveness of Nebraska school districts.

Estimated sources of inefficiency are then very useful in helping to determine district need for the purpose of computing state aid. We are able to construct indices of school district efficiency based on our models. We can use the models to estimate the cost frontier for districts, reflecting the least cost attainable, given the experience of districts in the sample. Based on that computation, we can then compute an adjusted measure of need for the purpose of computing state aid. Rather than defining need on the basis of average cost, as would be the case in using a conventional regression model, we can define need with reference to the cost frontier, taking into account favorable and unfavorable conditions in school districts. Such an application clearly demonstrates the very useful potential of these methods.

APPENDIX: THE DATA SET

Description of the Data

The period 1989-90 through 1991-92 was chosen as the time frame for the study. There were 274 K-12 school districts in operation during the time period. For these school districts, a data set containing the following variables was constructed: DPP, ADM, GR, AVGS, SP, and EDX. There were 280, 277, and 277 K-12 school districts in Nebraska in 1989-90, 1990-91, and 1991-92 respectively. Thus, the data set includes nearly all of the K-12 school districts in each of three years.

Summary statistics for the data set are presented in Tables A.1, A.2, and A.3. Disbursement per pupil (DPP) includes the following: disbursements for administration, instruction, principal, operation, maintenance, and transportation. Average daily membership (ADM) is a measure of average attendance of students in a school district. Graduation rate (GR) is based on the number of graduates out of the number of seniors in a given year.

Teachers' average salary (AVGS) statistics were calculated for teachers who met the following criteria: teach in public schools, hold a contract, teach in only one district, and have at least 170 contract days. The measure of special education students (SP) in a year for a school district was defined as the ratio of total disabled students to total enrollment in that year. Total disabled students include: students with behavioral disorder (BD), deaf-blindness (DB), hearing impairments (HI), mental handicap (MH), multiple impairments (MI), orthopedic impairments (OI), other health impairments (OHI), specific learning disabilities (SLD), speech-language impairments (SLI), and visual impairments (VI). Average educational experience of teachers (EDX) is a proxy of teaching skill.

Table A.1. Summary Statistics for Nebraska School Districts (1989-90)

Variable	Number of Districts	Mean	Standard Deviation	Minimum	Maximum
Disbursement per pupil ($)	274	4,975.90	1,214.60	3,091.40	11,208
Average daily membership (number of students)	274	901.68	3,166.70	70.46	40,056
Graduation Rate (%)	274	92.66	12.87	35.71	100
Average salary per full-time equivalent teacher ($)	274	22,991	2,594.80	16867	32,810
Proportion of special-need category students (Ratio)	274	0.11099	$3.74^{*}10^{-2}$	$3.00^{*}10^{-2}$	0.25
Valuation per resident student ($)	274	$0.22781^{*}10^{6}$	98,902	8242	$5.95^{*}10^{5}$
Average educational experience of teachers (Year)	274	13.538	2.763	5.70	22.50

Table A.2. Summary Statistics for Nebraska School Districts (1990-91)

Variable	Number of Districts	Mean	Standard Deviation	Minimum	Maximum
Disbursement per pupil ($)	274	5,205.60	1,259.10	3,434.70	10,219
Average daily membership (number of students)	274	9,14.92	3,224.70	60.68	40,678
Graduation Rate (%)	274	96.053	6.027	50	100
Average salary per full-time equivalent teacher ($)	274	23,857	2,655.70	18,371	34,303
Proportion of special-need category students (Ratio)	274	0.11712	$4.54^{*}10^{-2}$	$2.00^{*}10^{-2}$	0.32
Valuation per resident student ($)	274	$0.24441^{*}10^{6}$	$1.07^{*}10^{5}$	10,968	$5.74^{*}10^{5}$
Average educational experience of teachers (Year)	274	13.832	2.595	6.20	20.10

Table A.3. Summary Statistics for Nebraska School Districts (1991-92)

Variable	Number of Districts	Mean	Standard Deviation	Minimum	Maximum
Disbursement per pupil ($)	274	5,401.20	1,338.60	3,607.70	12,649
Average daily membership (number of students)	274	9,34.80	3,291.20	56.60	41,314
Graduation Rate (%)	274	95.99	5.631	66.67	100
Average salary per full-time equivalent teacher ($)	274	24,644	2,736.80	17,997	35,109
Proportion of special-need category students (Ratio).	274	0.11748	$5.06^{*}10^{-2}$	$3.00^{*}10^{-2}$	0.68
Valuation per resident student ($)	274	$0.24830^{*}10^{6}$	$1.13^{*}10^{5}$	9,049	$7.75^{*}10^{5}$
Average educational experience of teachers (Year).	274	14.062	2.717	3.0	21.20

Source: Nebraska Department of Education.

REFERENCES

Afriat, S.N. 1972. Efficiency Estimation of Production Functions, *International Economic Review*, Vol. 13, No. 3, (October).

Barrow, M.M. 1991. Measuring Local Education Authority Performance: A Frontier Approach, *Economics of Education Review*, Vol. 10, No. 1, p. 19-27.

Battese, G.E. 1992. Frontier Production Functions and Technical Efficiency: A Survey of Empirical Applications in Agricultural Economics, *Agricultural Economics*, Vol. 7, p. 185-208.

Battese, G.E. and T.J. Coelli. 1992. Frontier Production Functions, Technical Efficiency and Panel Data: With Application to Paddy Farmers in India, *The Journal of Productivity Analysis*, Vol. 3, p. 153-169.

Battese, G.E. and T.J. Coelli. 1993. A Stochastic Frontier Production Function Incorporating a Model for Technical Inefficiency Effects, Working Papers in Econometrics and Applied Statistics, No. 69, Department of Econometrics, University of New England, Armidale, pp. 22.

Bradbury, et al. 1984. State Aid to Offset Fiscal Disparities Across Communities, *National Tax Journal*, Vol. 37, (June).

Chakraborty, et al. 1996. Measurement of Technical Efficiency in Public Education: A Stochastic Frontier Production Function Approach, *Economic Research Institute Study Paper*, ERI #96-37, Department of Economics, Utah State University, Logan, UT 84322-3530.

Coelli, T.J. 1994. A Guide to Frontier Version 4.1: A Computer Program for Stochastic Frontier Production and Cost Function Estimation. (October) Draft.

_____ . 1995. Recent Developments in Frontier Modeling and Efficiency Measurement, *Australian Journal of Agricultural Economics*, Vol. 39, No. 3.

Coelli, T.J. and G. Battese. 1996. Identification of Factors Which Influence the Technical Inefficiency of Indian Farmers, *Australian Journal of Agricultural Economics*, Vol. 40, No. 2, (August).

Cohn, E. 1968. Economics of Scale in Iowa High School Operations, *Journal of Human Resources*, Vol. 3, (Fall).

_____ . 1975. *The Economics of Education,* Ballinger, Cambridge, Massachusetts.

Coleman, J.S., et al. 1966. *Equality of Educational Opportunity: Summary Report*, U.S. Government Printing Office, Washington, D.C.

Darlington, J.K. and B.D. Cullen. 1984. Pilot Study of School Examination Performance and Associated Factors, Government Economic Service Working Paper No. 75, London: Department of Education and Science.

Downes, T.A. and T.F. Pogue. 1994. Adjusting School-Aid Formulas for the Higher Cost of Educating Disadvantaged Students, *National Tax Journal*, Vol. 47, (March).

Farrell, M.J. 1957. The Measurement of Productive Efficiency, *Journal of Royal Statistical Society*, Series A, Vol. 120, No. 3.

Fox, W. 1981. Reviewing Economies of Size in Education, *Journal of Education Finance,* Vol. 6.

Gyimah-Brempong, K. and A.O. Gyapong. 1991. Characteristics of Education Production Functions: An Application of Canonical Regression Analysis, *Economics of Education Review*, Vol. 10, No. 1.

Hanushek, E.A. 1979. Conceptual and Empirical Issues in the Estimation of Educational Production Functions, *The Journal of Human Resources*, Vol. 14, No. 3.

_____ . 1986. The Economics of Schooling: Production and Efficiency in the Public Schools, *Journal of Economic Literature*, Vol. 24, (September).

_____ . 1987. Educational Production Functions, *Economics of Education: Research and Studies*, George Psacharopoulos, ed., Oxford; New York: Pergamon Press.

Hough, J.R. 1981. A Study of School Costs: National Foundation for Educational Research, Nelson, Slough.

Huang, C.J. and J. Liu. 1994. Estimation of a Non-Neutral Stochastic Frontier Production Function, *The Journal of Productivity Analysis*, Vol. 3.

Hughes, Michael D. 1988. A Stochastic Frontier Cost Function for Residential Child Care Provision, *Journal of Applied Econometrics*, Vol. 3.

Husen, Torsten, and T. Neville Postlethwaite, editors. 1990. *The International Encyclopedia of Education: Research and Studies, Supplementary Volume 2.* Pergamon Press, Oxford.

Jimnez, E. 1986. The Structure of Educational Costs: Multiproduct Cost Functions for Primary and Secondary Schools in Latin America, *Economics of Education Review*, Vol. 5, No. 1.

Klitgaard, R.E. and G.R. Hall. 1975. Are There Unusually Effective Schools? *Journal of Human Resources*, Vol. 10.

Kumbhakar, et al. 1991. A Generalized Production Frontier Approach for Estimating Determinants of Inefficiency in U.S. Dairy Farms, *Journal of Business and Economic Statistics*, Vol. 9.

Levin, H.M. 1976. Concepts of Economic Efficiency and Educational Production, in J.T. Froomkin, D.T. Jamison, and R. Radner (eds.), *Education as an Industry*. Ballinger Press, Cambridge, MA.

Levit, M. and M. A. S. Joyce. 1987. *The Growth and Efficiency of Public Spending,* Cambridge University Press.

Lewis, W.C. and K. Chakraborty. 1996. Scale Economies in Public Education, *Journal of Regional Analysis and Policy*, Vol. 26, No. 1.

Loxley, W. 1987. Wastage in Education, *Economics of Education: Research and Studies*, George Psacharopoulos, ed., Oxford; New York: Pergamon Press.

McCarty, T.A. and S. Yaiswarng. 1993. Technical Efficiency in New Jersey School, Chapter 10 in Fried, *et al.* (eds), *The Measurement of Production Efficiency: Techniques and Applications*. New York: Oxford University Press.

Nebraska Department of Education (NDE), Office of School Finance. Valuation, Levy, Spending, Aid Data for 1988-89 through 1991-92, including only K-12 Districts that Existed all Four Years.

Nebraska Department of Education (NDE), (1989-92). Salary Statistics for Public District Personnel Who Serve Exclusively as Teachers.

_____ . (1989-92). Special Education Office. Nebraska Special Education Statistical Report.

_____ . (1989-90 to 1991-92). Data on Cost, Average Daily Membership and Graduation Rate.

Nebraska School Finance Review Committee, Annual Report, March 1, 1992.

Nebraska School Finance Review Commission. 1990. Funding Nebraska's Schools: Toward a More Rational and Equitable School Finance System for the 1990's. Final report to the Nebraska State Legislature, January 1, 1990.

Ratcliffe, K., *et al.* 1990. The Fiscal Condition of School Districts in Nebraska: Is Small Beautiful? *Economics of Education Review*, Vol. 9, No. 1.

Reifschneider, D. and R. Stevenson. 1991. Systematic Departure from the Frontier: A Framework for the Analysis of Firm Inefficiency, *International Economic Review*, Vol. 32, No. 3, (August).

Riew, J. 1966. Economies of Scale in High School Operations, *Review of Economics and Statistics*, Vol. 48, No. 8, (August).

Schmidt, P. 1985-86. Frontier Production Function. *Econometric Reviews*, Vol. 4, No. 2, p. 289-328.

Schmidt, P. and C.A.K. Lovell. 1979. Estimating Technical and Allocative Inefficiency Relative to Stochastic Production and Cost Frontiers, *Journal of Econometrics*, Vol. 9, p. 343-366.

Sengupta, J.K. and R.E. Sfeir. 1986. Production Frontier Estimates of Scale in Public School in California, *Economics of Education Review*, Vol. 5, No. 3.

Verry, D.W. 1987. Educational Cost Functions, *Economics of Education: Research and Studies*, George Psacharopoulos, ed., Oxford; New York: Pergamon Press.

Woodhall, M . 1987a. Cost Analysis in Education, *Economics of Education: Research and Studies*, George Psacharopoulos, ed., Oxford; New York: Pergamon Press.

_____ . 1987b. Economics of Education: A Review, *Economics of Education: Research and Studies*, George Psacharopoulos, ed., Oxford; New York: Pergamon Press.

Wyckoff, J.H. and J. Lavinge. 1991. The Relative Efficiency of Public Elementary Schools in New York. *Working Paper*, State University of New York, Albany.

In: Perspectives on International, State and Local Economics
Editor: Gerald V. Liu, pp. 141-158
ISBN 1-60021-099-6

Chapter 5

PUBLIC SERVICES EFFICIENCY PROVISION IN ITALIAN REGIONS: A NON-PARAMETRIC ANALYSIS

António Afonso[1] and Carla Scaglioni

ISEG/UTL - Technical University of Lisbon, Department of Economics, and CISEP – Research Centre on the Portuguese Economy, R. Miguel Lúpi 20, 1249-078 Lisbon, Portugal

University of Rome "Roma Tre" and CIFREL – Centro Interuniversitario di Finanza Regionale e Locale – Università Cattolica di Milano, Italy

ABSTRACT

We measure the performance of public spending in Italian regions regarding the provision of public services, by constructing a so-called total regional performance indicator for strategic sectors such as general administration, energy, water and sewage, solid waste, and transports for 2001. This composite indicator is then the output measure selected to assess expenditure efficiency for the Italian regions, using the non-parametric DEA approach. The computation of efficiency scores allows to rank the regions and to detect some room for improvement in terms of efficiency gains at the regional level.

Keywords: technical efficiency, DEA, regional expenditure, Italy

1 – INTRODUCTION

Some available studies assess the performance and efficiency of public sector spending, namely in terms of international comparisons. For instance, Fakin and Crombrugghe (1997) and Afonso, Schuknecht and Tanzi (2003) assess public expenditure in the OECD, Clements (2002) analysis education spending in Europe, Gupta and Verhoeven (2001) addresses education and health in Africa, while St. Aubyn (2003) and Afonso and St. Aubyn (2004) study health and education expenditure efficiency in the OECD. Nevertheless, the literature on the efficiency of local government is rather scarce. De Borger and Kerstens (1996) apply non-parametric analysis to public spending efficiency in Belgian municipalities, while Afonso e Fernandes (2003) also use a non-parametric approach for municipalities in the region of Lisbon, and Balassone, Francese and Giordano (2002) review non-parametric applications to some public services in Italy.

The purpose of this paper is to assess the efficiency of publicly provided private services at the regional level in Italy. We measure the performance of Italian regions regarding the provision of public services by constructing a so-called total regional performance indicator for strategic sectors such as general administration, energy, water and sewage, solid waste, transports. Using such composite indicator as an output measure, we then use a non-parametric methodology, Data Envelopment Analysis (DEA), to estimate efficiency scores for public spending in the 20 Italian Regions in 2001. By means of frontier analysis we are able to identify regions that might qualify as "performing well" from those were some improvement might increase their efficiency. To our knowledge, this is a first effort of checking efficiency and productivity in Italian Regions using non-parametric analysis. Moreover, the relationship between citizens and policy makers as far as the demand for efficient public services is concerned will also be discussed.

The paper is organised as follows. In section two we give some motivation and provide stylised facts regarding the Italian Regions. Section three briefly presents the analytical framework. In section four we compute a regional performance indicator, which is then used as the output measures in the DEA analysis whose results are then reported and discussed. Section five provides conclusions.

2 – Motivation and Stylised Facts

Italy has devoted the last decade to "reform" the public governance, shifting from a highly interventionist state towards a modern regulatory one, introducing transparent rules, market openness, and competition. According to the Regulator's aim, the reform should have been able to enforce the competition, but the reality was very complex, showing the presence of significant diversity among the Italian regions. In some cases, there was a bias either in granting long concessions or to maintain the direct control on the service delivery. Nevertheless, in other cases, there was openness towards a more competitive market, introducing the tender system. Consequently, as more powers have been delivered to regional and local governments, the task of monitoring and correcting competition problems in regulation has become more complex, highlighting the absence of a well-established culture of competition in local governments.

The Italian utilities and network industries have changed significantly during the last ten years. This process was due namely to the response that Italy gave to European obligations to liberalise the public utilities sectors, in line to what happended across the euro area. Consequently, Italy's governance and markets were reformed and new relations established between the State, citizens, and the market. In order to assess the performance and responsibilities of the Italian regions in providing public services, a brief overview of the local government institutional features and responsibilities is provided below.

[1] email: aafonso@iseg.utl.pt.

Still far of being a federal state, Italy is nowadays a regional state, whose local government is organised in three subnational levels as shown in Figure 1.

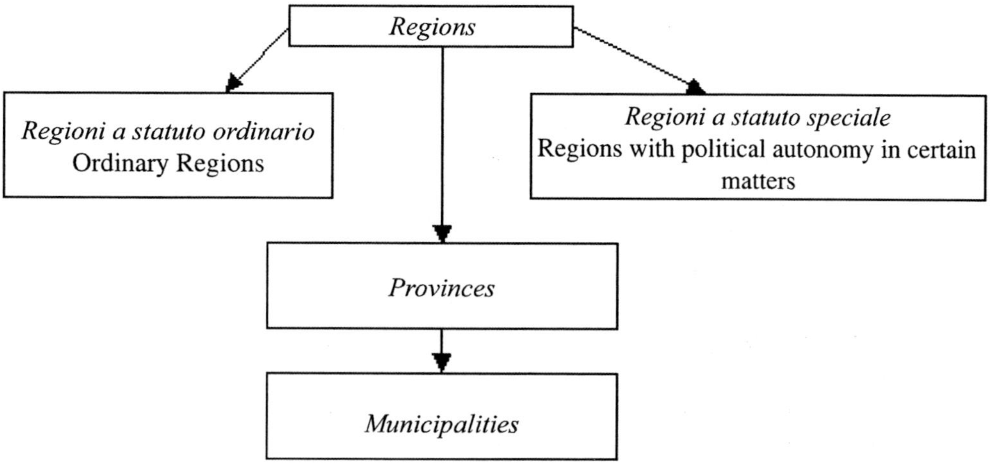

Note: Ordinary regions (Abruzzo, Basilicata, Calabria, Campania, Emilia – Romagna, Lazio, Liguria, Lombardia, Marche, Molise, Piemonte, Puglia, Toscana, Umbria, Veneto); regions with relative political autonomy (Valle d'Aosta, Trentino Alto Adige, Sicilia, Sardegna and Friuli Venezia Giulia).

Figure 1 – The organization of the local government in Italy

The first level includes the 20 Italian regions, which are divided in Ordinary Regions *(regioni a statuto ordinario)* and regions with political autonomy in certain matters *(regioni a statuto speciale)*. While the latter *(Valle d'Aosta, Trentino Alto Adige, Sicilia, Sardegna* and *Friuli Venezia Giulia)* were formally established between 1943 and 1963, the former were only created in 1970. The choice of the distinction was due mainly to the pressing demand of authonomy according to the peculiar etnical culture of those regions. Despite this regional organisation being in place for more than twenty years, the country was characterised by a highly centralised model, where the others local entities at the second level, Provinces and Municipalities had only a residual power.

Since 1997, after the introduction of the so-called "Bassanini reforms", a significant programme for public sector revitalisation helped the country in improving its use of best practice tools for regulatory quality. Legislation identifying the specific tasks of the regions and of the other local entities was introduced in order to guarantee the so-called *territorial empowerment,* reinforcing the effectiveness of the local policies.[2] Moreover, the Constitutional Reform that occurred in 2000, has modified .substantially the regions' competences giving them new powers.[3] In particular, two main innovations should be mentioned:

[2] 1 Laws n. 59/1997 and n. 127/97 modified by Laws n. 19 1/98 and n. 50/99

[3] Constitutional Law n. 3/2001.

a) The range of competencies on which regions can legislate was fully modified, i.e. the law mentions that the regions have the legislative power on all the topics not expressly reserved to the national government;[4]
b) A series of exclusive competences are attributed to the regions, on which the national government has no longer power.

As shown in Table 1, regions have *de facto* implemented their local power, both on the provision of public goods and on the definition of the local regulatory system.[5]

Table 1 – Main areas on which the Italian regions have both legislative and administrative competence

Social Services	Planning and use of the territory	Government of Economics
- Health care system - School sid - Cultural supply - Professional training - Social sid - Welfare assistance	- Urban and territorial planning - Water and sewage system - Defence of the territory - Protection of the environment - Transport planning with the possibility to give transfer funds in order to help local inefficient public companies	- Tourisme - Commerce - Agriculture - Fishery - Handicrafts

Source: Scaglioni (2004).

During the last decade a variety of incentives, such as service contracts *(Contratti di servizio)* and citizens charts *(Carte dei Servizi)* for public services were introduced in order to improve the quality of the public services (transports, sanity, energy, communications), and to provide commitments to performance criteria and compensation for customer non-satisfaction. Moreover, an effort was made to liberalise local public utilities, with the attempt to introduce market principles in water distribution, energy (other than electricity), public transport, and waste management, and a series of laws were approved to change the regulatory framework.[65]Alongside with the aforementioned institutional reforms, it was possible to notice the increase of both investment and employment levels in local public services. For instance, investment in total public services increased significantly in Italy between 1998 and 2002, around 33.9 per cent, while investment in local public services increased even more, by 43.3 per cent (see Figure 2). Additionally, and considering the

[4] This broadens the number of competences that can be regulated by the regional autorities. For an *historical excursus,* see Giarda (2004).

[5] In the Appendix, more detailde information is provided concerning the main interventions that occurred in some public utilities sectors.

[6] In the Appendix we provide an illustration of the key regulatory interventions occurred in the sectors we are considering

variation of employment, Figure 3 shows that employment in local public services broadly stabilised in the same period, vis-à-vis a decrease of some 10 per cent in total public services.

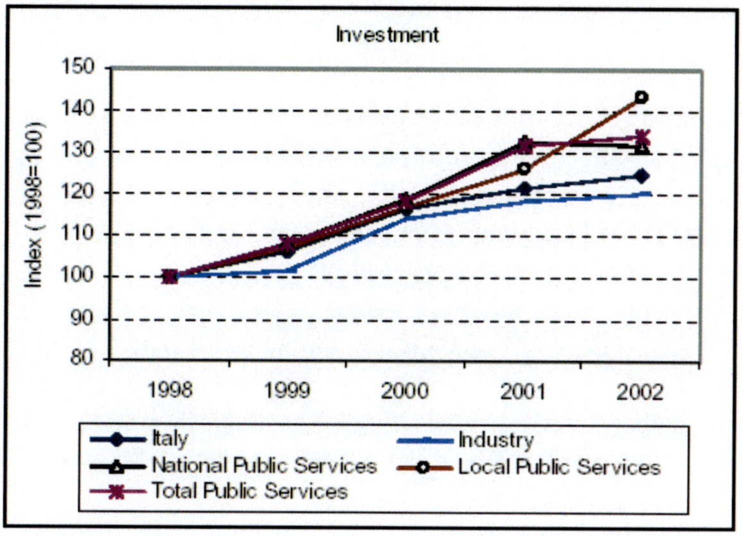

Source: adapted from Confservizi (2004).

Figure 2 – Investment developments

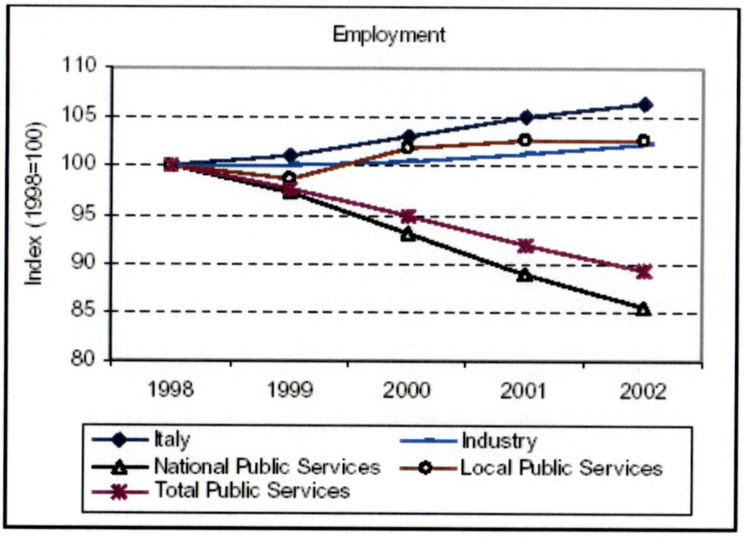

Figure 3 – Employment developments (1998-2002)

The objective of the reforms was to promote competition, even if its effectiveness depended mainly on the support given by the local governments. In practice, the results were mixed across the Italian regions. In some cases, there was a strong will to maintain the direct control of the service delivery, while there was also openness towards a more competitive market, introducing the tender system.[7]

As more powers have been devolved to regional and local governments, the task of monitoring and correcting regulatory competition problems has become more complex. This stems partly from the fact that the culture of competition is still not well established in local governments. Many concession-granting powers remain under local and regional governments' control including licensing, land use, and planning and development. One of the possible disadvantages of the reform was a potential for confusion between supervision and management, together with a long transition process, which may have weakened the force of competition or reinforced the pre-existent monopolies.

3 – Analytical Framework

Data Envelopment Analysis, originating from Farrell (1957) seminal work and popularised by Charnes, Cooper and Rhodes (1978), assumes the existence of a convex production frontier, a hypothesis that is not required for instance in the Fred Disposable Hull approach. The production frontier in the DEA approach is constructed using linear programming methods. The terminology "envelopment" stems out from the fact that the production frontier envelops the set of observations.[8]

DEA allows the calculation of technical efficiency measures that can be either input or output oriented. The purpose of an input-oriented study is to evaluate by how much input quantity can be proportionally reduced without changing the output quantities. Alternatively, and by computing output-oriented measures, one could also try to assess how much output quantities can be proportionally increased without changing the input quantities used. The two measures provide the same results under constant returns to scale but give different values under variable returns to scale. Nevertheless, and since the computation uses linear programming, not subject to statistical problems such as simultaneous equation bias and specification errors, both output and input-oriented models will identify the same set of efficient/inefficient producers or Decision Making Units (DMUs).[9]

The analytical description of the linear programming problem to be solved, in the variable returns to scale hypothesis, is sketched below. Suppose there are k inputs and

m outputs for n DMUs. For the i-th DMU, y_i is the column vector of the outputs and x_i is the column vector of the inputs. We can also define X as the $(k \times n)$ input matrix and Y as the $(m \times n)$ output matrix. The DEA model is then specified with the following mathematical programming problem, for a given i-th DMU: [10]

[7] As in the case of the local public transports in Rome and in Valle d'Aosta. For a review on local public transports, see Boitani and Cambini (2001).

[8] Coelli et al. (2002), and Thanassoulis (2001) offer good introductions to the DEA methodology.

[9] In fact, the choice between input and output orientations is not crucial since only the two measures associated with the inefficient units may be different between the two methodologies.

[10] We simply present here the equivalent envelopment form, derived by Charnes et al. (1978), using the duality property of the multiplier form of the original programming model.

$$
\begin{aligned}
& MIN_{\theta,\lambda}\theta \\
& \text{s. to } \; -y_i + Y\lambda \geq 0 \\
& \qquad \theta x_i - X\lambda \geq 0 \\
& \qquad n1'\lambda = 1 \\
& \qquad \lambda \geq 0
\end{aligned}
\qquad (1)
$$

In problem (1), θ is a scalar (that satisfies $\theta \leq 1$), more specifically it is the efficiency score that measures technical efficiency of unit $(x_i, \; y_i)$. It measures the distance between a decision unit and the efficiency frontier, defined as a linear combination of best practice observations. With $\theta < 1$, the decision unit is inside the frontier (i.e. it is inefficient), while $\theta = 1$ implies that the decision unit is on the frontier (i.e. it is efficient).

The vector λ is a $(n \; x \; 1)$ vector of constants, which measures the weights used to compute the location of an inefficient DMU if it were to become efficient. The inefficient DMU would be projected on the production frontier as a linear combination, using those weights, of the peers of the inefficient DMU. The peers are other DMUs that are more efficient and therefore are used as references for the inefficient DMU.

$n1$ is a n-dimensional vector of ones. The restriction $n1'\lambda = 1$ imposes convexity of the frontier, accounting for variable returns to scale. Dropping this restriction would amount to admit that returns to scale were constant. Additionally, notice that problem (1) has to be solved for each of the n DMUs in order to obtain the n efficiency scores.

In a simple example, three different hypothetical regions display the following values for indicator y and expense level x, as reported in Table 2:

Table 2 – Values for regions A, B and C

	Indicator	Expenditure
Region A		65800
Region B		681150
Region C		751000

Expenditure is lower in region A, and the output level is also the lowest. Region C does not exhibit the highest expenditure, and attains the best level of output. Region B may be considered inefficient, in the sense that it performs worse than region C. The latter achieves a better status with less expense.

Figure 4 illustrates DEA frontiers with the data of Table 2. The variable returns to scale frontier unites the origin (not depicted) to point A, and then point A to point C.

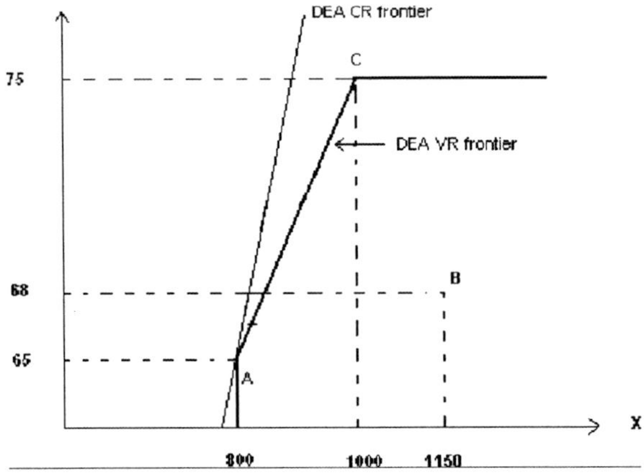

Figure 4 – DEA frontiers

4 – Non-Parametric Efficiency Analysis o Regional Spending in Italy

In our analysis we assess the efficiency for strategic sectors such as general administration, energy, water and sewage, solid waste, transports of the 20 Italian Regions in 2001. As inputs we use both public sector employees and public expenditure. Particularly, we use the database on Regional Public Accounts (MEFDPS, Banca Dati Conti Pubblici Territoriali) collected by the Italian Ministry for Economics and Finance. Regarding the output measure we first construct a composite indicator that tries to take into account the several areas of public provision of services and goods.

4.1 – Total Regional Performance Indicator (TRPI)

In this subsection we construct our measure of performance for Italian regions in providing public services to the population, by computing the so-called total regional performance indicator (TRPI) for 2001. This composite indicator is a simple average of seven sub-indicators of regional public performance: water provision, waste collection, frequency of the accidental long interruptions of the electrical service, public transportation utilization, railway utilization, motorway network, and houses provide with gas.[11]

We compile the performance indicator from the various indices giving equal weight to each of them[12].. This weighing up of the variables is quite straightforward and economically intuitive (even though it is still somewhat ad hoc). It avoids the problem of lack of economic justification of a more complex statistical approach such as principal component analysis that might come to mind in this context.

[11] The data and the respective sources are provide in the Annex.
[12] For example, water provision contributes 1/7 per cent to the total regional performance indicator

For those indicators where higher numbers are less favourable (e.g., irregularity in water provision, frequency of the accidental long interruptions of the electricity provision),we use the inverse of the original values. In order to facilitate the compilation, we normalised the values and set the average for all indices equal to unity (following the methodology adopted by Afonso et al. (2003)). The values for each region are then recalculated relative to the average. Table 1 presents the results for the constructed TRPI indicator for the year 2001.

Table 3. Total regional performance indicator (TRPI), 2001 (Sub-indicators are normalised to unity)

Region	Irregularity in water provision	Waste collection	Electric service failures	Public transport utilization index	Railway utilization index	Motorway network (km/ square km)	Gas (% houses provided	TRP (equal weights 1/)
Abruzzo	0.43	1.04	0.90	1.09	0.62	0.92	1.14	0.88
Basilicata	0.33	0.94	0.62	1.24	0.43	0.65	0.84	0.72
Calabria	0.18	0.66	0.37	1.09	0.89	0.90	0.39	0.64
Campania	0.49	0.86	0.61	1.29	1.43	1.01	0.92	0.94
Emilia - Romagna	1.59	1.14	1.39	0.72	0.93	0.66	1.48	1.13
Friuli - Venezia Giulia	4.22	0.92	1.72	0.82	0.85	0.61	1.30	1.49
Lazio	0.67	1.00	0.73	1.45	1.60	0.77	1.41	1.09
Liguria	1.77	1.01	1.23	1.48	2.83	0.69	1.24	1.46
Lombardia	1.20	0.98	1.66	1.22	1.56	0.92	1.58	1.30
Marche	0.96	0.97	1.23	0.78	0.41	1.69	1.22	1.04
Molise	0.44	0.90	0.75	1.27	0.39	0.16	1.03	0.71
Piemonte	1.25	0.95	1.14	0.98	1.40	3.13	1.35	1.46
Puglia	0.31	0.89	0.83	0.86	1.07	3.51	0.97	1.21
Sardegna	0.22	1.02	0.41	0.96	0.70	0.45	0.02	0.54
Sicilia	0.24	0.75	0.52	0.80	0.40	1.13	0.49	0.62
Toscana	0.82	1.28	0.91	0.78	1.04	0.63	1.39	0.98
Trentino - Alto Adige	2.09	1.04	0.86	1.07	0.76	0.24	0.57	0.95
Umbria	0.73	1.27	1.34	0.75	0.77	0.25	1.24	0.91
Valle D'Aosta	1.00	1.23	1.68	0.52		0.07	0.19	0.78
Veneto	1.05	1.15	1.11	0.82	0.92	1.60	1.23	1.13
Average	1.00	1.00	1.00	1.00	1.00	1.00	1.00	1.00
Maximum	4.22 (FVG)	1.28 (TOS)	1.72 (FVG)	1.48 (LIG)	2.83 (LIG)	3.51 (PUG)	1.58 (LOM)	1.49 (FVG)
Minimum	0.18 (CAL)	0.66 (CAL)	0.37 (CAL)	0.52 (VDA)	0.39 (MOL)	0.07 (VDA)	0.02 (SAR)	0.54 (SAR)

1/ Each sub-indicator contributes 1/7 to total indicator.

Note: Abruzzo – ABR; Basilicata – BAS; Calabria – CAL; Campania – CAM; Emilia - Romagna – ER; Friuli - Venezia Giulia – FVG; Lazio – LAZ; Liguria – LIG; Lombardia – LOM; Marche – MAR; Molise – MOL; Piemonte – PIE; Puglia – PUG; Sardegna – SAR; Sicilia – SIC; Toscana – TOS; Trentino - Alto Adige – TAA; Umbria – UMB; Valle D'Aosta – VDA; Veneto – VEN.

The computed sub-indicators suggest large differences in public services provision performance across regions. Regions with the highest values for sub-indicators include Friuli Venezia Giulia (water provision, and electricity provision), Toscana (waste collection), Liguria (public transports and railway utilisation), Puglia (motorway network), and Lombardia (gas provision). Regions such as Friuli - Venezia Giulia, Liguria, Piemonte, Lombardia, Puglia, Emilia-Romagna, and Veneto report high TRPI indicators.

The derived TRPI will be used ahead in the next sub-section as our chosen output measure for the DEA analysis.

4.2 – DEA INPUTS

We use two input measures: a financial measure, *X1,* which is the overall per capita spending in the region, and a quantitative measure, *X2,* the number of civil servants employed in each region defined as follows (data and sources are again reported in the Annex):

X1 - total spending in the region/inhabitants in the region;
X2 - civil servants per 1000 inhabitants = (civil servants/inhabitants)* 1000.

We first use a one input (regional spending per capita) and one output (TRPI) model. Afterwards we expand the analysis to a two-input (regional spending and civil servants) and one output (TRPI) model. Since the number of DMUs is not that large, one has to be careful in not using too many inputs or outputs, which would then increase the number of efficient by default DMUs.[13]

4.3 – DEA Analysis And Results

The general relationship for the theoretical production possibility frontier that we expect to test, regarding efficiency in regional provision on public services, can be given by the following function for region *i:*

$$Y_i = f(X1_i, X2_i),\ i=1,\ldots,n \tag{2}$$

where Y_i is the TRPI, and $X1_i$ and $X2_i$ are the previously defined two inputs for each region.

In Table 4 we report the DEA analysis results obtained with the one input, *X1,* and one output, TRPI, for the 20 Italian regions, both in terms of input and output oriented efficiency scores for 2001.

From the results it is possible to see that three regions would labelled as most efficient and located on the theoretical production frontier: Emilia – Romagna, Friuli – Venezia Giulia, and Piemonte. Interestingly, these are all regions from the north of Italy, as is also the case of the regions ranked fourth and fifth, respectively Veneto and Lombardia. One should also mention that there is no DMU that is efficient by default, in other words all DMUs on the frontier are at least once a peer of a non-efficient region.

---

[13] With less than three DMUs per input and output there is the risk that too many DMUs will turn out to be efficient.

Table 4. DEA results for Italian regions, 2001,1 input (expenditure) and 1 output (TRPI)

Region	Input oriented		Output oriented		Peers	CRS TE
	VRS TE	Rank	VRS TE	Rank	Input/output	
Abruzzo	0.879	6	0.605	14	Emilia – Romagna/ Piemonte, Emilia – Romagna	0.604
Basilicata	0.482	12	0.488	16	Emilia – Romagna/ Friuli - Venezia Giulia, Piemonte	0.272
Calabria	0.462	14	0.433	18	Emilia – Romagna/ Friuli - Venezia Giulia, Piemonte	0.232
Campania	0.330	18	0.633	12	Emilia – Romagna/Friuli - Venezia Giulia	0.244
Emilia - Romagna	1.000	1	1.000	1	Emilia – Romagna/Emilia – Romagna	0.883
Friuli - Venezia Giulia	1.000	1	1.000	1	Friuli - Venezia Giulia/ Friuli - Venezia Giulia	0.423
Lazio	0.462	15	0.738	8	Emilia – Romagna/ Friuli - Venezia Giulia, Piemonte	0.394
Liguria	0.588	11	0.984	4	Friuli - Venezia Giulia, Piemonte/ Friuli - Venezia Giulia, Piemonte	0.436
Lombardia	0.882	5	0.893	6	Emilia – Romagna, Piemonte/ Friuli - Venezia Giulia, Piemonte	0.837
Marche	0.688	8	0.710	9	Emilia – Romagna/ Friuli - Venezia Giulia, Piemonte	0.559
Molise	0.360	16	0.474	17	Emilia – Romagna/Friuli - Venezia Giulia	0.199
Piemonte	1.000	1	1.000	1	Piemonte/Piemonte	1.000
Puglia	0.825	7	0.828	7	Emilia – Romagna, Piemonte/ Friuli - Venezia Giulia, Piemonte	0.754
Sardegna	0.350	17	0.363	20	Emilia – Romagna/Friuli - Venezia Giulia	0.148
Sicilia	0.465	13	0.417	19	Emilia – Romagna/ Friuli - Venezia Giulia, Piemonte	0.225
Toscana	0.673	9	0.668	10	Emilia – Romagna/ Friuli - Venezia Giulia, Piemonte	0.515
Trentino - Alto Adige	0.080	19	0.634	11	Emilia – Romagna/Friuli - Venezia Giulia	0.059
Umbria	0.600	10	0.618	13	Emilia – Romagna/ Friuli - Venezia Giulia, Piemonte	0.426
Valle D'Aosta	0.064	20	0.524	15	Emilia – Romagna/Friuli - Venezia Giulia	0.039
Veneto	0.966	4	0.930	5	Emilia – Romagna/Emilia – Romagna	0.852
Average	0.608		0.697			0.455

Notes: CRS TE - constant returns to scale technical efficiency. VRS TE - variable returns to scale technical efficiency.

According to the average efficiency scores, there seems to scope for an improvement of around 39 per cent and 30 per cent respectively in terms of input efficiency and of output efficiency.In a different specification, we added the number of civil servants per 1000 inhabitants as a second input in other words we include *X2* in the production function (2). Table 5 reports this new set of results.

From this new set of results now five regions are seen as most efficient: Emilia – Romagna, Friuli – Venezia Giulia, and Piemonte, as before, plus Puglia and Veneto. In addition, Veneto is now efficient by default in the output oriented DEA analysis. Moreover, with this alternative specification using two inputs, on average the same level of outputs might be obtained with 19 per cent less resources. On the other hand, regions might have able to increase their outputs by 28 per cent using the same resources.

Table 5. DEA results for Italian regions, 2001, 2 inputs (expenditure, civil servants) and 1 output (TRPI)

Region	Input oriented		Output oriented		Peers	CRS TE
	VRS TE	Rank	VRS TE	Rank	Input/output	
Abruzzo	0.942	8	0.605	14	Puglia, Veneto/ Piemonte, Emilia – Romagna	0.604
Basilicata	0.884	9	0.538	15	Puglia/Piemonte, Puglia	0.528
Calabria	0.770	14	0.439	18	Puglia/ Friuli - Venezia Giulia, Piemonte	0.409
Campania	0.870	11	0.696	10	Puglia/ Piemonte, Puglia	0.681
Emilia - Romagna	1.000	1	1.000	1	Emilia - Romagna/Emilia – Romagna	0.883
Friuli - Venezia Giulia	1.000	1	1.000	1	Friuli - Venezia Giulia/ Friuli - Venezia Giulia	0.705
Lazio	0.884	10	0.815	8	Puglia/ Piemonte, Puglia	0.800
Liguria	0.954	7	0.997	6	Friuli - Venezia Giulia, Piemonte/ Friuli - Venezia Giulia, Piemonte	0.844
Lombardia	0.978	6	0.965	7	Puglia, Piemonte, Veneto/ Piemonte, Puglia	0.963
Marche	0.808	12	0.710	9	Puglia, Piemonte/ Friuli - Venezia Giulia, Piemonte	0.651
Molise	0.735	16	0.483	17	Puglia/ Friuli - Venezia Giulia, Piemonte	0.43 1
Piemonte	1.000	1	1.000	1	Piemonte/Piemonte	1.000
Puglia	1.000	1	1.000	1	Puglia/Puglia	1.000
Sardegna	0.644	18	0.366	20	Puglia/ Friuli - Venezia Giulia, Piemonte	0.289
Sicilia	0.750	15	0.422	19	Puglia/Friuli - Venezia Giulia, Piemonte	0.383
Toscana	0.801	13	0.669	11	Puglia, Veneto/ Friuli - Venezia Giulia, Piemonte	0.616
Trentino - Alto Adige	0.253	19	0.634	12	Puglia/ Friuli - Venezia Giulia	0.198
Umbria	0.715	17	0.618	13	Puglia, Veneto/ Friuli - Venezia Giulia, Piemonte	0.510
Valle D'Aosta	0.215	20	0.524	16	Puglia/ Friuli - Venezia Giulia	0.139
Veneto	1.000	1	1.000	1	Veneto/Veneto	0.852
Average	0.810		0.724			0.624

Notes: CRS TE - constant returns to scale technical efficiency. VRS TE - variable returns to scale technical efficiency.

Figure 5 provides an alternative presentation of the ranking of the regions' efficiency scores from Table 5 for the input oriented analysis. Again, all the efficient regions are located in the north of Italy, the exception being Puglia. This last region, already well ranked in the one input analysis (seventh place) is now labelled efficient because it has the lowest ratio of civil servants per 1000 inhabitants in the sample.

Figure 5 – Ranking of efficiency scores for the Italian regions, 2001.(DEA input oriented, 2 inputs, 1 output)

Notice however, that it is not easy to accurately identify the effects of regional spending on public services outcomes and separate the impact of spending from other influences. For instance, it is difficult to assess to what extent does irregularity in water provision and electricity service failures reflect public intervention rather than other factors such as climate, and geographical conditions. On that line of reasoning, adverse geographical conditions may also impair on the quality and cost of a regional communications infrastructure.

5 – CONCLUSION

In this paper, we have evaluated efficiency in providing public services across Italian regions by assessing a so-called TRPI index, our output measure, against the inputs used: regional per capita spending and the number of regional civil servants per 1000 inhabitants.

With data for 2001, we constructed the performance index as a composite index of seven sub-indicators of regional public performance: water provision, waste collection, frequency of the accidental long interruptions of the electrical service, public transportation utilization, railway utilization, motorway network, and houses provide with gas.

Input and output efficiency scores were then estimated by solving a standard DEA problem with the 20 Italian regions as DMUs. The results that inefficiencies may be significant and some improvements may be possible across regions. On average, and using the results from the one output and two input analysis, regions could have increased their output by 28 percent using the same resources (as can be seen from the average output score from Table 5), with a region like Sardegna having a theoretical margin for potential output improvement of 63 percent. On the other hand, on average, regions could have decreased their inputs by 19 percent and still obtain the same output, with a region like Valle D'Aosta displaying scope for a potential improvement of 78 percent.

To our knowledge, this is the first attempt at computing a performance composite indicator for public services provision at the Italian regional level. This same is true for the subsequent non-parametric efficiency analysis. However, all these first results have to be seen as indicative and need to be interpreted with great care. Indeed, and for instance, it would be useful to use only the number of civil servants that are more directly involved in the provision of regional public services. This additional analysis may be pursued in future work if and when such data limitations can be overcome.

AKNOWLEDGEMENTS

We thank Assunta Draicchio and Emma Galli for helpful comments, and MEF-DPS, Banca Dati Conti Pubblici Territoriali, for providing the data on regional expenditure. The opinions expressed herein are those of the authors and do not necessarily reflect those of the author's employers.

REFERENCES

Afonso, A. and Fernandes, S. (2003). "*Efficiency of local Government Spending: Evidence for the Lisbon Region,*" WP 09/2003/DE/CISEP, ISEG/UTL – Technical University of Lisbon

Afonso, A.; Schuknecht, L. and Tanzi, V. (2003). "Public Sector Efficiency: An International Comparison," ECB Working Paper n 242, July, forthcoming in *Public Choice.*

Afonso, A. and St. Aubyn, M. (2004). "Non-parametric Approaches to Public Education and Health Efficiency in OECD Countries," ISEG-UTL, Working Paper nº 1 /2004/DE/CISEP/UECE, forthcoming in the *Journal of Applied Economics.*

Balassone, F.; Francese, M. and Giordano, R. (2002). "Efficienza nei servizi pubblici: una rassegna della letteratura," in *L 'eficienza nei servizi pubblici,* Banca d'Italia, Roma.

Boitani, A. and Cambini, C. (2001). "La riforma del trasporto pubblico locale in Italia: problemi e prospettive," *Hermes - Working Paper* 5, 2001.

Charnes, A.; Cooper, W. and Rhodes, E. (1978). "Measuring the efficiency of decision making units," *European Journal of Operational Research,* 2 (6), 429–444.

Clements, B. (2002). "How Efficient is Education Spending in Europe?" *European Review of Economics and Finance, 1(1),* 3-26.

Coelli, T., Rao, D. and Battese, G. (2002). *An Introduction to Eficiency and Productivity Analysis,* sixth edition, Massachusetts, Kluwer Academic Publishers.

Confservizi (2004). "*Servizi Pubblici, sviluppo regolazione, compatibilità sociale e ambientale. Rapporto Confservizi sui Servizi Pubblici Locali 2004,*" quaderni n. 5/2004.

De Borger, B. and Kerstens, K. (1996). "Cost Efficiency of Belgian Local Governments: A Comparative Analysis of FDH, DEA, and Econometric Approaches", *Regional Science and Urban Economics,* 26(2), 145-170.

Fakin, B. and de Crombrugghe, A. (1997). "Fiscal Adjustment in Transition Economies: Social Transfers and the Efficiency of Public Spending, a Comparison with OECD Countries", *Policy Research Working Paper* 1803, Washington, The World Bank.

Farrell, M. (1957). "The Measurement of Productive Efficiency," *Journal of the Royal Statistical Society, serie A, General,* 120, 253-81.

Giarda, P. (2004). "Decentralization and intergovernmental fiscal relations in Italy: a review of past and recent trends," *mimeo.*

Gupta, S. and Verhoeven, M. (2001). "The Efficiency of Government Expenditure – Experiences from Africa", *Journal of Policy Modelling,* 23, 43 3-467.

Istat (2001). *I servizi pubblici e di pubblica utilità: utilizzo e soddisfazione*, Roma.

OECD (2001). Regulatory reform in Italy, Paris, *OECD Reviews of Regulatory Reform*, April.

Scaglioni, C. (2004). "The Local Agencies for the Public Services. The Italian case," in *Proceedings of the 6th European Evaluation Society Biennial Conference*, Governance, Democracy and Evaluation, Berlin, September 30– October 2, 2004.

St. Aubyn, M. (2003). "Evaluating Efficiency in the Portuguese Education Sector", *Economia,* 26, 25-51.

Thanassoulis, E. (2001). *Introduction to the Theory and Application of Data Envelopment Analysis*, Kluwer Academic Publishers.

Appendix

Table A1 – Main interventions that occurred in some public utilities sectors: water and waste

Industry	Regulatory Framework	Regulatory Governance
Water supply and waste water management	Law 36/94, (so called Galli Law) has aimed to introduce competition within water service sector in order to ensure efficiency in production and management of the resource.	The Law has established new local water authorities Autorità d'ambito Territoriale Ottimale (*ATOs*) and a separation between water resource planning and the operation of water utilities. ATOs, whose borders are set by the Italian Regions, have the task of -defining the resource planning; -assigning the operation to a private provider, selected through auction; -setting the price (tariff) cap for the water utilities (including aqueduct systems, sewage systems and treatment plants); -drawing up the Piano d'Ambito (a 30 year plan) which includes the timing and level of infrastructure investments, and ensures that the provider respects the contract requirements.
Waste management	EU Directive 91/156/CE EU Directive 91/689/CE EU Directive 94/62/CE Legislative Decree 22/1997 (so called Ronchi Decree) Legislative Decree 389/1998 Law 426/1998 Law 326/2004	This group of legislative interventions covers collection, treatment and disposal of waste. It has introduced through several steps an increasing process of decentralisation of competences from the State to the Regions and the others local entities. The regulatory governance is based on the definition of the integrated management of waste through regional and provincial plans. The ATOs have the task to ensure the operation and the management of the waste according to the plans and in collaboration with the Regions, Provinces and Municipalities The law has introduced the tariff mechanism to cover the operational costs, which should have replaced the TaRSU, a specific tax on waste, but by law the transition period was prorogated from Jannuary 1999 to jannuary 2005.

Source: Elaboration on OECD (2001) and Confservizi (2004).

Table A2 – Main interventions that occurred in some public utilities sectors: energy sector

Industry	Regulatory Framework	Regulatory Governance
-Electric power	Law 481/95 established the *Authority for Electricity and Gas* (AEEG).	There is an Independent National Authority called *Authority for Electricity and Gas* (AEEG), created in 1997. It has regulatory powers such as the determination of *i)* pricing ; *ii)* quality level of services i, *iii)* economical and technical conditions of the network access and interconnession.
	EU Directive 96/92/CE Legislative Decree (so called Bersani Decree) 79/1999 liberalised the sector, promoting competition into generation and provision to liberalised customers	The production, import/export and distribution are liberalised The transmission network is still public and managed by the State through the *Trasmission System Operator* (Gestore della Rete di Trasmissione), which has a concession contract, with the owner *Terma Spa*, a company of the *Enel Group*, the former monopolist public provider, transformed in a joint-stock company in 1999. The *Operator* is obliged to connect to the network all the requiring providers, which have to pay a fee determinated by the AEEG. The market is divided in two: one part is captive and the other free. In the first case the providers pay a fee determinated by the AEEG and in the second a price determinated by the market. In addition, the reform allows for only one concession for distribution on the territory of each municipality The *Operator* has created the so called *Single Buyer* (Acquirente Unico) and the *Electric Market Manager* (Gestore Mercato elettrico). The former is encharged to sell the energy to those providers operating in the captive market. The tariffs are in this case regulated by AEEG.The latter has the task to regulate the generation market, ensuring the matching between demand and supply in acompetitive framework. In this case the price is determinated within the market. The principle of uniform tariff is now applied only for captive consumers.
-Natural Gas	EU Directive 98/30/CE Delegated legislative Decreee 625/96 eliminated the legal monopoly of ENI, the public monopolist Delegate Legislative Decree 164/2000 (so called Letta Decree)	Starting from 2003 small customers and household are free to choose the providers, which cannot exceed a ceiling of 75% of total imports and production (decreasing by 2% a year, down to a 61% ceiling in 2010) nor to exceed a ceiling of 50% of the sales to final consumers. Both ceilings will be removed in 2010. The AEEG has the task to regulate Third Party Access to the storage, transmission and distribution networks. It fixes the tariffs for transmission, distribution and the captive customers (Decision 138/03), on the basis of price caps. Concessions for distribution are managed by the Municipalities through auctions

Source: Elaboration on OECD (2001) and Confservizi (2004).

Table A3 – Main interventions that occurred in some public utilities sectors: transports sector

Industry	Regulatory Framework	Regulatory Governance
-Railway Sector	EU Directive 95/18/CE EU Directive 95/19/CE President of the Republic Decree-Dpr 277/1998, introduced the access to international operators and the accounting separation President of the Republic Decree-Dpr 146/1999 implemented the criteria for licencing and allocation of infrastructure capacity Law 326/2004	In 1992 *Ferrovie dello Stato*, the former monopolist became a joint stock company, still owned by the Ministry of Treasury. The legal separation between the network operator (RTF) and the service company *(Trenitalia)* took place in 2000, after the inroduction of the accounting separation in 1999. The State responsabilities for local railways have been decentralised to the regions. Competition for local should have been introduced in 2003, but the Budget Law of 2004 has prorogated the transition period, for the local public services The international freeight segment has been liberlised during 2000 (licens has been granted. All other segments have been liberalised with the Budget Law of 2000 and 4 licences already issued for the international segment have been extended. In October 2000 the network operator has adopted a Network code for non-discriminatory access
-Transports on roads	CIPE Decision n.319/1996 IT Directive 1998 (so called Ciampi-Costa Directive)	The road network is still public and managed by the State through the *ANAS*, which has a concession contract, with the different companies and the former main operator
	Legislative Decree 400/1999 Law 448/2001 Law 326/2004	Società Autostrade transformed in a joint-stock company and privatised. ANAS has to define the parameters, which each company needs in order to determinate the price cup and consequently the tariff or toll. The Legislative Decree 400/1999 has -given a new definition of subsidy transfer mechanisms for minimum services by the Regional Governments; -introduced the adoption of service contracts to regulate the relationship between the granting Authority and the service provider; -affirmed the compulsory public tenders for the assignment of services by the end of 2003; Additionally all the special companies and consortia should have been transformed into joint stock companies or cooperatives (within 31st December 2000); Eeach Regional Government had to established a regional fund for transport replacing the old national transportation fund. The Budget Law of 2004 has prorogated the transition period, for the local public services and pushed towards the adpotion of the "in house" provision, stopping the liberation process, which was confirmed in the Budget Law of 2001

Source: Elaboration on OECD (2001) and Confservizi (2004).

In: Perspectives on International, State and Local Economics ISBN 1-60021-099-6
Editor: Gerald V. Liu, pp. 159-183

Chapter 6

REINVESTMENT MOTIVES OF HOMEOWNERS AND HOUSE PRICES: JERUSALEM AND HAIFA AS CASE STUDIES

Boris A. Portnov[1]
Department of Natural Resources & Environmental Management,
Graduate School of Management, University of Haifa, Mt.Carmel, Haifa, Israel 3190.

ABSTRACT

Households may undertake housing changes and modifications (HCMs) for two basic reasons – increasing property value and gaining personal utility. In environmentally unfavorable or physically deteriorated neighborhoods, in which no substantial price gain can be expected, HCMs may be motivated mainly by improving personal utility, rather than by maximizing return on HCMs. As a result, in such neighborhoods relatively little accumulation of HCMs may occur. To verify this hypothesis, eight residential neighborhoods in two large cities of Israel – Jerusalem and Haifa, - were analyzed. The incidence of HCMs was found to be related to neighborhood and building characteristics, while the amount of accumulated post-occupancy HCMs helped to explain the variation of selling prices of apartments and houses.

INTRODUCTION

Neighborhood amenities, building patterns, and housing characteristics may appear to affect housing prices *only directly*, which is not always true, as we shall argue later in this chapter. The direct link between neighborhood and building characteristics, on the one hand, and housing prices, on the other, is indeed fairly straightforward. Whereas a lake view or proximity to open areas bring a price premium to homeowners (Benson et al., 1998; Bond et al., 2002; Des Rosiers et al., 2002; Morancho, 2003), structural wear is likely to lessen a

[1] Tel.: +972-4-8288532; Fax.: +972-4-8249971. E-mail: portnov@nrem.haifa.ac.il

building's value, and housing prices near a noisy road tend to be low (Asabere and Huffman, 1995; Ryan, 1999; Wilhelmsson, 2000). The reverse link – between housing prices and neighborhood change – is also investigated in depth in the literature on residential succession and gentrification (Smith, 1979; 1987; Palen and London, 1984; Banzhaf and Walsh, 2004; Sieg *et al.,* 2004).

In our view, however, such direct links may somewhat be oversimplified. Why do housing prices tend to be low in a heavily polluted neighborhood? Because apartments and houses in such a neighborhood are unattractive to buyers, the appraisal theory readily tells us. Yes, it is definitely correct, but only in part. Will individual property owners in such a neighborhood invest much in the maintenance and expansion of their properties – in building additions, renovations, and gardening? The answer to this question is likely to be *no*. The reason is simple: In an environmentally disadvantageous or poorly located neighborhood, any future price gain can hardly be expected. As a result, such a neighborhood will naturally become *a disincentive for rehabilitation decisions.*

Why do individual homeowners modify their properties? In general, they may invest in post-occupancy HCMs for two basic reasons – *increasing property value and improving personal utility*. For instance, homeowners may modify their houses, expecting a future price premium on current investment. Thus, a property owner may decide to add a porch (at the construction costs of \$5,000) to the house currently priced \$100,000, expecting that the modified house will sell for \$110,000, bringing a net profit of some \$5,000. However, post-occupancy HCMs are not always profit-driven. Thus, a homeowner may choose to replace windows in the house, in order to improve the views of open areas, or to add another room, to satisfy family needs (Portnov *et al.*, 2006).

Our distinction between basic motivations for HCM decision-making is thus based on the size of *a potential market premium a particular housing improvement may bring to the homeowner*. If a homeowner makes a HCM at a cost greater than the property price increment attributed to the improvement in question, such a HCM is likely to be driven mainly by personal needs (utility), rather than by return maximization.

According the explanation we propose, the link between *neighborhood conditions, HCM activity of homeowners and housing prices* works as follows. In an environmentally disadvantageous, inaccessible or physically deteriorated neighborhood, where no substantial price gain can be expected (P3; Fig. 1), HCMs may be motivated *mainly* by improving personal utility, rather than by maximizing return on HCMs. As a result, in such a neighborhood *relatively little accumulation of HCMs* may occur.

The second hypothesis we attempt to test in this study is that housing modifications accumulated in residential neighborhoods help to explain the variation of selling prices of local apartments and houses. We can reflect this "HCM-price" link by introducing an additional component into the basic "attributes–value" model (Fig. 2-i). In the proposed model (see Fig. 2-ii), HCM efforts of homeowners serve as an intermediary between neighborhood/building attributes and housing prices.

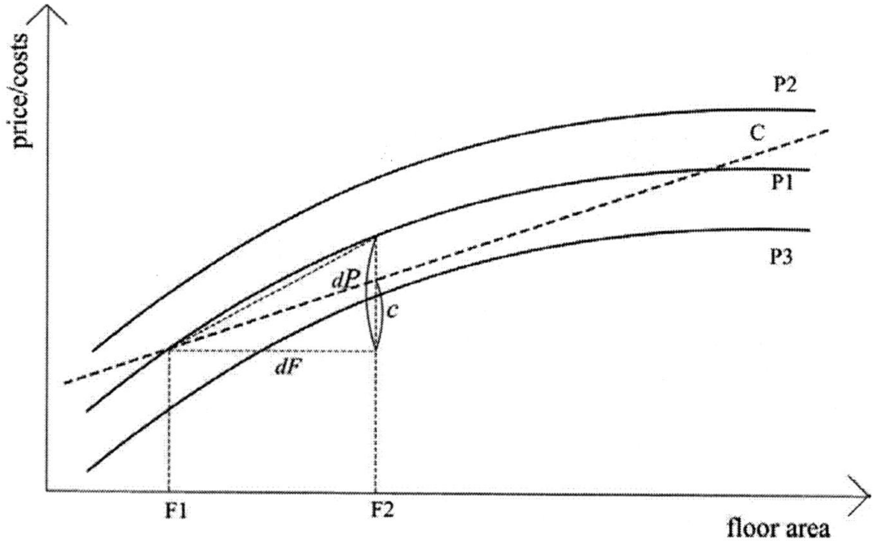

Figure 1: Housing changes and modifications (HCMs), construction costs and housing price change As argued, the number of HCMs in residential neighborhoods depends on the construction costs (C) associated with the implementation of a particular HCM (e.g., change in the floor area: F1->F2) and the neighborhood-specific price increment curve (P1...P3). Thus, in environmentally disadvantageous, inaccessible or physically deteriorated neighborhoods, where no substantial price gain can be expected (e.g., P3), HCMs may be motivated mainly by improving individual utility, rather than by maximizing return on HCMs. As a result, in such neighborhoods, there are likely to be relatively little accumulation of HCMs. If c denotes the construction costs associated with the F1->F2 transition, and dP stands for the market price change of a property after the modification is undertaken, then the choice between HCM motivations is as follows: if dP > C, HCM is justified by profit considerations (i.e., gaining property value), while if dP ≤ C, HCM is undertaken for a sole reason of gaining personal utility, disregarding any potential economic gain (or lack thereof) that the HCM in question may bring to the homeowner.

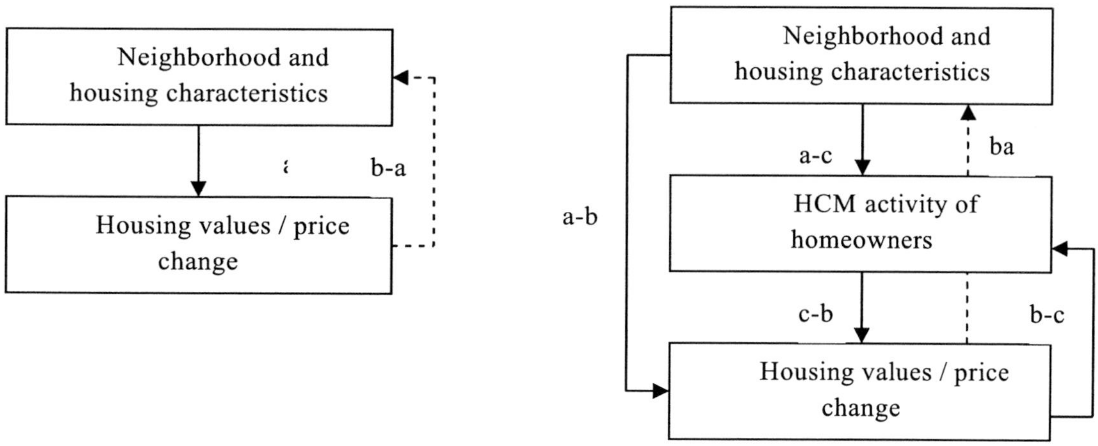

Figure 2: Interaction between neighborhood/building factors and housing values – traditional approach (i) and proposed model (ii)

The present chapter attempts to verify these hypotheses by investigating the incidence of HCMs in *eight* residential neighborhoods located in two large cities of Israel - Jerusalem (650,000 residents) and Haifa (300,000 residents). In particular, the study attempts to answer the following two main questions:

- Does the incidence of HCMs vary by neighborhood depending on local building characteristics and environmental attributes?
- Do HCM efforts of homeowners translate into a price premium?[2]

The chapter is organized as follows. It begins with a brief outline of previous studies dealing with post-occupancy housing changes and modifications in residential neighborhoods and their effects on housing prices. Then, the research methodology is introduced and the recent trends of housing price change in the neighborhoods under study are analyzed. In the following sections, various modeling techniques (ranging from ordinary least squares to spatial lag models) are used to identify and measure the effect of HCMs on housing prices, and the effect of housing and neighborhood characteristics on the incidence of HCMs. As the analysis indicates, the incidence of HCMs appears to be related to neighborhood and building characteristics (such as distance to major roads, number of floors, etc), while the amount of accumulated HCMs helps to explain the variation of selling prices of apartments and houses. In general, the neighborhoods with large numbers of HCMs tend to exhibit more rapid average price increases and higher rates of housing turnover than neighborhoods with little HCM accumulation.

HOUSING MODIFICATIONS AND HOUSING PRICING – A BRIEF SUMMARY OF PREVIOUS STUDIES

Post-occupancy HCMs are often associated with *neighborhood gentrification*. This term was coined by Ruth Glass, who used it to describe the influx of middle-class people into the working-class inner city neighborhoods in London in the early 1960's. As a result of the gentrification process, run-down neighborhood properties were converted into comfortable and expensive homes.

The rental gap theory developed by Smith (1979) explains the economic forces behind residential gentrification. According to this theory, a fall in the price of inner-city land (relative to land price in the suburbs) forms a rental gap between the actual and potential use of land in the inner-city areas. The rental gap phenomenon implies the difference between "the actual capitalized ground rent (land value) of a plot of land given its present use and potential ground rent that might be gleaned under a 'higher and better' use" (Smith, 1987, p.462). In Smith's view, the rent difference attracts developers to reinvest in inner-city properties.

Owing to the complexity of the gentrification phenomenon, it has been defined differently in professional literature. Some studies consider gentrification as the process of

[2] In this study, HCMs refer to post-occupancy housing changes and modifications that were implemented prior to sales and are thus not expected to affect sale prices that were negotiated *before* these modifications were made.

population displacement, based on class or racial pressure and dislocation (Palen and London, 1984; Slater et al., 2004). In more recent studies, however, the "environmental" facet of gentrification has been emphasized (Walsh, 2003; Banzhaf and Walsh, 2004; Sieg et al., 2004). The term "environmental gentrification," set forward by Sieg and his colleagues (ibid.), refers to the renovation process which results in an environmental improvement, such as better air quality or more open spaces. As the neighborhood's amenities improve, wealthy households move in, driving up home prices and rents (Walsh, 2003; Banzhaf and Walsh, 2004).

The links between housing modifications, socio-economic and environmental features of residential neighborhoods have also been investigated in a number of field studies dealing with the process of housing renewal (Ding et al., 2000; Simons et al., 1998; McMillen, 1996; Gloves and Niner, 1998, DETR, 2000). As these studies indicate, there is, in general, a positive association between rehabilitation efforts of homeowners and property values. However, as these studies acknowledge, the longitudinal benefits of such investment are rather limited. That is, although social and environmental improvements in the neighborhood may encourage the property owners to invest in the repair, maintenance and rehabilitations of their properties, crime, air pollution and the lack of open spaces may lead eventually to housing deterioration and drop in property prices (Gloves and Niner, 1998; Cole and Reeve, 2001).

Field studies on housing quality, satisfaction of tenants, and post-occupancy housing evaluations deal extensively with housing modifications undertaken by homeowners (see *inter alia* Ellen and Turner, 1997; Bridge et al., 2003, Sungur and Çağdaş, 2003). Thus, Sungur and Çağdaş (2003) list the following factors that may influence post-occupancy changes in dwellings: building type, greenery, cleanliness, quality of construction, landscape views, neighborhood location, and low traffic volumes.

Dweller-initiated housing modifications have been also investigated in conjunction with the general patterns of residents' use of urban space (Shiferaw, 1998; Wilkinson and Kardash, 1992; Ikejiofor, 1999). These studies indicate that proper neighborhood design is a decisive precondition for post-occupancy improvements and modifications. In contrast, Etzion *et al.* (2001) attribute post-occupancy HCMs to the inadequacy of the original housing design, and poor performance of buildings under location-specific climatic conditions, acknowledging, however, that environmental and socio-economic externalities may also affect the household's motivation either to initiate such changes or to refrain from them.

While previous studies of HCMs in residential neighborhoods deal mainly with specific cases, they analyze only general causes of such modifications and their socio-economic consequences. In particular, these studies offer no general theoretical framework explaining the links between environmental conditions in residential neighborhoods, post-occupancy HCMs and housing prices. Portnov *et al.* (2006), in their study of the factors affecting housing modifications and pricing in Haifa, Israel attempt to fill this gap by proposing an explanatory model of the linkages between neighborhood characteristics and the HCM activity of homeowners. According to this model, property values and neighborhood factors interact through the reinvestment decisions of homeowners. While the present analysis builds upon the theoretical foundation laid down by the former study, it furthers it in some respects. In particular, the present analysis clarifies the reinvestment motives of homeowners, and investigates in some detail the dynamic aspect of the HCM-housing price links, such as HCMs vs. residential turnover and longitudinal price change.

Research Methodology

To verify the initial research assumption that building and neighborhood factors influence the HCM activity of homeowners and that this activity leads, in turn, to a price premium (Fig. 2-ii), the analysis was carried out in three phases: a) neighborhood survey; b) the analysis of price change and housing turnover, and c) multivariate modeling. These phases are described in brief in the following subsections.

Neighborhood Survey

Since HCMs accumulate slowly (Etzion et al., 1999; Portnov et al., 2006), *well-established* neighborhoods are required. The neighborhoods built in the early 1970's through 1980's as mass construction meet well this requirement. First, these neighborhoods are old enough for various housing modifications and additions to occur. Second, they are formed by houses and apartments of similar size and design, which facilitates comparative analysis.

The basic physical characteristics of the neighborhoods selected for the present survey are featured in Appendix 1, and their location is shown in Figs. 3-4.

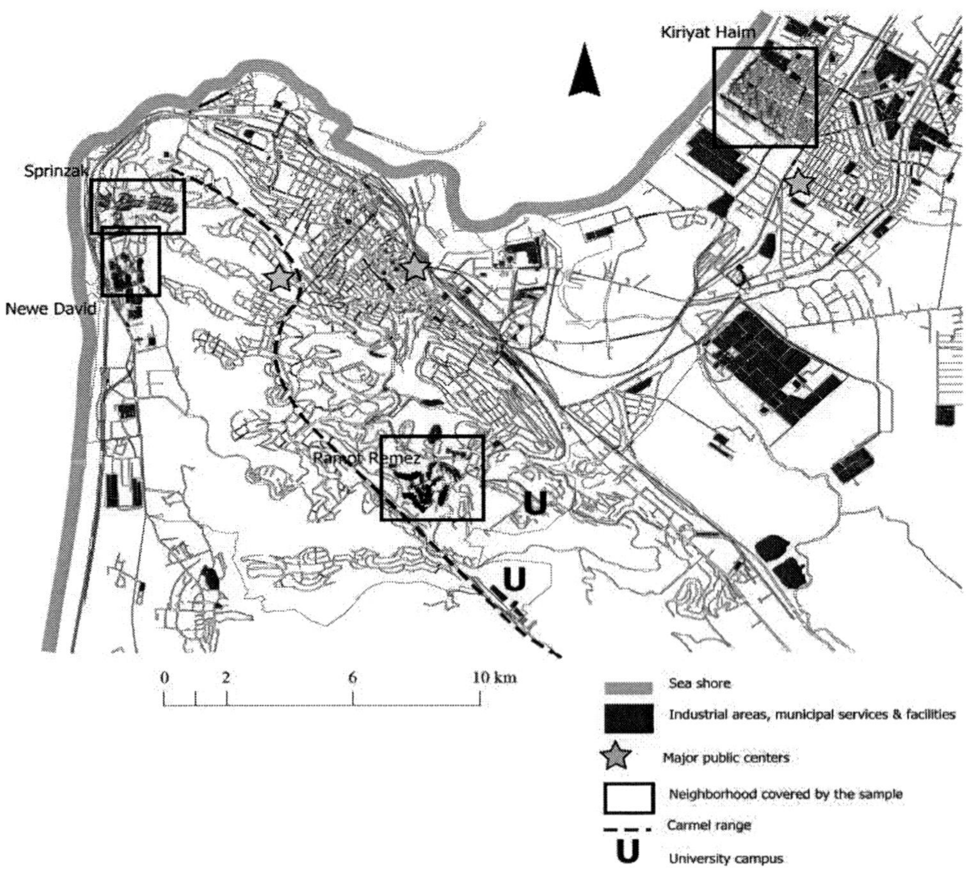

Figure 3: Haifa - Location Of The Neighborhoods Covered By The Research Survey

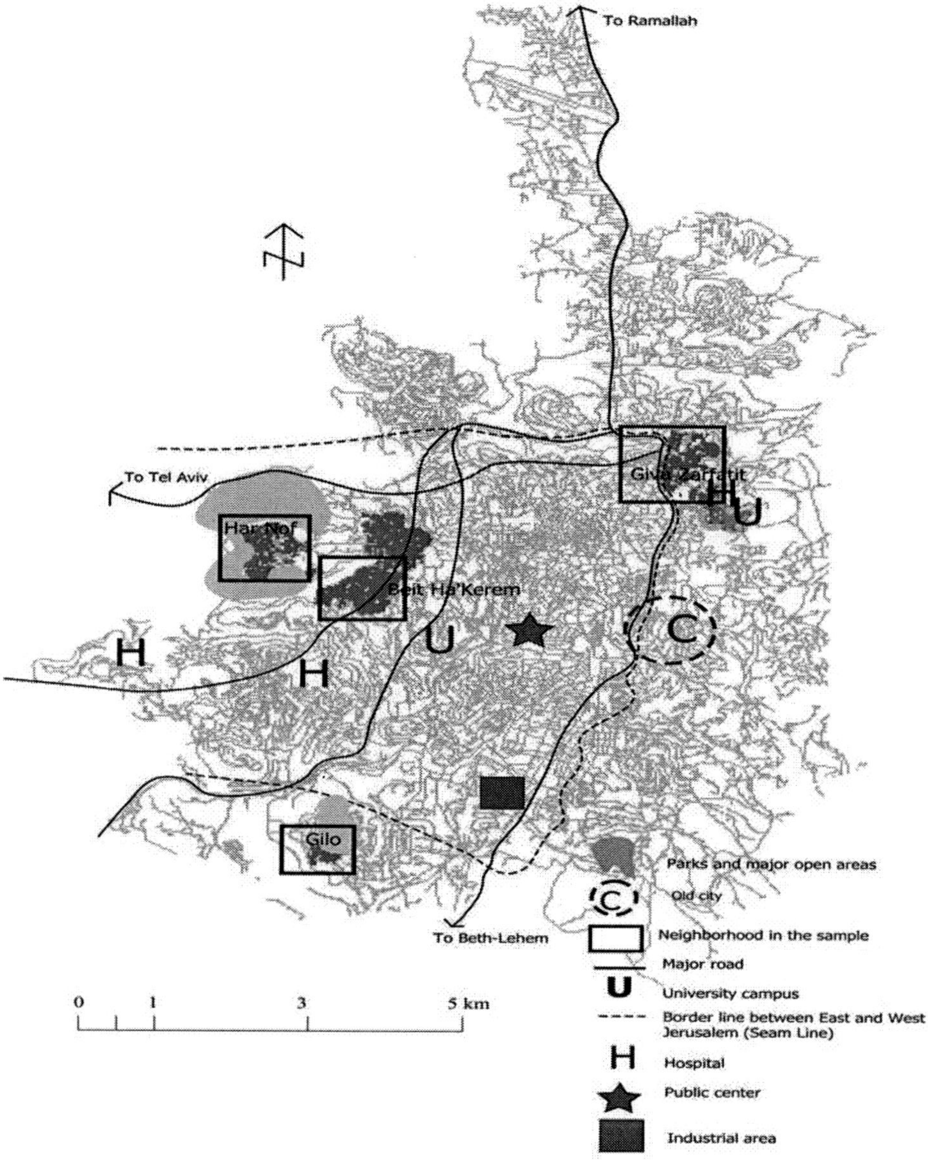

Figure 4: Jerusalem - Location Of The Neighborhoods Covered By The Research Survey

A sample of recently sold housing units in each neighborhood was drawn from the Apartments and Houses' Sales Database, maintained by the Israel Tax Office. This database contains the actual sale prices of individual apartments and houses, their street addresses, and the date on which a particular transaction took place; it also reports some essential physical characteristics of apartments and houses, such as floor area, number of rooms, etc.

In each neighborhood, between 100 and 300 individual housing units were covered by the study: 449 housing units were surveyed in Jerusalem and 754 units - in Haifa (see Appendix 1). All the apartments and houses covered by the study are privately owned.[3]

In addition to basic physical characteristics of properties, reported in the Tax Office database, we recorded post-occupancy HCMs, using a specially designed field table (see Appendix 3). The table assigns numerical codes to most typical changes (01,02,..N), and provides open-ended numbering for earlier unobserved changes and modifications (Etzion *et al.,* 2001). After the field survey was completed, the overall number of HCMs for each apartment was transferred into the main field table (Appendix 3B: Change coding). We also differentiated between major HCMs (such as room, roof additions and permanent storages) and minor modifications (such as window and door replacements, installation of air conditioners, etc.).

Building patterns and development options may affect the incidence of HCMs. In this sense, *outset* development rights may result in both higher prices initially paid for the properties and in a greater number of building additions. To facilitate a cross-neighborhood comparison, we ascertained that *none* of the neighborhoods was defined by the city building plans as having outset development rights: i.e., each HCM in these neighborhoods must be approved on the individual basis by the local planning commissions.

For obvious reasons, HCMs may be more frequent in single-family housing than in multi-story development, where HCMs must often be implemented simultaneously by several property owners. Furthermore, the owners of apartments located in the ground floors of multi-story buildings may find it easier to make external modifications than homeowners whose apartments are situated in the middle floors of such multi-story structures. In order to account for these differences, the list of explanatory variables included both building characteristics and neighborhood variables. The complete list of factors covered by the analysis and scales used to measure their effects are given in Appendix 2

Proximities to neighborhood amenities and disamenities (Appendices 1 and 2: distance to parks, to roads, etc.) are important research variables. This information was assembled in two steps. First, all the major amenities and disamenities in the neighborhood and in their vicinity, which may (at least in theory) affect HCM decision of the local property owners, were identified during field surveys and positioned on the neighborhood maps. At the next phase, these environmental features were transferred into ArcGIS9™ databases, and aerial distances from each of them to individual apartments and houses were calculated using the 'spatial join' tool (for more detail, see Minami, 2001).

A sizable part of investment in residential properties (viz., furnishing, layout change, renovation, and plumbing) occur inside apartments and houses and *cannot* be traced from outside. Investment intentions of property owners are another important indicator of the homeowners' response to neighborhood conditions and building characteristics, which cannot be investigated by a field survey, without entering individual properties. The present study

---

3 In Israel, there is practically no rental housing owned by commercial firms. Instead, public housing agencies (such as *Amidar* and *Amigur*) own a substantial portion of the housing stock in many localities. There is also a fairly well-developed market for rental of privately owned apartments and houses. However, by law, tenants are not allowed to modify properties without getting an explicit approval from the property owners. The local housing market is volatile, and housing prices fluctuate considerably. Hence only recent sales (recorded within past 3-4 years) are covered by the sample. The apartments and houses are drawn from the database at random, in order to minimize sampling bias.

deals solely with *external HCMs,* assuming that follow-up studies may focus on the survey of interior modifications and direct interviewing of homeowners.

Price Change and Housing Turnover

As assumed, well-maintained neighborhoods and neighborhoods with multiple HCMs should have high turnover rates and maintain higher housing prices, due to their attractiveness to buyers and the ability of local homeowners to capitalize on the elevated demand. The best way to verify these assumptions is to compare the annual rates of HCM accumulation with price dynamics and turnover rates across individual neighborhoods. However, as the field surveys and the analysis of building permits indicated, the number of such permits was magnitude smaller the actual number of HCMs recorded in the neighborhoods. This implies that most HCMs were undertaken without getting proper building permits, as required by the law. Therefore, in the present analysis, the average housing prices in the neighborhoods and turnover rates were compared with *the average numbers* of HCMs per housing unit, accumulated in the neighborhoods over their *entire 'life-span'* (as recorded by the field surveys), rather than with annual HCM accumulation rates, as would be preferable.

The analysis covered the period of 13 years, between 1990 and 2002, for which completed and comparable data were available. In the analysis, housing turnover data covered all the properties sold in the neighborhoods (see Figs. 2-3), while housing prices were obtained for a 20% sample of the neighborhoods' properties. The sampling was required due to a labor-intensive process of obtaining individual price records from the Tax Office database.

Multivariate Modeling

Although residential neighborhoods may differ substantially in the incidence of HCMs, these differences *may not* necessarily be attributed to the effect of neighborhood factors and building characteristics. For instance, HCMs may be more frequent in wealthy neighborhoods, whose residents can afford them. Since the data on the incomes of individual homeowners were unavailable for the study, the average per capita income in the neighborhood was used as a proxy for the local welfare levels. The list of dependent and explanatory variables used in the analysis is given in Appendix 2.

Research Results

Price Change and Housing Turnover

Notably, all the neighborhoods covered by the study appear to exhibit similar trends of housing price change: a rapid price increase in 1990-1994 (Jerusalem) and 1990-1996 (Haifa), followed by a price drop since 1994 in Jerusalem and since 1996 in Haifa (see Fig. 5). The underlying causes of these changes are macro-economic, rather than local. They include a rapid deterioration in the security situation (especially since 1996), a continuous drop in the foreign immigration to the country after 1992-93, and the overall economic slowdown, which became evident in the late 1990's. Similar trends appear to have affected the entire housing market in Israel and are well documented in other studies (see *inter alia* Gat, 1998; Fleishman and Odish, 2003a, 2003b). A detailed analysis of these macroeconomic trends lies far beyond the scope of the present study, which focuses on individual neighborhoods. In the following discussion, we shall thus discuss only on the differences between the neighborhoods surveyed in their relative price levels and housing turnover rates.

Over 13 years covered by the study, the price ranking of the neighborhoods hardly changed. Thus, in 1990, Beit Ha'Kerem led Jerusalem's neighborhood list with \$1800 per m^2 of floor area, while Gilo brought up the rear with \$1300 per m^2 (see Fig. 5A). Virtually the same neighborhood sequence remained in 2002: Beit Ha'Kerem (\$2500/m^2), Har Nof (\$2250), Giva Zarfatit (\$2100) and Gilo (\$1700). Only two neighborhoods - Har Nof and Giva Zarfatit – switched their ranking between 1990 and 2002. However, the relative price change was relatively minor: ±\$50 per m^2. Characteristically, in 1995/96, at the peak of the price hike, the price gap between the leading (Beit Ha'Kerem) and lagging (Gilo) neighborhood was widest – ca. \$1000 per m^2. However, it shrunk by some 20% a few years thereafter, when the local housing market showed the signs of price decline.

Neither in Haifa, the price ranking of the neighborhoods under study changed substantially between 1990 and 2002 (see Fig. 5B). Thus, in 1990, Ramot Remez led the neighborhood group with \$1300 per m^2 of floor area and retained its leading position 13 years thereafter with \$1600 per m^2. The Newe David neighborhood brought up the rear with \$750 per m^2 in 1990 and remained lagging in 2002, with \$1100 per m^2 of floor area. However, unlike in Jerusalem, the price gap between the leading and lagging neighborhood (Ramot Remez and Newe David) remained virtually unchanged over the years, reaching some \$500 per m^2 in both 1990 and 2002 (Fig. 5B).

Notably, in Jerusalem, the highest rates of residential turnover are documented in the neighborhoods with relatively cheap housing – Gilo and Giva Zarfatit (see Fig. 5A). In contrast, in Haifa, relatively more expensive neighborhoods – Sprinzak and Ramot Remez – appeared to sell best (see Fig. 6B). At least in part, this tendency may be explained by the difference in the average levels of housing prices in the two cities - \$2000 per m^2 in Jerusalem vs. \$1000 per m^2 in Haifa. Considering that the average annual per capita income in Jerusalem reaches only one half of that in Haifa (\$5,500 and \$10,000, respectively), the marked preference of Jerusalem's buyers for cheaper apartments becomes explicable.

HCMs Vs. Housing Price Change And Turnover Rates

Fig. 7 compares the average annual rates of price change and the incidence of housing changes and modifications (HCMs) in the neighborhoods under study. In order to account for the local environmental qualities, the neighborhoods are ranked according to three environmental factors – proximity to major roads, proximity to parks, and the share of apartments with panoramic views of open areas (see Appendix 1). In the diagrams (Figs. 7A-B), the neighborhoods are sorted from left to right, from least environmentally favorable (Giva Zarfatit in Jerusalem and Kiryat Haim in Haifa) to most environmentally attractive places (Gilo in Jerusalem and Ramot Remez in Haifa).

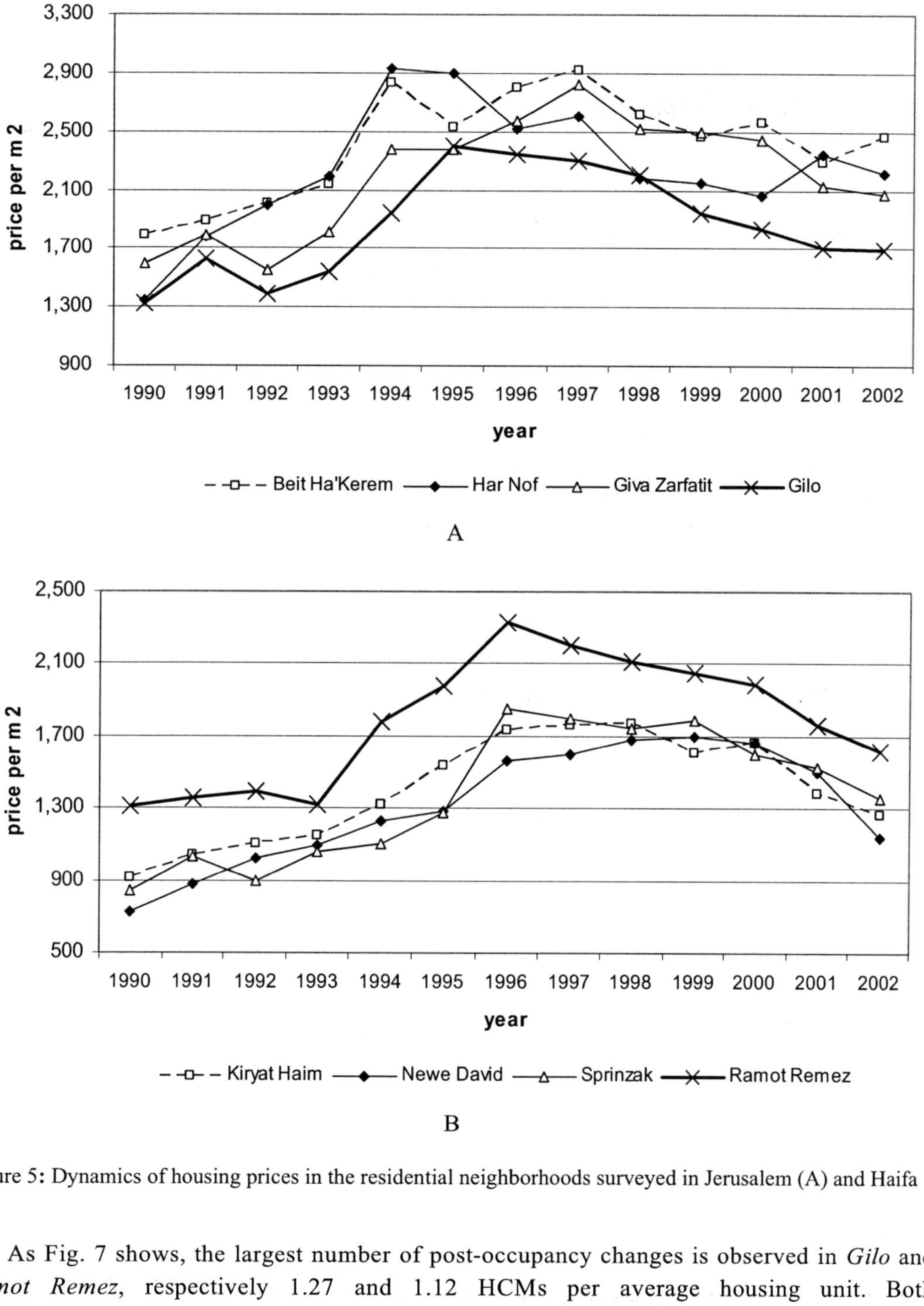

Figure 5: Dynamics of housing prices in the residential neighborhoods surveyed in Jerusalem (A) and Haifa (B)

As Fig. 7 shows, the largest number of post-occupancy changes is observed in *Gilo* and *Ramot Remez*, respectively 1.27 and 1.12 HCMs per average housing unit. Both neighborhoods are characterized by relatively favorable environmental conditions: they are situated on high elevations, surrounded by open areas, and more than a half of the apartments, covered by our survey in these neighborhoods, have attractive panoramic views of built or open areas (see Appendix 1). Notably, both neighborhoods are also characterized by relatively high rates of housing turnover (see Fig. 6). This is clearly in line with the research assumption that neighborhoods with considerable HCM accumulation attract more buyers. However, it is also possible that a frequent change of ownership leads to more HCM accumulation, since new owners may try to adapt apartments and houses to their needs.

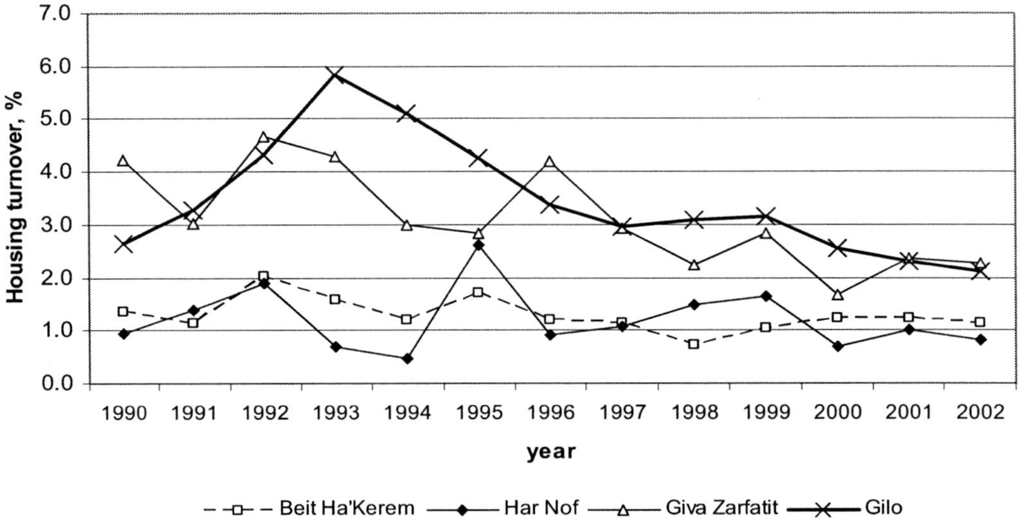

A

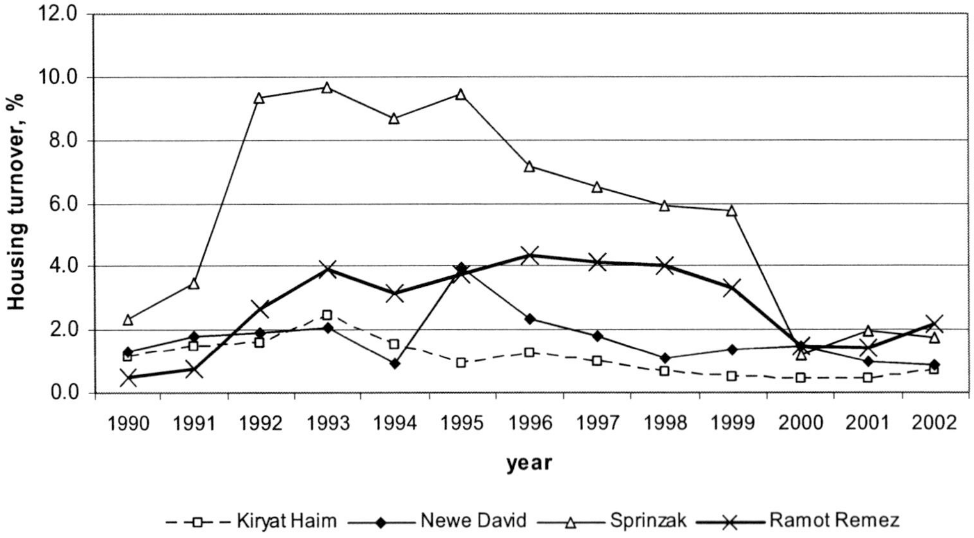

B

Figure 6: Residential turnover in the neighborhoods surveyed [the overall number of annual sales as percent of the total number of housing units in the neighborhood] Jerusalem (A) and Haifa (B)

HCMs are fewest in the Giva Zarfatit (Jerusalem) and *Kiryat Haim* (Haifa) neighborhoods, respectively 0.84 and 0.14 HCMs per average housing unit (see Fig. 7). Both neighborhoods are situated far away from green areas and offer relatively little panoramic views (see Appendix 1). In addition, Giva Zarfatit is located in the Eastern part of the capital.

This part of the city is adjacent to the Seam Line and disputed between Israel and the Palestinians. The neighborhood's location in such a place is a clear disincentive for HCM decisions of homeowners, due to uncertainty. Moreover, most buildings in Giva Zarfatit are designed without porches, and this kind of modification (i.e., porch or balcony), which is very common elsewhere, is not allowed in this neighborhood. The relative scarcity of HCMs in *Kiryat Haim* (see Fig. 7B) may also be explained by its location disadvantages, viz. low elevations (ca. 5 m above the sea level), and close proximity to major roads and industrial areas, such as oil refineries (see Fig. 3).

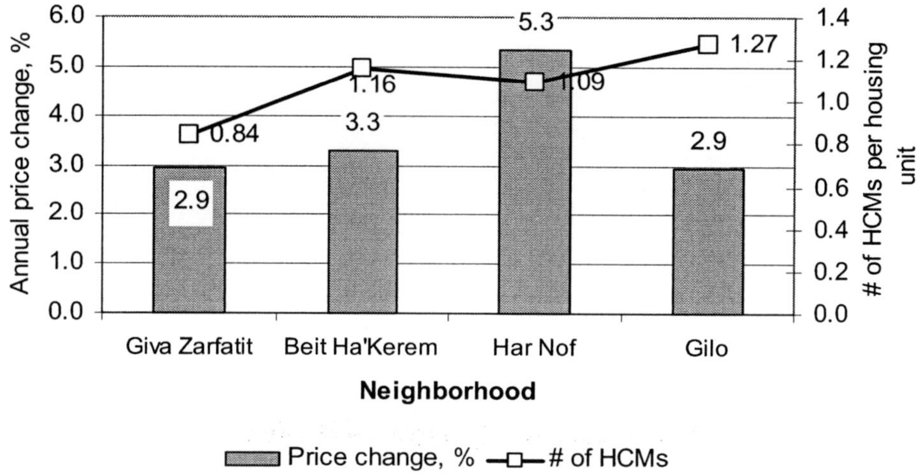

A

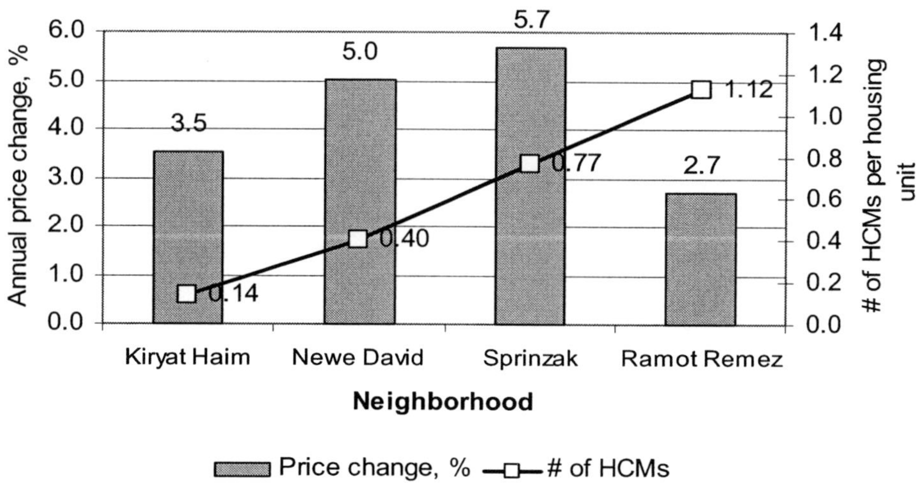

B

Note: The neighborhoods are ranked according to their environmental conditions, from worst (left) to best (right)

Figure 7: The average numbers of HCMs per housing unit and annual price change in the neighborhoods surveyed in Jerusalem (top) and Haifa (bottom)

In general, the average number of post-occupancy changes accumulated in the neighborhoods correlates with annual price change (Fig. 7). However, a relatively small number of cases (four neighborhoods in each city) does no allow us to draw any firm statistical conclusions from a simple inter-neighborhood comparison and thus limits our discussion of these relationships to most general observations, pending a more advanced statistical analysis, reported in one of the following sub-sections (see pp.16-17).

With a notable exception of Gilo in Jerusalem and Ramot Remez in Haifa, the relationship between the average number of post-occupancy changes accumulated in the neighborhoods and annual price change appears to be fairly straightforward: *the neighborhoods with large numbers of HCMs tend to exhibit more rapid average price increases*. Thus, in Haifa (Fig. 7B), the Sprinzak neighborhood (0.77 HCMs per average dwelling) exhibited in 1990-2002 the average annual price increase of some 5.7%, whereas Kiryat Haim (0.14 HCM) witnessed a price increase of only 3.5% per annum.

Notably, Gilo (Jerusalem) and Ramot Remez (Haifa) clearly deviate from these trends. In these neighborhoods, the relatively large incidence of HCMs is accompanied by relatively slow annual price increments – 2.9% and 2.7%, respectively (see Fig. 6). In both neighborhoods, housing additions and modifications are relatively easy to implement due to the presence of small (3-4-story) buildings with a relatively large share of ground floor apartments. Concurrently, residential properties in Ramot Remez are relatively expensive (\$1600 per m^2 as opposed to \$1000-1200 per m^2 in other neighborhoods surveyed in Haifa), which renders any substantial price increase in this neighborhood rather unlikely, due to ongoing economic recession and the availability of cheaper accommodations in the neighborhood's vicinity, specifically in the Ramot Itzhak neighborhood built nearby. As for the Gilo neighborhood in Jerusalem, its relatively slow price increase can be blamed on the severe deterioration of security situation in this part of the capital, bordering on the Palestinian autonomous areas.

Fig. 8 may also help to explain why HCMs are common in some neighborhoods and scarce in others and why HCMs are relatively more frequent in Jerusalem than in Haifa (see Fig. 7). Thus, as Fig. 8 shows, in the Beit Ha'Kerem neighborhood, an increase of apartment floor area from, for instance, 80 to 100 m^2 (with can be accomplished at the total construction costs of \$20,000-25,000, including taxes) is likely to raise the selling price of the apartment, on the average, from \$200,000 to \$230,000, i.e., by some \$30,000 (Fig. 8A). It makes such a building addition profitable. In contrast, the addition of the same room in the Giva Zarfatit neighborhood will cause a net economic loss to the homeowner, since it may raise the apartment's price by only \$20,000, from \$180,000 to \$200,000 (Fig. 8A). Characteristically, in *no* neighborhood in Haifa, physical expansions of properties is economically justifiable (Fig. 8B), since the construction costs are always higher than any potential price gain that may accrue from them. As a result, as hypothesized form the outset of the analysis (see Fig. 1), whatever HCMs homeowners may undertake in these neighborhoods, they undertake them solely for improving personal utility, rather to profit considerations.

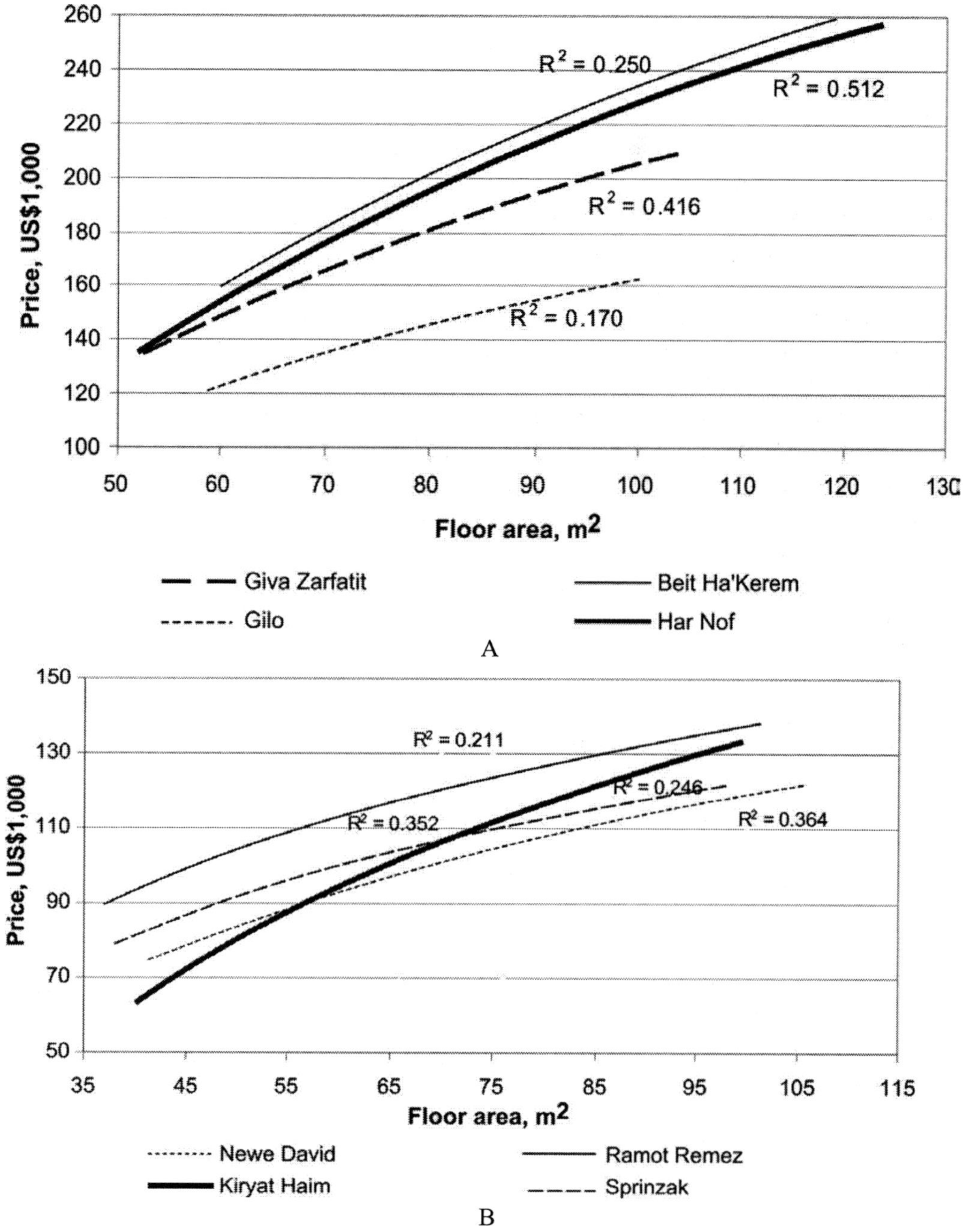

Figure 8: Average sale prices of apartments of different size in Jerusalem (top) and Haifa (Bottom) – logarithmic fits

Multivariate Analysis – Sale Prices

As Table 1 shows, in *Jerusalem*, ten factors are filtered out by the SMR as statistically significant. They are: floor area, the number of HCMs, cleanness, elevator, green view, parking, physical condition, sale year, urban view, and Beit Ha'Kerem (T>3.0; P<0.05; Table

1: Variables in the model). Thus, the sale prices (LOG) tend to be higher in large apartments (AREA: B=0.007; P<0.001), in buildings with elevators (ELEVATOR: B=0.084; P<0.001), in apartments with private parking (PARKING: B=0.049; P<0.01), and in apartments located in buildings characterized by sound structural conditions (PHYSICAL CONDITION: B=0.090; P<0.001). Cleanness of the open areas around a building also increases the sale price (CLEANNESS: B=0.040; P<0.001), so does the location of an apartment in the Beit Ha'Kerem neighborhood (B=0.158; P<0.001).

Table 1. Factors affecting the sale prices of housing units in Jerusalem (1st run: dependent variable – PRICE (LOG); method – SMR)

Explanatory variable	B[a]	Beta[b]	t[c]	sign.[d]	VIF[e]
A. Significant variables (variables in the model)					
(Constant)	85.964		12.421	0.000	
AREA	0.007	0.483	14.860	0.000	1.667
BEIT HA'KEREM	0.158	0.256	8.990	0.000	1.279
CHANGE	0.017	0.059	2.290	0.023	1.051
CLEANNESS	0.040	0.101	3.563	0.000	1.279
ELEVATOR	0.084	0.163	4.487	0.000	2.073
GREEN VIEW	0.116	0.175	5.646	0.000	1.510
PARKING	0.049	0.090	3.262	0.001	1.206
PHYSICAL CONDITION	0.090	0.194	6.102	0.000	1.594
SALEYEAR	-0.037	-0.275	-10.825	0.000	1.022
URBAN VIEW	-0.040	-0.069	-2.376	0.018	1.328
No of observations	449				
R^2	0.723				
R^2 adjusted	0.716				
F	114.056			0.000	
RSS[f]	8.172				
B. Insignificant variables (excluded variables)					
	Beta In[b]	t[c]	sign.[d]	Partial Correlation	VIF[e]
AP_FLOOR	-0.003	-0.105	0.916	-0.005	1.250
BUILDYEAR	-0.054	-1.467	0.143	-0.070	2.109
DPARK (LOG)	0.037	1.703	0.089	0.081	1.651
DROADS (LOG)	0.050	0.915	0.361	0.044	1.495
DSCHOOL (LOG)	-0.018	-0.747	0.455	-0.036	1.278
FLOOR	-0.009	-0.314	0.754	-0.015	1.339
FLOORS	-0.028	-0.655	0.513	-0.031	2.857
GARDEN	0.039	1.465	0.144	0.070	1.101
GILO	-0.105	-2.202	0.028	-0.105	3.638
GIVA ZARFATIT	0.101	2.202	0.028	0.105	3.323
INDUSTRIAL VIEW	0.016	0.541	0.589	0.026	1.346
RELATIVE CONDITION	-0.059	-1.916	0.056	-0.091	1.484
STORAGE	-0.006	-0.165	0.869	-0.008	1.802
VEGETATION	0.032	0.864	0.388	0.041	2.101

[a] regression coefficient; [b] standardized regression coefficient; [c] *t*-statistic; [d] significance of *t*-statistic; [e] - variance inflation factor (collinearity diagnostic); [f] residual sum of squares

Table 2. Factors affecting the sale prices of housing units in Haifa (1st run: dependent variable – PRICE (LOG); method – SMR)

Explanatory variable	B	Beta	t	Sign.	VIF
A. Significant variables (variables in the model)					
(Constant)	58.158		18.742	0.000	
AREA	0.003	0.450	18.405	0.000	1.104
ELEVATION (LOG)	0.053	0.365	11.222	0.000	1.961
SALEYEAR	-0.027	-0.404	-17.254	0.000	1.012
RELATIVE CONDITION	0.033	0.149	6.248	0.000	1.052
SINGLE	0.056	0.098	3.777	0.000	1.240
STORAGE	0.026	0.127	4.555	0.000	1.430
GARDEN	0.024	0.062	2.277	0.023	1.390
PARKING	-0.015	-0.074	-2.543	0.011	1.568
AP_FLOOR	0.004	0.056	2.188	0.029	1.222
MAJOR CHANGE	0.011	0.059	2.084	0.037	1.458
No of observations	754				
R^2	0.598				
R^2 adjusted	0.592				
F	110.457				
RSS	3.070				
B. Insignificant variables (excluded variables)					
Explanatory variable	Beta In	t	Sign.	Partial Correlation	VIF
BUILDYEAR	0.004	0.151	0.880	0.006	1.401
CLEANNESS	0.005	0.198	0.843	0.007	1.346
DPARK (LOG)	0.026	0.881	0.378	0.032	1.612
DROAD (LOG)	0.020	0.571	0.568	0.021	2.222
FLOOR	-0.007	-0.285	0.776	-0.010	1.131
FLOORS	-0.035	-1.193	0.233	-0.044	1.587
GREEN VIEW	-0.012	-0.489	0.625	-0.018	1.149
GROUND_FLOOR	0.013	0.544	0.586	0.020	1.058
INDUSTRIAL VIEW	0.002	0.107	0.915	0.004	1.009
PHYSICAL CONDITION	0.050	1.394	0.164	0.051	2.389
SEA VIEW	-0.041	-1.653	0.099	-0.061	1.124
URBAN VIEW	0.026	0.829	0.407	0.030	1.824
VEGETATION	-0.038	-1.515	0.130	-0.056	1.175

See note to Table 3

Concurrently, urban views and the sale year reduce the price (P<0.05). The negative sign of the latter variable (SALEYEAR) clearly reflects the trend of the price drop in past years (see Fig. 5A). The views of built areas appear to be unattractive for the local buyers (URBAN VIEW: B=-0.040; P<0.05), as opposed to green views which tend to raise apartment prices (GREEN VIEW: P=0.116; P<0.01).

As hypothesized, the presence of HCMs increases the sale prices of properties (CHANGE: B=0.017; P<0.05), indicating that there indeed appears to be *a price premium* associated with rehabilitation efforts of homeowners.

Characteristically, the sale prices of apartments and houses in *Haifa* are affected by similar factors – floor area, relative physical conditions of buildings, the presence of storage, parking and private garden (see Table 2). As Table 2 shows, the sale prices of apartments and houses (log) tend to rise as the floor area increases (B=0.003; P<0.001). In addition, *ceteris paribus,* the sale prices tend to be higher in single family dwellings than in multi-story structures (SINGLE: t=3.777; P<0.001), and in apartments located on higher elevations (B=0.053; P<0.001; see Table 2). As expected, the presence of major HCMs[4] also tends to increase the sale price (P<0.01; see Table 2).

In our view, however, the actual contribution of the HCM component is likely to be underestimated. First, some of the effects of the HCM factor may be captured, at least in part, by other variables in the models. For instance, a change in an apartment's floor area may be captured by the AREA variable (B>0). Although the multicollinearity of explanatory variables was checked and found within tolerable limits (VIF<4; see Tables 1 and 2), even these, relatively low collinearity levels may lessen the actual contribution of the HCM variable. Second, as previously noted, many HCMs (viz., furnishing, layout change, renovation, and plumbing) occur *inside* apartments and houses and was not covered by the present survey. Further studies, involving the assessment of *interior* HCMs, may thus be needed to assess the full extent of the influence of HCM activity of homeowners on the selling prices of apartments and houses.

Multivariate Analysis – HCMs as Dependent Variable

Only in Haifa, a reasonably good regression model of the incidence of HCMs in residential neighborhoods could be obtained (R^2=0.405; see Table 3). This model is discussed below in some detail.

As Table 3 shows, there appears to be more HCMs in apartments located on higher elevations (ELEVATION: B=0.472; P<0.001). The presence of a private garden and parking also increase the propensity of homeowners to modify their properties. There are also significantly more HCMs in large apartments (AREA: B=0.006; P< 0.001), and in well-maintained buildings (PHYSICAL CONDITION: B=0.176; P< 0.001), than elsewhere. Concurrently, the presence of a private storage decreases the number of HCMs (STORAGE: B=-0.234; P<0.001). Apparently, storage sheds minimize the residents' need to expand their properties, by adding verandas and balconies which can serve as temporary storages for household goods. As expected, there are fewer HCMs in multi-story buildings than elsewhere (FLOORS: B=-0.035; P< 0.001). The matter is that in multi-story buildings, making external modifications may be either expensive or impracticable, specifically in residences occupying middle floors. A large number of HCMs in single family houses (SINGLE: B=0.330; P<0.001) further supports this explanation.

Notably, the number of HCMs drops, *ceteris paribus,* as the log distance from major roads increases. This trend may have a simple explanation. Thus, homeowners whose apartments are located near a noisy road may tend to invest more in particular types of

[4] Include room and roof additions, arbors, and permanent storages. Although in initial stages of the analysis, HCMs were represented separately by all changes (variable – CHANGE) and major changes (variable – MAJOR

housing changes and modification (e.g., closing a balcony, redoubling windows, etc.), in order to reduce the negative impact of traffic noise, as indicated by the present survey.

Expectedly, the number of HCMs tends to be larger in wealthy neighborhoods (INCOME (LOG): B=1.016; t=10.268; P<0.01). The number of external HCMs also increases with PRICE CHANGE (B=0.170; t=8.313; P<0.01; see Table 3), which is fully in line with the initial research assumption that in neighborhoods, in which no substantial price gain can be expected, relatively little accumulation of HCMs occurs.

Table 3.Factors affecting the number of major HCMs in apartments and houses (dependent variable – MAJOR CHANGE; method – SMR)

Explanatory variable	B[a]	Beta[b]	t[c]	t-sig[d]	VIF[e]
A. Significant variables (variables in the model)					
(Constant)	5.881		1.559	0.119	
AREA	0.004	0.114	3.499	0.000	1.321
BUILDYEAR	-0.007	-0.125	-3.582	0.000	1.510
DROAD (LOG)	-0.194	-0.161	-4.028	0.000	1.994
FLOORS	-0.031	-0.138	-3.988	0.000	1.501
GARDEN	0.687	0.337	9.826	0.000	1.469
INCOME (LOG)	1.016	0.586	10.268	0.000	4.061
PARKING	0.187	0.176	4.072	0.000	2.335
PHYSICAL CONDITION	0.191	0.204	6.669	0.000	1.172
PRICE CHANGE	0.170	0.310	8.313	0.000	1.738
SINGLE	0.304	0.101	3.363	0.001	1.136
STORAGE	-0.236	-0.219	-6.360	0.000	1.482
URBAN VIEW	-0.152	-0.132	-3.292	0.001	1.993
No of observations	754				
R2	0.405				
R2 adjusted	0.396				
F	42.125			0.000	
B. Insignificant variables (excluded variables)					
Explanatory variable	Beta In	t	Sig.	Part.Cor.	VIF
AP_FLOOR	-0.037	-0.988	0.323	-0.036	1.715
CLEANNESS	0.006	0.167	0.867	0.006	1.398
DPARK (LOG)	0.000	0.007	0.994	0.000	2.052
ELEVATION (LOG)	0.086	0.543	0.587	0.020	31.286
ELEVATOR	0.019	0.443	0.658	0.016	2.272
FIRST_FLOOR	0.035	1.184	0.237	0.043	1.064
FLOOR	-0.034	-1.058	0.291	-0.039	1.298
GREEN VIEW	-0.024	-0.776	0.438	-0.029	1.179
INDUSTRIAL VIEW	-0.007	-0.251	0.802	-0.009	1.009
RELATIVE CONDITION	-0.029	-0.726	0.468	-0.027	1.946
SALEYEAR	-0.031	-1.079	0.281	-0.040	1.029
SEA VIEW	0.042	1.257	0.209	0.046	1.382
VEGETATION	0.032	0.991	0.322	0.036	1.269

*See footnote to Table 3.

CHANGE; see Appendix 3), only the best performing variables (i.e., MAJOR CHANGE for Haifa and CHANGE for Jerusalem) are reported in this paper.

CONCLUSIONS

Homeowners may choose to modify their properties for two basic reasons – enhancing personal utility and maximizing return on HCMs in terms of property value. If C denotes the construction costs of a particular HCM (e.g., a room or roof addition), and dP represents the change of a property's market price after the modification is undertaken, then the choice between the aforementioned HCM motivations may be expressed as follows:

1. $dP > C$: HCM is justified by rational economic considerations (i.e., gaining property value) while it may also be undertaken to enhance personal utility;
2. $dP \leq C$: HCM is undertaken for a sole purpose of gaining personal utility, without any value-rise justification (see Fig. 1).

According to the explanation we propose, in an environmentally disadvantageous, inaccessible or physically deteriorated neighborhood, where *no* substantial price gain can be expected, HCMs may be motivated *mainly* by improving personal utility, rather than by value-rise considerations. As a result, in such a neighborhood, little accumulation of HCMs may occur.

As the present analysis indicates, in both cities covered by the study, there indeed appear to be more HCMs in environmentally favorable neighborhoods. In particular, in Haifa, for which a reasonably good explanatory model of the factors affecting the incidence of HCMs in residential neighborhoods could be obtained, the incidence of HCMs appears to depend significantly on the neighborhood-specific price change, apartment's floor area, distance to major roads, elevation above the sea level, physical condition of the building, number of floors, and other building and neighborhood factors. The research also points out that there appears to be a price premium associated with HCM efforts of homeowners. In particular, the inclusion of the HCM component in the traditional hedonic model helps to improve the model's fit and generality.

We also witnessed that, despite considerable fluctuations of housing prices, the neighborhoods characterized by a relatively large accumulation of post-occupancy HCMs, tend to retain their relative price levels and exhibit relatively high rates of housing turnover. This observation is in line with the initial research assumption that neighborhoods with considerable HCM accumulation attract more buyers. However, it is also possible that frequent change of ownership leads to more HCM accumulation, since new owners may try to adapt apartments and houses to their needs.

The limitations of data, obtained via external field surveys carried out in a relatively small number of neighborhoods, restrict on how the proposed hypotheses can be verified by the empirical results, thus necessitating further studies. Investment intentions of property owners are another important indicator of the homeowners' response to environmental conditions, which cannot be investigated by a field survey, without entering individual properties. Therefore, the follow-up studies should focus both on the survey of interior housing modifications and on direct interviewing of homeowners. The results of such studies should thus help to determine whether past investment and investment intentions of property owners indeed differ significantly by neighborhoods, depending on their environmental conditions and building characteristics, as hypothesized in the research model (Fig. 2-ii).

ACKNOWLEDGMENTS

The author's gratitude is due to Yakov Odish, Orit Kruss and Haim Yehoshua, real estate appraisals, for providing apartment price data for the present study. The author is also thankful to Dr. Larissa Fleishman for assisting with literature survey, and to graduate students of the Department of Natural Resources and Environmental Management of the Haifa University for their assistance in field surveys.

REFERENCES

Asabere, P. K., and F.E. Huffman. (1996) "Thoroughfares and apartment values", *The Journal of Real Estate Research* 12 (Jenuary), 9-16.

Banzhaf, H.S., and R.P. Walsh. (2004). Testing for Environmental Gentrification: Migratory responses to Changes in Environmental Quality, Working paper for 2004 AERE Workshop, Estes Park, CO.

Benson, E.D., J.L. Hansen, A.L. Schwartz, Jr. and G.T. Smersh. (1998). "Pricing residential amenities: The value of a view," *Journal of Real Estate Finance and Economics* 16 (January), 55-73.

Bond M.T., Seiler V.L and M.J. Seiler (2002) Residential Real Estate Prices: A Room with a View, *Journal of Real Estate Research* 23(1/2): 129-138.

Bridge C., Flatau P., Whelan S., Wood G., and J. Yates. (2003). *Housing Assistance and Non-Shelter Outcomes,* Australia Research Centre, Sydney.

Cole I., and K. Reeve. (2001). *Housing and Physical Environment Domain: A Review of the Evidence Base*, Centre for Regional Economic and Social Research, Sheffield Hallam University, Sheffield.

Des Rosiers F., Thériault M., Kestens Y. and P.Villeneuve (2002) Landscaping and House Values: An Empirical Investigation, *Journal of Real Estate Research* 23(1/2): 139-162.

DETR. (2000). *Low Demand Housing and Unpopular neighbourhoods*, Department of Employment Training and Rehabilitation, London

Ding C., Simons R., and E. Baku. (2000). "The effect of residential investment on Nearby Property Values: Evidence from Cleveland, Ohio", *Journal of Real Estate Research* 19 (January-February), 23-48.

Ellen I., and M. Turner. (1997). "Does neighbourhood matter? Assessing recent evidence", *Housing Policy Debate,* 8 (April), 833-866.

Etzion Y., B.A. Portnov, E. Erell, I. Meir and D. Pearlmutter. (2001). "An open GISframework for recording and analyzing post-occupancy changes in residential buildings – a climate-related case study", *Building and Environment* 36, 1075-1090.

Fleishman L., and Y. Odish. (2003a). "The effect of urban parks on residential real estate prices", Working paper, Department of Real Estate Appraisal, Ministry of Justice, Israel.

Fleishman L., and Y. Odish. (2003b). "The influence of traffic noise on the values of residential property: A case study of Jerusalem, Israel", *Working paper*, Department of Real Estate Appraisal, Ministry of Justice, Israel.

Gat, D. 1998. "Urban Focal Points and Design Quality Influence Rents: The Case of the Tel Aviv Office Market", *Journal of Real Estate Research* 16 (February), 229-247.

Glass, R. (1964). "Aspects of Change," in (MacGibbon and Kee, eds), *Aspects of Change,* Centre for Urban Studies, London.

Groves R. and P. Niner. (1998). *A Good Investment? The Impact of Urban Renewal on an Inner City Housing Market,* Policy Press, West Sussex.

Ikejiofor, U. 1999. *"If past traditions were building blocks. A perspective on low income housing in Nigerian cities," Building and Environment* 34, 221-230.

McMillen, D.P. (1996). "One Hundred Fifty Years of Land Values in Chicago: A Nonparametric Approach," *Journal of Urban Economics* 40, 100-124.

Minami, M., *Using ArcMap,* Redlands, CA: Environmental Systems Research Institute, 2001.

Morancho, A.B. (2003). "A Hedonic Valuation of Urban Green Areas", *Landscape and Urban Planning* 66, 35-41.

Palen, J., and B. London (eds.). (1984). *Gentrification, Displacement and Neighborhood Revitalization.* State University of New York Press, Albany.

Portnov B.A., Odish Y. and L. Fleishman (2006). "Factors Affecting Housing Modifications and Housing Pricing: A Case Study of Four Residential Neighborhoods in Haifa, Israel," *Journal of Real Estate Research* 27(4): 371-407.

Ryan S. (1999). "Property values and transportation facilities: finding the transportation-land use connection", *Journal of Planning Literature* 13 (April), 412-427.

Shiferaw, D. (1998). *Self-initiated transformations of public-provided dwellings in Addis Ababa,* Ethiopia. Cities 15, 437-448.

Sieg, H.V., V.K. Smith, H.S. Banzhaf, and R. Walsh. (2004). Estimation general Equilibrium Benefits of Large changes in Spatially Delineated Public Goods," *International Economic Review.*

Simons, R.A., R. Quercia and I. Maric. (1998). "The Value Impact of New Residential Construction and Neighborhood Disinvestment on Residential Sales Prices," *Journal of Real Estate Research* 15 (Jenuary-February), 147-162.

Slater, T., W. Curran, and L. Lees. (2004). "Gentrification research: New directions and Critical scholarship," *Environment and Planning A* 36 (July), 1141-1150.

Smith, N. (1979). "Toward a theory of gentrification: A back to the city movement by capital not people," *Journal of the American Planning Association* 45, 538-548.

Smith, N. (1987). "Gentrification and the Rent-Gap," *Annals of the Association of American Geographers* 77 (March), 462-465.

Sungur C.A., and G. Çağdaş (2003). *Effects of housing morphology on user satisfaction,* 4th International Space Syntax Symposium, London.

Walsh, R.P. (2003). *Analyzing Open Space Policies in a Location Equilibrium Model with Endogenous Landscape Amenities,* Mimeo. Boulder, CO: University of Colorado.

Wilhelmsson, M. (2000). "The impact of traffic noise on the values of single-family houses", *Journal of Environmental Planning and Management* 43 (June), 799-815.

Wilkinson, H., and H. Kardash. (1992). "Development within development: distribution of responsibilities in aided self-help in Egypt's new city settlements," *Third-World Planning Review* 14, 297-312.

APPENDIX 1

Selected Characteristics of the Neighborhoods Surveyed

Neighborhood	Total No of housing units	No of apartments surveyed	Price, $/m2 (2-bdr)	Annual price change in 1990-2002, %	Housing turnover per annum, %	No of HCMs per housing unit	Distance to parks, m	Distance to roads, m	Green views, %	Urban views, %	Elevation above the sea level, m	Vegetation (1-3)*	Cleanness (1-3)*	Structural condition of buildings (1-3)*
Jerusalem														
Giva Zarfatit	2,106	153	2,198	2.9	3.1	0.84	232	109	0.0	39.2	820	2.8	2.7	3.0
Beit Ha'Kerem	3,871	100	2,189	4.3	1.3	1.16	168	60	6.0	9.0	765	2.5	2.6	2.4
Har Nof	3,323	96	2,247	5.3	1.2	1.09	102	27	79.2	1.0	750	1.5	2.4	3.0
Gilo	8,911	100	1,864	2.9	3.5	1.27	41	67	0.0	52.0	830	1.4	1.9	1.9
Total:	18,211	449												
Haifa														
Kiryat Haim	10,584	168	1,374	3.5	1.1	0.14	444	36	0.0	0.0	5	1.4	2.0	2.0
Newe David	1,878	117	1,290	5.0	1.7	0.40	160	68	8.5	0.0	26	1.8	2.1	2.2
Sprinzak	1,673	152	1,338	5.7	5.2	0.77	33	161	30.3	3.3	59	1.6	2.0	1.9
Ramot Remez	2,161	327	1,749	2.7	2.6	1.12	71	217	17.4	66.1	271	1.3	2.1	1.7
Total:	16,296	764												

See legend to Appendix 2 for explanation

APPENDIX 2

Description of research variables

Variable	Description
A. Dependent variables	
CHANGES	Overall number of changes in a apartment [see Appendix 3B – Total # of changes]
MAJOR CHANGES	Overall number of major changes in an apartment [a]
PRICE (LOG)	Logarithm of apartment sale price [US$]
UNIT_PRICE	Apartment sale price per m^2 of floor area [US$]
B. Explanatory variables (neighborhood and apartment characteristics)	
AP FLOOR	Number of apartments per floor
AREA	Total area of the apartment/house [m^2]
BUILDYEAR	Year of the apartment/house construction
CLEANNESS	Cleanness of spaces around building: 1 = poor; 2 = reasonable; 3 = good
DPARK (LOG)	Distance to nearby public park [m]
DROAD (LOG)	Distance to the closest arterial road [m]
DSCHOOL (LOG)[d]	Distance to nearby school [m]
ELEVATION (LOG) [c]	Log of elevation of the building above the sea level [m]
ELEVATOR	Elevator in the building = 1; no elevator = 0
FLOOR	Floor on which apartment is located
FLOORS	Number of floors in the building
GARDEN	Private garden = 1; no garden = 0
GREEN VIEW	Green view = 1; no green view = 0
GROUND FLOOR	Location on the ground floor (1 = ground floor; 0 = elsewhere)
INCOME (LOG)	Average income level in the area [US$ per capita]
INDUSTRIAL VIEW	View of industrial area = 1; no industrial view = 0
PARKING	Private parking = 1; no private parking = 0
PHYSICAL CONDITION	1 = poor; 2 = average; 3 = good
PRICE (LOG)[d]	Log of apartment sale price [US$]
PRICE CHANGE	Average annual price change in the neighborhood in 1990-2002 [%]
RELATIVE CONDITION	Relative condition (compared to nearby buildings): 1 = worse; 2 = same; 3 = better
SALEYEAR	Year of sale
SEA VIEW [c]	Sea view = 1; no sea view = 0
SINGLE [c]	Single family dwelling = 1; multi-family dwelling = 0
STORAGE	Private storage shed = 1; no storage =0
URBAN VIEW	Panoramic urban view = 1; no view = 0
VEGETATION	Few = 1; some = 2; a lot = 3
C. Explanatory variables (neighborhood dummies - Jerusalem)[b]	
BEIT HA'KEREM	1 for an apartment located in the Beit Ha'kerem neighborhood, 0 – location elsewhere
GILO	1 for an apartment in the Gilo neighborhood, 0 – location elsewhere
GIVA ZARFATIT	1 for an apartment in the Giva Zarfatit neighborhood, 0 – location elsewhere
D. Explanatory variables (neighborhood dummies - Haifa)[b]	
KIRIYAT HAIM	1 for an apartment/house in the Kiriyat Haim neighborhood, 0 – location elsewhere
NEWE DAVID	1 for a apartment/house in the Newe David neighborhood, 0 – location elsewhere
SPRINZAK	1 for a apartment/house in the Sprinzak neighborhood, 0 – location elsewhere

a Include only room and roof additions, permanent storages and balconies; b tested during the exploratory stages of the analysis but excluded later on from the models due to strong collinearity with the ELEVATION (LOG) variable; c available for Haifa only; d available for Jerusalem only; d tested during the exploratory stages of the analysis but excluded later on from the models due to strong collinearity with the INCOME (LOG) variable.

APPENDIX 3

A. Field survey table - data sources and examples of records

Address				Building								Apartment				Location (Proximity to…)				
Apartment ID	Street	House #	Apart. #	# of floors	Apart per floor	Physical condition	Relative condition	Changes	Elevator	Greenery	Cleanness	Storage	Parking	Private court-yard	View	Disamenity (ies)	Open spaces	Major road	Commercial centre	Elev. above sea level
Scale→				#	#	*	*	#/cost	yes/no	*	*	yes/no	yes/no	yes/no	*	meters	meters	meters	meters	meters
Source	Sale database			Field survey								Field survey				GIS calculation				
1	Pel yam	23	7	5	2	3	2	8/36100	yes	3	3	yes	yes	yes	4	458	56	120	1200	450
…																				
n	Naviim	15	45	4	3	1	3	2/13000	no	1	2	no	no	no	5	53	1236	45	540	24

LEGEND (*):

Physical condition		Relative condition (compared to adjacent buildings)		Greenery		Cleanness		View	
1	Poor	1	Worse	1	Few	1	Poor	1	No view
2	Average	2	Same	2	Some	2	Reasonable	2	Sea view
3	Good	3	Better	3	A lot	3	Good	3	Green view
								4	Urban view
								5	Industrial view

B. Change coding and examples of records

Address				No of changes by change type														
Apartment ID	Street	House #	Apartment #	1-window	2-door	3-solid roof	4-arbor	5-room	6-storage	7-balcony	8-paving	9-air. Conditioner	10-wall, fence	11-gate	12-stairs	13-other	Total # of changes	Estimated cost
1	Pel yam	23	7	1	2		1	1			1	2					8	36100
…																		
n	Naviim	15	45	1	1												2	1300

Note: Apartment ID1 (street address Pelyam 23/7) : 1 new window; 2 doors added; 1 arbor; 1 room addition; paving; 2 air co1nditioners added

In: Perspectives on International, State and Local Economics
Editor: Gerald V. Liu, pp. 185-208
ISBN 1-60021-099-6

Chapter 7

Economic Growth and International Trade in the Mediterranean Area: An Empirical Analysis

Lucio Laureti
Lum Jean Monnet, Casamassima (Ba) Dmqte, Univ. G. D'annunzio, Pescara
Action Jean Monnet, Bruxelles

Abstract

One of the goals of the integration process between EU and MED countries, is the MED countries growth increase. Another goal that the process wants to reach is the increase of intra-area trade by reducing tariffs and non tariffs barriers. The aim of this paper is to verify if a positive relationship between economic growth and international trade in the examined area exist. The empirical evidence (confirmed in this paper) starts from a Johnson model application adapted in the Mediterranean area, by introducing demographic rise. The results of regressions seem to confirm that if the Barcelona integration process goes on, with a constant but continuous increase in trade, Med countries economic growth will also increase. If we exclude from the analysis two countries: Turkey and the Palestinian Authority, we obtain more reliable results.

Introduction

The study of the influence of trade on economic growth has aroused a lot of interest in connection with long term economic outlooks. The existing different theories on this subject seem to confirm the existence of a positive correlation between economic growth and international trade, however it is really difficult to divide accurately the effects of commercial liberalization on the growth from the effects of other virtuous policies made by each nation in other fields, such as the financial, fiscal and social ones. But, it has demonstrated that the countries which have liberalized their economies, through increasing imports and exports, the enlargement of the market, the increasing of productivity and of specialization, are usually rewarded with a growing per capita GDP.

The main aim of this work is to identify the relationship between economic growth and international trade: the countries studied are the 12 partners Countries of the Mediterranean area (MPC – 12) which signed the Barcelona declaration in 1995 with the European Union with the main aim of creating a free trade area by 2010.

For the empirical analysis we have chosen the Johnson Model, formulated around the middle of 50's, that puts in relationship the fluctuation of the balanced development rate of a Country A with the fluctuation of the export flow of this country towards a Country B. Starting from Johnson's fundamental equation and making some changes to this equation, we have produced a new equation according to which the fluctuation of a balanced development of a country (for us one of the MED countries) depends on the fluctuation of the income and of the exports flow during the time. After appropriate manipulations, we have used the classic model of linear regression in order to estimate the parameters that express the sign of the relationship that links the two variables in this study.

The years studied are from 1991 to 2000 that, even if they are not enough to verify the convergence in the national growth, they show us the influence of the globalization process and even of the effects of the Barcelona declaration as far as the relationship between growth and trade is concerned.

The Johnson Model

Keynesian theory has been extended to the analysis of economic development by the introduction of investment-production capacity relationship of the Keynesian relationship between investment and effective demand. A combination of the two relationships gives us a measure of the *balanced development rate*, defined as a rate that sustains full supply capacity[1]. This balanced development rate will be a fundamental variable for the relationship between economic growth and international trade[2].

This analysis considers an open economy where we know the export demand development rate. Furthermore it moves by the hypothesis that the balance of payment equilibrium is obtained with loans.

The fundamental development model includes two relations:

$$I_t = s \cdot Y_t \qquad (1)$$

where I_t is the investment rate required for total capital use, s is the part of saved income, constant by hypothesis, and Y_t is the existing supply rate at the time t.

The production capacity growth obtained by the investment is:

---

[1] Alternatively, the model can be used for specifying the development rate that maintains a "normal" degree of excess of capacity

[2] The development of this model has been, till then, confined to a closed economy, with the exception of some remarks of R.F. Harrod, Johnson for the first time expand this model to an international economy made by two countries in order to draw conclusions on the balanced development of such economy.

$$\frac{dY_t}{dt} = \frac{I_t}{k} = a \cdot I_t \tag{2}$$

where k is the capital coefficient or the capital-product relationship (constant by hypothesis), and a is its reciprocal, the production coefficient or product-capital relationship.

Substituting (1) for (2), we obtain the investment increase rate and sustainable GDP of full employment of the production:

$$r = \frac{dY_t}{dt} = a \cdot s \cdot Y_t \qquad \Rightarrow \qquad r = \frac{1}{Y_t} \cdot \frac{dY_t}{dt} = a \cdot s \tag{3}$$

This shows another hypothesis of the model: the working population must grow at least at the rate to avoid the capital stock exceeding the needed work to cover investment costs.

Furthermore, for the sake of mathematical simplicity, in the study of the international aspects, the model considers that the level of prices is constant, that the price of one unit of product corresponds to one unit of money and that the exchange rate between the currencies is initially equal to one.

This model, at the beginning, was applied to a close economy where investments were the only destination of the savings. In an open economy, on the contrary, imports and savings are dispersions of the effective demand while the exports and investments cover the existing differences between internal demand and supply for each level of production capacity. The equation (1), became:

$$(s + m) \cdot Y_t = I_t + X_t \tag{4}$$

where m is the import expenditure/GDP relation (constant by hypothesis) and X_t the current export flows; the equation (3) became:

$$r_t = \frac{dY_t}{dt} = a \cdot (s + m) \cdot Y_t - a \cdot X_t \Rightarrow r_t = a \cdot \left[s + m - \frac{X_t}{Y_t} \right] \tag{5}$$

and can be written in the form:

$$r_t = a \cdot (s - b_t) \tag{5a}$$

where $b_t = \dfrac{X_t}{Y_t} - m$ is the current export surplus of the country, expressed as a fraction of the production.

From the last two equations, we can make the following conclusions: if the export surplus decreases in time, the development balanced rate (r_t) increases; if, on the contrary, the surplus increases, that means that the export rate is over the import rate, so the balanced development rate (r_t) decreases. This second result is obtained differentiating equation (5):

$$r_t = a \cdot \left[s + m - \frac{X_t}{Y_t} \right]$$

where x is the export development rate and Y_t is positive by hypothesis.

In these terms the analysis is attractive, but probably misleading, because production, exports, balanced development rate and the export surplus are not constant but they are variables depending on the system constants.

In order to be sure of the results, we must resolve the differential equations in Y contained in the equation that defines r_t :

$$r_t = a \cdot \left(s + m - \frac{X_t}{Y_t} \right)$$

The solution is:

$$Y_t = Y_0 \cdot e^{a \cdot (s+m) \cdot t} + \frac{a \cdot X_0}{x - a \cdot (s+m)} \cdot \left(e^{a \cdot (s+m) \cdot t} - e^{x \cdot t} \right)$$

where Y_0 and X_0 are respectively the starting levels of supply capacity and the exports.

If the starting balanced development rate level is:

$$r_0 = a \cdot \left(s + m - \frac{X_0}{Y_0} \right) = a \cdot (s - b_0)$$

we can reach the following results:

if $x < r_0$ so $r > x$ and increases in the time reaching the asymptote $r_\infty = a \cdot (s + m)$

if $x < r_0$ so $r > x$ and increases in the time reaching the asymptote $r_\infty = a \cdot (s + m)$

if $x > r_0$ so $r < x$ and decreases continuously in time, with the consequence of a final inversion of the production

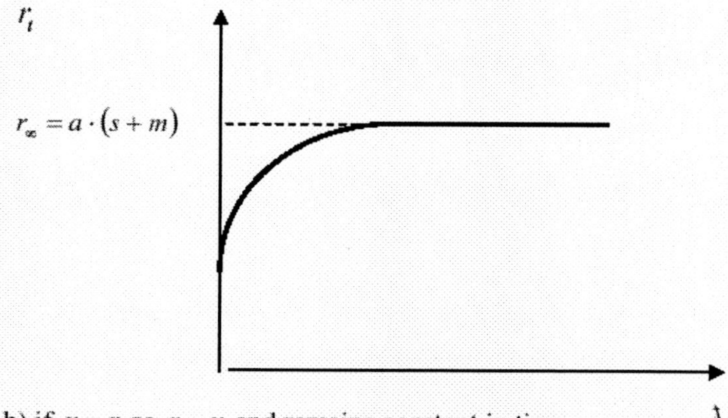

b) if $x = r_0$ so $r = x$ and remains constant in time

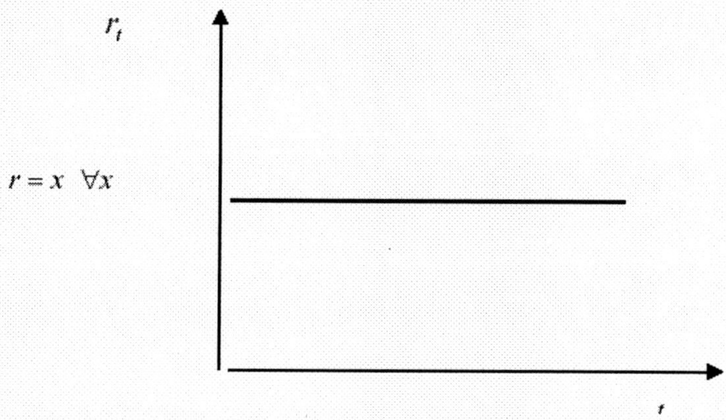

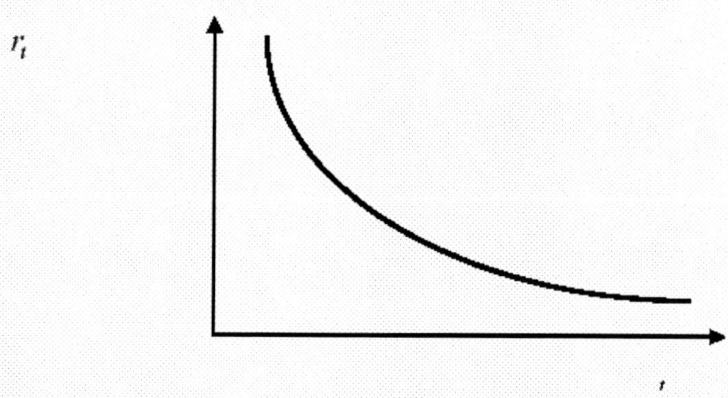

The economic evidence of these results are the following:

a) if the balanced development rate of a country is greater than the export demand increase rate, this country must grow at an increasing speed if we require the effective demand to be equal to the product capacity;

b) if the balanced development rate is less than the export demand increase rate, so this country must grow at a decreasing speed if we require the effective demand to be not greater than the product capacity;
c) only if the balanced development rate of a country is equal to the export demand increase rate, will equilibrium be maintained between effective demand level and productive capability at a constant speed.

A TRANSFORMATION OF THE ORIGINAL JOHNSON EQUATION

We are going to study the existing relationships for economic growth of each MED country and international trade, for the period 1991 and 2000, seen as, in this case, a trade between a single MED country and EU[3]. We will take the Johnson equation (5) by the hypothesis of a two countries world and a fixed price level. In this case, increasing productivity would be resolved in a proportional increase of the balanced develop rate. The above equation is the following:

$$r_t = a \cdot (s+m) - a \cdot \frac{X_t}{Y_t}$$

We can re-write the equation (5) in terms of incremental ratio developing the balanced development rate which changes during time:

$$\frac{dr_t}{dt} = -a \cdot \frac{X_t}{Y_t} \cdot \left[\frac{dX_t}{dt} \cdot \frac{1}{X_t} - \frac{dY_t}{dt} \cdot \frac{1}{Y_t} \right] \tag{5.1}$$

Dividing by $\frac{1}{r_t}$ we obtain the following equation:

$$\left(\frac{1}{r_t} \cdot \frac{dr_t}{dt} \right) = a \cdot \frac{X_t}{Y_t} \cdot \frac{1}{r_t} \cdot \left(\frac{dY_t}{dt} \cdot \frac{1}{Y_t} \right) - a \cdot \frac{X_t}{Y_t} \cdot \frac{1}{r_t} \cdot \left(\frac{dX_t}{dt} \cdot \frac{1}{X_t} \right) \tag{5.2}$$

It says that the balanced development rate change in time, is related with the difference on the change, in time, of the export flows.

We have already said that we aimed to study the relationship, if one exists, between economic growth of the MED countries and international trade with the EU in the last years. The obtained equation can be taken, at a starting point, to construct such a relationship, considering the balanced development rate as an economic growth indicator and the export flows as an international trade indicator.

[3] In other words we want to examine how EU and Med countries trade affects the Med countries growth

Taking the last equation obtained and expressing it as a logarithm:

$$\ln\left(\frac{r_{i(T)}}{r_{i(0)}}\right)=a\cdot\frac{X_t}{Y_t}\cdot\frac{1}{r_t}\cdot\left[\ln\left(\frac{Y_{i(T)}}{Y_{i(0)}}\right)\right]-a\cdot\frac{X_t}{Y_t}\cdot\frac{1}{r_t}\cdot\left[\ln\left(\frac{X_{i(T)}}{X_{i(0)}}\right)\right] \quad (5.3)$$

where:

- $Y_{i(T)}$, $Y_{i(0)}$ show the domestic per-capita productivity of each MED country (i marked), respectively at T time (in particular it will correspond to the year 2000, the latter of the 10 observed) and at 0 time (in particular it will correspond to year 1991, the first of the 10 observed);
- $X_{i(T)}$, $X_{i(0)}$ show the single MED country (i) toward EU, respectively at the time T and 0;
- $r_{i(T)}$, $r_{i(0)}$ show the balanced develop rate of the single MED country, respectively at the time T and 0.

Multiplying each term of the equation (5.3) by $\frac{1}{T}$, where T represents the examined number of years of this work, that is 10 years[4], we can reach the following equation:

$$T^{-1}\cdot\ln\left(\frac{r_{i(T)}}{r_{i(0)}}\right)=T^{-1}\cdot a\cdot\frac{X_t}{Y_t}\cdot\frac{1}{r_t}\cdot\left[\ln\left(\frac{Y_{i(T)}}{Y_{i(0)}}\right)\right]-T^{-1}\cdot a\cdot\frac{X_t}{Y_t}\cdot\frac{1}{r_t}\cdot\left[\ln\left(\frac{X_{i(T)}}{X_{i(0)}}\right)\right] \quad (5.4)$$

Applying logarithm properties[5] and introducing an average error term at 0 time and T time ($\delta_{i(0,T)}$) the previous equation became:

$$T^{-1}\left[\ln\left(r_{i(T)}\right)-\ln\left(r_{i(0)}\right)\right]=T^{-1}a\frac{X_t}{Y_t}\frac{1}{r_t}\left[\ln\left(Y_{i(T)}\right)-\ln\left(Y_{i(0)}\right)\right]+ \quad (5.5)$$

$$-T^{-1}a\frac{X_t}{Y_t}\frac{1}{r_t}\left[\ln\left(X_{i(T)}\right)-\ln\left(X_{i(0)}\right)\right]+\delta_{i(0,T)}$$

that represents our fundamental equation.

[4] T will assume a different value by 10 in all cases in which available data, for each country, covers an inferior year number: for example for 8 years or 6, T will assume the same number of the years available.

[5] In this specific case we apply the ratio logarithm property.

We can conclude that our equation allows us to verify if the economic growth of each single MED country is positively related to a more open market among MED and EU countries.

DATA

The twelve MED countries, object of our study, are the following: Algeria, Morocco, Tunisia, Egypt, Jordan, Lebanon, Syria, Israel, Palestinian Authority, Cyprus, Malta e Turkey.

We will take, in the period 1991 - 2000, the Johnson variables which the model requires. In particular we will present: *i)* the GDP per-capita historical series, as a fundamental variable to obtain the MED countries and EU balanced development rate; *ii)* MED countries and EU import and export flow historical series; *iii)* MED countries annual unemployment historical series[6].

In the first step to obtain GDP, we use EU and each MED country[7] annual GDP per-capita data, in million of EURO[8], both at constant prices with base year 1996.

The EU countries original data were showed in EURO, at constant prices, with base year 1996, so non transformation was required.

Table 1 – EU per-capita GDP, at constant prices, in million of EURO, (1996=100)

1991	17.289
1992	17.432
1993	17.268
1994	17.688
1995	18.056
1996	18.291
1997	18.700
1998	19.202
1999	19.652
2000	20.235

Source: EUROSTAT, 2002

On the contrary, the twelve MED countries data were shown, in millions of EURO, at current prices. For this reason, data were transformed in constant prices with base year 1996. This transformation was made with a specific deflation method[9], because the harmonized prices index historical series, for each MED countries were available and followed in table 2.

6 All data presented, both referred to the MED single country and to the whole EU, are obtained from EUROSTAT data bank and are expressed in EURO.

7 Each MED single country data are reported to the SCN (United Nations National Accounting System).

8 Before January 1999, values were expressed in ECU.

9 If we have a goods and services price index I_p that forms an aggregate, an evaluation of it is possible, at the current time, dividing current value for the price index; so we obtain deflation: $\left(\sum P_0 Q_t\right) I_p$ = current time volume ≡ constant prices value.

Table 2 – MED countries consumer prices index, (1996=100)

	1991	1992	1993	1994	1995	1996	1997	1998	1999	2000
Algeria	31,7	41,8	50,3	64,9	84,3	100,0	105,7	111,0	114,0	114,3
Morocco	78,3	82,7	87,0	91,5	97,1	100,0	101,0	103,8	104,5	106,5
Tunisia	78,8	83,4	86,8	90,8	96,5	100,0	103,7	106,9	109,8	113,0
Egypt	65,5	71,0	79,6	86,0	93,3	100,0	104,6	108,2	111,6	114,6
Jordan	82,5	85,7	88,5	91,7	93,9	100,0	103,0	106,2	103,6	104,3
Lebanon(1)	:	:	:	:	:	:	:	100,0	100,7	:
Syria	59,0	65,5	74,2	85,6	92,4	100,0	101,9	101,8	99,6	98,7
Israel	58,5	65,5	72,7	81,6	89,8	100,0	109,0	114,9	120,9	122,2
Pal. Aut.	:	:	:	:	:	100,0	108,0	114,0	119,9	123,3
Cyprus	81,0	86,2	90,4	94,7	97,2	100,0	103,6	105,9	106,8	112,1
Malta	85,1	86,5	90,0	93,8	97,5	100,0	103,2	105,6	107,8	110,4
Turkey	4,9	8,4	14,0	31,1	55,4	100,0	185,8	342,9	565,5	875,9

Source: EUROSTAT
Data not available
base change (1998=100)

Table 3 shows GDP per-capita historical series among 1991 to 2000, expressed in millions of EURO, at constant prices, in the twelve MED countries.

Table 3 – MED GDP per-capita, at constant prices, in millions of euro (1996 = 100)

	1991	1992	1993	1994	1995	1996	1997	1998	1999	2000
Algeria	4.634	3.455	3.217	1.998	1.359	1.294	1.380	1.318	1.315	1.668
Morocco	1.163	1.054	1.026	1.073	989	1.074	1.065	1.105	1.109	1.165
Tunisia	1.622	1.710	1.674	1.640	1.597	1.695	1.750	1.817	1.875	1.971
Egypt	835	815	888	871	835	873	1.025	:	:	:
Jordan	1.114	1.254	1.369	1.395	1.293	1.245	1.363	1.406	1.446	:
Lebanon(1)	:	:	:	:	:	:	:	:	:	:
Syria	1.366	1.192	1.181	1.092	970	944	954	912	998	:
Israel	16.566	15.179	14.818	14.447	13.504	13.490	14.083	13.097	12.782	15.606
Pal. Aut.	:	:	:	:	:	1.537	1.389	1.358	1.368	:
Cyprus	:	:	:	:	10.905	10.800	11.100	11.615	12.059	12.667
Malta	6.463	6.705	6.333	6.503	6.769	6.900	7.461	7.670	8.163	8.967
Turkey	:	:	:	5.788	3.791	2.300	1.453	817	477	365
Total	33.763	31.364	30.506	34.807	42.012	42.152	43.023	41.115	41.592	42.409
Average	4.220	3.921	3.813	3.867	4.201	3.832	3.911	4.112	4.159	6.058

We have before defined the balanced development rate as the national product (GDP) level that maintains product capacity at the full employment level. This variable is fundamental in the economic growth and international trade relationship analysis. In this case it takes the role of depending variable after export variation flows.

The balanced develop rate can be interpreted as "potential" GDP, that is the GDP that a country could reach if the whole workforce were employed. "Potential" GDP, therefore, is the sum of the "effective" GDP of a country (table 3) and "theoretic" GDP that could reach that percentage of unemployed population.

To reach the potential GDP, we must use the 1991 - 2000 unemployment rate historical series of each MED country, using the following formula:

$$\bar{Y} = \frac{(u - \bar{u})Y_t}{[1 - (u - \bar{u})]}$$

where $\bar{Y}$ is the theoretic GDP, u is the annual unemployed rate (table 4), $\bar{u}$ is the frictional unemployed rate and Y_t is the effective GDP (table 3).

Table 4 – Annual unemployment rate in % (1991-2000)

	1991	1992	1993	1994	1995	1996	1997	1998	1999	2000
Algeria	26,9	27,0	23,2	24,4	28,1	29,7	26,4	26,9	27,0	29,8
Morocco	14,8	14,9	15,0	16,0	16,0	17,8	15,0	14,8	13,9	13,6
Tunisia	15,6	15,5	15,5	15,6	15,4	15,6	15,7	15,7	15,8	15,6
Egypt	9,4	9,5	10,9	11,0	11,1	8,9	8,4	8,2	8,1	9,0
Jordan	15,5	15,6	18,7	15,0	14,2	12,0	13,2	12,6	10,3	13,7
Lebanon(1)	:	:	:	:	:	:	:	:	:	:
Syria	8,9	8,9	8,4	8,8	7,0	8,8	8,9	8,9	9,5	9,5
Israel	8,3	8,2	10,0	7,8	6,9	6,7	7,7	8,5	8,9	8,8
Pal. Aut.	18,3	18,4	18,3	18,5	18,2	23,8	20,3	14,4	11,8	14,1
Cyprus	3,4	3,3	2,7	2,7	2,6	3,1	3,4	3,4	3,6	4,9
Malta	5,1	5,2	5,2	4,8	4,2	5,0	5,5	5,6	5,8	5,0
Turkey	7,5	7,6	8,8	8,4	7,5	6,5	6,7	6,8	7,7	6,6
EU-15	9,3	9,4	10,1	10,5	10,1	10,2	10	9,4	8,7	7,8

Table 5 – MED countries theoretic GDP (1991-2000)

	1991	1992	1993	1994	1995	1996	1997	1998	1999	2000
Algeria	1461.8	1276	814	543	455.4	471	421.6	415.8	415	610.7
Morocco	157.9	143.2	139.4	160.3	147.8	186.6	144.7	150.1	135.1	138.1
Tunisia	232.6	245.2	240	236.4	228.9	243	254.6	260.5	275.2	284.1
Egypt	57	56.3	76.2	75.7	63.8	54.7	58.5	59.4	61.6	77
Jordan	158.9	178.8	254.9	190.2	163	123.1	154.8	149.3	113.9	180.2
Lebanon(1)	:	:	:	:	:	:	:	:	:	:
Syria	86.1	75.1	67.4	68.8	40.4	59.5	60.1	57.2	69.4	69.8
Israel	923.4	846.1	1115.3	728.4	548	518.3	694.5	762.2	801.4	1049.2
Pal. Aut.	:	:	:	:	:	403.6	290.6	174.7	132	:
Cyprus	:	:	:	:	0	10.8	44.6	46.6	72.8	245.3
Malta	140.7	146	367.4	119.2	82.2	140.8	191.3	204.7	235.1	183
Turkey	:	:	:	330.4	178.6	72.6	55.8	32.3	23.5	13.6

We can suppose that the frictional unemployment, so called "research", is 3%.

Table 5 shows theoretic GDP historical series (1991-2000), at constant prices, (1996=100), in million of EURO.

We can now proceed to calculate the balanced development rate or potential GDP (in symbol r_t), with the sum among effective GDP Y_t and theoretic GDP $\overline{Y}$. The balanced development rate historical series of each MED country, in the years 1991 to 2000, showed in table 6, is obtained with the sum of the historical series contained in tables 3 and 5, for each MED country.

Table 6 – MED countries balanced development rate or potential GDP, at constant prices, in millions of euro (1996 = 100)

	1991	1992	1993	1994	1995	1996	1997	1998	1999	2000
Algeria	6095.8	4731	4031	2541	1814.4	1765	1801.6	1733.8	1730	2278.7
Morocco	1320.9	1306.2	1165.4	1233.3	1136.8	1260.6	1209.7	1255.1	1244.7	1303
Tunisia	1854.6	1955.2	1914	1876.4	1825.9	1938	2004.6	2077.5	2150.2	2255
Egypt	892	871.3	964.2	946.7	898.8	927.7	1083.5	1141.8	1208.6	1283
Jordan	1272.9	1432.8	1623.9	1585.2	1456	1368.1	1517.8	1555.3	1559.9	1684.2
Lebanon[(1)]	:	:	:	:	:	:	:	:	:	:
Syria	1452.1	1267.1	1248.4	1160.8	1010.4	1003.5	1014.1	1969.2	1067.4	1073.8
Israel	17489	16025	15933	15175.4	14052	14008	14777.5	13859	13583	16655
Pal. Aut.	:	:	:	:	:	1940.6	1679.6	1532.7	1500	:
Cyprus	:	:	:	:	10905	10811	11145	11662	12132	12912.3
Malta	6603.7	6851	6700.4	6622.2	6851.2	6149.8	76543	7874.7	8398.1	9150
Turkey	:	:	:	6118.4	3969.6	2075.6	1508.8	849.3	500.5	378.6

We will use annual data, in millions of EURO, in the period 1991-2000, for imports and exports. These refer to the import and export level, from and toward EU, of each MED country (base year 1996).

Table 7 – MED countries imports from EU, in millions of EURO, at constant prices (1996=100)

	1991	1992	1993	1994	1995	1996	1997	1998	1999	2000
Algeria	25110	17074	12962	9482	5746	5449	7910	6146	6821	14435
Morocco	4157	4110	3988	4144	4136	4237	4702	5137	5309	5633
Tunisia	3000	2992	2914	3387	3473	3637	3872	4017	4337	4867
Egypt	3576	3607	2859	3323	2347	2774	2518	2338	2143	2966
Jordan	99	113	3141	1646	1437	171	1689	1506	1631	1917
Lebanon[(1)]	:	:	:	:	:	:	:	154	2055	:
Syria	2349	2364	2300	1880	1877	2025	1987	1444	2169	3444
Israel	6082	5314	4907	5237	5187	5283	5751	6022	6313	8101
Pal. Aut.	:	:	:	:	:	:	:	:	:	:
Cyprus	7851	7076	8097	6663	7582	564	3590	4098	5627	8920
Malta	8390	10069	9655	10959	11046	797	6792	7244	7866	9057
Turkey	1329	8166	48821	25360	16685	10191	6388	3971	2661	1997

(1) base change (1998=100)

Table 8 – MED countries exports toward EU, in millions of EURO, at constant prices (1996=100)

	1991	1992	1993	1994	1995	1996	1997	1998	1999	2000
Algeria	14442	9897	8473	7439	5607	4063	4118	4745	4575	5337
Morocco	4905	4937	5014	4908	4868	4703	5275	6361	6330	7230
Tunisia	4008	4306	4308	4293	4306	4343	5096	5411	5475	6460
Egypt	7073	5476	5952	5699	5376	5729	6455	7024	7108	6806
Jordan	836	984	1150	1196	1114	1189	1164	1072	1205	1534
Lebanon(1)	:	:	:	:	:	:	:	2820	2641	:
Syria	1619	1730	1925	1987	1491	1403	1328	1506	1671	1824
Israel	10482	10408	10941	11525	10758	10414	10555	9476	10580	12848
Pal. Aut.	:	:	:	:	10	30	50	92	120	81
Cyprus	1952	2494	2174	2203	2073	1937	1880	2008	2193	2765
Malta	1680	1824	1977	2014	2066	1867	1936	1872	1921	2536
Turkey	175816	104024	88636	29936	24168	18243	12053	6470	3634	3391

(1) base change (1998=100)

THE EMPIRICAL ANALYSIS: ESTIMATE OF MODEL PARAMETERS

The referring sample, in order to make our study, is made of 11 MED countries and not of 12 as we have no data on Lebanon. On the basis of the collected data[10], the referring variables will be shown with:

Δr_t the variable which expresses the balanced economic growth of each MED country between 1991 and 2000. Following the statement of the Johnson modified equation, this variable will be calculated with the following expression:

$$T^{-1}\left[\ln\left(r_{i(T)}\right)-\ln\left(r_{i(0)}\right)\right]$$

ΔX_t is the variable which shows the fluctuation of the trade level between each MED country and UE, from 1991 up to 2000, of the exports flow from each Med country towards UE:

$$T^{-1}\left[\ln\left(X_{i(T)}\right)-\ln\left(X_{i(0)}\right)\right]$$

In this case, the table of remarks will be the following:

[10] Tables 6, 8.

Table 9 – Observed variables (1991-2000)

Countries	Δr_t	ΔX_t
Algeria	-0,0983	-0,0995
Morocco	-0,0014	0,0387
Tunisia	0,0200	0,0477
Egypt	0,0360	-0,0038
Jordan	0,0280	0,0607
Syria	-0,0300	0,0119
Israel	-0,0049	0,0203
Palestinian Authority	-0,0064	0,3465
Cyprus	0,0280	0,0348
Malta	0,0326	0,0410
Turkey	-0,3975	-0,3948

The existing relationship between the two considered variables could be represented on a dispersion diagram which will lead to a eleven points cloud (Scatter of remarks). Supposing that between the two variables will exist a linear relationship, we will refer to a two-variable linear regression model, one depending, Δr_t, and one independent, ΔX_t.

In order to study the link between the economic growth of MED countries and the international trade between these countries and the UE, we take equation (5.5) as reference that expresses the way in which the dependent variable is determined by the independent variable, in other words it expresses the relationship, that we have assumed to be linear, that exists between the two observed variables. For clearness of exposition we can re-write the equation (5.5) stating with $y_{i(0,T)}$ the dependent variable and with $x_{i(0,T)}$ the independent one:

$$y_{i(0,T)} = \gamma + \beta x_{i(0,T)} + \delta_{i(0,T)} \tag{6}$$

With the study of the regression we practically want to identify a function that will be an estimate of a straight line of the model represented by the equation (6), and in particular of the straight line:

$$\Delta r_t = \gamma + \beta \Delta X_t + \delta_t \tag{7}$$

In order to identify the kind of hypothesized linear link that exists between the two variables Δr_t and ΔX_t, we must estimate statistically, according to our remarks, the unknown parameters of equation (7). In particular the parameters to be estimated are:

- parameter γ, that shows in the expression that we have obtained the term $T^{-1} a \frac{X_t}{Y_t} \frac{1}{r_t} \left[\ln\left(Y_{i(T)}\right) - \ln\left(Y_{i(0)}\right) \right]$, which represents the constant that is the interceptor of the regression straight line; the parameter β, that shows in the equation that we have obtained the term $-a\frac{X_t}{Y_t}\frac{1}{r_t}$, that represents the angular coefficient of the regression straight line (7), that is the coefficient of the variation ratio of the opening degree of MED countries towards UE[11].

Before making the estimates of the two above mentioned parameters, we should make some considerations on the stochastic component $\delta_{i(0,T)}$. This term represents the average of errors in the slot [0,T].

We can hypothesized that the errors $\delta_{i(0,T)}$ will distribute themselves with an average equal to 0, a constant variance equal to a σ^2_δ and will be linked in order that the different values of $\delta_{i(0,T)}$ are obtained independently one from the other. In symbols we will have:

E($\delta_{i(0,T)}$) = 0;

(1) Var($\delta_{i(0,T)}$) = E($\delta^2_{i(0,T)}$) = σ^2_δ = k $\forall i$ (Hypothesis of homoskedasticity according to which the variance of the errors, in the linear regression model, is constant);

(2) Cov($\delta_{i(0,T)}, \delta_{j(0,T)}$) = E($\delta_{i(0,T)}, \delta_{j(0,T)}$) = 0 $\forall i \neq j$ (that is the covariance calculated between the i-th error and the j-th error and when the j-th error is equal to 0).

Then the model depends on the unknown parameters γ, β e σ^2_δ.

Now it is possible to make the estimates of the parameters of the model, in order to do it we will use the method to estimate the ordinary least squares (OLS) as, according to the Gauss-Markov theorem, can give some BLUE estimators (Best Linear Unbiased Estimator). These estimators, which in this case are showed with $\hat{\gamma}$ and $\hat{\beta}$, represent respectively the values estimated by the two unknown parameters of the equation (7), γ and β, and enjoy three important statistic properties:

- They are a linear function of the dependent variables $y_{i(0,T)}$. In symbols, this property can be showed as follows: $\hat{\gamma} = f(y_{i(0,T)})$ e $\hat{\beta} = f(y_{i(0,T)})$ (supposing, naturally, that *f* represents a linear function);
- They are correct, in the way that the average of the estimators is equal to the same parameter. In symbols we will have: E($\hat{\gamma}$) = γ and E($\hat{\beta}$) = β;
- They are efficient, that is they are the best estimators that can be obtained in the class of linear and correct estimators as, inside this subclass, they have the minimum

[11] This parameter, in general, shows how is the average variation of the character y when an unit of character x changes.

variance[12]. The principle at the base of the methods of minimum squares, is to chose $\hat{\gamma}$ and $\hat{\beta}$ in order to minimize the squared distance between the value observed of the dependent variable $y_{i(0,T)}$ and the theoretical value of the same $y^*_{i(0,T)}$. Knowing that the difference $(y_{i(0,T)} - y^*_{i(0,T)})^2$ is equal to $\delta^2_{i(0,T)}$, to apply the method of the minimum squares means to identify the values of the parameters $\hat{\gamma}$ and $\hat{\beta}$ that make the function minimum:

$$\sum_{i=1}^{n} \delta^2_{i(0,T)} = \sum_{i=1}^{n} (y_{i(0,T)} - y^*_{i(0,T)})^2$$

The results of the estimate made on the observation period, 1991 – 2000, are quoted in the following table:

Table 10 – Results of the regression of Δr_t on ΔX_t

	Coefficient	Standard Error	**t**	P>t	(Interval of confidence at 95%)	
ΔX_t	0,58328	0,1479	3,9437	0,003	0,24860	0,91786
Constant	-0,041297	0,024292	-1,7	0,123	-0,09625	-0,01365
R^2	0,63345					
s	0,080436					

In order to verify the relationship that exists between the Med countries economic growth and the variation ratio of the degree of openness of these countries towards UE, it has not a great importance to consider the result of the estimate of the constant γ, but the most interesting thing is the analysis of the result of the estimate of the parameter β as it expresses the relation that we are looking for.

---

[12]In fact, the efficiency is measured in terms of variance, in this way to say that an estimator is efficient means that the variance of the estimator obtained with the method of minimum squares is inferior to the variance of another estimator which belongs to the class of linear and correct estimators. The terms $\delta^2_{i(0,T)}$ can have a value either positive or negative accordingly that the points which show the remarks are over and under the estimated straight line. The sum of the squares of these remnants or deviations coming from it gives a non negative value that will change directly with the distance of the remarks of the estimated straight line. As a consequence, different couples of values of $\hat{\gamma}$ and $\hat{\beta}$ will lead to different straight lines and for this reason to different values of the sum of the squares of the remnants. For this reason we could write the following relation: $\sum_{i=1}^{n} \delta^2_{i(0,T)} = f(\hat{\gamma}, \hat{\beta})$.

As we can see in table 10, the estimated coefficient ΔX_t has a positive value equal to 0,58328. This shows the existence of a direct relationship between the examined variables, in particular a positive relationship between the MED countries economic growth and the degree of opening of these countries towards UE: the more the variation ratio of the degree of opening of MED countries towards UE (ΔX_t) increases, the more, proportionally, (a proportion equal to the coefficient β), the ratio of variation of the balanced development rate grows, Δr_t, which is the indicator of the economic development indicator of MED countries.

In order to confirm what we have said up to now further, it is useful to introduce briefly the concept of the Standard Error (SE) of estimator $\hat{\beta}$, in this case equal to 0,1479.

Graphically the equation (5.5) can be represented with a straight line which interpolates the scatter of the remarks as follows:

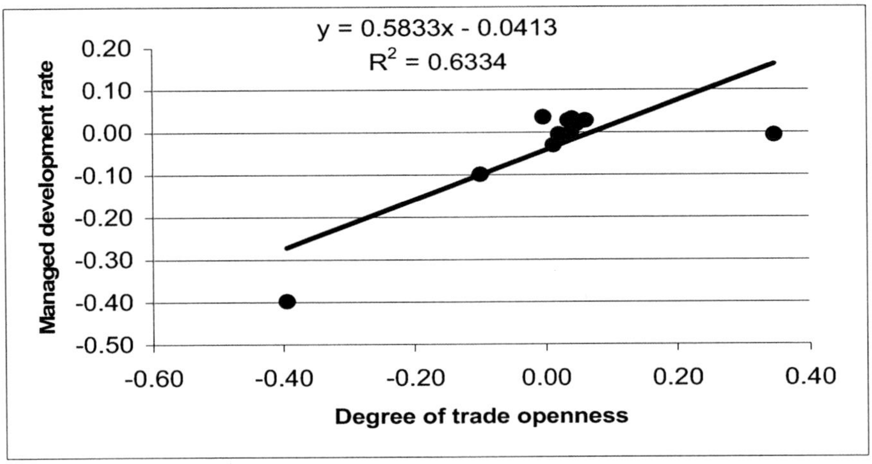

Linear regression of Δr_t (balanced development rate) on ΔX_t (degree of openness to trade)

The graph confirms what we have analytically verified: the regression straight line has a growing trend with an angular coefficient β equal to 0,58328 and intercepts γ equal to –0,041297.

We have verified if the stated hypothesis on the value of the regression coefficient β can be considered exact or not according to the remarks, through a test. We have used the distribution Student t with n-2 degrees of freedom (gl) expressed even as a relationship between a standardized Gaussian random variable and an independent distribution χ^2 related to their degrees of freedom. The statistic test of this check of hypothesis, shown with t, assumes the shape of a relationship between the estimator $\hat{\beta}$ and its standard error (SE):

$$t = \frac{\hat{\beta}}{SE(\hat{\beta})} \approx T_{(n-2)}$$

We have set a significance level equal to 5%, with which is defined the region R of rejection, and a region A of acceptance.

Table 10 gives us the statistics (t) for the estimators $\hat{\gamma}$ e $\hat{\beta}$: in particular the test statistic for the estimator $\hat{\beta}$ is 3,9437 and a region R of rejection of this hypothesis at a significance level (α) is equal to: $\left\{|t| \geq t_{1-\frac{\alpha}{2}}\right\}$ where $t_{1-\frac{\alpha}{2}}$ is the quantile of a *Student t* with n-2 (in this case 11-2=9 remarks) degrees of freedom at a level α = 5%. In this case this value is: $t_{1-\frac{\alpha}{2}}$ = 2,2622.

Therefore, as t($\hat{\beta}$) = 3,9437 > 2.2622 (the test falls in the rejection region), the hypothesis of independence between the variables Δr_t and ΔX_t is rejected to the level α = 5%.

The reliability of the result of the parameter can also be verified by observing the *P-value*, that is the probability P$\left\{|X| \geq t\right\}$, where $X \approx t_{(n-2)}$. Then it deals with the level of significance of the test and shows the probability that our test falls in the region of acceptance.

In our case, as the *P-value* is 0,003 is really lower than the level α = 5% (0,05), so, it has a statistically meaning, we can refuse the hypothesis of non significance of the estimate and again that of independence between the two examined variables.

Moreover, we have interpreted a level of confidence for the set: in our case we consider another time a statistic t that follows the law T of *Student* with n-2 degree of freedom. Once a level of probability (1-α)has been settled it will be possible to find two values t_1 and t_2 such as:

$$P(t_1<t<t_2)= 1-\alpha$$

And this can be done for each $0<\alpha<1$.

Now we are going to show the proceeding of the estimate of an interval of confidence for $\hat{\beta}$ and for $\hat{\gamma}$, those extremes are represented in table 10. So we have:

$$(*)\left[\hat{\gamma} - s\sqrt{\frac{1}{n}+\frac{\bar{x}^2}{\sigma_x^2}}t_{1-\frac{\alpha}{2}(n-2)}, \hat{\gamma} + s\sqrt{\frac{1}{n}+\frac{\bar{x}^2}{\sigma_x^2}}t_{1-\frac{\alpha}{2}(n-2)}\right]$$

$$(**)\left[\hat{\beta}-\frac{s}{\sigma_x}t_{1-\frac{\alpha}{2}(n-2)},\hat{\beta}+\frac{s}{\sigma_x}t_{1-\frac{\alpha}{2}(n-2)}\right]$$

are intervals of confidence of level 1-α (95%) respectively for $\hat{\gamma}$ and $\hat{\beta}$. Where s (table 10) is the square root of what we show with s^2, that is a non-distorted estimator of σ_δ^2, n (11) is the number of the sample remarks, $\bar{x}$, equal to 0,00941 calculated with the usual formula $\frac{1}{n}\sum_{i=1}^{n}x_i$, is the average of the remarks and σ_x^2, equal to 0,29577 calculated with the usual formula $\frac{1}{n}\sum_{i=1}^{n}(x_i-\bar{x})^2$, is the variance of the remarks .

In this case the intervals are:

[0,24860 < $\hat{\beta}$ < 0,91786]

[-0,09625 < $\hat{\gamma}$ < -0,01365]

As we can notice these are intervals of confidence at 95%, really little for both the estimators. This means that the estimate of the minimum squares has given a value which belongs to the interval of the acceptable values of $\hat{\beta}$ and of $\hat{\gamma}$ with a good accuracy.

We must still analyze the index R^2 in table 10, that is if the regression straight line well interprets the scatter of remarks. This quantity is *the ratio of variation of y which is explained by the model* and is showed in the following way:

$$R^2=\frac{DEV(R)}{DEV(Y)}=1-\frac{DEV(E)}{DEV(Y)}$$

$$\Rightarrow R^2=\frac{\sum_{i=1}^{n}\left(y_{i(0,T)}^{*}-\bar{y}\right)^2}{\sum_{i=1}^{n}\left(y_{i(0,T)}-\bar{y}\right)^2}=1-\frac{\sum_{i=1}^{n}\left(y_{i(0,T)}-y_{i(0,T)}^{*}\right)^2}{\sum_{i=1}^{n}\left(y_{i(0,T)}-\bar{y}\right)^2}$$

where:

DEV(R) represents the deviance of regression given by $\sum_{i=1}^{n}\left(y_{i(0,T)}^{*}-\bar{y}\right)^2$;

DEV(Y) represents the total deviance given by $\sum_{i=1}^{n}\left(y_{i(0,T)}-\bar{y}\right)^2$;

DEV(E)represent the deviance of the error given by $\sum_{i=1}^{n}\left(y_{i(0,T)} - y^{*}_{i(0,T)}\right)^2$.

As, in the second expression of R^2, the denominator $\sum_{i=1}^{n}\left(y_{i(0,T)} - \bar{y}\right)^2$ is greater than the numerator $\sum_{i=1}^{n}\left(y_{i(0,T)} - y^{*}_{i(0,T)}\right)^2$, the ratio is less than one, and then $0 \le R^2 \le 1$. In this case the value of the determination index R^2 is equal to 0,63345, so we can assert that the regression straight line interpolates in a satisfying way the scatter of the remarks.

A RECOVERY OF THE ANALYSIS: THE CASES OF TURKEY AND OF THE PALESTINIAN AUTHORITY

Analyzing the regression we have just made, even if the statistical tests of significance have given good responses, the results are influenced in a negative way by the presence of two of Med countries whose remarks contribute to distort the result of the estimate: in particular we speak about Turkey (Δr_t= -0,3975 ; ΔX_t= -0,3948) and of the Palestinian Authority (Δr_t= -0,0064 ; ΔX_t= 0,3465). In fact from the one side Turkey presents a ratio of variation really negative as far as opening degree to trade and to balanced development growth are concerned, and the Palestinian Authority presents a high rise ratio of the flow of exports as regards all the other countries.

We try to estimate again the parameters of the model excluding from our sample Turkey and the Palestinian Authority. The regression gives the following results:

Table 11 – Results of the regression of Δr_t on ΔX_t excluding Turkey and the Palestinian Authority

	Coefficient	Standard Error	t	P>t	(Interval of confidence at 95%)	
ΔX_t	0,76294	0,18294	4,1703	0,004	0,33086	1,19502
Constant	-0,011757	0,008798	-1,3362	0,223	-0,08017	-0,05666
R^2	0,71302					
s	0,024719					

In this second regression the estimate of parameter β will have a value equal 0,76294, greater that the value of the parameter of the first regression: this means that if the degree of opening to trade of MED countries towards the UE grows the balanced development rate grows more proportionally for a factor equal to 0,76294.

The straight line of regression has a growing trend with an angular coefficient β equal to 0,76294 and intercepts γ equal to–0,011757.

The standard Error of the estimators $\hat{\gamma}$ and $\hat{\beta}$ are both minimal and they show us a satisfying accuracy degree of the estimators.

As far as the verification of the hypothesis is concerned, if we stop for a moment on the analysis of estimator $\hat{\beta}$, the statistical test for estimator $\hat{\beta}$ is 4,1703 and a region R of rejection for this hypothesis at a level of significance (α) is equal to: $\left\{|t| \geq t_{1-\frac{\alpha}{2}}\right\}$ where $t_{1-\frac{\alpha}{2}}$ is the quantile of a *Student t* with n-2 (in this case 9-2=7 remarks) degree of freedom at a level α = 5%. In our case, this value is: $t_{1-\frac{\alpha}{2}} = 2{,}3646$.

Therefore, as t($\hat{\beta}$) = 4,1703 > 2.3646 (the test falls in the rejection region), the hypothesis of independence between the variables Δr_t e ΔX_t (null hypothesis H_0) is still rejected to the level α = 5%.

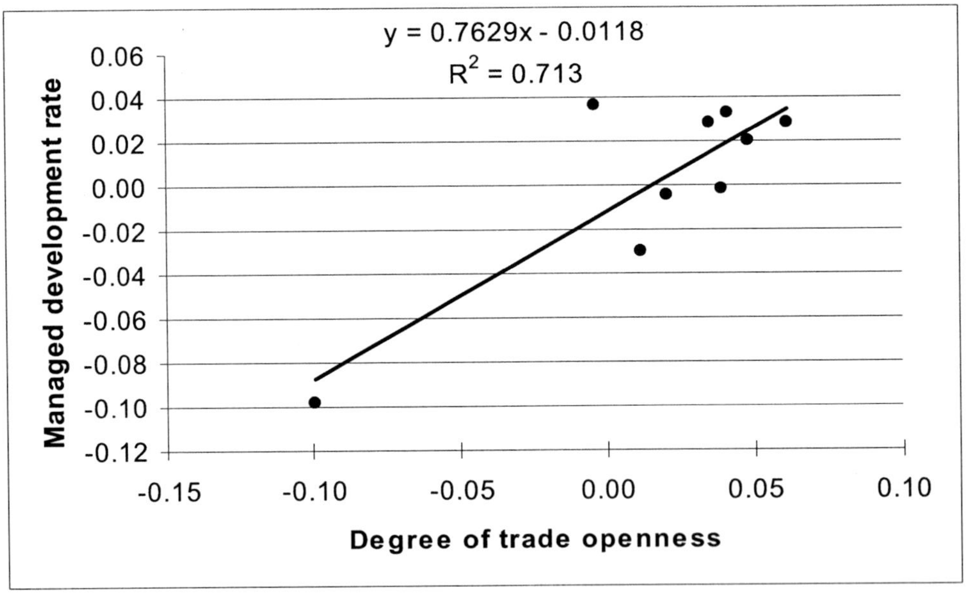

Linear regression of Δr_t on ΔX_t (excluding Turkey and the Palestinian Authority)

As far as the significance of the test is concerned, from table 11 we see that the P-value is equal to 0,004, and even in this second regression it is really lower at the level α = 5% (0,05), and so it has a statistical significance.

The intervals of confidence at 95% for the estimators $\hat{\gamma}$ and $\hat{\beta}$ are respectively:

$[-0{,}08017 < \hat{\gamma} < -0{,}05666]$

$[0{,}33086 < \hat{\beta} < 1{,}19502]$

In short, what is of particular importance is the index of determination R^2 and then the effectiveness of our model excluding Turkey and the Palestinian Authority. In fact the assumed value (table 11) from R^2 is 0,71302, near to the maximum value 1. Going from the first regression to the second one, the model can explain more than 70% of the change of the dependent variable, and then a better effectiveness of the model excluding Turkey and Palestinian Authority emerges.

As far as Turkey is concerned this apparent anomaly finds its justification in two key factors: from one side, the customs union with UE and from the other side the financial crisis of Turkey at the beginning of 2001.

In January 1996 the customs union with UE, that comes from the Association Agreement of 1963 (Ankara Agreement) came into force. It was a step forward that has facilitated the trade of goods between the two partners producing great expansion of the trade between Turkey and the EU. The EU represents 54% of Turkish trade activity and is to date the most important trade partner of this country.

The indicator ΔX_t has been calculated according with the exports at constant prices (table 8), as consumer prices grow remarkably during the period of reference, the flow of exports at constant prices decreases during the examined ten-year period because of the high inflation

This caused high financial crisis in Turkey, that had its climax from February 2001 with the subsequent slump of the Stock exchange and of the Turkish lira (-60% in few days). Thanks to this crisis we have the ratio, really negative, of the change of GDP per capita. Because of this economic collapse, the worst in the country's history, which came about also due to a delay in the privatization of Turkish Telecom, a million and half of people lost their jobs, with a lost of the per-capita income from 3.100 to 2.100 dollars per year.

Moreover Turkey had, even in the past, a very high foreign debt, 118 billion dollars

Nowadays, even if not all the Turkish problems have been solved, this country is recovering. The launching of structural reforms and privatization, the intervention of the IMF for help amounting to 31 billion dollars are giving the hoped for results.

As far as the Palestinian territories are concerned the economic growth and the development models present, on the contrary, a number of problems at a structural level: the direct control of Israel, from 1967 and the imposition of heavy customs barriers, tariff and non-tariff ones, has radically modified the trade and economic structures.

During 80's, on the contrary, we had a contraction of the economy, in correspondence with the worsening of Israel-Palestinian relations, heavier were the effects of the Gulf war: during that year (1991) the GDP had a decrease of 4.1%. Moreover, the incidence of the closure policy made by Israel has been particularly negative, between 1993 and 1996. The economic problems of the Palestinian Territories and the complicated historical events have effectively contributed to restrain the economic growth of this country.

CONCLUSIONS

The regression linear model has shown satisfactory but different results if we take into consideration the whole sample of countries.

On the whole, a great part of the MED countries is living a good economic growth phase. The Barcelona Conference, as we can see from this study, is giving the hoped returns and the process of integration is giving positive effects.

The huge efforts made in several fields by the UE, which is the greater trade partner of the countries of the Association (50% of foreign trade of the region as far as goods and services are concerned) both from MED counties, whose inter-regional trade is only the 5% of the volume of their exchanges, will be able to improve the growth of these countries located on the South of the Mediterranean sea.

If results of the present work are acceptable, the whole area development process can no longer proceed with the classic cooperation instruments. The only cooperation possible is the commercial one, where the MED countries can produce goods and services for the EU countries according to the comparative advantages theory. So, international trade must develop in the primary sector (specifically agricultural) and in the secondary one with a high labor intensity.

If commercial relationships increase in the future, we have demonstrated that also economic growth will rise with advantages for all countries in the area.

REFERENCES

Balassa B., (1978), Exports and Economic Growth: further evidence, *Journal of Development Economics*, 5, pp. 181–189.

-- (1985), Exports, Policy Choices and Economic growth in Developing Countries after the 1973 oil shock, *Journal of Development Economics*, 18, pp. 23–35.

Barro R. J., (1991), Economic growth in a cross section of countries, *Quarterly Journal of Economics*, vol. 106, n. 2, may.

Barro R. J., Sala I. Martin X., (1991), Convergence across States and Regions, Brooking Papers on Economic Activity, n. 1.

-- (1992), Convergence, *Journal of Political Economy*, n. 100, april.

Clements K. W.; Frenkel J. A., (1980), Exchange Rates, Money and Relative prices: The Dollar - Pound in the 1920s, *Journal of International Economics*, 10, pp.249-262.

Colombatto E., (1992), «Crescita e commercio estero dei paesi in via di sviluppo», UTET, Torino.

Daveri F., (1996), Economia dei paesi in via di sviluppo, Bologna, Il Mulino.

Domar E. D., (1941), Essays in the theory of economic growth, Oxford University Press.

Dornbusch R., (1976), Expectations and Exchange Rate Dynamics, *Journal of Political Economy*, 84, pp. 1167-1176.

-- (1982), Expectations and Exchange Rate Dynamics, *Journal of Political Economy*, February 1982, 90(1), pp. 158-165.

Emery R. F., (1967), The relation of exports and economic growth, *Kyklos*, 20, 2, 470–486.

Eurostat, (2001), Statistiques Euro-Mediterranèennes, Luxembourg, Commission europèenne, Office des pubblications officielles des Communautès europèennes.

Feder G., (1983), On Exports and Economic Growth, *Journal of Development Economics*, 12, 59–73.

Fischer S., (1984), Real Balance, the exchange rate and indexation: real variables in disinflation, *National Bureau of Economic Research Working Paper*, n. 1497.

Frankel J. A, (1986) International Capital Mobility and Crowding-out in the U.S. Economy: Imperfect Integration of Financial Markets or Goods Markets? in *How open is the U.S. economy?* Ed: RIK W. Hafer. Lexington: Lexington Books, pp. 33-67.

-- (1990), Zen and the Art of Modern Macroeconomics: A Commentary, in *Monetary policy for a volatile global economy*, Eds.: W.S. Haraf and Th.D. Willett. Washington, DC: American Enterprise Institute for Public Policy Research, pp. 117-23.

Fratianni M., Salvatore D. and Jurgen Von Haven, eds., (1997), Handbook of Macroeconomic Policies in Open Economies, Westport Conn: Greenwood Press.

Friedman M., (1977), Nobel lecture: Inflation and Unemployment, *Journal of political Economy*, 85, pp. 451-472.

Hoekman B., Djankov S.,(1996), Catching up with Eastern Europe? The European Union's Mediterranean free initiative, *Policy Research Working Paper*, n. 1562, The Word Bank, Washington.

Johnson H. G., (1976), Commercio internazionale e sviluppo economico, La Nuova Italia, Firenze.

Kuznets S., (1965), Economic Growth and Structure, W.W. Norton, New York.

Kravis I. B., Lipsey R. E., (1983), Toward an explanation of national price levels, *Princeton Studies in International Finance,* n. 52. NJ International Finance Section, Dept. of Economics, Princeton U.

Laureti L., (2000), Unique Currency and Mediterranean: Which is the Best Monetary System to opt For?, *Working Paper Fordham University*, n. 112, May.

-- (2001), Purchasing Power Parity and integration. Empirical evidence in the Mediterranean countries, Journal of Policy Modeling, 23, pp. 731-751.

Levine R., Renelt D., (1992), A sensitivity analysis of cross country growth regressions, *American Economic Review*, n. 4.

Maddison A., (1982), Phases of Capitalist Development, Oxford University Press.

Mankiw N. G., Romer D., Weil D. N., (1991), A contribution to the Empirics of Economic Growth, *Quarterly Journal of Economics*, may.

Mcnown R., Wallance M. S., (1989), National Price Levels, Purchasing Power Parity and Cointegration: A Test of Four High Inflation Economies, *Journal of International Money and Finance*, December 1989, 8(4), pp. 533-545.

Morris C. T., (1984), The measurement of economic development: quo vadis?, in Ranis G., West R.L., Leisersen M.W. and Morris C.T., Comparative development perspectives, Westview Press, Boulder Colorado.

Navaretti G. B., Faini R., (1997), Nuove prospettive per la cooperazione allo sviluppo, Il Mulino.

Padoan P. C., (1997), Integrazione e Sicurezza nel Mediterraneo, Franco Angeli.

Rogoff, K.,(1992), Traded Goods Consumption Smoothing and the Random Walk Behavior of the Real Exchange Rate, *Bank of Japan Monetary and Econ. Stud.,* Nov. 1992, 10(2), pp. 1-29.

Rosen S. and Shapouri S. (1989), Export growth instability and shortfall: the impact on economic performance in Africa, *Canadian Journal of Agricultural Economics*, 37, 1241–1250.

Salvatore D., (2001), Economia Internazionale, Etas, Milano.

-- (2003), Globalization, Comparative Advantage and Europe's Double Competitive Squeeze, Global Economy Quarterly, June 2003.

Samuelson Paul A.,(1964), Theoretical Notes on Trade Problem, *Rev. Econ. Statist.,* May 1964, 46(2), pp. 145-54.

Selvanathan S., (1998), Empirical regularities in OECD Consumption, *Discussion Paper n. 88.01, Department of Economics*, The University of Western Australia, Perth.

Theil, H., (1967), Econometric and Information Theory, Amsterdam, North. Holland.

Tsoukalis L., (1998), Nuova Economia Europea, Il Mulino.

Unctad (1995), Recent Developments in International Investments ad Transnational Corporation, Geneva, *United Nations Conference on Trade and Development.*

Williamson J., (1965) The Crowding Peg, Essay in *International Finance* n. 50, Princeton University Press.

-- (1994),. Estimating equilibrium exchange rates, Washington, DC: Institute for International Economics.

In: Perspectives on International, State and Local Economics ISBN 1-60021-099-6
Editor: Gerald V. Liu, pp. 209-234

Chapter 8

AN ECONOMIC ANALYSIS OF NUCLEAR ACCIDENTS IN JAPAN*

Akihiro Watabe[1]
Department of Economics, Kanagawa University
Yokohama, Kanagawa 221-8686
Japan

Under the terms of the Kyoto Protocol on Climate Change, Japan must reduce the emission of greenhouse gases to a target level of six percent below the 1990 base level by the first compliance period covering 2008 to 2012. To achieve this target, the Japanese Government has drafted a national energy plan which calls for the construction of ten additional nuclear power plants. Nuclear power in Japan is regulated by the Nuclear Liability Act (NLA) of Japan. As stated in Article 1, the NLA aims both to promote the sound development of the nuclear energy industry and to protect the victims and the environment from a nuclear accident. In practice, however, the NLA has several weaknesses which prevent it from achieving both policy objectives in a fair, balanced manner. This paper draws upon the economic analysis of accident law, as well as Japan's first nuclear criticality accident at the JCO plant, to identify these weaknesses and suggest possible remedies, thereby aiding Japan's adherence to the Kyoto Protocol.

1. INTRODUCTION

The reliance on nuclear power for energy supply is one of the greatest concerns to the Japanese public. In particular, the two recent accidents in the Japanese nuclear power sector have rekindled public awareness and anxiety about the safety of nuclear energy. In September 1999, Japan's first criticality nuclear accident occurred at JCO in Tokaimura. The accident resulted in severe damages for the environment, health and regional business, including the death of two JCO employees. It was classified as a level four event by the

---

* The author would like to thank Rudy Yaksick, Satoshi Morosaka and Kaoru Yamaguchi for comments and discussions.
[1] E-mail: watabe89@kanagawa-u.ac.jp

International Atomic Energy Agency (IAEA).[2] Surprisingly, the accident was caused by the use of non-approved and illegal operating procedures for the handling of the uranium solution. Even though the accident occurred four years ago, the form of compensation for neighboring residents is still unresolved (Yomiuri Shinbun, September 2, 2002).

The second disturbing event was the revelation that for the past two decades electric power companies, including Tokyo Electric Power Company (Tepco) and others, were covering up the falsification of records identifying structural weaknesses of nuclear reactors. Even more troubling was the fact that the falsification was found by a whistle-blowing employee (Wall Street Journal, September 18, 2002). Because of this illegal cover-up, fifteen of Tepco's seventeen nuclear power plants were obliged to shut down, resulting in an energy crisis.

Meanwhile, the Japanese government proposed a new energy plan which places a higher reliance on nuclear energy. This policy shift toward nuclear energy was prompted by the Kyoto Convention on Climate Change in December 1997.[3] According to the government's new energy plan, CO_2 emissions, caused by generating electricity, will have to be cut by nine percent by 2010. This emissions reduction target was based on the long-term energy demand and supply plan (Japan Agency for Natural Resources and Energy, 1998).[4] The long-term plan assumes an annual growth rate of electricity demand to be about 1.2 percent per year.

In setting this target, the Japanese government and the electric utility industry reached a basic agreement to increase the reliance on nuclear power generation by ten percent over the next decade. Consequently, at least ten additional nuclear power plants are needed to supply the additional electricity.[5] As of July 2003, construction had already started on four plants, with eight plants in the planning and preparation stage (Ministry of Economy, Trade and Industry, 2003). However, proceeding with the planning is becoming increasingly difficult due to the growing opposition of the proposed sites by the residents as well as the local governments.[6]

The motivation for the policy shift towards nuclear power is easily understood when one examines the recent data on Japanese CO_2 emissions. Japanese energy consumption in 2000 represented an increase of 16.2 percent, relative to the 1990 level. Commensurate with that energy increase is the increased level of CO_2 emissions, estimated to have reached 1.16 billion tons and representing nearly a 10 percent increase, relative to the 1990 level. The increase in CO_2 emissions implies that Japan must reduce the level of CO_2 emissions by about 16 percent over the next decade in order to be in compliance with the Kyoto Protocol. Against this backdrop of increased CO_2 emissions, nuclear energy appears to be perhaps one of the most effective means to comply with the Kyoto Protocol. This conclusion is based on the fact that the electric utility industry is the major source of CO_2 emissions in Japan, currently contributing about one fourth of total Japanese CO_2 emissions. Moreover, the

---

[2] IAEA evaluates a nuclear accident by five levels, with the most severe accident receiving a level five designation, the highest level.

[3] Under the Kyoto Protocol on Climate Change, Japan must reduce the emission of greenhouse gases to a target level of six percent below the 1990 base level. The deadline for meeting this target is the first compliance period covering 2008 to 2012.

[4] Energy conservation by households and industries is included in this plan.

[5] In 1996, nuclear power plants supplied about 35 percent of electricity. They are expected to supply about 41 percent of electricity by 2010.

[6] Before the incidence on the falsification of records by Tepco, fifty two nuclear power plants were operating in Japan.

construction of a single nuclear power plant is expected to cut, on average, 0.7 percent of the total CO_2 emissions (Prime Minister of Japan and His Cabinet, 2002).[7]

Since the nuclear accident at JCO and the cover up at Tepco and other facilities, there is much debate about the safety of nuclear energy, including the use of more stringent regulation and monitoring systems for nuclear facility operations. Meanwhile, the Japanese government consistently asserts that nuclear power stations are safe enough to continue their operation. On the one hand, the incidences at JCO and, in particular, Tepco sound the alarm if there is an increased reliance on nuclear power. On the other hand, however, we need to carefully analyze the expected benefits and risks of nuclear energy. As several academic studies have shown, subjective risks are often quite different from objective risks--as quantified in risk-benefit analyses. In addition, experts always perceive nuclear energy to be safer than the general public's view of safety (Slovic et al., 1990).

It is widely accepted that the likelihood of a nuclear accident is very low; i.e., a nuclear accident leading to off-site exposure will occur between one-in-ten thousand (1 in 10^4) and one-in-ten million (1 in 10^7) reactor-years (Trebilcock and Winter, 1997). If the worst scenario happens, however, total uninternalized damages could reach 145.68 billions in 1995 Canadian dollars (Heyes and Heyes, 2000).[8] Hence, if a nuclear energy policy is adopted, compensation for damages related to nuclear accidents is equally important as engineering safety. However, a careful, unbiased analysis of the policy leads one to conclude that the Japanese government's interest leans more toward the safety of nuclear energy. Moreover, the analysis finds that the government lacks sufficient policy tools for the compensation of the victims of nuclear-related accidents.

The Nuclear Liability Act of Japan (NLA) was established in 1961. As stated in Article 1, the NLA aims both to promote the sound development of the nuclear energy industry and to protect the victims and the environment from a nuclear accident. In particular, the NLA was designed to achieve two policy objectives: nuclear facility operators will be induced to take efficient precaution against the accident and, at the same time, the victims (both human and the environmental) of the accident will be efficiently indemnified after the accident occurs. In practice, however, there are several weaknesses of the NLA regarding fair and timely compensation, efficient allocation of resources, and appropriate safety behavior by nuclear facility operators. The purpose of this paper, therefore, is twofold. First, we aim to identify the weaknesses of the NLA; secondly, to evaluate possible remedies as well as propose desirable changes in the NLA.

---

[7] Of course, there are several alternatives for curbing greenhouse gases, mainly CO_2 emissions. These include: carbon taxes, emission trading and clean development mechanism (CDM). CDM, also called the "Kyoto mechanisms", aims to reduce CO_2 emissions between developed and developing countries through joint emission abatement projects. A developed country can get a credit, relative to its target level of CO_2 emissions reduction under Kyoto Protocol by investing in abatement technologies located in developing countries to help them reduce CO_2 emissions. Japan is currently working on several CDM projects with China, Thailand and other developing countries. The Japanese government estimates that emission trading can reduce CO_2 emissions by at least 1.6 percent. Carbon taxes will be introduced from April 2007.

[8] Heyes and Heyes (2000) used numerical simulation to estimate the off-site damage of the worst scenario in the Canadian case. Given existing "expert" views about worst case accidents (i.e., probability of an accident is the range between 1 in 10^6 and 1 in 10^5, and off-site damage inflicted by the accident is the range between 1 billion dollars and 100 billion dollars), they computed the total expected damage of the worst case by estimating the annual probability of the reactor incurring the worst case off-site damage under the Canadian Nuclear Liability Act, which limits nuclear operators' liability to 75 million Canadian dollars.

The remainder of this chapter is organized as follows. In section 2, we provide some background by introducing the components of nuclear power systems and reviewing the key definitions and provisions of the NLA. In section 3, we discuss the basic economic principles of accident law. These principles guide our analysis of safety and compensation issues related to the NLA. Implementation issues and accident remedial measures are examined in section 4. The last section concludes the chapter.

2. Nuclear Power Systems and the NLA

This section provides some background information on the Japanese nuclear power industry and fuel cycle. In particular, we first summarize the size of the nuclear power industry in Japan. Then, we illustrate the key elements of the nuclear fuel cycle. Next, we define the key terms, as contained in the NLA, of a "nuclear accident" and "nuclear damage", as well as discuss the major restrictions placed on nuclear operators by the NLA. This information enables the reader to more easily grasp the problems and weaknesses of the NLA

2.1 Nuclear Power Industry

As of July 2003, there are sixty four nuclear power plants in Japan. Of these, fifty two plants are currently operating, four plants are under construction, and eight plants are in the construction planning stage. The fifty-two operating plants generate 45.9 million kilowatts (kW) of electricity. The plants that are either under construction or in the planning stage are expected to generate 14.4 million kW. When all the plants are operational, they will supply 60.3 million kW of electricity. Although some of the plants are expected to finish construction after 2010, the Japanese government is planning to increase the electricity supply by nuclear power plants from 31 percent in 2002 to about 41 percent in 2010, and then maintain the same share after 2010 (Japanese Ministry of Economy, Trade and Industry, 2003).

By way of contrast, the U.S. and France each have more nuclear power plants than Japan. The U.S. currently has 103 nuclear power plants that generate a total of 101.9 million kW, 19.8 percent of the electricity supply. France has fifty nine nuclear power plants that generate 65.9 million kW, 76.4 percent of the electricity supply (Japanese Ministry of Economy, Trade and Industry, 2002).

2.2 Nuclear Fuel Cycle

The entire cycle of nuclear fuel creation, conversion, enrichment, reprocessing, and disposal is illustrated in Figure 1. Within this cycle, there is a circular flow (illustrated by the 3-dimensional arrows) that is called *nuclear fuel cycling*. This flow is of particular interest since the previously mentioned accident at JCO occurred in the *Re-conversion Plant*. In this plant, uranium hexafluoride is converted to enriched uranium dioxide, which is then transferred to the fuel fabrication plant.

This figure illustrates the scope of nuclear power-based threats to human health, industry, and the environment. Note, that the components of the system are linked by a transportation system. That is, highways and railroad networks are used to transport nuclear materials and radioactive wastes. Hence, the transportation system is another source of threats to humans and the environment. Fortunately, the scope of the NLA is rather broad, covering accidents which can occur anywhere shown in the Figure 1. The NLA define the operators of a nuclear reactor, a reprocessing plant, conversion, enrichment, re-conversion, and fuel fabrication plants as nuclear operators.

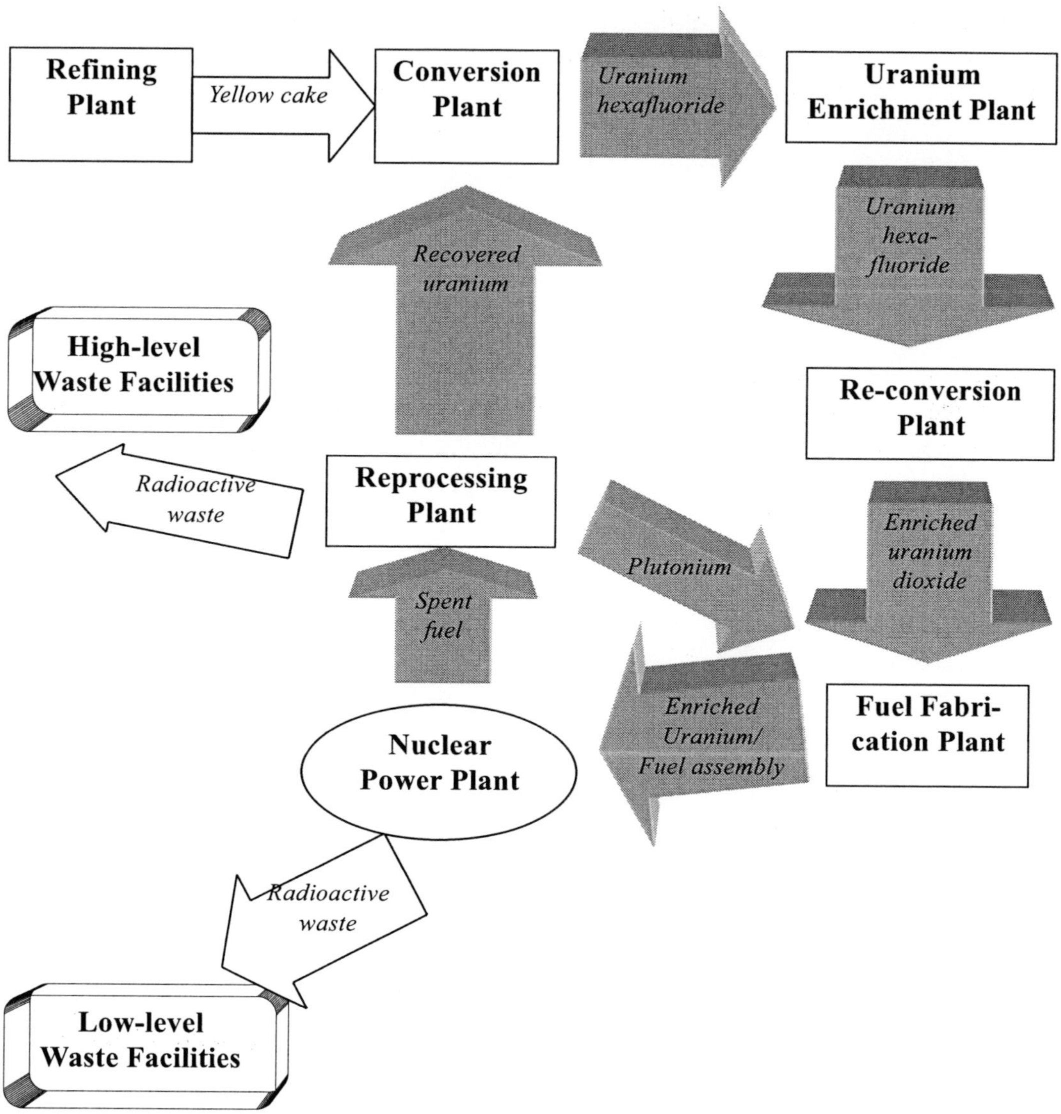

(Source: The Japan Atomic Power Company Co. Ltd., 1998)

Figure 1: Nuclear Fuel Cycle

2.3 Definitions of Nuclear Accidents and Nuclear Damage

The NLA defines nuclear accidents as the casualty of damage occurring in the five main operation processes, including: (i) the operation of nuclear reactors, (ii) processing nuclear fuel materials, (iii) reprocessing nuclear fuel materials, (iv) the use of nuclear fuels, and (v) the disposal, the storage and the transportation of nuclear fuels or wastes. In the context of the nuclear fuel cycle flowchart in Figure 1, (i) refers to *Nuclear Power Plant*, (ii) refers to *Conversion Plant*, *Uranium Enrichment Plant* and *Fuel Fabrication Plant*, and (iii) refers to *Reprocessing Plant* and *Re-conversion Plant*, (iv) refers to each plant in the cycle and (v) refers to each plant within the cycle and both *High-level Waste Facilities* and *Low-level Waste Facilities*.

The NLA defines nuclear damage associated with nuclear accidents as the damage caused by either radioactive or toxic effects of nuclear fuels or materials on human bodies. Note, that the NLA does *not* define environmental damage *per se*, such as radioactive pollution of groundwater, land or seawater. Instead, the NLA deals with environmental damage as the idiosyncratic damage harming unspecified areas as well as unidentified victims.

2.4 Key Provisions of the NLA

The NLA, as stated in Article 1, aims to promote the sound development of the nuclear energy industry and, at the same time, to protect the victims and the environment from nuclear accidents. To achieve these policy objectives, the NLA contains four key provisions spelling out the liability and compensation rules applicable to nuclear operators, insurance companies and victims.

First, the NLA requires strict liability be applied *only* to nuclear operators for damages incurred by third parties of nuclear accidents. Other participants in the nuclear fuel cycle, such as waste handlers and transporters of nuclear fuels are exempted from liability. However, shippers--who tend to be nuclear operators--are liable. And, product liability is not applicable to suppliers of nuclear plant and equipment. Consequently, suppliers of nuclear technology and plants are also exempt from liability. In short, liability is strictly held for nuclear operators, regardless of who is negligent for an accident.

Second, through mandatory liability insurance required of all nuclear operators, the NLA provides for a limit of about 480 million dollars on the total liability of a nuclear operator for nuclear accident-related damages. The limit depends on the *type* of the nuclear operator. More specific, the NLA provides for (i) a limit of about 480 million dollars for nuclear reactors that generate 10,000 kW or above and for reprocessing, (ii) a limit of about 48 million dollars for nuclear reactors that generate between 100 kW and 10,000 kW, operators handling plutonium and for the storage of nuclear wastes, and (iii) a limit of about 8 million dollars for nuclear reactors that generate less than 100 kW and for processing but not reprocessing.

Third, when the total damages exceed the above limits--and the operators are not financially able to pay/compensate the residual damages, even after the liability insurance provides payment to victims--the government provides compensation for the remaining damages.[9] Furthermore, any nuclear accidents resulting from natural disasters--such as earthquake, typhoon and volcano--are ineligible for compensation by the liability insurance. Instead, liability caused by natural disasters is compensated by the government, based on the contracts made between the government and the nuclear operators prior to the occurrence of such disasters.

Finally, the victims of a nuclear accident are able to claim damages only for a period up to twenty years after the occurrence of the nuclear accident. Moreover, these claims must be made under the civil law (Article 724).

3. Economic Principles of Accident Law[10]

This section reviews the basic economic principles of accident law that are relevant to our critique of the NLA. There are two basic objectives of the economic analysis of accident law. The first is to explain or predict how various legal liability rules affect the level of precaution taken by injurers and victims against accidents of various types. The second objective is to use the analytical framework of economics to identify the socially optimal level of precaution taken by both parties.

We begin by introducing several key concepts. There are many types of *accidents*, including: hitting a pedestrian with a car, running an oil supertanker aground, occurrence of chemical leaks at waste sites, medical malpractice, nuclear accidents, etc. For each type of accident, there are *injurers*, those who cause accidents, and *victims*, those who suffer from accident damage.[11] Accident *risk*, defined in this chapter as the probability of the accident occurring multiplied by the magnitude of accident damage, depends both on how injurers and victims participate in risky activities and the attributes of the risky activities, e.g., production technology and processes.

3.1. Nuclear Accidents

There are three distinguishing characteristics of a nuclear accident. First, the accident is unilateral in nature. That is, only nuclear operators (i.e., injurers) affect both the probability of the accident and the magnitude of damage. Unlike car accidents in which a pedestrian's involvement and extent of injuries may be due to careless walking, the probability and severity of a nuclear accident is solely determined by safety measures of nuclear operators. People living near nuclear power plants (i.e., victims) cannot reduce the accident probability by taking protective measures.

The safety measures of nuclear operators also affect the magnitude of damage. If nuclear operators would make relatively higher expenditures on safety technology, the resulting damage could be smaller. Meanwhile, victims are generally unable to control the magnitude of the damage. Of course, people living near a nuclear power plant can reduce the magnitude

9 The decision of providing compensation and the amount of compensation are authorized by the Parliament.

10 This section is based on Shavell (1986, 1987).

11 Injurers and victims can be identical persons for some accidents. For example, when a car crashes into a guardrail, the driver may also be injured.

of damage by relocating to residential locations outside the risky zone. Nonetheless, for a variety of psychological, economic, and sociological reasons, there are people living within the risky zone, for example, within a 10-mile radius of the nuclear power plant. Moreover, given the lethal nature of radioactive materials released during a nuclear accident, residents can do very little to protect themselves from exposure to harmful levels of radiation.

Second, victims are third parties to injurers. That is, we assume that there are no contractual or employer-employee type relationships between nuclear operators and residents. In other words, all plant employees live outside the risky zone. Moreover, there are no agreements, other than the NLA, between nuclear operators and community residents with regard to accident liability and victim compensation.

Third, nuclear operators do not have to fully compensate accident victims, if the total damage related liability exceeds the post-accident market value of the assets of nuclear operators, after deducting the nuclear accident insurance payments made to victims. In other words, a nuclear operator cannot be forced to make compensation payments that will, in turn, force the operator into declaring bankruptcy. According to Park (2003), if the worst-case nuclear accident occurs in Japan, it will possibly create expected damages totaling close to $800 billion. And, there are no Japanese nuclear operators who have the financial ability to make compensation payments of this magnitude yet remain solvent.

3.2. Social Optimum for Accident Precaution

Since only nuclear operators affect the risk of a nuclear accident, the socially optimal level of accident precaution should reflect how much a nuclear operator spends on accident precaution. Hence, the socially optimal level of precaution balances the costs of exercising precaution against the benefits of a reduction in expected accident damages. The social optimum will minimize total accident costs, defined as the sum of the costs of exercising precaution and the expected accident damage. At a conceptual level, expected damage is computed by multiplying the accident probability by the magnitude of damage, given that an accident occurs.

For a nuclear accident, the damage generally includes both financial and non-pecuniary damages. The latter category of damages includes: death, chronic diseases caused by radiation exposure, loss of physical integrity, emotional distress, and so on. If non-pecuniary damage is added to pecuniary damages, the socially optimal level of precaution will be higher than otherwise.

However, several vexing problems are encountered when one attempts to compute the socially optimal level of precaution. First, how should non-pecuniary damages be measured? Such damages cannot be represented by an *equivalent* basket of goods and money. And, this lack of an equivalent basket prevents the court from imputing the *value* of damages. Second, courts cannot directly observe emotional/psychological damages. Thirdly, the causation of an accident and the latency of health and psychological damages are additional complexities. Finally, each victim's level of *suffering* and determination of *value* is entirely subjective. Thus, a victim's notion of "being made whole" is entirely subjective and personal. In other words, each victim's calculation of the level of compensation required to make her whole depends on the each victim's subjective, unique level of *utility* (e.g., psychological payoff) resulting from both monetary and in-kind compensation. Hence, the measurement problems associated with non-pecuniary damage could lead to misestimation of accident damages, which, in turn, results in nuclear operators adopting socially inefficient levels of accident precaution.

3.3. Liability Rules

In this subsection, we summarize the impact on nuclear operator accident precaution of both the strict liability rule (adopted by the NLA) and the negligence liability rule. Note, that this discussion rests on the unrealistic assumption that the occurrence of accident and resulting damages are known with certainty; this assumption is relaxed in subsequent sections. Under strict liability, nuclear operators must pay all the damage caused by an accident. Each profit-maximizing nuclear operator will, therefore, have an incentive to minimize total accident costs, which is equal to the sum of the cost of exercising precaution plus the expected accident damage. Hence, each nuclear operator's cost-minimizing behavior results in the socially desirable level of accident precaution.

Suppose, however, that nuclear operators are financially unable to compensate total victim damage. These financially strapped operators are, thus, able to compensate only the portion of the damage equivalent to the post-accident market value of their assets. Hence, in this insolvency scenario, accident costs imposed on nuclear operators are less than the total accident damages. In reality, given the insurance provisions of the NLA, nuclear operators compute their compensation payments net of the liability insurance payments made to victims.[12] So, the minimization of accident costs--net of insurance payments--by nuclear operators results in a socially suboptimal level of precaution. Furthermore, since nuclear operators will, in all likelihood, be imposed liability less than actual damages, they may engage in an excessive level of power generation, relative to the socially optimal level. The reason is that liability is limited by the post-accident market value of their assets so that any incremental damage generated by the excessive power generation beyond the market value of their assets does not affect the amount of liability payments. We will discuss the impact of nuclear operator insolvency later on.

Next, consider the negligence rule. If the negligence rule is adopted, nuclear operators will be held liable for accident-related damage only if they were negligent. That is, only if their level of precaution was less than the *due care* standard. The level of due care is determined by the court system. For nuclear plants, for example, the capacity of power plants and the technology of power generation are different across electric power companies. Hence, the socially optimal level of care will vary among nuclear operators and levels of due care will also vary among them. If courts cannot distinguish the differences in the cost of taking care among nuclear operators, courts may choose a uniform level of due care in determining negligence for all operators.

If the court sets due care according to efficient resource allocation rules, then the socially optimal level of due care is that level at which the marginal cost associated with adding another unit of accident precaution equals the marginal benefit associated with the commensurate decrease in expected accident damages. Since the socially optimal level of due care is efficient, i.e., minimizes the total accident costs, spending one unit less on

[12] See section 2.4.

accident precaution, relative to the due care standard, implies that the total accident costs will be higher. Hence, rational, honest, profit-maximizing nuclear operators find it in their best self-interest to obey the due care standard. So, if the court sets due care at the socially optimal level, the level of precaution will be socially optimal, assuming all operators obey the court's choice of the level of due care.

Unfortunately, as we experienced from Tepco and other electric companies' covering up the falsification of structural troubles of nuclear reactors, there exist dishonest operators who may deviate from the due care standard, hoping that the court or regulator will not detect their illegal behavior. Compounding the problem is the fact that the regulator cannot always detect the behavior of dishonest operators. Fortunately, this illegal behavior can be remedied by using enforcement programs, e.g., unannounced, surprise safety inspections, and fines for violating the standard (Polinsky and Shavell, 1979).

This desirable outcome arises because rational, profit-maximizing nuclear operators have no incentive to incur costs associated with precaution levels in excess of the due care standard. If they implement a precaution level less than due care, they must pay for accident damages--which translates into higher expected costs, hence lower expected profits. Hence, rational, honest nuclear operators clearly set the level of precaution equal to the due care standard in order to avoid liability claims.[13] An additional benefit of the negligence rule is that nuclear operators can avoid insolvency and, in turn, no need to enter the bankruptcy process by setting the level of precaution equal to the due care standard. There remains the additional issue: who should pay for the damage if an accident actually occurs?[14]

Finally, we note that it is very difficult, if not impossible, to accurately compute expected accident costs, prior to an accident. Inaccurate cost estimates will be made since there is a lack of the information regarding nuclear operators' precise level of precautionary care and cost of safety technologies, as well as scientific uncertainties regarding radiation-induced health effects. We discuss these issues in the following subsections.

3.4. Uncertainties: Hidden Information and Lack of Knowledge

When there are uncertainties with regard to either frequency of accidents or loss magnitudes (i.e., accident severity), the socially optimal level of prevention will not result from either the strict liability or the negligence rule. That is, when the technologies and safety expenditures of nuclear operators are proprietary and hidden information, or when we have scientific uncertainties, such as the magnitude of damage arising from unknown latency periods, the total accident costs cannot be accurately computed either prior to or even after the occurrence of an accident. Hence, courts will fail to set the level of due care at a social

[13] In Japan, negligence is determined as follows. Injurers will be negligent if their behaviors violate the terms specified by articles (e.g., due care standard) in the civil law. In such a case, injurers certainly know the level care they are exercising, hence, they will know if they will be negligent prior to an accident. But, if there are no articles that refer to due care standard, injurers will not certain if they will be negligent prior to an accident. In particular, courts do not release general due care principles prior to an accident and thus injurers will be uncertain if they will be negligent prior to an accident. Negligence depends on how courts judge the injurers' behaviors after the accident.

[14] Calabresi (1970) has argued, from a fairness perspective, that victims should receive compensation from injures.

optimum as well as to determine the magnitude of damage. Furthermore, nuclear operators will, likewise, misestimate damages.[15]

Aside from liability rules, when nuclear operators misestimate damages, the misestimation will affect their decisions regarding the level of accident precaution and the purchase of insurance contracts. These issues have been studied, within the context of the strict liability rule, but without the possibility of injurer insolvency, by Yaksick (1986). Although he analyzed the issues by a general framework, he obtained interesting results for policy implications. That is, in the presence of moral hazard, the level of accident precaution is indeterminate when injurers misestimate damages in purchasing coverage. Moreover, even if injurers correctly estimate the severity of damage, the level of accident precaution can be less than the socially optimal level. This result depends on two conditions holding: (i) the insurance coverage is either relatively small (and less than the first-best level of full coverage) or, (ii) the cost of accident precaution is sufficiently high to induce the injurer to purchase a level of coverage nearly equal to full coverage. The related issue of insurance coverage will be discussed in subsection 3.6.

3.5. Plant Operator Insolvency

In the event of a severe, perhaps, catastrophic nuclear accident, a nuclear operator can become insolvent when liability-related damages, net of insurance payments to victims, exceed the post-accident market value of the operator's assets. Even without the uncertainties discussed above, the insolvency of nuclear operators will also distort the level of precaution under the strict liability and the negligence liability rules.

Under strict liability, the level of precaution will be less than the social optimum. The reason is that the expected accident damage is not fully taken into account when the operator takes a decision on investing in risk reduction technologies and practices. In particular, the operator can have lower costs (equivalently, higher profits), by shirking on safety, during the time period before the occurrence of an accident. And, once an accident occurs, the operator can avoid payment of total accident damage claims by filing for bankruptcy, due to insolvency.[16]

Under the negligence rule, operators may exercise due care to escape from accident liability. However, if accident damages, net of insurance payments to victims, far exceeds the post-accident market value of the assets (e.g., there is a catastrophic accident in which all physical assets are destroyed or the assets have low market value), nuclear operators will

---

[15] For example, the damages paid to third party victims of the Three Mile Island accident in 1979 were totally $26.3 million. There were many unsettled claims for personal injury associated with more with the panic caused than with radioactivity. In February 1985, there were settlements signed with 280 claimants for an unknown amount in excess of $4 million (Smets, 1987).

[16] Of course, there is a cost to filing for bankruptcy. In particular, the long-run viability of the business may be threatened by relying on bankruptcy as a shield to avoid accident damage claims. For example, after declaring bankruptcy, the operator may have more difficulty obtaining both equity and debt capital, required for replacement of damaged/destroyed physical assets. Moreover, by shirking on safety effort, the operator faces the increased probability of a catastrophic accident in which the entire plant becomes contaminated ala the Chernobyl catastrophe. In this scenario, shareholder (equity) value is destroyed and bond holders have no hope of being repaid. When this occurs, the operator is viewed as a credit risk and may never be able to raise capital at a price consistent with economically viable power generation projects.

again tend to exercise less care than the due care standard. The reasoning is the same as that outlined in the preceding, strict liability case.

3.6. Insurance

As the previous section has demonstrated, third-party liability insurance plays two key, dual roles of providing incentives for operators to take precautions as well as sharing risks, assuming that the government does not subsidize the operator's insurance premium. For an insurer (i.e., the seller of insurance), the type of contract offered to operators depend on whether or not the insurer can observe the precautionary care of an accident taken by insureds (i.e., the buyer of insurance). If a nuclear operator's care is unobservable to the insurer, then the selling of insurance to the operator may induce the operator to shirk on the level of precautionary care stated in the insurance contract, resulting in moral hazard. Given the unilateral nature of nuclear accidents, unobservability of the precautionary care crucially affects the available set of insurance contracts and the resulting level of precautionary care. We will first consider non-mandatory third-party liability insurance under both the strict liability and negligence rules. We argue that mandatory liability insurance required by the NLA is preferable to the payment of liability compensation to victims.

- *Negligence Rule*

First, consider the case of non-mandatory liability insurance combined with the possibility that, if an accident occurs, nuclear operators will be insolvent due to a relatively high level of accident liability. Under the negligence rule, nuclear operators will not purchase coverage, regardless of both their risk attitudes (risk averse or risk neutral) and the observability of their precautionary care. Of course, nuclear operators can avoid liability by exercising due care. Hence, their decision to purchase coverage depends on the tradeoff between the level of expenditure associated with the level of due care compared with spending less monies than that required to satisfy the due care standard, but then incurring expected accident costs plus certain insurance premiums payments.

If the insurer can accurately observe the level of the operator's safety precaution (denoted x), he can provide full coverage (denoted l) at an actuarially fair premium. That is, the premium paid by each insured is equal to the expected insurance payment to each victim, if an accident occurs. That is, the premium each insured will pay for full coverage equals the amount of coverage multiplied by the accident probability $p(x)$, that is, $p(x)l$. So, insureds will spend $x + p(x)l$, which is equivalent to the expected accident cost.

Moreover, when care is accurately observable, courts can set the mandatory due care level so as to minimize expected accident costs. Hence, when the operator invests in safety at the due care level, the expected accident cost is x, which is less than $x + p(x)l$. Consequently, rational nuclear operators will not purchase full coverage insurance at an actuarially fair premium.[17]

[17] This argument is based on risk neutral insureds (plant operators). However, the same argument holds for risk averse insureds. See Shavell (1986) for a detailed analysis.

In reality, the insurer cannot accurately observe the operator's level of precautionary care; only the operator knows its level of care. This asymmetric distribution of information may result in a moral hazard type behavior of insureds. In particular, when the insurer cannot observe the precautionary care x, he cannot compute the actuarially fair premium: actual expected accident damages are different from contractually agreed expected damages. The reason for this difference between actual and expected damages is that the insured's morally hazardous behavior results in a different accident damage probability distribution than the probability distribution used by the insurer to compute the actuarially fair premium. Hence, given the possibility that insureds--who purchase full coverage insurance--may shirk their care, the insurer will set a premium much higher than an actuarially fair rate in order to compensate for higher accident damages or insurance claims.

Meanwhile, the insurer can sell a partial coverage contract to insureds. Given the partial coverage, insureds are not entirely free from accident risk so that they will not shirk the level of care, as much as the case of full coverage, hence, mitigating morally hazardous behavior. However, when the insurer cannot accurately observe the insured's precautionary care, the insurer will still set a premium higher than the actuarially fair rate. Hence, the premium payments of insureds are higher than the expected reduction of accident liability covered by insurance. Consequently, profit-maximizing nuclear operators will not purchase accident insurance, in the presence of the negligence rule.

- *Strict Liability*

Under strict liability, if the insurer can observe the level of precautionary care, nuclear operators will purchase full coverage and pay the actuarially fair premium. However, if the market value of their assets are significantly low relative to expected damages (e.g., catastrophic accidents), no coverage will be purchased. The reason is that the insurance premium will exceed the value of the insured's assets. In reality, this is unlikely to occur. Suppose that the probability of catastrophic accidents by Japanese nuclear operators is similar to other industrial nations. Then, it lies between1 in 10^6 and 1 in 10^5 (Heyes and Heyes, 2000). Suppose also that the total damages of catastrophic accidents are $800 billion (Park, 2003). Then the total amounts of the insurance premium paid by nuclear operators--the probability of catastrophic accidents multiplied by the total damages--will be far less than the value of their assets.

If the insurer cannot accurately observe the level of precautionary care, the insurer will set a very high premium for full coverage, as discussed in the negligence rule case. Consequently, nuclear operators will not purchase insurance, if the value of their assets (post-accident) is high relative to expected damages. These relatively high valued assets can be used to pay damage claims. On the other hand, if the value of their assets (post-accident) is low relative to expected damages, they will purchase partial coverage since the full coverage premium is too expensive.

If a catastrophic accident occurs (e.g., Chernobyl), the physical assets of nuclear operators will have no market value, even as scrap. Thus, if nuclear operators' decision to purchase insurance coverage is based on the expected post-accident market value of assets, they will purchase no coverage. The reason is that the insurer will set a very high premium due to unobservability of precaution care. Hence, the premium will greatly exceed the post-accident market value of assets.

- *Misestimated Damages*

So far, we have assumed that the accident damage is observed and known to the public (i.e., nuclear operators, insurers and courts). However, given fundamental scientific uncertainties, such as the magnitude of radiation exposure and its resulting latent damage, accident damage will not be accurately estimated, even after an accident occurs. Yaksick (1986) studied the impact of misestimated accident damages on the injurer's decision to purchase insurance coverage as well as the choice of the level of accident precaution under strict liability. He showed that when risk-averse injurers overestimate damages in the presence of moral hazard, they may *ex ante* purchase partial coverage that may equal the victims' realized *ex post* damage. On the other hand, if the injurers underestimate damage when moral hazard is present, they will purchase coverage that is less than the socially optimal (first-best) level of coverage.

When damage is overestimated, the associated optimal level of partial coverage may, in fact, equal the full coverage level associated with accurate estimation of damages. Hence, it is possible to observe *ex post* first-best efficient accident precaution. If this is the case, the victims will also be fully compensated via insurance coverage. If damage is underestimated, the result is very intuitive. Thus, the accuracy of damage estimation by nuclear operators will be crucial to compensation for victims. In relation to the NLA, Yaksick's analysis is relevant to relatively small scale accidents, for example, accidents by small scale reactors and fuel processing. The limited scope of relevance is due to the fact that bankruptcy is disregarded in his paper. And, given the overestimation of damage, the potential bankruptcy of nuclear operators will further dilute the incentives to purchase insurance coverage.

- *Policy Implications*

The potential insolvency of nuclear operators may diminish their desire to purchase non-mandatory third-party liability insurance. The above arguments, therefore, justify the requirement of mandatory liability insurance under the NLA, in particular, for catastrophic accidents. Hence, an important policy issue is: what is the socially efficient level of required insurance coverage under the framework of the NLA?

In reality, insurers are reluctant to provide coverage for nuclear accidents. The reason is that there is the lack of actuarial data for nuclear accidents since nuclear accidents have very low probability. Hence, the insurers need to assess non-actuarial risk to determine the premium. For example, the rate of the premium paid by Japanese nuclear operators for the compulsory coverage of $240 million in 1998 was about 7.9 percent of coverage. This is equivalent to $18.9 million (Japan Science and Technology Agency, 1998).

Every scenario for a nuclear accident results in a wide range of damages. In the worst case scenario, Park (2003) concluded that estimated damages are expected to far exceed $500 billion. However, the NLA only requires insurance coverage, with a ceiling set at $480 million. Given the worst case scenario estimate, as well as our experience with the JCO accident, it is fair to state that the NLA requires nuclear operators to purchase partial coverage. If full coverage were required, however, nuclear operators will take no care. The fundamental reason for this undesirable behavior is that insurers cannot observe the true level of precautionary care, after insurance coverage is sold to the plant operator. And, in the presence of unobservable care--combined with full coverage--nuclear operators can shirk on care, yet remain completely free from bearing risks.

4. Weaknesses of the NLA and Remedial Measures

Recall that the NLA aims to promote the sound development of the nuclear energy industry as well as to protect the victims and the environment from a nuclear accident. To be more precise, the objectives of the NLA are twofold: (i) to induce nuclear operators to take the socially optimal level of accident precaution *ex ante*, and (ii) to allocate *ex post* damage efficiently when a nuclear accident occurs. In this section, we identify several weaknesses of the NLA legislation, which prevent the achievement of these objectives in a balanced manner. We then examine several remedial measures for these weaknesses.

We begin the critique of the first objective by analyzing the liability rule adopted by the NLA. In doing so, we rely heavily on the basic economic principles of accident law discussed in section 3. The essence of liability rules in accident law is to induce injurers to take the socially optimal level of precaution. However, liability rules are relatively silent on issues related to fair compensation of victims. Nuclear operators may partly escape from their liability compensation obligations. That is, regardless of liability rules, the total accident liability is likely not to be compensated fully by nuclear operators. Hence, to examine the second objective, we will consider the scope and the magnitude of accident liability with the relation to the liability rules examined earlier.

4.1. Liability Rule under the NLA

The NLA adopts strict liability *only* for nuclear operators; other participants in the nuclear fuel cycle are ignored (see section 2.4). Nonetheless, there are two potential advantages of strict liability. One is that nuclear operators are induced to take the socially optimal level of precaution against an accident and victims will be compensated by nuclear operators and the liability insurance coverage. The other advantage is that in accidents which involve several injurers--such as nuclear operators, suppliers, transporters, etc.--the strict liability rule can avoid delays in both identifying an injurer (i.e., the party causing the accident) and providing compensation to victims, since the necessary insurance capacity, assembled by the insurance industry, can be concentrated on the nuclear operators.

On the other hand, the present strict liability system has several flaws. First, drawing upon the arguments made in sections 3.3 to 3.5, we anticipate that nuclear operators will not be motivated to take the socially optimal level of precaution, if they will be insolvent after a major accident. Second, other participants in the nuclear fuel cycle, such as plant suppliers and transporters of nuclear fuels and wastes, will not take sound precautionary care, since they are exempt from any accident liability. Furthermore, the exemption from accident liability of the suppliers and transporters removes, to some extent, barriers to entry for new firms, thereby increasing market competition between potential entrants and incumbents in the transportation industry. This market competition will reveal itself in the form of price competition. Hence, incumbent suppliers and transporters would tend to reduce costs by shirking safety effort.

The recent incidences at Japanese electric power companies can be interpreted as providing some evidence of this shirking behavior due to the exemption of suppliers and transporters from the liability rules. For example, beginning in the 1980s, Tepco avoided repair costs by covering up the falsification of records concerning cracks found in the core structures of 13 nuclear reactors (Wall Street Journal, 2002). Other electric power companies such as Chubu Electric Power Company and Tohoku Electric Power Company also concealed structural troubles at two nuclear reactors. Although electric power companies will be held liable for large damages, if a catastrophic or major accident occurred, why did they conceal the important structural deficiencies and continue their operations? One admittedly favorable interpretation is that the companies are very confident about the safety of their plant; the companies did not perceive cracks as constituting a material threat to plant safety.[18] From the perspective of accident law, however, the companies' behavior is entirely predictable: they will certainly fail to take any precautionary care, if they are rational--cost minimizing--managers. If a major accident occurs, the post-accident market value of their assets is significantly lower than accident liability, thereby diluting the incentives to take precautionary care.

Even with the possible insolvency of nuclear operators, strict liability should nonetheless be implemented for a nuclear accident. This is because nuclear operators possess the most complete and accurate information, which is proprietary, about the condition of their generating technologies. Thus, nuclear operators should be able to accurately calculate the probability of an accident and the associated level of damages. Hence, nuclear operators should know whether or not they will face the potential of bankruptcy.

In practice, nuclear operators will consider a cost to filing for bankruptcy. Once financial markets respond to filing for bankruptcy, it may be very difficult for nuclear operators to obtain both equity and debt capital, required for replacement of destroyed plants (see footnote 16). Hence, bankruptcy may not be an inevitable result. It seems plausible, therefore, that operators will take appropriate precautionary care to avoid bankruptcy, and this will be more supportive if nuclear operators tend to be more risk averse than other participants in the fuel cycle, e.g., power plant suppliers and transporters, who have smaller market value of the assets than nuclear operators. Consequently, the strict liability rule, combined with more effective safety monitoring systems, are the desirable set of policy tools for achieving the two objectives of the NLA.

Meanwhile, in theory, the negligence rule can induce nuclear operators to take the socially optimal level of precaution, even if they face potential insolvency since nuclear operators can escape from accident liabilities by taking the due care standard. And, they will do so when the post-accident market value of assets exceeds the costs of precaution by exercising the due care.

However, courts must observe the level of precaution and safety technologies adopted by nuclear operators to determine if the operators violated the due care standard. Furthermore, although the probability of a catastrophe is exceedingly low, we cannot

[18] Electric power companies concluded that the reactors were safe enough to continue their operation, based on their internal safety inspections and judgment. However, this conclusion lacks credibility since shutting down nuclear reactors for one month created incremental costs in excess of one hundred million dollars, due to the shifting of nuclear power to thermal power for electricity generation (Nikkei Net, 2002)

eliminate the possibility of its occurrence. Hence, in the presence of the negligence rule, the court faces the problem of determining the required level of accident prevention expenditures in order for nuclear operators to escape from liability. In other words, the courts must decide: how safe is safe enough?

Next, consider the market failure caused by the fact that the NLA does not hold power plant suppliers and transporters of nuclear fuels and waste responsible for the liability they cause. Observe that the application of product liability law to power plant suppliers can mitigate nuclear safety problems. The reason is that power plant suppliers will be held liable for damages if an accident is caused by defectively constructed plants.[19]

The same argument is true for transporters. Hence, transporters should also be liable for damage they cause. However, there still remain the problems arising from insolvency, in particular, for transporters. The hazardous waste transportation industry tends to be dominated by small businesses with commensurately small value of assets.

To eliminate this weakness in the NLA, we propose that suppliers and transporters face joint and several liability with nuclear operators. That is, nuclear operators will be responsible for the remaining accident liability, when the suppliers or transporters are not sufficiently solvent to satisfy victims' damage claims, net of insurance payments. This chain of liability compensation creates strong incentives for nuclear operators, suppliers and transporters to sign multi-party contracts in which all parties agree to adopt sound safety operations. At the same time, this form of contracting also motivates the mutual monitoring of operations by each participant in the chain. Thus, joint and several liability can weaken the threat of moral hazard (Jost, 1996; Shavell, 1987; Watabe, 1999).

In relation to the above issues, vicarious liability is another effective measure for increasing safety incentives.[20] There are circumstances where all or some of the liability one party causes is imposed on another party. That is, vicarious liability expands from an agent to a principal. A typical example is the situation in which the employer (principal) is liable for torts (accidents) caused by the employee (agent).[21] Under vicarious liability, the principal wants to use incentives to induce the agent to take an appropriate level of precautionary care. We consider such a possibility in the next section.

- *JCO Accident*

Now, let us consider the JCO criticality accident. As a result of this accident, JCO became insolvent due to the magnitude of the estimated damage.[22] Sumitomo Metal and Mining Co. (SMMC), the parent company of JCO, therefore, decided to assume the liability compensation for JCO. How liability is shifted from one firm to another significantly affects

---

[19] Whenever potential power plant suppliers or transporters find the markets to be profitable, they will enter the markets and the number of firms in the markets will increase. Polinsky (1980) has shown that when the number of firms is variable in the long run, strict liability leads firms to take the efficient level of care, but negligence fails to do so.

[20] Vicarious liability is defined where one person may be held responsible for the torts committed by another. Where this happens, the third party is said to be "vicariously liable" for the tortfeasor's acts (see p.407, Cooter and Ulen, 1988).

[21] For the nuclear fuel cycle in Japan, an accident caused by the employee is responsible for the employer.

[22] The total equity capital of JCO was about $ 9 million at the time of the accident and the estimated damage was about $125 million (JCO Criticality Accident Comprehensive Assessment Committee, 2000). JCO remained all value of the physical assets after the accident.

risks of activities and the resulting social welfare. In particular, liability shifting affects the economic incentives to mitigate the likelihood of an accident, especially in the case of potential bankruptcy (Watabe, 1999).

The liability shifting from JCO to SMMC created two major faults in exercising precautionary care. First, SMMC took the decision of assuming the liability *after* the accident occurred. Thus, there was no consideration of the possibility of vicarious liability beforehand. Hence, SMMC failed to provide *ex ante* the proper incentives to induce JCO to take efficient precaution against the accident. As a matter of fact, the criticality accident was caused by non-approved operating procedures applied to the uranium solutions. Second, JCO and SMMC are in a parent-child corporate relationship. Hence, they are bound together in a less effective economic relationship for intensifying safety measures, relative to firms facing each other in a competitive setting.

Aside from vicarious liability, these problems can be remedied by requiring that risky activities can be conducted only under the terms of contracts awarded via competitive bidding amongst different firms (Laffont, 1995; Lewis and Sappington, 1999). Under competition, a large firm may prefer to not enter into a contract with a smaller firm, such as JCO, because the smaller firm is more likely to go bankrupt than a large firm in the event of an accident. As a result, the larger firm predicts that accident liability compensation is shifted to its own, as a deep pocket. Thus, a competitive setting forces the smaller firm to engage in higher safety effort in order to become a more attractive contracting partner to the larger firm.

Financial market impact is another incentive mechanism to induce appropriate safety technology and behavior. After the JCO accident, the price of SMMC stock dropped by 60 percent from $5.20 to $2.00 over a two-month period. Hence, the shareholders--some of whom may be senior members of the company management team--bear some of accident costs through a reduction in shareholder wealth. Therefore, shareholders, especially institutional shareholders such as pension funds, may well engage in increased monitoring of the corporation's safety effort. Moreover, if the threat of bankruptcy or huge reduction of future cash flows looms large, investment capital will tend to be allocated away from the nuclear sector.

Lastly, for *ex post* liability of nuclear operators, it is often argued that the nuclear power industry is so heavily regulated that nuclear power safety is achieved more efficiently through regulation, rather than increasing the liability share of the industry (Trebilcock and Winter, 1997). However, a socially appropriate choice of liability rules is essential to safety measures. As we discussed earlier, regulators cannot always observe morally hazardous behaviors of nuclear operators. As we experienced, although nuclear operators are required to submit safety records to the Japan Nuclear and Industry Safety Agency, Tepco and others falsified the reported safety records. Nuclear operators will have incentives not to reveal truthful information on their safety unless it is beneficial for them to do so. Hence, stringent regulation alone is obviously not enough to meet the objectives of the NLA. Finally, previous studies also suggest that the optimal combination of regulation and liability rules jointly induce firms to take efficient precaution against accidents (Trebilcock and Winter, 1997; Kolstad et al., 1990; Shavell, 1984a, 1984b).

4.2. The Scope and the Magnitude of Accident Liability

The scope and the magnitude of accident liability rely heavily on the definitions of nuclear damage and environmental damage (see section 2.3). And, the measurement of accident liability is central to the design of efficient and fair compensation schemes. We shall now address three major issues, related to the damage concept, raised by the NLA.

- *Definition of Damages*

First, the NLA defines nuclear damage as the damage inflicted only on human bodies. This definition of nuclear damage rules out the compensation for *indirect damage*, such as evacuation costs from an accident area, business losses by temporary closure of firms, and so on. That is, if an evacuation or temporary closure of business occurred in order to avert radiation exposure, compensation for evacuees and business owners will not be guaranteed by the NLA. The exclusion of indirect damage implicitly implies that the government insurance will also not be provided. For example, the radiation leaks at Tsuruga Nuclear Power Plant in 1981 led to the radioactive contamination of seawater near the plant and harmed local fishing business. Nonetheless, the business losses were neither compensated under the NLA nor by government insurance.

Second, the NLA does not define environmental damage *per se*, such as radioactive pollution. The NLA indirectly recognizes environmental damages by allowing for idiosyncratic damage, i.e., damages incurred by unspecified areas and victims. This indirect notion of environmental damage is analogous to the case in which asthma is caused by air pollution of automobiles or factories. Hence, the damaged areas and the number of the victims are indeterminate in the absence of scientific proof of a linkage between ambient air pollution and each victim's health status. That is, compelling statistical evidence of causation is required in order to compensate for the restoration of the environment as well as victims' health. Furthermore, the burden of proof of causation rests with the victims suffering from health problems, rather than nuclear operators. Consequently, the victims need to have the financial resources to hire the necessary experts to compile evidence supporting the victims' damage claims. And, when the victims lack a "voice", i.e., the ecosystem is damaged, damage costs will undoubtedly be borne by society: either in the form of higher tax revenues or reallocation of tax revenues away from non-accident projects to accident clean-up and restoration projects.

- *Latent Damage Claims*

The NLA has no provisions regarding the limitation period for pursuing damage claims related to latent health or environmental effects.[23] And, latent health and environmental

[23] Japan is not a signatory to the Paris Convention that requires nuclear operators to be liable for damages up to ten years after an accident occurs. The basic argument underlying the omission of the limitation period from the NLA is that the determination of latent damage caused by the nuclear accident relies on many uncertain factors with respect to scientific and medical evidence. In other words, latent damage is a probabilistic concept due to fundamental scientific and medical uncertainties. Thus, it is inappropriate to impose problematical, i.e., probabilistic, burdens on nuclear operators for a long period, since the operators are already burdened by stringent regulation.

effects are the most obvious "idiosyncrasy" category of nuclear damages. The reason is that in the presence of latent effects, causation is not easily verified. There are many intervening effects, e.g., personal behavior and genetic resistance (i.e., predisposition) between dosage and manifestation of the bad outcomes. The victims of a nuclear accident have a 20-year period (post-accident) in which they are able to submit a damage claim. But, a limitation period for the commencement of claims by the victims is obscure under the NLA.

Victims experiencing latent damages only have one venue for pursuing their claims: the civil legal system, with its prolonged processes and related costs. Hence, this class of victims must abide by civil law, when claiming compensation for life and health problems caused by a past accident. More specifically, the claims for retrospective liability must follow Article 724 of the Civil Law. This Article deals with industrial tort cases in general such as air pollution or water pollution by oil spills; the Act is not designed to deal with nuclear accidents as special cases. The claimants are required to demonstrate the proximate causes of the retrospective liability created by a nuclear accident. Hence, the proof of causation is central to the compensation of latent damage, whose processes are neither simple nor short-term.[24] In particular, the nature of nuclear accidents obliges the courts to deal with the proof of causation separately on a case by case basis.

In sum, although nuclear operators are held strictly liable for accident-related damages, the NLA restricts the magnitude of accident liability by preventing victims from filing claims for indirect and latent damages. By ignoring indirect and latent damages, the NLA is placing a ceiling on damage claims. And, this omission places a ceiling on the amount of liability insurance coverage provided under the NLA. In particular, only victims who exhibit immediate and direct damages are eligible for compensation.[25]

Given this ceiling on damage, hence insurance payments, a large portion of the damage created by a nuclear accident will be borne by the victims, as in the JCO accident. Ultimately, society will bear uncompensated accident damages via the use of general tax revenues to compensate victims. Moreover, recall from section 3, that truncating liability will adversely affect the precaution level of a plant operator. And, eliminating the liability of handlers, transporters and other suppliers would possibly lead them to take no precautionary care. These are some of the weaknesses of the NLA.

To develop a recommendation for this policy gap, we researched the issue and found that the limitation period differ across countries. For example, the U.K., Germany and Switzerland have a limitation period of thirty years. France specifies the limitation period of ten years. The French government, however, makes compensation for latent damage claimed for five years after the limitation period is passed. The limitation period of the U.S. varies across the states, since the period depends on each state law. But the Price-Anderson Act of the U.S. provides for a second level of coverage in the form of retrospective liability of 75.5 million dollars per reactor in a mutual risk sharing agreement (U.S. Nuclear Regulatory Commission, 1985).

[24] Baram (1987) discusses the difficulty of the proof of causation for chemical industrial hazards case.

[25] In the JCO accident, residents living within 500m radius from the accident site were exposed to the level of radiation that exceeds the legally allowable level of radiation one can be exposed in one year. Residents living within 150m radius were exposed more than 50 mSV (milli-Sievert) of radiation by the JCO facility accident (Koide, 1999). According to past scientific statistics, people can develop cancer, after a latency period lasting a few decades, by being exposed to radiation levels in excess of 50 mSV (Mabuchi, 1997).

4.3. Analysis of JCO Accident

The JCO criticality accident serves as a good case study to illustrate the weaknesses of the NLA discussed above. The accident occurred during fuel conversion processes. The NLA provided about 8 million dollars of compensation via liability insurance payments (see sections 2.3-2.4). The estimated total damages were, however, approximately 125 million dollars; far less than the coverage of liability insurance. The estimated total damages included such indirect damages as lost sales of agricultural products and temporary closure of firms in the vicinity of the accident area.[26] Regardless of the exclusion of indirect damages, however, nearly all of the damages have not been indemnified under the NLA. Consequently, the compensation of remaining liability as well as indirect damage relies on a legal decision, unless JCO and the victims voluntarily reach a compensation agreement.

However, as stated previously, the SMMC assumed liability compensation for JCO.[27] SMMC allocated about 127 million dollars, which is about 6.7 percent of their equity capital, in the special budget in 2000 in order to satisfy damages claims for the JCO accident. SMMC asserts that it has settled about 98 percent of a total of 6,985 claims made by the victims (Mainichi Interactive, 2000). Meanwhile, 663 people were reported to be exposed to radiation by the accident. And, none of the claims surrounding life and health problems are yet settled (Yomiuri Shinbun, 2002). Every firm, including SMMC, prefers to minimize compensation payments, since the payments reduce profits. Indeed, there is much criticism that SMMC intends to hasten the settlement in order to evade liability at a later stage of the limitation period. That is, an earlier settlement may enable SMMC to avoid compensation payments for latent life and health problems that surface in the future. And, this strategy obviously eliminates or reduces their future financial burdens (JCO Criticality Accident Comprehensive Assessment Committee, 2000).

Finally, when SMMC assumed responsibility for the payment of compensation, the government insurance was practically precluded. The reason is that SMMC is solvent for accident liability born by JCO accident and thus, there is no need to use the government insurance. When SMMC tries to minimize the compensation payments, the compensation payments by SMMC, rather than the government insurance, would be insufficient to meet the damages suffered by victims.

4.4. Weaknesses of the NLA

There are several weaknesses of the NLA. First, when a nuclear accident occurs and the compensation for victims is taken place, the insurance coverage is first used to pay victims. If total damages exceed the insurance coverage, then the nuclear operator must be responsible for the payment of the residual liability after the coverage is provided to victims. When the nuclear operator is insolvent, however, the NLA assures that the remaining liability, after the nuclear operator makes payment by using all financial resources, is compensated by the government insurance. But, government insurance was not applied in

[26] Latent damage is excluded from the estimated total damage estimate.

[27] SMMC's assumption of liability is viewed as being motivated by the company's desire to avoid gaining a negative reputation. From this viewpoint, SMMC's decision was not motivated by vicarious liability.

the JCO-SMMC accident. The reason is that SMMC is solvent for accident liability and thus, liability can be fully compensated by SMMC without the government insurance. Rigorously speaking, the NLA was not fully implemented for the JCO accident. As discussed above, SMMC attempts to minimize the payments of liability by hastening the settlement with claimants at an earlier stage of the limitation period. This partial implementation problem can be remedied by vicarious liability, combined with new regulation that shifts liability to a party of injurers that are connected via the fuel cycle process.

Second, this compensation system precludes indirect damage. And, indirect damage should be included in liability, since such damages generates social losses. For efficient compensation--the second objective of the NLA--liability must be equal to social losses. Costs of evacuation and business losses are observable, immediate pecuniary damages incurred by households and businesses. Thus, one can easily calculate the magnitude of the damages. For example, in the U.S., residents of the Three Mile Island area were reimbursed costs incurred due to the evacuation.[28] The exclusion of indirect damage from the NLA implies that residents and business firms incurring losses must bring a lawsuit against the nuclear operator in order to receive compensation. When considering litigation costs and potential social costs, which will be accrued in the future, it would be socially efficient (cost minimizing) to include indirect damage in the NLA legislation.

As a matter of fact, evacuation statistics of past industrial accidents show that the number of evacuees in a nuclear accident is not necessarily large, compared with other major industrial accidents. For example, 5,000 people were forced to evacuate by the Three Mile Island accident, compared with the Bhopal accident in which 200,000 people were forced to evacuate (Smets, 1987). This is because nuclear power stations tend to be located in less populated areas.

Another weakness is that the limits of insurance coverage are fixed by the types of operators. However, operator type can be independent of the level of accident damages, for example, the levels of the severity of nuclear accidents classified by IAEA. Admittedly, it is easy to classify coverage limits into the relatively same configuration or grouping of operators in order to reduce administrative costs and to simplify the provision of insurance coverage. However, it is more appropriate, from an efficient risk-sharing perspective, to determine coverage limits by the expected level of an accident.

Fourth, the most difficult compensation issue is to define the scope and the magnitude of liability for non-pecuniary damages. In particular, retrospective liability is heavily influenced by the location of radiation exposure, individual physical conditions, preexisting environmental conditions and many other factors that cause the duration of the latency period and the magnitude of the future damage.

Fifth, the accident investigation process needs to become more transparent. When a nuclear accident occurs in Japan, the Nuclear Safety Commission (directed by the Japan Nuclear and Industry Safety Agency) appoints industrial experts and scientists to investigate the scope and the magnitude of the resulting damage. The Commission estimates the scope and the magnitude of the damage based on the proof of causality. Then, the level of nuclear damage will be set to enable the computation of compensation. Finally, the NLA provides insurance coverage for the realized damage.

[28] $1.3 million were paid for evacuation costs of 3,170 families, including $92,400 for loss of earnings by 636 claimants, for the Three Mile Island accident case (Smets, 1987).

This process contains several weaknesses. During the investigation stage, the precise information about the accident, such as the degree of causality and the related evidence on the estimated damages, is very rarely disclosed to the public. Non-disclosure of the information can lead the public to perceive that causality and accident responsibility is being hushed up. Note, that a transparent investigation process can reduce the probability of erroneous judgment being made regarding the degree of responsibility of the injurer, thereby avoiding uncompensated liability being borne by society, as well as avoidance of future litigation costs against the nuclear operator.

For the JCO criticality accident, the Japanese government concluded two months after the accident that marked health problems of residents caused by radiation had not been observed. However, the Ibaraki Prefecture government, where JCO is located, disagreed with this conclusion (Yomiuri Shinbun, 2002). It is well known that the proof of causality requires complex statistical techniques, particularly to estimate possible latent health and environmental effects due to radiation exposure. Hence, it is quite natural to ask how the Japanese government required only two months to draw such a definitive conclusion. The only way to address this question is to have the government release to the public the detailed information that is used to make its decision. Note, that the government's conclusion of no health problems negatively affected the victims in terms of compensation as well as the possible need to enter into a lengthy, costly litigation processes.[29] Furthermore, when the government, under the terms of the NLA, takes over compensation for the residual liability due to an insolvent operator (like JCO), the government insurance coverage could be less than social losses.[30]

It is argued in accident law that the scope of liability depends on whether or not the dilution of precautionary care actually causes a corresponding increment in damages. In other words, the precautionary care must be linked to the prevention of damage. The difficulty for nuclear accidents is that victims may develop, for example, cancer without being directly exposed to radiation. For example, consumers in urban areas may consume agricultural products contaminated with radiation, while the crops were being grown in a distant rural area. Hence, the city dwellers may develop cancer even though they lived a great distance from a nuclear accident that occurred in a rural, farming area. Hence, it is extremely difficult to determine the scope of liability in an efficient manner. In short, we need to follow the present system of investigation. But, it is essential that nuclear accident damages be evaluated efficiently, honestly and in a transparent, timely manner.

Lastly, the NLA needs to include a provision specifying the statue of limitation period for the commencement of claims on retrospective liability. For Japan, as stated above, the NLA has no provisions specifying the limitation period for filing damage claims. Thus, the victims of a nuclear accident must claim for damages through the Civil Law. Under the Civil Law, the limitation period for the commencement of claims is twenty years. The difficulty of the inclusion of retrospective liability in the NLA is that most insurers do not like to offer the

---

[29] After the JCO accident, Japan Nuclear and Industry Safety Agency (1999) reported that the level of radiation exposure must exceed approximately 200 mSV in order to develop latent health effects such as cancer. The area within 10-20m from the site was exposed to the radiation over 200 mSV. Thus, they concluded that latent health effects should not be the immediate concern to JCO accident. A scientific study shows, however, that people can develop cancer by being exposed to radiation over 50 mSV (see footnote 25).

[30] In reality, compensation processes will, thereafter, be shifted to legal processes. Compensation for liability depends on how the courts judge accident-damage causality examined by the government.

coverage. Moreover, by relying on government third-party liability insurance, the nuclear industry can transfer the costs of internalizing accident damages onto society. And, we know that the government's subsidization of private activities distorts resource allocation away from efficiency (Radetzki and Radetzki, 2000).

5. Conclusions and Policy Recommendations

This chapter uses widely-accepted economic principles of accident law to identify the weaknesses of the NLA. Based on these principles, we then analyze possible remedies and propose necessary revisions and additions to the NLA. Although the NLA imposes four major restrictions on nuclear operators for nuclear damage, the NLA has one major weakness: accident liability is limited to direct damages only. This exclusion is socially counterproductive since it would result in an inefficient level of precaution against an accident. The second major weakness is that only nuclear operators are liable for accident damages; handlers and transporters of nuclear fuels or waste and other suppliers are exempted from liability for damages. And, this exclusion cannot provide safety: handlers and transporters with the incentive to shirk their accident prevention and/or damage control efforts in order to reduce their operating costs.

The weaknesses of the NLA can be eliminated through the inclusion of indirect damages into the NLA as well as the requirement of mutual risk sharing among nuclear reactors for latent damage, such as retrospective liability. A potentially good model might be the mutual risk sharing program among nuclear operators, as implemented in the U.S. However, the effectiveness depends on the amount each operator is required to contribute to the compensation fund. Suppose that each operator is required to provide the same amount as the U.S., that is, \$75.5 million per reactor. Then, the required amount will be, on average, about 35-40 percent of profits of all electronic power companies. If the required amount is \$50 million per reactor, it will be about 25-30 percent of their profits. Given that the likelihood of off-site exposure will be between 1 in 10^4 and 1 in 10^7 reactor-years, it should not be too difficult to introduce this form of risk sharing among operators.

In addition, the imposition of liability on handlers, transporters and other suppliers, rather than strict liability applied only to nuclear operators, will induce proper incentives to increase safety measures and effort throughout the entire nuclear power cycle. Another improvement can be made in the situation when liability is transferred from one firm to another in the search for "deep pockets". In this situation, the NLA should specify *ex ante* the acceptable parameters of such a transaction in order to avoid the shirking of safety effort. Our experience with previous nuclear accidents amply demonstrates the weaknesses of current policy.

Complementing the remedial policies for the NLA, is the need for clarification regarding the proof of causality between radiation exposure and damages. This proof is central to compensation for liability. Finally, to avoid additional social costs--including undervalued damages, excessive litigation costs, emotional distress, etc.--the damages should be evaluated efficiently and fairly via a transparent, timely and independent investigation process.

REFERENCES

Baram, M.S. (1987) "Chemical Industry Hazards: Liability, Insurance, and the Role of Risk Analysis," in *Insuring and Managing Hazardous Risks: From Seveso to Bhopal and Beyond*, eds. by P. Kleindorfer and H. Kunreuther, Berlin: Springer-Verlag.

Calabresi, Guido (1970) *The Costs of Accidents,* New Haven: Yale University Press.

Cooter, Robert and Thomas Ulen (1988) *Law and Economics,* New York: Harper Collins Publishers.

Heyes, Anthony and Catherine Heyes (2000) "An Empirical Analysis of the Nuclear Liability Act (1970) in Canada," *Resource and Energy Economics,* 22, 91-101.

Japan Agency for Natural Resources and Energy (1998) *A Long-Term Outlook for Energy Demand,* The Original Bill, (in Japanese).

Japan Atomic Power Company (1998) *Power Station Guide, http://www.japc.co.jp.*

Japan Nuclear and Industry Safety Agency (1999) *On the Effects of JCO Accident on the Nearby Environment* (in Japanese), Report of Nuclear Safety Division, November 4, 1999.

Japan Science and Technology Agency (1998) *An Insurance Premium for Nuclear Liability Insurance* (in Japanese), *http://sta-atm.jst.go.jp.*

Japanese Ministry of Economy, Trade and Industry (2002) *Nuclear Power 2002* (in Japanese), Tokyo: Japanese Government Printing Office.

Japanese Ministry of Economy, Trade and Industry (2003) *A State of Nuclear Power Stations in Japan, http://www.atom.meti.go.jp/genjyo/main01.html.*

JCO Criticality Accident Comprehensive Assessment Committee (2000) *JCO Criticality Accident and Japanese Nuclear Power Administration* (in Japanese), Tokyo: Nanatsumori Shokan.

Jost, P.-J. (1996) "Limited Liability and the Requirement to Purchase Insurance," *International Review of Law and Economics,* 16, 259-276.

Koide, Hiroaki (1999) "Radioactive Pollution and Radiation Exposure," (in Japanese), *Gijutsu to Ningen.*

Kolstad, C., Ulen, T. and G. V. Johnson (1990) "Ex Post Liability for Harm vs. Ex Ante Safety Regulation: Substitutes or Complements?" *American Economic Review,* 80, 888-901.

Laffont, Jean-Jacques (1995) "Regulation, Moral Hazard and Insurance of Environmental Risks," *Journal of Public Economics,* 58, 319-336.

Lewis, Tracy R. and David E.M. Sappington (1999) "Using Decoupling and Deep Pockets to Mitigate Judgment-proof Problems, *International Review of Law and Economics,* 19, 275-293.

Mabuchi, Haruhiko (1997) "The Effect of Low Level Radiation and Linearity Hypothesis Based on Risk Evaluation in Epidemiology," (in Japanese), *Japanese Journal of Health Physics,* 32, 5-7.

Mainichi Interactive (2000) "Compensating Damage for JCO; 125 million dollars," *http://www.mainicih.co.jp/eye/feature/article/tokai/001028-1.html.*

Nikkei Net (2002) "Tepco's Nuclear Power Troubles – Economic Burdens Exceed 20 Billion yen Monthly," (in Japanese), November 15, 2002.

Park, Seung-Joon (2003) "Estimation of Nuclear Accident Damage: A Case of No.3 Reactor at Ohi Power Plant," (in Japanese), *Gijutsu to Ningen.*

Polinsky, A. Mitchell (1980) "Strict Liability vs. Negligence in a Market Setting," *American Economic Review Papers and Proceedings,* 70, 363-367.

Polinsky, A. Mitchell and Steven Shavell (1979) "The Optimal Tradeoff between the Probability and Magnitude of Fines," *American Economic Review,* 69, 880-891.

Prime Minister of Japan and His Cabinet (2002) *Guidelines for Measures to Prevent Global Warming,* March 19, 2002.

Radetzki, Marcus and Marian Radetzki (2000) "Private Arrangements to Cover Large-Scale Liabilities Caused by Nuclear and Other Industrial Catastrophes," *Geneva Papers on Risk and Insurance,* 25, 180-195.

Shavell, Steven (1984a) "A Model of the Optimal Use of Liability and Safety Regulation," *RAND Journal of Economics,* 15, 271-280.

Shavell, Steven (1984b) "Liability for Harm versus Regulation of Safety," *Journal of Legal Studies,* 13, 357-374.

Shavell, Steven (1986) "The Judgment Proof Problem," *International Review of Law and Economics,* 6, 45-58.

Shavell, Steven (1987) *Economic Analysis of Accident Law,* Cambridge: Harvard University Press.

Slovic, Paul, Fischoff, Baruch and Sarah Lichtenstein (1990) "Rating the Risks," in *Readings in Risk,* eds. by T. Glickman and M. Gough, Washington D.C.: Resources for the Future.

Smets, H. (1987) "Compensation for Exceptional Environmental Damage Caused by Industrial Activities," in *Insuring and Managing Hazardous Risks: From Seveso to Bhopal and Beyond,* eds. by P. Kleindorfer and H. Kunreuther, Berlin: Springer-Verlag.

Trebilcock, Michael and Ralph A. Winter (1997) "The Economics of Nuclear Accident Law," *International Review of Law and Economics,* 17, 215-243.

U.S. Nuclear Regulatory Commission (1985) *The Price-Anderson Act: The Third Decade,* Washington D.C.: U.S. Government Printing Office.

Wall Street Journal (2002) "Executives Resign in Nuclear Scandal at Japan's Tepco," September 18, 2002.

Watabe, Akihiro (1999) "The Effect of Liability Sharing Rules in Delegating Hazardous Activities," *International Review of Law and Economics,* 19, 349-368.

Yaksick, Rudy (1986) "Strict Liability and Insurance under Loss Misestimation," in *Insurance and Risk Theory* (Vol. 171 in NATO ASI Series C: Mathematics and Physical Sciences), eds. by M. Goovaerts, F. del Vylder and J. Haezendonck, Dordrecht, Holland: D. Reidel Publishing Company.

Yomiuri Shinbun (2002) "JCO Criticality Accident," (in Japanese), September 2, 2002 evening edition.

INDEX

A

B

C

D

E

F

G

H

I

J

K

L

M

Q

R

S

T

U

V

W